LANDMARK ESSAYS ON ARCHIVAL RESEARCH

Landmark Essays on Archival Research gathers over twenty years of essays addressing archival research methodologies and methods. These works give readers a sense of how scholars have articulated archival research over the last two decades, providing insight into the shifts research methods have undergone given emerging technologies, changing notions of access, concerns about issues of representation, fluid definitions of what constitutes an archive, and the place of archival research in hybrid research methods.

This collection explores archival research involving a range of disciplinary interests, and will be of interest to scholars working on topics related to postmodern, feminist, working class, and cultural issues. With archival research now ubiquitous, illustrated by the recent number of published collections, journal articles, conference sessions, and pedagogical treatises devoted to the topic, this volume appeals to a broad range of scholarly fields and areas of study.

Primary, archival investigation leads to novel insights and publications, and has a place in most of the research being conducted by compositions and rhetoric scholars. This volume will chart the recent historical trends of archival research and suggest future directions for investigation.

Lynée Lewis Gaillet is Professor of Rhetoric and Composition and Chair of the English Department at Georgia State University.

Helen Diana Eidson is Assistant Professor of English at Auburn University.

Don Gammill, Jr. is a PhD student and teaching fellow at Georgia State University.

THE LANDMARK ESSAYS SERIES

Landmark Essays is a series of anthologies providing ready access to key rhetorical studies in a wide variety of fields. The classic articles and chapters that are fundamental to every subject are often the most difficult to obtain, and almost impossible to find arranged together for research or for classroom use. This series solves that problem.

Each book encompasses a dozen or more of the most significant published studies in a particular field, and includes an index and bibliography for further study.

Series Editors:
James J. Murphy
Krista Ratcliffe

Landmark Essays on Archival Research
Edited by Lynée Lewis Gaillet, Helen Diana Eidson, and Don Gammill, Jr.

Landmark Essays on Tropes and Figures
Edited by Roberto Franzosi

Landmark Essays on Rhetoric and Feminism: 1973–2000
Edited by Cheryl Glenn, Andrea Lunsford

Landmark Essays on Speech and Writing
Edited by Peter Elbow

Landmark Essays on Basic Writing
Edited by Kay Halasek, Nels P. Highberg

Landmark Essays on ESL Writing
Edited by Tony Silva, Paul Kei Matsuda

Landmark Essays on Rhetoric and Literature
Edited by Craig Kallendorf

Landmark Essays on Contemporary Rhetoric
Edited by Thomas B. Farrell

Landmark Essays on Aristotelian Rhetoric
Edited by Richard L. Enos, Lois P. Agnew

Landmark Essays on Bakhtin, Rhetoric, and Writing
Edited by Frank Farmer

Landmark Essays on Rhetoric and the Environment
Edited by Craig Waddell

Landmark Essays on Rhetoric of Science: Case Studies
Edited by Randy Allen Harris

Landmark Essays on Advanced Composition
Edited by Gary A. Olson, Julie Drew

Landmark Essays on Writing Centers
Edited by Christina Murphy, Joe Law

Landmark Essays on Rhetorical Invention in Writing
Edited by Richard E. Young, Yameng Liu

Landmark Essays on Writing Process
Edited by Sondra Perl

Landmark Essays on Writing Across the Curriculum
Edited by Charles Bazerman, David R. Russell

Landmark Essays on Rhetorical Criticism
Edited by Thomas W. Benson

Landmark Essays on Voice and Writing
Edited by Peter Elbow

Landmark Essays on Classical Greek Rhetoric
Edited by A. Edward Schiappa

Landmark Essays on Kenneth Burke
Edited by Barry Brummett

Landmark Essays on American Public Address
Edited by Martin Medhurst

LANDMARK
ESSAYS ON ARCHIVAL RESEARCH

Edited by
LYNÉE LEWIS GAILLET, HELEN DIANA EIDSON,
AND DON GAMMILL, JR.

NEW YORK AND LONDON

First published 2016
by Routledge
711 Third Avenue, New York, NY 10017

and by Routledge
2 Park Square, Milton Park, Abingdon, Oxon, OX14 4RN

Routledge is an imprint of the Taylor & Francis Group, an informa business

© 2016 Taylor & Francis

The right of the editors to be identified as the author of the editorial material, and of the authors for their individual chapters, has been asserted in accordance with sections 77 and 78 of the Copyright, Designs and Patents Act 1988.

All rights reserved. No part of this book may be reprinted or reproduced or utilised in any form or by any electronic, mechanical, or other means, now known or hereafter invented, including photocopying and recording, or in any information storage or retrieval system, without permission in writing from the publishers.

Trademark notice: Product or corporate names may be trademarks or registered trademarks, and are used only for identification and explanation without intent to infringe.

Library of Congress Cataloging in Publication Data
Names: Gaillet, Lynée Lewis. | Eidson, Diana. | Gammill, Don, Jr.
Title: Landmark essays on archival research / [edited by] Lynée Lewis Gaillet, Diana Eidson, and Don Gammill, Jr.
Description: New York, NY : Routledge, 2016. | Series: Landmark essays series | "In this collection, we gather twenty-five years of landmark essays addressing archival research methodologies and methods, bringing to the foreground theories and practices defining this essential form of scholarly inquiry." | Includes bibliographical references and index.
Identifiers: LCCN 2015027162 | ISBN 9781138897861 (hardback) | ISBN 9781138897878 (pbk.)
Subjects: LCSH: Archives—Research—Methodology.
Classification: LCC CD972 .L36 2016 | DDC 027—dc23
LC record available at http://lccn.loc.gov/2015027162

ISBN: 978-1-138-89786-1 (hbk)
ISBN: 978-1-138-89787-8 (pbk)

Typeset in Minion
by Keystroke, Station Road, Codsall, Wolverhampton

Printed and bound in Great Britain by
TJ International Ltd, Padstow, Cornwall

For Win, 1922–2014

CONTENTS

Acknowledgements ix

INTRODUCTION 1

SECTION 1
CLAIMING GROUND **11**

1. Panel Organized by James J. Murphy, [Octalog I:] The Politics of Historiography (1988) 13
2. Robert J. Connors, Dreams and Play: Historical Method and Methodology (1992) 50
3. Cheryl Glenn, Remapping Rhetorical Territory (1995) 63
4. Jacqueline Jones Royster, When the First Voice You Hear is Not Your Own (1996) 78

SECTION 2
ACCESSING THE ARCHIVES **89**

5. Panel Organized by Richard Leo Enos, Octalog II: The (Continuing) Politics of Historiography (1997) 91
6. Linda Ferreira-Buckley, Rescuing the Archives from Foucault (1999) 111
7. Richard Leo Enos, Recovering the Lost Art of Researching the History of Rhetoric (1999) 117
8. Hui Wu, Historical Studies of Rhetorical Women Here and There: Methodological Challenges to Dominant Interpretive Frameworks (2002) 130
9. Shirley K. Rose and Irwin Weiser, The WPA as Researcher and Archivist (2002) 145
10. Barbara A. Biesecker, Of Historicity, Rhetoric: The Archive as Scene of Invention (2006) 156

SECTION 3
DOING ARCHIVAL RESEARCH **163**

11. Elizabeth (Betsy) Birmingham, "I See Dead People": Archive, Crypt, and an Argument for the Researcher's Sixth Sense (2008) 165
12. Barbara E. L'Eplattenier, An Argument for Archival Research Methods: Thinking Beyond Methodology (2009) 171

13 Cheryl Glenn and Jessica Enoch, Drama in the Archives: Rereading Methods, Rewriting History (2009) — 183
14 Sammie L. Morris and Shirley K. Rose, Invisible Hands: Recognizing Archivists' Work to Make Records Accessible (2010) — 200
15 Tarez Samra Graban, Emergent Taxonomies: Using Tension and Forum to Organize Primary Texts (2010) — 218

SECTION 4
RETHINKING THE ARCHIVES — 231

16 Panel Organized by Lois Agnew, Laurie Gries, and Zosha Stuckey, Octalog III: The Politics of Historiography in 2010 (2011) — 233
17 Jonathan Buehl, Tamar Chute, and Anne Fields, Training in the Archives: Archival Research as Professional Development (2012) — 256
18 Kelly Ritter, Archival Research in Composition Studies: Re-Imagining the Historian's Role (2012) — 280
19 Lynée Lewis Gaillet, (Per)Forming Archival Research Methodologies (2012) — 295

Index — 313

ACKNOWLEDGEMENTS

I feel as though I am coming full circle in so many ways with the publication of this Landmark Essays Series volume addressing archival research. When I came to Georgia State University as a newly minted Assistant Professor in Rhetoric and Composition in the early 1990s, the English Department provided me with a stipend to buy books, since rhetoric and composition was a field new to the University and library holdings were woefully slim. I asked if I might have some of those funds parceled out so that I could buy the promised and forthcoming volumes of the Landmark Essays Series. Over the next decade, I collected all the books in the series, eagerly awaiting the arrival of the next mint green volume.

I am so fortunate now to have the opportunity to compile essays that have influenced me and so many other scholars new to rhetoric, communication, and composition studies. The first Octalog was published the year I entered graduate school, and was the first article I read in Dr. Jim Baumlin's History of Rhetoric I seminar at Texas Christian University. Brave New World indeed! The next semester, I enrolled in Dr. Winifred Bryan Horner's History of Rhetoric II seminar and was introduced to methods for doing archival research. I wish to thank Dr. Horner for the sea change she wrought in my life—in ways that led to the production of this volume. I also wish to thank Jerry Murphy for supporting my work in so many ways over the last two decades. He is an inspiration to generations of scholars, and his energy, enthusiasm for new projects, and breadth of knowledge is astounding. Thank you to Jerry and the brilliant Krista Ratcliffe for renewing the Landmark Essays Series and including *On Archival Research* in this fine lineup, and to Ross Wagenhofer, editor extraordinaire. Ross is always patient, encouraging, wise, quick to respond and ever-cheerful.

Of course, this volume owes its greatest debt to the contributors, the theorists, archivists, and teachers whose work codified the messy and sometimes elusive acts of archival research, who questioned traditional approaches to primary investigation, and expanded access to collected materials. These scholars sometimes asked hard questions of archival researchers and demanded transparency in ways we represent ourselves, our subjects, and our findings. Finally, I wish to thank Diana Eidson and Don Gammill, two new archival researchers and fabulous collaborators, who bring clarity and enthusiasm to primary investigation and expand in their research traditional notions of what constitutes an archive. Diana and Don represent the future of archival investigation; the field is in good hands indeed.

Lynée Lewis Gaillet

INTRODUCTION
On Archival Research: Methodology and Method
Lynée Lewis Gaillet, Helen Diana Eidson, and Don Gammill, Jr.

In this collection, we gather twenty-five years of landmark essays addressing archival research methodologies and methods, bringing to the foreground theories and practices defining this essential form of scholarly inquiry. This body of work explores archival research involving a range of disciplinary interests. For example, scholars interested in postmodern, feminist, working class, and cultural rhetorics have vigorously engaged in recovery and revision research in order to reclaim and redefine the rhetorical canon, and to discover rhetorical instruction and engagement occurring outside traditional venues, spaces, and communities. Compositionists have looked to archival research for a "usable past," seeking case studies, cultural events, and pedagogical practices to determine the field's origins. In some cases, scholar-teachers sought to ameliorate perceptions of composition's narrow association with current-traditional instruction, rescue and recover the work of predecessors in the field, and locate origins for contemporary teaching practices.

Since the first Octalog panel addressing historiography and archival research was held at the Conference on College Composition and Communication (CCCC) in 1988, the research pendulum has routinely swung between scholarly discussions of archival methodology and method, asking researchers to closely examine and, in some cases, justify their archival research methodologies—then, subsequently, calling for more training in how to *do* archival research. Twenty-first century scholars are just now, in great numbers, fully answering Linda Ferreira-Buckley's 1999 call for increased training of archivists, pragmatically addressing the previous dearth of procedures and tools for investigating primary materials.

Archival research, while historically an ongoing scholarly concern, is now ubiquitous, illustrated by the recent number of published collections, journal articles and special issues, conference sessions, and pedagogical treatises devoted to the topic—as well as the burgeoning number of courses grounded in this methodology. Attesting to the prevalence of archival inquiry, the first four essays of the September 2012 special issue of *College Composition and Communication* (dedicated to "Research Methodologies") specifically addressed archival research: historiography and representation, methodologies and methods, ethical considerations, and sustainability. Archival scholars aren't just historians, librarians, or curators; elements of archival research already own a place within most methods currently defining the work of rhetoric, composition, and communication scholars. As the field moves away from mutually exclusive research methods and towards greater consideration and adoption of hybrid models of investigation, understanding the role of archival research across fields of study becomes increasingly important.

Traditionally, archival researchers visited holdings of primary materials to see what the collections could tell us about X (the subject at hand). Librarians and curators served as guides to help researchers discover predetermined answers to their questions. But what happens in the wake of archival digitization and the accompanying increased access outside our narrow disciplinary divisions—changes that make possible shifting conversations about archives and about interpreting materials in ways that curators and archivists who collated those materials may never have anticipated? For example, composition scholars often investigate materials not originally assembled with writing instruction or teachers in mind. As archival scholars, they bring their own research agendas/questions to primary materials rather than searching the archives for pre-ordained answers and authenticated assumptions.

The often-cited essays and book chapters collected in this volume thoughtfully address these fundamental archival research issues. We organize the following materials chronologically, demonstrating the trajectory of archival methodological/method conversations as they grew out of the three decennial Octalog panels; just as logically, we could have divided the works into methodology and method sections. As it turns out, this chronological scheme also works thematically. Concerns addressed in the selections move from providing a rationale for archival research ("Claiming Ground"), to questions of access and method ("Accessing the Archives" and "Doing Archival Research") to an overall re-envisioning of the possibilities of archival research ("Rethinking the Archives"). Collectively, these works revisit the established tradition of historiography and (largely through new approaches to archival investigation) move in uncharted directions.

The foundational Octalog I, "The Politics of Historiography" (1988), was the first of three roughly decennial colloquia on the subject and laid the groundwork for an ongoing conversation about historiographical theories and practices. Held at the CCCC, this session brought together eight scholars across a spectrum of methodological beliefs. Moderated by James J. Murphy, the panel format consisted of an introduction and overview, a series of three-minute speeches by each participant, a dialogue among the panelists, and a question-and-answer session. The panel featured James Berlin, Robert J. Connors, Sharon Crowley, Richard Leo Enos, Susan C. Jarratt, Nan Johnson, Jan Swearingen, and Victor J. Vitanza. Several prominent themes emerged from the debate. In order to theorize epistemology and ethics, panelists explored their ideological stances, their views of the "Truth" or "truths" historiography could potentially uncover, whether or not historiography could be truly inductive, and how the subfield of rhetoric and composition could more effectively define itself in the field of English Studies. Subsequent published works took up these issues.

A participant in the inaugural Octalog, Robert Connors authored one of the first published works to offer both theoretical and practical considerations for archival researchers in his "Dreams and Play: Historical Method and Methodology" (1992), a touchstone for subsequent discussions of the role serendipity "plays" in archival method. He asserts that historians bring three "pieces of information" to the task of solving historical problems: "present awareness, archival retrieval, and the realization of prejudice." Historians always begin their research with a hypothesis that lends purpose and focus to their efforts. The hypothesis, articulated in research questions, stems from preconceptions and bias, allowing for what Connors calls "play," a "directed ramble" analogous to an "August mushroom hunt." Connors delineates three archival tasks: "external criticism, internal criticism, and synthesis of materials." Following a pragmatic look at the nature of archival research, he explores the epistemology of historiography. Ultimately, Connors asserts the value of what composition historians do through their recovery of composition history, the "telling of stories about the tribe that make the tribe real."

Cheryl Glenn's "Remapping Rhetorical Territory" (1995) charts new territory in discussions of archival research by tracing the map of rhetorical history's development, thereby taking archival scholarship in new directions. The initial map defines privileged white males from the canon, but more recent historiographies have expanded the map to include rhetorical contributions of marginalized populations. By claiming a feminist historiography based in gender studies, Glenn asserts that scholars can examine questions of power rather than merely focusing on gender identity. Her postmodern approach to historiography challenges historians to problematize the map in order to explore new territory. This mapping method yields a more nuanced and complete (though never wholly comprehensive) topography of rhetorical theory and practice across millennia. Investigating Aspasia of Miletus, Glenn also demonstrates ways in which this method enables us to infuse new ideas and energy into our scholarship and pedagogy and how we might position ourselves on the map.

Likewise, Jacqueline Jones Royster's "When the First Voice You Hear is Not Your Own" (1996) directs attention to the relations of subject position and discourse, offering a dialectic of research ethics from a position of marginalization. Royster develops a theory of "cross-boundary discourse" emerging from her work on nineteenth-century African American women. For her, "'subject' position really is everything," and she introduces concepts of positionality and overt examinations of the researcher's position into archival research. Recalling three "scenes" from her lived experience, Royster focuses on voice. These scenes show her as being silenced, as speaking but not being heard or believed, and as speaking but not being perceived as authentic and authoritative. She describes voice as not only a "phenomenon" that is expressed orally and visually, but also as "a thing heard, perceived, and reconstructed." Widely cited and anthologized, this article offers scenarios in which researchers might enact this cross-boundary space pedagogically, in discourse with post-secondary administrators, and within professional organizations.

The next "shifts" in the trajectory of archival research are represented in 1997's "Octalog II: The (Continuing) Politics of Historiography," the second colloquium delivered at CCCC. This panel, while revisiting ideological and epistemological concerns raised in the inaugural Octalog, also rejuvenated debates involving technology, literacies, identities, and the body. Richard Leo Enos and Theresa Enos organized this panel (in memory of James Berlin). Octalog II's format varied somewhat from the first iteration; Edward P.J. Corbett chaired the session and Thomas Miller served as respondent. Janet Atwill, Linda Ferreira-Buckley, Cheryl Glenn, Janice Lauer, Roxanne Mountford, Jasper Neel, Edward Schiappa, and Kathleen Welch comprised this panel. As Miller notes, these talks show rhetorical history moving away from "The Rhetorical Tradition" and toward "the experiences of women, people of color, and the working classes."

Cited often as a pivotal shift in the focus of rhetorical historiography from theory to practice, Linda Ferreira-Buckley's "Rescuing the Archives from Foucault" (1999) challenges scholars to engage in the hard work of closely examining primary materials and to train the next generation of archivist-researchers in practical investigative matters. She chastises historians, stating that in their expanding of the canon, they seem to have forgotten that history was once a branch of rhetoric and should be (rightly) regarded with a healthy skepticism. She argues that "one's theory and one's approach ... are not coterminous and that methodological approaches per se do not indicate a political position—at least not in any simple way." Including an analysis of Thomas P. Miller's *The Formation of College English Studies* (1997), Ferreira-Buckley reminds readers that traditional methodologies represent the best vehicle for social change, and that progressive historians should therefore master both traditional and emerging methodologies.

Richard Leo Enos also makes a powerful case for our discipline's return to the archives. In his 1999 article "Recovering the Lost Art of Researching the History of Rhetoric," he insists on rigorous primary research rather than commentaries based on secondary sources. Some rhetoricians have focused on methods to the exclusion of attending to intellectual problems. Other rhetoricians perceive the possibilities of interdisciplinary collaboration now that rhetoric has established and defined itself as a concentration in English Studies. Unfortunately, as Enos points out, too few engage in the "basic research" of historiography: primary scholarship that yields new contributions to the discipline. Enos maintains that many scholars only enact close readings of secondary texts, or write metatheory, or wage debates on ideological questions in the epistemology of the field. Of note, Enos urges readers to expand their notions of texts and to explore a range of artifacts that provide diachronic and intertextual readings of primary materials.

Hui Wu, in "Historical Studies of Rhetorical Women Here and There: Methodological Challenges to Dominant Interpretive Frameworks" (2002), echoes Enos's call for an active emphasis on primary historical research and urges scholars to reject conventional frameworks in order to engage in a progressive methodology embracing the nuanced nature of an engaged praxis. Her work contributes to the subfield of rhetorical history by framing and explicating a debate about alternative methodologies such as feminist historiography. Wu cites a case in point—a debate waged in *College English* (2000) among three scholars: Xin Liu Gale, Cheryl Glenn, and Susan C. Jarratt. She criticizes Gale's article, in which Gale "reduced feminist histories to research techniques and ... confusingly paralleled [them] with postmodernism." This misunderstanding, Wu maintains, stems from a lockstep adherence to "established interpretive frameworks." Aligning her work with Glenn and Jarratt, Wu highlights alternative methodologies that challenge, both ethically and politically, these dominant frameworks. Wu argues that feminist methodology performs research in order to exert power over research methods themselves, or to act as "subject-producers of history."

Building upon previous theories of archival method, Shirley K. Rose and Irwin Weiser advocate expanding archival work into writing program administration. In "The WPA as Researcher and Archivist" (2002), they encourage program administrators to see themselves as researchers *and* archivists. WPAs who develop these strategies can run programs effectively, contribute to writing studies, and establish a rich source of data for future research. WPA research exhibits qualities that distinguish it from other types of research in terms of location, stakeholders, and kairos. The WPA, they contend, must understand the process of developing the archive as a multi-step, reflective, recursive enterprise. Rose and Weiser offer practical considerations for this process and remind WPAs that the best outcomes arise from a comprehensive, holistic view which mixes theory and practice by integrating roles: teacher, mentor, administrator, researcher, and archivist.

Many of the works assembled here disturb traditional notions of archives and artifacts. For example, Barbara A. Biesecker's "Of Historicity, Rhetoric: The Archive as Scene of Invention" (2006) deconstructs truth claims of archival artifacts by redefining our perceptions of the archive itself. Biesecker maintains that whatever else an archive may be, it "always already is the provisionally settled scene of our collective invention . . ." That is, the archive only appears as materiality and thereby shores up the veracity of conclusions drawn from it. She relates the *Enola Gay* controversy as a way to work out this conundrum for rhetorical historiographers: The Smithsonian planned an exhibition that would have shown photographs of dead and maimed Japanese civilians. Outside pressure put a halt to the project, but a decade later a documentary film aired on television that showed these photos without any fallout. Biesecker speculates that artifacts "authorize" rather than "authenticate." She advocates for scholarship that foregrounds our strategic and situated uses of archives. In so doing, she shatters the faith that many archival researchers had placed in their ability to approximate veracity in their work.

In a similar challenge to dominant notions of positionality and researcher ethics, Elizabeth Birmingham expands notions of the role of archival researchers in "'I See Dead People': Archive, Crypt, and an Argument for the Researcher's Sixth Sense" (2008). In the film *The Sixth Sense* (1999), the child protagonist possesses the gift of seeing dead people who do not know they are dead. Birmingham claims the archive as a space in which the dead not only talk to us, but also befriend us. She presents her investigation of architect Marion Mahony Griffin (1871–1961) as an apt case study to develop this metaphor. Birmingham describes working *with* Griffin rather than *on* her. She first encountered Griffin's work while researching her husband Walter Burley Griffin; existing research on Mr. Griffin did not acknowledge the talent and influence of his wife. Birmingham's work illustrates how our sixth sense as researchers opens up the possibility that our dead subjects "will help us recover ourselves, help us discover that we did not know that we were the dead. . . ." Despite the fact that a scholar may be alone, surrounded by forgotten archival materials in a cold, dusty place, a potentially profitable human-to-human dynamic still exists—a relationship archival researchers should seek.

Another contribution to the emerging trend focused on the practicalities of actually doing archival work, Barbara E. L'Eplattenier's opinion piece, "An Argument for Archival Research Methods: Thinking Beyond Methodology" (2009), fulfills three purposes: arguing for focus on practical, robust primary method; distinguishing between method and methodology; and explaining key considerations of writing a methods section in the presentation of our work. Discerning differences between "methodology" and "method" (and pointing out the dearth of materials addressing method), L'Eplattenier outlines the contributions of historical scholars such as Glenn ("Remapping") and Crowley ("1988 Octalog") toward an appropriate methods section in historiographies, arguing ultimately for the methods section's worth and highlighting approaches for effectively crafting one.

Also addressing practical ways to approach archival investigation, Cheryl Glenn and Jessica Enoch's "Drama in the Archives: Rereading Methods, Rewriting History" (2009) contributes a useful overview of the historical research trajectory, adopting Kenneth Burke's dramatistic pentad as an extended metaphor and theoretical tool to underscore this contentious dynamic. Using the ratios among those research acts, as well as Burke's notion of "trained incapacities" (the bias and ideology of each researcher), Glenn and Enoch depict this archival drama as it has unfolded in the past five decades. In "Act I," Glenn and Enoch look at Burke's "act:purpose" ratio, highlighting the importance of entering the archives with a purpose while remaining flexible and resourceful. In the next "act," they look at agent and purpose by describing the various agents in the archives, including colleagues and archivists. "Act III" unpacks the purpose:agency ratio, which concerns the relationship between means and ends. Finally, Glenn and Enoch offer these analyses as a heuristic for future archival explorations.

Impressively, Sammie L. Morris and Shirley K. Rose's "Invisible Hands: Recognizing Archivists' Work to Make Records Accessible" (2010) illustrates ways to perform the role of researcher-archivist. Morris and Rose give us an inside look at the work archivists undertake to make materials available. Long-time, Purdue-affiliated collaborators, Morris and Rose catalogue and curate the James Berlin Papers, and in the process provide excellent descriptions of key concepts and practices in archival work: provenance, original order, archival preservation, and archival arrangement and description. Collaborating enabled Morris and Rose to not only understand each other's disciplinary work but also to discern the interplay between rhetorical theory and archival practice. Understanding the working habits of archivists provides researchers with strategies for addressing ethical concerns, for working more efficiently, and for triangulating data.

Similarly, Tarez Samra Graban, in "Emergent Taxonomies: Using Tension and Forum to Organize Primary Texts" (2010), creates a useful tool for collecting and coding archival data for purposes of discourse analysis. Works such as Morris and Rose's piece and this one represent emerging scholarly emphases on organizing, cataloguing, and accessing archival materials. As Graban processed eleven boxes of material collected from the work of Helen Gougar, a nineteenth-century American suffragist, she discerned differences between the archivist's desire to preserve original order and her own desire to make sense of artifacts. Using Carolyn Heald's notion of diplomatics (a postmodern method of reading documentary texts) and Cindy Johanek's contextualist research paradigm, Graban developed a taxonomy for developing research questions and for sorting and cataloguing Gougar's work. Adopting Karlyn Kohrs Campbell's notion of the *double bind* or tension faced by women speakers, as well as James Porter's notion of the *forum* or two-way exchange between rhetor and audience, she developed an instrument to classify and code Gougar's discourse. Graban's unique taxonomy provides a tool for researchers to discover the contextual and intertextual factors in archival artifacts. Few existing works address the difficulty in organizing and coding archival findings, and Graban's essay provides a model for encouraging archivist-researchers to make transparent the ways in which they investigate primary materials.

"Octalog III: The Politics of Historiography in 2010," the third decennial colloquium, demonstrated that historiography remains a vibrant and contested practice in our field. Lois Agnew organized this session, and Victor Vitanza provided a response to the eight panelists: Vicki Tolar Burton, Jay Dolmage, Jessica Enoch, Ronald L. Jackson II, LuMing Mao, Malea Powell, Arthur E. Walzer, and Ralph Cintron. This panel demonstrated that while historians have expanded notions of the canon and have sought to move beyond the wealthy European white male perspective, the discipline "still negotiate[s] multiple and contested understandings of what constitutes the history of rhetoric, how to study it, and rhetoric's role in forming and promoting the common good." Panelists urged the audience to examine issues such as power, identity, spaces, corporeality, and citizenship. As we see in these three panels, the need for an ongoing examination of "The Politics of Historiography" has not diminished, and the topics under discussion remain kairotic. Many of these talks encourage scholars to expand the realm of the researcher-archivist.

Taking up notions of method and instruction—and Ferreira-Buckley's 1999 challenge to teach students how to do archival work—Jonathan Buehl, Tamar Chute, and Anne Fields' "Training in the Archives: Archival Research as Professional Development" (2012) establishes a model for introducing archival research to graduate students. Buehl, who taught the archival course in collaboration with archivist Chute and English subject librarian Fields, launched the class discussion on inquiry-based research and archival research by using an artifact: a newspaper clipping from 1959 about a college student teaching literacy at a Native American school. Six themes emerged from the researchers' interviews with the archival course students: interest in learning practical aspects of archival work, in diversifying their search strategies, in theorizing the rhetoric of historiography, in understanding their subfield by practicing historical research, in articulating what they need from methods training, and in teaching archival methods to their own students. This work represents a recent trend to proliferate pedagogical materials for training a new generation of archivists.

Kelly Ritter offers yet another way of thinking about archival research. In "Archival Research in Composition Studies: Re-Imagining the Historian's Role" (2012), she suggests an alternative research approach that mitigates the problems of subjectivity, representation, and truth claims perennially experienced by researchers using a narrative approach. To address concerns about positionality, Ritter outlines a method long used by professionals in library and information science: the archival ethnography. This method enables the historian to present (rather than represent) a community as shaped by the archivist herself rather than one that naturally occurs. Ritter points to John Brereton's *The Origins of Composition Studies in the American College, 1875–1925: A Documentary History* (1999) as the closest example of archival ethnography yet produced in our field.

The final essay in our collection, Lynée Lewis Gaillet's "(Per)Forming Archival Research Methodologies" (2012), serves as a conclusion to this volume. Based on a survey of recent scholarship and interviews with experienced archival researchers, this overview of the current status of archival research both complicates traditional conceptions of archival investigation and encourages scholars to adopt the stance of archivist-researcher.

Looking Ahead

In *Theorizing Histories of Rhetoric* (2013), a recent collection of research methodology essays, Editor Michelle Ballif reexamines historiographical approaches to the late-twentieth-century reclamation work proliferating in the twenty-first. Ballif traces the often-heated discussions about historiography in the '80s and '90s and examines the subsequent unprecedented trend of "doing" history rather than theorizing about it. Contributors to *Theorizing Histories of Rhetoric* once again ask readers to revisit their methodological approaches to archival research, thus ushering in a new phase of discussion about archival research theory.

And a new trajectory of rhetoric and composition scholarship targets *pedagogy*, blending theory and method to explore ways the field might incorporate primary or archival research into writing/research classes to train the next generation of primary researchers. Until recently, book-length treatises and course surveys of research methods glossed over primary research—the lifeblood of academic writing. Given the recent scholarly attention focused on archival research theories and methods, pedagogical implications of primary investigation now seem ripe for exploration, evidenced by recent and forthcoming scholarship that extends archival training to *undergraduate* students. Works such as Wendy Hayden's "'Gifts' of the Archives: A Pedagogy for Undergraduate Research" (*CCC* 2015) and Lynée Lewis Gaillet and Michelle Eble's textbook *Primary Research: People, Places, and Spaces* (2015) make introducing archival research methodologies and methods to undergraduate students and beginning researchers far easier than before.

These materials have fulfilled a distinct need in our field for pedagogies that engage students in inquiry-based, locally focused research. Getting students into the archives opens up new worlds of possibility in building multimodality and critical thinking skills and in encouraging service learning and civic engagement. Both undergraduates and graduate students are addressing real rhetorical situations through performing on-site and digital archival research and sharing their research both in digital spaces and in a wide variety of print formats. In addition, writing instructors increasingly write about their uses of archives in the classroom, often in collaboration with special collections librarians and archivists in journals such as *Pedagogy* and *Provenance*.

Future directions in archival research are explored more fully in the final essay of this volume, but in particular, scholars should now seek to address issues related to digital archives and documentary records. Essays such as Elizabeth Yakel's "Searching and Seeking in the Deep Web: Primary Sources on the Internet" (in Alexis E. Ramsey, Wendy B. Sharer, Barbara L'Eplattenier, and Lisa S. Mastrangelo, eds., *Working in the Archives*, 2010) provide instruction for researchers who must delve into the "deep web" (beyond library finding aids and engine searches) to ascertain holdings and find materials. However, technology changes so fast that published materials quickly become outdated. We asked the noted archival scholars who edited *Working in the Archives* for their thoughts on next steps in archival research. Barb L'Eplattenier's answer is definitive: we need more work about researching online and on curating online collections. We need to investigate

> how to negotiate and locate electronic versions of documents—the uncentralizing of archival finding aids. There's so much—I don't know if it is just because we are not trained historians or librarians, but the sheer amount of texts/images/video/interviews online is overwhelming. Additionally, how to deal with multi-modal histories as publishers/writing manuscripts . . . Our history is electronic and it's both inaccessible and overwhelming.
> (Message to Lynée Lewis Gaillet)

In response, Wendy Sharer expands upon L'Eplattenier's comments:

> I wonder if we aren't at a critical moment when more of our focus should be on methods of archiving rather than/in addition to methods of archival research. I'm thinking about how many hard-copy only correspondences didn't get saved, how many student projects were tossed out with the syllabi and other records of pedagogical work when someone retired, how many meeting minutes were never copied and put into files for keeping, and the list goes on. Part of the issue was the fact that those responsible for producing and circulating these texts didn't see a value in keeping them, but another part of the issue was the time and expense of copying, sorting, filing, finding storage, etc.
> (Message to Lynée Lewis Gaillet)

Sharer also points out that the time is now right for rhetoric scholars "to establish a more systematic, centralized way of talking about/naming archival materials that are particularly relevant to Rhetcomp, materials that might not be seen as valuable or promising to other researchers, or at least not valuable in the same ways." And adding to the conversation about future archival concerns, Lisa Mastrangelo notes a new direction in archival research, specifically the feminist approach to archival investigation advocated by Jacqueline Jones Royster and Gesa Kirsch in *Feminist Rhetorical Practices: New Horizons for Rhetoric, Composition, and Literacy Studies*:

> [T]hinking about Royster and Kirsch['s methodology] helps me with my "method." My initial [archival] method, like most, was the recovery and reinscription that so many of us do and have done. But I love their idea of moving beyond that to the ideas of critical imagination, strategic contemplation, social circulation, and globalization. For me, this has just been such a great way of moving beyond "Here's something really cool" and instead thinking about how I know what I know, how it might be placed in its place and time, and how it might have travelled more widely from there.
> (Message to Lynée Lewis Gaillet)

These issues, along with others noted in the final essay of this volume, point to logical future directions in scholarship about archival research and pedagogy. In particular, we see the place for further conversations about the role of archival investigation working in tandem with texts such as the forthcoming collection *Microhistories of Composition* (Utah State Press). This volume includes a brilliant introduction to new methodological uses of microhistories by Bruce McComiskey, collection editor. He explains that in microhistories, "the researcher's point of view [or positionality] becomes an intrinsic part of the account. The research process is explicitly described and the limitations of documentary evidence, the formulation of hypotheses and the lines of thought followed are no longer hidden away from the eyes of the uninitiated." He goes on to explain ways in which microhistories enact a new relationship with the audience, change the power dynamics between researcher/material under scrutiny, and rely heavily on archival sources that reflect local knowledge, not abstract trends.

While the term "archives" is often associated with dusty attics, cold basements, and fragile documents, the essays assembled herein point to the vibrancy of primary research, the possibilities within this research method, and its centrality to current scholarly investigations. By redefining what constitutes an archive and how we access, query, and report archival findings, these scholars bring to light new venues, new voices, and new perspectives. This landmark volume provides snapshots of the history of archival research methods and methodology—serving as a guide to issues that have been investigated, and, more importantly, suggesting those that have yet to be explored.

Works Cited

Ballif, Michelle, ed. *Theorizing Histories of Rhetoric*. Carbondale: Southern Illinois UP, 2013. Print.

Gaillet, Lynée Lewis and Michelle Eble. *Primary Research: People, Places, and Spaces*. New York: Routledge, 2015. Print.

Hayden, Wendy. "'Gifts' of the Archives: A Pedagogy for Undergraduate Research." *CCC* 66.3 (2015): 402–426. Print.

L'Eplattenier, Barbara. E-mail message to Lynée Lewis Gaillet. 19 February 2015.

Mastrangelo, Lisa. E-mail message to Lynée Lewis Gaillet. 19 February 2015.

McComiskey, Bruce, ed. *Microhistories of Composition*. Forthcoming Utah State UP. Print.

Ramsey, Alexis E., Wendy B. Sharer, Barbara L'Eplattenier, and Lisa S. Mastrangelo, eds. *Working in the Archives: Practical Research Methods in Rhetoric and Composition*. Carbondale: Southern Illinois UP, 2010. Print.

Roster, Jacqueline Jones and Gesa E. Kirsch. *Feminist Rhetorical Practices: New Horizons for Rhetoric, Composition, and Literacy Studies*. Carbondale: Southern Illinois UP, 2012. Print.

Sharer, Wendy. E-mail message to Lynée Lewis Gaillet. 20 February 2015.

Yakel, Elizabeth. "Searching and Seeking in the Deep Web: Primary Sources on the Internet." In Alexis Ramsey, Wendy Sharer, Barbara L'Eplattenier, and Lisa Mastrangelo, eds. *Working in the Archives: Practical Research Methods in Rhetoric and Composition*. Carbondale: Southern Illinois UP, 2010. Print. 102–118.

SECTION 1

CLAIMING GROUND

1.
[OCTALOG I:] THE POLITICS OF HISTORIOGRAPHY
Panel Organized by James J. Murphy

Prologue

It is from the ancient Greek term *polis* that we derive our modern word *politics*. Aristotle declares that it is the aim of men living in a community (a *polis*) to work together for the common good; just as Ethics is the study of how individuals work toward what they perceive as goods, so Politics is the examination of how communities work toward their commonly perceived goods. For Aristotle it is the choice of Final Causes (purposes) which determines the Efficient Causes (ways of action) which a community pursues.

In Aristotelian terms, then, an historian's reason for writing his or her account of things will shape the way in which the task is undertaken.

As reasons differ, so ways will differ. The one event may be to one observer a biographical phenomenon, to another a sign of demographic trend, or to another a proof of dialectical synthesis. Or to put it in Archimedean terms, the place where one stands will have a great influence on what the historian's lever can move.

It should not be surprising, then, to discover that historians can differ widely about the efficient causality of their craft when they clearly differ so widely about the "why" of what they are doing. These differings are essentially disagreements about the nature of the common good for the *polis*, which in turn lead to disagreements about ways and means.

It is probably natural that this should be. History seems to be a public enterprise. The poet who notes that "Many a gem of purest ray serene" is born to blush, then die unseen would certainly not say the same of a history. The term *private history* would be not only an oxymoron, but a contradiction in terms. By the same token, the term *Politics of Historiography* is a redundancy. The writer of history is a grapher of the *polis*.

The reader of the following pages must therefore bear in mind that what is at stake here is not differings in methodology alone but varying perceptions of what ought to be discovered for the good of the community. Those variations in perception lead inevitably to variations in focus, in choice of data, in mode of presentation. The multilogue format of an eight-person discussion may bewilder the reader at first reading, but it might be profitable to approach this text the way one can read a new play—that is, read rapidly through to the end to get the gist of the plot, then return to savor the

---

Murphy, James J. "The Politics of Historiography." *Rhetoric Review* 7 (1988): 5–49. Print.

interplay of the characters. And, since the Editor views this particular drama as actually Act One of a continuing Brechtean exchange, the reader can interject Self as a character in Act Two by responding to what is spoken here.

James J. Murphy
University of California, Davis

Panelists' Statements

DIALECTICAL HISTORIES OF RHETORIC

James Berlin, Purdue University

The historian of rhetoric must deny pretensions to objectivity, looking upon the production of histories as a dialectical interaction between the set of conceptions (the terministic screen) brought to the materials of history and the materials themselves. The data chosen for interpretation and for exclusion will be determined by this governing framework. The data itself, however, can also disrupt the scheme which selected it, challenging in a genuine dialectic its adequacy to events. There are no definitive histories since no historian's ruling perceptual network can ever account for the entire historical field, or even for the field it itself has selected. Thus, there must be multiple histories of rhetoric, each identifying its unique standing place—its grounds for seeing—and the terrain made available from this perspective. Most important, each history endorses an ideology, a conception of economic, social, political, and cultural arrangements that is privileged in its interpretation. These must be made self-reflexively available to scrutiny. In brief, historians must become aware of the rhetoricity of their own enterprise, rhetoric here being designated the uses of language in the play of power.

ENGLISH COMPOSITION AS A SOCIAL PROBLEM

Robert J. Connors, University of New Hampshire

Composition historians live by necessity in a polemical universe of discourse. Since our discipline has a unique genesis—having been created to solve a social problem and not by the evolution of a body of knowledge—we are forced to make judgments and take sides in everything we write. The hypotheses we evolve are all either implicitly or explicitly a commentary on what is going on in the teaching of writing and its meaning in our culture today. Since, more than most other college-level courses, the teaching of writing is tied in with larger cultural goals, dreams, and fears, our history, to be useful, must show us how this connection has developed and worked in the past. How, in other words, has the culture created rhetoric, and how has rhetoric then recreated the culture? Composition history cannot exist in a narrow valley of "history of ideas," because all of our disciplinary ideas have been based in people's struggle for a better life. Purely philosophical history is mandarin history. Meaningful historical writing must teach us what people in the past have wanted from literacy so that we may come to understand what *we* want.

PEDAGOGICAL GOALS

Sharon Crowley, Northern Arizona University

Few historians of rhetoric and composition, I take it, write essays or books about early nineteenth-century writing instruction for the pure pleasure of adding to the growing body of historical research in this area. Rather, we undertake our work with pedagogical goals in mind; we want, in general, to guide teachers of composition in making pedagogical choices by acquainting them with those which have been made in the past. To paraphrase Professor Connors, we write history because we still live in a professional world which is directly shaped by our intellectual and institutional histories. Historians of rhetoric and composition are also more sensitive than are many professional historians to the fact that histories are constructed narratives, that there exists no objective means of finding, interpreting, or assembling historical data which could guarantee the truth of the resulting narrative. And yet we often find that the intellectual categories we introduce in our histories, or the figures we study, are reified by our readers in such a way as to award them quasi-metaphysical status. For example, we have been charged with canon-formation, something I am sure none of us intended when we began to study influential figures in our history. A major irony resides in the fact that the potential reification of our work is a direct result of the pedagogical bent of our profession, where the first question asked of any research is "What use is it in the classroom?"

LURCHING TOWARD MT. OLYMPUS: THE *POLIS* AND POLITICS OF HISTORIOGRAPHY IN CLASSICAL RHETORIC

Richard Leo Enos, Carnegie Mellon University

What constitutes "proof," or the validity warranting historical interpretation has a direct impact on the meaning one gives to historical phenomena. Akin to the notion of a *polis*, a community of scholars exist who regulate, adjudicate and establish standards and methods of analysis. Often for the sake of the pristine and venerable, however, sources of proof tend to be linked to the exegesis of literary texts as the dominant if not sole source for evidence. An openness and attention toward the development of new sources of evidence and methodologies for analysis will replace a disposition toward conventional methods of research for the sake of conformity and tradition with the laudable quest for a more sensitive understanding of the history of rhetoric. In this sense the *polis* of historians of rhetoricians places the Olympian value of its *paideia*, or quest toward intellectual excellence, ahead of any yearning that places conformity to Victorian ideals as its primary criterion for scholarly contribution.

POLITICS AND HISTORIOGRAPHY

Victor J. Vitanza, University of Texas, Arlington

My political/rhetorical/hysteriographical positions cannot be paraphrased; they can be only performed. Therefore, forced to write a paraphrase, I lie ... and therefore at best give contra/dictory stage directions: (1) *"There is no History of Rhetorik."* Hegel says that there is no consciousness without self-consciousness. It follows then: If there is no consciousness without self-consciousness, there can be no Histories/Hysteries of Rhetorics without historiographies/hysteriographies. (2) *"There is, however (quite ironically), 'The History of Rhetorik.'"* But what are we to think of it? since it gives so little, if any, thought to itself? Its historiography—can it even be labeled as such?—is "common sense realism"; it is unselfconscious ... without suspecting itself ... of political suppression, ... without even suspecting itself ... of being politically ideological. (3) *"The History of Rhetorik is a 'Philosophical' History of Rhetorik"* ... which is written out of the fear of the "bewitchment" of language ... out of the fear of *"The Other"* untold Histories of Rhetorics, "Hysteries of Desire." (4) *"Histories-of-Desire, Histories of Rhetorics, are Hysteries of Discourses in their plural, forever non-homogenized, heterological (Hysterical) artistic-anarchistic forms."* They are Hysteries of Rhetorics as "aphoristic mis/representative political antidotes," which are based on Lacan's *"lalangue"* Lecercle's *"délire."* Kristeva's "semiotic," or Cixous' "laugh of the medusa" (her "flying in language and making it fly"). They are Hysteries, as Cixous would say, against "the false theater of phallogocentric representationalism." They are Hysteries of Rhetorics that have as their locus "the body hysteric"; they are Hysteries of Rhetorics as irrepressible Laughter breaking up the logos of phallogocentric philosophical rhetorik.

THE POLITICS OF TEXT SELECTION IN HISTORY OF RHETORIC

Susan C. Jarratt, Miami University

In past decades, historians of rhetoric have taken as their materials for the most part texts explicitly calling themselves "rhetorics." They are usually sets of student lectures, and their investigation has lent power and value to their commentators largely by dint of their obscurity. That is, they are not titles "owned" by other disciplines. Aristotle's *Rhetoric,* for example, becomes a primary text not only because it establishes a discipline by naming it, but because it is generally ignored by other disciplines—classics, philosophy, literary theory. The primary historiographical trope at work here is the rediscovery and possession of forgotten treasures. An alternative position would entail the appropriation and redefinition of texts currently "held" by other disciplines, which, despite their names, concern rhetorical issues. Examples are Thucydides' histories, Coleridge's "Essay on Method," and Marx's introduction to *Capital.* As daring usurper (rather than marginalized hoarder), rhetoric could step into its role as meta-discipline and create opportunities for dialogue among historians, critics, and theorists across several disciplines.

MY IDEOLOGICAL STANCE

Nan Johnson, University of British Columbia

My ideological stance toward historiography falls somewhere in the middle of the continuum of beliefs ranging from an orthodox confidence in the expository nature of history (the notion that writing history is a straightforward matter of uncovering and explaining essentials and orders that are there to be discovered) to a poststructuralist self-consciousness of history as a form of literary narrative (the notion that the substance of history is figurative not actual). I proceed on the assumption that historical research and writing are archaeological *and* rhetorical activities. As an historian, I am responsible both to the claims of historical evidence *and* to the burden of proclaiming my enterprise as an attempt to tell "true stories."

THE INSTITUTIONALIZATION OF RHETORIC AND THE INSCRIPTION OF GENDER

Jan Swearingen, University of Texas, Arlington

Two social contexts for rhetorical theory and practice have been omitted from extant histories of rhetoric during the classical period, an omission that has distorted subsequent understanding of rhetoric and public language alike during that period. First, the spread of early literacy (*c.* 450–50 BC) was contemporaneous with the institutionalization of rhetoric in Greek and Roman schools, and should be a consistent context for examining early rhetoric. It has instead been more common to examine rhetoric as an oral milieu, an emphasis that obscures the mutual influence of rhetoric on literacy and literacy on rhetoric. Second, women were increasingly excluded from schooling, rhetoric, and public assemblies during precisely the period when rhetoric and literacy were in the ascendant, a pattern that is now known to have occurred in other cultures of the ancient near east. Literacy in virtually every culture brought with it exclusion of women from the inscribed culture, whether that culture was philosophical, religious, or literary. In the exclusion of women from the schools of rhetoric there is a seldom-noted pattern that merits further study: women were included well into the 4th century AD in schools of philosophy. Why were women included in Plato's Academy but barred from Aristotle's Lyceum? Are the agonistic patterns in rhetorical argument and dialectic an inscription of gender along the lines suggested by Walter Ong, and if so, what alternate patterns of discourse will we find in retrieving the women philosophers of the classical period?

Philosophical Statements

JAMES J. MURPHY: Let me read you a portion of what I sent these eight panelists. Each panelist is allotted three minutes, one hundred and eighty seconds, to make a statement in addition to what is on the handout—that's on the handout that the first hundred of you received. This is a sort of bonus for early arrival. Following these statements, which will go on consecutively without comments, the panel will, if they have anything to say to each other, have thirty minutes to say it. Following that, if they will limit themselves, you will have fifteen minutes to say whatever you want to say to whomever you wish to say it, and then I will take three minutes at the end to tell you what you all said. I had planned initially to do a short history of rhetoric for you. But since that, I was told that I could only have three minutes too. And since the theme of today is not charity but justice, I decided to forego that instead and just give you the history of the world with two examples.

I assume you are here for some reason. As Aristotle says, "Whatever occurs, occurs for some reason." Perhaps it's true of the 4Cs as well. My reason is that, to go back to an ancient wall inscription in Greece, the one that says, "He who does not study rhetoric can be the victim of it," he or she who does not study the history of rhetoric will be the victim of the reinvention of the wheel. And we see that all the time. These people are interested in bringing whatever has already been done by other people into the presence of us, to see whether we're doing new things, old things, bad things, good things. They had their varying reasons.

We're going to let them troop up here in the order in which they are in the program, which may be slightly different from the one that's on the handout, but you can probably figure it out. We have a high tech method of time control: I'm going to show them this when there's one minute to go. When there's less than time left, I'm going to show them this. And if they go on beyond a human breath, I'm going to use the British method; I'm going to stand in silent disapproval. And I hope you will reinforce this social control should that occur in the unlikely event of an overtime statement.

So let us begin in the order of the program, which is—I don't have mine handy.

JAMES BERLIN: A rhetoric, any rhetoric, ought to be situated within the economic, social, and political conditions of its historical moment, if it is to be understood. A rhetoric is a set of rules that attempts to naturalize—an ideology—to make one particular arrangement of economic, social, and political conditions appear to be inevitable and ineluctable, inscribed in the very nature of things. To understand a rhetoric, it is thus necessary to examine its position in the play of power in its own time. This means looking at it within its material conditions. The difficulty for the historian is that, even when evidence is available and extensive, the writing of history is itself a rhetorical act. The historian is herself underwriting a version of the normal, of the proper arrangement of classes, races, and genders. History does not write itself, having in itself no inherent pattern of development. Historians cannot escape this play of power, inherent in all signifying practices. They must instead attempt to locate themselves in this play, to find their predilections and to forward them, making them available to their auditors. This ideological screen makes the historical record readable to the historian, influencing what he sees as significant and what he finds to be meaningless.

Historians must, however, also strive for a dialectical relationship with the evidence, remaining sensitive to the impossibility of totality, of accounting for everything. But this is a negative dialectic (in the sense that Adorno uses the term), the recognition that all accounts are limited and subject to revision. All histories are partial accounts, are both biased and incomplete. The good histories admit this and then tell their stories. The bad attempt to dominate the past, pretending at the same time to be mere recorders of the facts.

We then must have *histories* of rhetoric, multiple versions of the past, each version acting as a check, a corrective to the others. This, of course, also means that we will have differences and disagreements, and these are not to be denied.

Rhetorical histories are important to the writing teacher. They explore the relationship of discourse and power, a rhetoric again being a set of rules that privilege particular power relations. A rhetoric explores discursive practices, ways of using language that are found in numerous political practices. Since a rhetoric is best understood in its difference from other rhetorics, from competing versions of normal discourse, it reveals the conflicts of an historical moment.

In all of this, rhetorical histories reveal us to ourselves. We do not read and write rhetorical histories to avoid repeating the past. We could not repeat the past if we tried. As economic, social, and political conditions change, so do the rhetorics that inscribe the discourse rules that are a part of these conflicts. We read and write histories to understand better our differences from the past and this difference provides the point of illumination for the present. Thank you.

ROBERT CONNORS: I write history to try to make my world a better place, to try to brighten the corner in which I live and work. And in order to do this at all, I have to accept certain things in my epistemological world, as assented to by you, by people who read what I write, by the community of discourse in which I live. I have to accept the idea that truth for us is consensually created by our assent to it. I have to accept the idea that there is an "I" who can assent and persuade, and a "you" who can assent and be persuaded. I have to accept the idea that there is evidence that we can agree exists, and good reasons for accepting or not accepting it. I have to accept the idea that persuasion and assent are sought for both practical and ethical reasons.

There are accusations against accepting these ideas. Some people would claim that they are politically naive which, frankly, is an accusation I think hurts any of us: to be called "naive" in the academic world is a mortal blow against certain elements of our pride. These ideas might also be called insufficiently aware of the ideology that supports them. And against this, I can only say that I feel that to live I must act; otherwise, ideologies competing within me can create an endless hall of mirrors that will prevent any action on my part.

I've written a number of histories of certain problems in composition studies, and bizzarely enough, I'm down here at the far end of the table with the "establishment historians." In my own mind, all the historical pieces that I've written have been meant to be profoundly anti-systematic. They've been meant to attack certain genuine practical problems that I've seen in the teaching of writing, trace them back to sources, and try to figure out where or when things began to go this way in the culture and the educational establishment, to find out whether or not we can do anything about that today.

Is propaganda part of what a composition or rhetorical historian has to engage in? Well, if we look at the word *propaganda* in its original sense, as propagation of a faith, I think yes. A faith that I subscribe to, and that I think most people here subscribe to, is that we must come to an idea or vision of truth together by the exchange of good reasons. That is a faith to which I will openly admit I subscribe. I have to reject what Pat Bizzell in a session yesterday called the "epistemological *Weltschmerz*" that can too often accompany a close examination of the ideological reasons for accepting ideologies. I'm done.

SHARON CROWLEY: We're physically closer up here than we are intellectually. Very interesting, a sort of contrast. I've been thinking very hard for about six months about why one would want to write the history of composition studies. I've read Victor Vitanza's arguments for revisionist histories. I've reread Professor Connors' work, which I admire, and I think his account of it is an accurate one. And I've almost come to the conclusion that it's impossible to write history. I feel almost paralyzed by the impossibility of writing history and I'll tell you why that is.

If I get excited about tracking down an idea or a tradition—for instance, if I discover that the five-paragraph theme, which is so ubiquitous in traditional composition pedagogy, has an intellectual history. That intellectual history is called "method" and it's all bound up with the notion that one *thinks* first, one goes through an act of investigation first, then one moves to presentation. And I've discovered that this is an invention of modern thought, invented in the 17th century. (I don't know the day and the time yet, but I'll find them.) And then I begin to reread forward through historical texts and I discover in Isaac Watts a discussion of method. (Isaac Watts was a logician whose *Logick* first came out in 1724, and enjoyed many, many editions. It was a popular school textbook.) And I discover in Watts *unity, coherence,* and *emphasis.* They're right there on the page. And then I finally get my hands on a copy of Rippingham's composition textbook, which appeared in this country in 1802, and there's Watts and there's a theory of invention there that is tied to methodical progression. That's very exciting and that's a lot of fun.

But since I am a historian of composition studies, I have to remember that my ideas are going to be read by people who have very pragmatic aims. "Of what use is this to me in my teaching?" they will ask.

I am afraid that the things I write may get reified. For instance, Professor Murphy has taught us that there are three major traditions in medieval rhetoric: the art of letter writing, the art of sermon making, the art of poetry making. It strikes me that it's very easy to turn that into an exam question: What are the three major traditions of medieval rhetoric? I'm sure Professor Murphy doesn't intend to have that happen to his work; we certainly wouldn't want that to happen to any of our work. But it does. That's the problem with writing history in composition studies. It's the fun, but it's also the bane. I'll stop.

RICHARD ENOS: Notice that these people are on my left in my perspective, and I'm on the right.

If not the only, there's at least one salient issue that captures my position on the politics of historiography, and fittingly it's the same issue that is at the center of Aristotle's rhetoric: What constitutes proof on issues of opinion requiring judgment?

The tenor of that issue can easily and appropriately be transferred to research in the history of rhetoric. That is, what forces shape validity in historical study? Historians of rhetoric tend to follow a classical form of historical research: thesis, hypothesis, analysis, and synthesis. Our academic *polis* establishes what Pat Bizzell calls "foundational standards" and great importance is placed on the cogency of the last phase, the synthesis phase. That is, the ability to draw together meaning and advance inferences about the "proof" evidenced at the analysis phase. Unlike Bizzell's disparaging view on foundationalism, however, I equate it here with a sense of *paideia;* that is, an unceasing effort to seek, establish, and refine standards of intellectual excellence. From that perspective, the *paideia* of historiography is to determine by the admissibility of proof, and the openness to accept, new sources of evidence. What constitutes proof, or the validity warranting historical interpretation, has a direct impact on the synthetic meaning one gives to historical phenomena.

In this respect, historians of rhetorics exist in a tacit academy. The community of researchers participate in a dialectic in which research is articulated and responded to primarily through journal essays, books, and reviews. Not enough attention, however, is paid to the categories of evidence brought under analysis nor the creation of new methodologies. And it is this point which I wish to stress. For the sake of the pristine and venerable, sources of proof tend to be linked to the exegesis of literary texts as the dominant, if not sole, source of evidence. A conservative orientation to what constitutes valid evidence in historiography promotes a closed system that risks limited acquisition of evidence, and ultimately an imprecise understanding that fails to account adequately for forces shaping the subject under study. For the sake of time, I will limit myself to an analogy and I'll just mention it here.

Heinrich Schliemann, the father of modern archaeology, was vilified because others believed that dirtying one's hands through actually going to see what was at Troy was something that scholars shouldn't do, but rather make armchair explanations based solely upon the *Iliad* and the *Odyssey*. But his innovation established new methods and new insights to the homeric world. Unfortunately, many researchers in the history of rhetoric have taken the prevailing disposition of the *polis,* our scholarly community, with tacit acceptance and have not learned from Schliemann and have been reluctant to "dirty their hands" in such a manner of research, but rather perpetuate and even glorify the armchair, venerable methods of analysis in the history of rhetoric.

Would it be, for us, a question of "dirty hands," for example, to actually go to Sicily and examine artifacts that may tell us more about Corax, Tisias, and Gorgias, than what literary fragments alone would have to yield? Would it be unthinkable to immerse oneself in the study of Greek archaeology and history in order to learn about cultural forces shaping Greek thought and expression? And lastly, would it be unthinkable for us, unlike our colleagues who have done such a good job in the social sciences, to develop new methodologies and new *theories* to try to account for the evidence that they present in the formulation of their theories? Thank you.

VICTOR VITANZA: i. . . . faraway voices are telling us: Of arms and the *mask*uline and its history of rhetorik. We do not sing; instead, of "the body hysteric" and its histeries of the antibody rhetorics, We do sing.

ii. In the nineteenth century, Walt Whitman wrote, "I sing the body electric."

iii. Is this singing transcendentally above/beyond us? No! (To repeat, ever again) it is in the body hysteric; ... its locus is the body-*politic*-hysteric. ...

iv. In the seventeenth century: Sir Thomas Browne wrote, "We are only that *amphibious* piece between a corporal and spiritual essence. ... Man [is] that great and true *amphibium,* whose nature is disposed to live not only like other creatures in diverse elements but in divided and distinguished worlds. For though there be but one to sense, there are two to reason: the one visible, the other invisible. ..."

vi. In the nineteenth century: Herman Melville wrote, "Oh man! admire and model thyself after the whale. Do thou, too, remain warm among ice. Do thou, too, live in this world without being of it."

vii. In the twentieth century: Helene Cixous "flies" and "steals" away while she "sings." "They [the phallologocentric world] riveted us between two horrifying myths: between the Medusa and the abyss. That would be enough to set half the world laughing, except that it is still going on, [this] phallologocentric sublation is with us, and it's militant, regenerating the old patterns, anchored in the dogma of castration. ... You [YOU!] only have to look at the Medusa straight on to see her. And she's not deadly. She's beautiful and she's laughing. ... Men say that there are two unrepresentable things: death and the feminine sex. ... Let's get out here."

viii. Let us, then, return to the laughing rhapsodic voices: They sing, "we are no longer—as you have lied to us with the 'clarity' of your metaphors—political 'amphibians,' but political 'amphibolies'; that is, many contra/dictary, ka(e)rotic voices in laughter." Cixous sings: "break up the 'truth' with laughter." Deleuze sings: "Laughter—and not meaning. Schizophrenic laughter or revolutionary joy." The voices sing: Let us resist ... their history across laughter, ... their common sense, realist historiography across the body-*politic*-hysteric, ... across the am*phib*olous, ka(e)rotic *hyster*iographies. ... Let's get out of here!

SUSAN JARRATT: The printed offering that is on the sheet that you have makes a case for text selection, a kind of practical outcome of a certain kind of historiography, and that case dealt with the politics of disciplines. What I'd like to do with my three minutes is to give an example of the way in which that practice has worked for me in a class that has an outcome that has to do with the politics of gender.

In a class that I'm teaching right now on the history of rhetoric from the 17th through the 19th centuries, I look at the canon and I don't see any women. This is no surprise, right? So what do I do? I decided to include Mary Wollstonecraft's "A Vindication of the Rights of Woman" plus a selection of Eliza Haywood's work, "The Invisible Spy," which is a parody of Addison and Steele's *Spectator.* So what this does for me in my class is it shows two kinds of rhetorical practice, both of which can be gauged in relation to the people who are in the canon—those Scots, Blair and Campbell, and Whately also, the Brit—to show how, in the one case, a woman takes on the hegemonic forms of discourse in order to make her way from a subordinate power position, and, in the other hand, how Eliza Haywood rejects those. She rejects a kind of prepositional argument. She uses magic, she uses narrative, but she does the same kind of social commentary and criticism that Wollstonecraft is doing. It has the same goal. So, this is a way in which I see a kind of historiography working in my classroom and having a kind of political impact.

NAN JOHNSON: What I want to do here is to speak quite personally about how I have come to view history and the writing of history. In particular I'd like to extend my position statement regarding the archaeological and rhetorical nature of this type of enterprise.

In likening historical research to archaeology, I am upholding in part the traditional, and I would say common-sensical, bias that historical investigation can unearth material evidence. But my present notion of historical research as a type of archaeological dig recognizes much more about history. It recognizes the heuristic and epistemic nature of historical research. Historical scholarship is heuristic in the sense that the active research itself creates and recreates conceptual directions as well as an emerging hierarchy of topical and procedural priorities. Research is epistemic in the sense that methodological activity itself becomes the means of coming to know the past in a particular way. The understanding which the historian comes to bears the unique mark of how the investigative method has proceeded and of the inevitable hierarchy of topics and conclusions that have emerged to guide conceptual development.

One of the particular political implications of viewing historical research as archaeological is that it mitigates against intellectual righteousness. If method implicates conclusions and vice versa, claims to "right" answers have to be taken with a grain of salt, and method becomes a process to scrutinize quite critically.

Why I believe history is rhetorical as well as archaeological is already implied by my view toward historical research. If methodological motion can shape the topical hierarchy which emerges in an investigation, then conceptual content, argumentative emphasis, formal structure, and style in historical writing can be predisposed as well, by the topical substance and propositional logic the historian adopts or forsakes. In this belief, I am showing what can be defined as a poststructuralist tendency to recognize that the propositionality of all texts resides in rhetorical structures and not in claims to "fact." After all, like literary narratives, the logic and substance of historical texts are invented and cannot be defined as transparent.

From this perspective, I cannot present the account of 19th-century rhetoric I am working on as a documentary because I know that it is figurative. It is an interpretive document. However, I submit, a self-consciousness of my role as a narrator does not prevent me from intending my tale to be accepted as a "true story" in the sense that, as an act of rhetoric, my history imposes formal shape on the probable, or on relative truth, while simultaneously seeking acceptance as a logical explanation of reality. Believing in history as an effort to persuade readers to accept one particular story of the past reminds me of the duplicity and the obligations which attend any rhetorical exchange. Although we can know that the nature of reality of past and present is negotiated, although we can know that what historians do is to compel an act of attention to a text which is itself an act of attention, although we can know that histories are just stories, historians and readers alike tend to *believe* and subsequently *proceed* as if some stories were truer than others. It is the energy of this contradiction that fuels the political impact of historiography and makes this business of accounting for the past a baffling responsibility.

JAN SWEARINGEN: I think it's possible to write history, and I would like to state outright that my ideology is an aggressive naivete and that I embrace the metaphysics of authenticity.

Two social contexts for examining rhetorical theory and practice in the classical period have been omitted from many histories of rhetoric in that period. This has been to the great disadvantage of our subsequent understanding of that period. First, the spread of early literacy between 450 and 50 BC coincided almost exactly with, and was virtually inseparable from, the development and subsequent institutionalization of rhetoric in the Greek schools and only slightly later in the Roman schools. Thus, I propose that rhetoric be reconceived and re-examined, and its history be rewritten, as a primary instrument of disseminating literacy in the classical era.

We should also examine the history of the exclusion of women from the schools of rhetoric and the interesting but seldom-noted pattern of their continuing inclusion in the nonrhetorical schools of antiquity. Plato's Academy, but not Aristotle's Lyceum, included women. The daughters of the Stoic Diodoros Kronos were renowned by dialectitions and grammarians in a later era. Stoicism in general rejected technical rhetoric. The Academic Skeptics, who evolved out of the original academy and the peripetetics descended from Aristotle's School, taught literacy and rhetoric to boys and young men who would use these skills in statecraft. Women were excluded from this schooling. Walter Ong has observed the effects of the exclusion of women from the universities for much later eras, for the Medieval and Renaissance periods. There has been a longstanding and persistent exclusion of women from training in argument through their exclusion from training in Latin, in rhetoric, and from access to the manuscript culture that characterized early literacy. Democritus railed that women should never be taught argument, suggesting that at the very dawn of formalized training in argument there was sentiment explicitly forbidding or discouraging women's participation in argument.

It is argument more than any other single element in early literacy, and rhetoric alike, which I propose seems most tenaciously associated with masculinity. This is an argument that Walter Ong has also made for a later era. An insidious domino effect that I think we need to study conceivably links exclusion from argumentation with exclusion from literacy in this early period. The institutionalized schools of rhetoric functioned as the core curriculum in classical and later eras. Exclusion from these schools meant exclusion from literacy as well. The seemingly gender-neutral phenomenon of literacy itself, if viewed through these ties to rhetoric and particularly to argumentation, can be re-viewed, I think, and should be, as a masculinizing influence on both culture and language within which we're still operating when it comes to argument.

JAMES J. MURPHY: In the very best restaurants, at least in California, I would be offered a bewildering menu of possibilities in a 17-page wine list from which to choose.

You begin your dinner with perhaps an hors d'oeuvre, then a salad, and then perhaps a fish dish. And then to whet your appetite, in a little flute glass, sugar, or some sweet. That's my function right here. I've been trying to think of something sweet to say to pursue this metaphor and I'm at a loss. So I'll invite you to use your imaginations. This is a bewildering array of very cogent ideas and I must confess I agree with every one of them. I should have taken some of the argumentation training that Jan was talking about while I was young, apparently. At this stage we would like to tap the ebulient spirits of the speakers to see if, perchance, they have anything that they would like to ask or say to each other. I've already been nudged at least once in this connection, and so to give primacy to the pushy element, I'll ask Bob what he wants to say.

ROBERT CONNORS: I'd like to address a question to both Jim and to Victor. I've read and heard both of them attack Santayana's famous cliché, "Those who cannot remember the past are condemned to repeat it." I don't think anybody would stand absolutely behind the idea that we're condemned to repeat it, but I almost seem to think I hear them saying that we can't usefully *learn* from the past, or that we can't learn enough to keep us from making similar mistakes though we study the past. An example that comes immediately to my mind is the example of the Harvard Book List and the Harvard Exams of the 1880s and 1890s, and how knowledge of what happened there might affect our vision of E.D. Hirsch's cultural literacy campaign. I think we can learn a tremendous amount from the Harvard experience and apply it today. I'd like to hear if you agree or disagree.

VICTOR VITANZA: I agree and I disagree with the statement. I want to situate myself in what a logician would usually call a contradiction; but, as a rhetorician, as a sophistic rhetorician, I would call a paradox. Yes, we can learn from history. I just don't think there is any doubt about that, and we have. Whether or not we can act on it in a rational manner, I'm not sure. What I want to do is to give a certain credence to the fact that we are not only rational creatures, but that we are nonrational creatures as well. I think there's something very perverse in us as human beings and, given the knowledge of the past and the knowledge of the mistakes of the past, we often repeat them nonetheless. So in that sense I have problems with Santayana's statement. It's not complex enough. It does not celebrate the true multiplicity of what it is to be a human being in history because there is something called "hystery."

JAMES BERLIN: I would say that what we are engaged in is a conflict of forces in which some people want us to make the same mistakes again because they benefit from us making the same mistakes again. I think that's what Hirsch's involved in. He's arguing for a particular class position that's also involved in gender and race as well. It is in the interest of this class and this gender and this race to keep repeating these mistakes. Now he is perfectly historical—in fact he *invokes* history in support of this project.

Now, the thing is, I would argue that there're a number of problems here. One thing, I don't think that the period of early monopolistic capitalism is that radically different from the period of monopolistic capitalism we are in right now. In other words, the tests designed were then to serve particular purposes in the American democratic university and now we have a profession of composition teachers who are designed to serve the same purposes. And we have E.D. Hirsch who writes *The Philosophy of Composition* and tells us that's what we're here for: we're here to maintain these dominant class and gender and race relations. What he's arguing for is a repetition of these mistakes. I don't think we can repeat these mistakes exactly as he would like us to repeat them and that's where we intervene in order to stop repeating these mistakes. What we need is something different from us.

The problem with this example is that I don't think this period is radically different from our current moment. That's a problem with the example. If we look at the class relations, for instance, that existed in the feudal period, look at the class relations that existed in ancient Greece, then I think we're in a different enough situation. When we begin to see, for instance in the case of the sophists, that we're seeing a rhetoric that is different from ours, we're seeing that it's attempting to address issues that are situated in a position that tells us something about our own kind. In other words, I think, for instance, the sophists were systematically excluded from history. I would speculate that their documents were destroyed because they were dangerous politically. The reason we don't have them—Richard Enos is going to look for these documents—is because they have been destroyed; they're just not available, and I don't think that's an accident that they're not available and Aristotle and Plato are.

JAMES J. MURPHY: Did we incautiously mention the word *sophist*?

RICHARD ENOS: I would like to just give some perspectives on the ideas that he just talked about. Are all historical accounts equally credible? In other words, is it an arbitrary decision? Is one historical account just as good as another or is there some sort of jurisprudential function that our community has which weighs and sifts evidence and arrives at what we think is not—I don't want to make it into an ontological sense, that's too "easy" of an argument to weigh the truth—but the best reasoned account of what we believe took place in the phenomenon? In that sense I'm saying dialectic, in the effort to reach a reasonable interpretation, an inferential statement. And I think that's what makes history good, and if there are politics in history, it's to promote that good.

SHARON CROWLEY: I don't think that what makes history good is a decision that is that simple. That's what I'm trying to get at in my remarks. Lots of times, the reasons we read histories is that they are written by somebody like Jim Berlin, who has a reputation as an excellent historian. In other words, the whole notion of the historian's *ethos* is very important. We know Jim's work well enough now to *know* what his attitude toward historiography is and if we want that version of 19th-century history, that's what we read. If we're more comfortable with a more traditional rendition, we pick up Bob Connors' work or Nan Johnson's work. I think they all argue reasonably, and they all assess evidence carefully, they're all excellent scholars. What makes us read a history is the authority that it bears, its *ethos*.

SUSAN JARRATT: I think I can follow up on Sharon's comment that we sort of fall in a range on a spectrum of the degree to which we're interested in facts. Bob and I were having a lot of discussion yesterday about facts, and I was really enjoying the rhetoric of the kind of self-deprecation or the problems of people who are "fact" people. Rich is saying we use armchair methods, or Rich is accusing us, and I'm really kind of polarizing us here in a rhetorical way. We have armchair methods, but they're the ones who get out and dirty their hands. Bob was asking me yesterday, "What's wrong with facts?" I don't think there's anything wrong with facts; it's just that, to use the example of the rediscovery of the sophists, I wonder where the *idea* comes from that we need to go back and look for the documents of the sophists. It may be that that idea comes from someone who is not quite as invested in, already, a project of uncovering a lot of facts, but rather someone who is maybe more in the armchair and is trying to get a little bit of distance from all that archaeological dirt.

JAN SWEARINGEN: I want to answer the question, "Why should we go back and dig up the sophists?" Or "Why should we go back and dig up all these lost women philosophers that we never heard of before? Why not start where we are and go forward?" There is a theoretical position, an ideological position, that says you can't get it back anyway because it doesn't exist or because the very concept of facts is simpleminded.

In an essay entitled "Storming the Toolshed," that some of you may know, concerning women's studies and particularly Virginia Woolf, Jane Marcus argues that before you ideologically question your history in different fields and in different areas, first you have to have a history. I for one am not comfortable with the idea of leaving a group of women philosophers, or sophists, or whatever the excluded group is, just lying there unresearched, unknown, on the grounds of a modern ideology that says history is fiction. I'm not comfortable with that, and Marcus makes this point for women's studies, too. We need to retrieve the women writers of the Middle Ages and the Renaissance. There are traditions there that should be reclaimed as a part of our history, in terms of which we define ourselves. So if there are those who wish to exclude that or ignore it or not pursue it, or problematize it, so be it but I think it's a worthy enterprise. You have to have something to problematize, and if you have no history at *all*, no knowledge at *all* of those people, than you're talking about a nonexistent problematic.

I'd also like to note, on the question of the sophists, that there's an alternate argument about their exclusion that I'm not sure if I'm convinced by, but it's very interesting. In a study of Plato's *Sophist* Stanley Rosen concludes that the sophists were by no means eliminated or excluded or excised from the tradition. They were so totally absorbed by the tradition that they disappeared and that what we have had in our negative dialectics ever since are several schools of sophistic thought guiding and directing traditions within rhetoric. His way of putting it is that "the triumph of sophistry was its disappearance."

VICTOR VITANZA: Stanley Rosen also after that statement—Stanley Rosen is a philosopher—says that he clearly favors rationality over nonrationality. He clearly favors rationality of language over the sophistic magic of language. He makes that very clear and he's passing a judgment, after he makes that particular statement. So I think that's something we need to keep in mind; that bias towards rationalism clearly comes through. When I look at the work on Aristotle, even though there's a difference of agreement—say, between Kinneavy and Grimaldi and other people as well—Aristotle, nonetheless, is always perceived as being—and I think this is something that I would go along with too—as being very, very rational. To be sure, he does give time to *ethos*. But *ethos* is always talked about in terms of rationality and always *checked* by rationality, just as *pathos* is. *Pathos* is *specifically* checked by rationality. Of the three major proofs, then, *logos*—rationality—is the thing that's there *to check* us all. Stanley Rosen makes that comment as well.

SUSAN JARRATT: I want to ask Jan why it is that knowing that histories are stories keeps you from wanting to go look for the women? Did you say that just now? And also Sharon says she's paralyzed by this. I'm thinking of something I heard out of some political pamphlet that says, despite the fact there are enough nuclear warheads to destroy us all several times, and despite the fact that there are apparently troops in Central America right now, American troops, you still make soup and eat bread. And I just wonder why that freezes you or paralyzes you from doing the kind of study women do.

JAN SWEARINGEN: It doesn't freeze *me*, but the position can clearly have that effect. We've had two people here talking about how warring ideologies inside their minds would make it impossible for them to write history. That's one statement of the paralysis. Another is a radical ideology of illusoriness that would say, "Look, you can't get back the original; there is no original." And the further back it is, the less retrievable it is. I am nonetheless interested in getting back whatever we can of those shards and so forth. I believe we can understand them. I don't think problematics necessarily constrains people. It doesn't constrain me.

SUSAN JARRATT: I have another question on sort of a different subject. It's for Bob. It's a less abstract question. In Bob Connors' statement he says that, "The hypotheses we evolve are all either implicitly or explicitly a commentary on what is going on in the teaching of writing and its meaning in our culture today." This sort of puts your position in a different place from mine. I'm trying to expand the field of rhetorical studies and look at a much larger group of texts, looking at everything as text actually. And you're saying it's only pertinent to rhetorical history to the extent that, implicitly or explicitly, it has to do with teaching writing in the classroom in America in 1988. And I just wondered if you could talk about how serious you are about that constriction and how you see the relationship between that activity and kinds of history that don't directly pertain to that.

ROBERT CONNORS: I suppose I was talking specifically about the history of composition in America, which is the greater bulk of the historical work that I myself have done. And it's impossible for me to look at what was being proposed for the classroom of 1841 and not think of what that might mean for my classroom of 1988.

I wouldn't attempt to make an argument that looking at sophistic rhetoric or looking at *ars dictaminis* necessarily always moves me back toward whether I'm going to teach sentence combining on Monday. Certainly the rhetorical world is wider than the world of teaching composition. But, for the purposes of composition history, I think it's inescapable that I always keep coming back to, "Is this attitude still with me; am I still this person?"

RICHARD ENOS: There was a time in the history of rhetoric when it wasn't sophistic rhetoric; it was just rhetoric, because that's what it was. And I think that sort of perspective and attention to adjectives causes us some problems.

A few days ago, one of my colleagues, Linda Flower, was talking to me about some ideas I was sharing with her about this and I was categorizing people as "presocratic philosophers" and then "rhetoricians." And she said, "What would happen if you just didn't have those labels and looked at what they said?" I think that sort of cogent point of view is something that I have to constantly keep in mind, because I recognize I am a product of Aristotelian thought and I'm trying to understand other ways of thinking and how they compare. And I think that's what's healthy about what's going on now, something we should pay attention to.

ROBERT CONNORS: This is, I suppose, a methodological, if political, question, but it keeps coming up for all of us. It keeps coming up for me in very practical ways. What is the balance we try to strike between inductive research and deductive research, the degree to which we dance around closure about issues before we start to let our closure on those issues affect the research paths we take? In a disagreement that Jim and I once had about a book that he wrote, I now tend to see the real disagreement as having been my implicit contention that he should have danced around closure longer before he made certain decisions that affected his research paths. I just wondered if anybody had any ideas about how we can strike that balance? When do we close up and start to follow some paths and not others?

JAMES BERLIN: In an essay in *PRE/TEXT*, that has just been released from its prison in Arlington, Texas, I argue for invoking Adorno's negative dialectic. We can't ever achieve totality. We can't ever explain everything. For one thing we have to limit the field; and then we can't even explain everything in that field. So what we have to do is, we then engage in this negative dialectic. Ordinary dialectic is I bring my ideas, my conceptual framework, to the material conditions and then we have this interaction. This negative dialectic, as Jameson says, is "thought about thought," it's "thought but once removed." What we're doing is realizing that we have to reach closure. We have to totalize. And yet we have to be constantly aware that our totalization is a fiction. And that we're *doing* it because it underwrites particular economic, social, and political arrangements, whether we want to or not. My contention is that we have to acknowledge that, we have to acknowledge that inscribed in our texts there's this political bias. And, of course, part of our judgment is whether or not one closed the field too soon, in other words, was not sufficiently dialectical.

One of the reasons I was moved in the direction of Marxism, neo-Marxism, is that people kept accusing me of being this radical relativist who said, "anything goes; anybody can say anything and it's true." That's strange, if that were the case, because certain kinds of economic, social, and political arrangements appear over and over again, and the same people are benefiting from them, over and over again, at the same time that alternative interpretations are being offered. It's the same problem I have with indeterminacy. Yes, there are indeterminate readings, but somehow, why are the same readings made in powerful positions? Congressmen keep reading things the same way. Somehow their indeterminate readings enable them to emerge from a particular political stance, with a particular distribution of the material goods of our experience. And I realize that material goods are themselves constructions; they're empirical, but we can never see them. The thing in itself will always evoke this conceptual framework.

My answer is that people can be open to the charge that they did reach closure too soon. There's no question about that. Facts were missed, obvious facts, in the field, in one's project, were missed.

SHARON CROWLEY: The distinction that Bob makes is a little too simple. When you find yourself in a large state library, working with dusty shelves that nobody has touched for a hundred years, reading yet one more textbook that's just like the one you just read, you ask yourself, "What in the hell am I doing here? I could be home watching *Dallas*." But my point is that *I* already made some decision that got me into that library to do what you're calling "inductive research." But it's impossible to do purely inductive research. When I read, say, D.J. Hill's *Science of Rhetoric*, I bring to it, as Jim would say, the whole framework that I have derived, not only from how I got interested in this project in the first place, but from my place in an institution where I've got to get promoted and do this kind of arcane research. There's no such thing as purely *in*ductive or purely *de*ductive historical research. Your motives are what govern all of your choices from the outset when you even decide to do research in the first place.

SUSAN JARRATT: This just reminds me a lot of Darwin, and Darwin was accused very adamantly of having formulated his hypothesis before he got his data. And he argued against that very vigorously because he was very committed to the hypothetical deductive method; he was very much at pains to prove that he was Baconian, that he didn't have an idea in his mind when he went and looked out at all those finches and plants and things. So, I think Sharon has said it very well, that you never go blind into a project. But what I think we're doing right now, why I think we're making this fairly extreme argument for a kind of historiography that is more story than fact, is that it serves a particular moment in the history of our discipline. That is, it is a kind of historiography for our time; that there have been histories in which the presuppositions were so well accepted, they were kind of blind, so we got the sense that there was a bunch of fact that we're being delivered. And now we're beginning to realize what those suppositions are and the kind of economic and political ramifications of them. So now we're kind of pulling away and saying, "Wait a minute; there are stories that are guiding these things." I think that this is the thing to say right now, to kind of adjust and move our histories in a beneficial direction for our field.

NAN JOHNSON: There seems to me a big difference between stories that "propose": "I'm telling a story that goes something like 'Well, you know, it seems to sort of have been like this; this is my interpretation;'" and "It was like this, and it was like this, and it was like this; *and* it was a pretty serious situation"—Those are very different kinds of histories. And I think there are very different kinds of motives. I think we need them all. The type of history that intends to account for a state of affairs that has gone wrong—which is fine; that's a good kind of history; that's a fine kind of history; we need that kind of history. It's *one* kind of history. A kind of history that says, "You know, we missed all of this in the original run through. All of these people were left out. This was missed, this was missed. Back to the home plate, let's go around the track"—is *another* kind of history. And I think that is really important to keep in mind. Having been accused—and I accept it—of being a traditionalist, I would like to say one thing that has not been even said once: Intellectual curiosity—Inquiry—Discovery—Who were we then? You know!

[**ROBERT CONNORS:** (sotto voce) How dare you enjoy history!]

JAMES J. MURPHY: You missed a remark. Bob said, "How dare you enjoy history!"

VICTOR VITANZA: That joyful phrase "reaching closure," along with induction and deduction referred to earlier by Sharon and then Susan: I wonder where that phrase conceptually comes from. "Reaching closure"? I can think of a number of other similar metaphors, but I will not because they will even bruise my sensibility. I think it's such a male-dominated notion of reaching closure. When I write, I try to maintain a sense of "discovery," of being on the joyful Road to Serrendip; or to maintain a sophistic sense of the motion of the whole. I don't have to resolve any of these issues that I juggle because so many of my other colleagues will resolve them. I think someone needs to maintain the sophistic motion of the whole. So my posture is that of "a nomad" on a trip but without any destination, taking a look at what there is along the landscape.

RICHARD ENOS: I'd like to talk for a little bit about feelings and sentiments. I think that these are the ideas I'd like to hear: be careful of your own perspectives; weigh your evidence carefully; remember your prejudices and biases. I *like* that kind of talk. What concerns me is that sometimes there is almost a cynicism or a folly to think that you might ever advance knowledge; that there's almost a despairing attitude that anything important could be said. And I will be quaint enough to say that I don't like that attitude because I believe that we now have the possibility to really contribute knowledge about very important phenomena that deal with composing. And this is, I think, a very exciting time to do that and not a sentiment of despair, cynicism, or relativism to the point of futility, and that's the attitude that I feel.

JAMES J. MURPHY: I said earlier that this would be a day of justice and not charity and I promised you that, in justice, we would give *you* a chance to talk. So I am turning my back literally so I can't see the frantic people behind me, and I'm sure there are some.

A couple of administrative matters. Those of you who came in after the first one hundred did not get a copy of the handout. We had no idea these people were so notorious and so we brought only a hundred handouts. There are two signup sheets here. If you want to put your name and address down afterwards, I will mail you one of these sheets. Each one was given one hundred and fifty words to write a statement and it's all on one sheet of paper, and it's free. Two administrative matters: our associate chairman, Dennis Quon, suitably on your left. Our recorder on your right, from Alabama State University, is T. Clifford Bibb. That's why he is so distanced from this group, you see, because he wants to have an objective, historical view of what's happening here.

Is it possible that any of you would like to address anything to anyone here? Now, we are trying to record this entire event. Theresa Enos, who is the most desperately interested person, because she hopes to publish all this, is in charge of this tape recorder down here and we have a person coming from the rear of the room, Theresa, as I speak, so turn it on. It would be helpful to identify yourself for the tape.

JANICE LAUER: I'm wondering about Rich's question about validity, evidence, and good reasons. That was posed and I don't think anyone engaged it terribly much. That may be because the rest of the panel thinks it isn't important to engage it. There are some implications that I hear. One of them is that, if you expose your presuppositions and your positions and you make your ideologies explicit with which you are dealing, whatever histories you're working with—that that makes what you're doing valid? Is the word *valid* meaningful in this context? Is the very act of juggling—Victor's juggling act—the fact that one is *doing* that and not coming to closure and playing that role in historiography. Because one is doing that makes this per se, whatever one is juggling, does it make it a valuable and valid act? I'd like this issue discussed.

JAN SWEARINGEN: I was about to respond to Rich's statement when our noble chairman decided it was time to start doing this instead, so I would like to respond to that first. I'm with Rich in his feeling about the validity of evidence and primary research. I also understand the theoretical position from which the problematizing position comes. I'm getting a little tired of it. But part of that is just attitude, taste, temper. I am a traditional historian in some ways and in others not. So I think we all do need to acknowledge our biases. I want to comment on that, too.

I think there's been a lot of talk today about bias and prejudices and how we've all got our prejudices and our biases and we have to acknowledge them all the time. One bias is objectivity and rationality and proof and evidence and the enjoyment that Nan was describing of finding something new and feeling like you are contributing something genuinely new. I have that feeling about some of these early women philosophers; knowledge of them in turn has plugged directly into my writing classes and pedagogy because I'm interested now in gender differences in patterns of reasoning that are reflected in discourse. We have modes of argument that we teach people to produce as if argument were logic, were thought. There are alternate paradigms that we can be teaching; and that to me is by no means unrelated to the early historical research. So on the question of bias, I'd like to hear us talk more, or equally, of bias as value. The things that we value. Bias is value, it's not always a bad thing. Yes, everything is biased; but, yes, people all have things that they value and in terms of which they are doing things. Those are the flip sides of one another. It is worthwhile to point out that there are bad kinds of bias, prejudices; but prejudice, too, means the position from which you're coming at something. You can prejudge certain things, and that is inevitable. That does not mean we shouldn't do those things. It just means, as Rich was saying, that we should be able to know where we're coming from and, if possible, defend them, as Nan and Rich have. I like the sense of contributing to knowledge. I think that can be done in a satisfying and legitimate way. That's my answer.

BOB JOHNSON: We've been talking a lot about opening up and I am all in favor of that. I think that's the way we should go. But we've also been calling this the politics of historiography here and I would like to pose a question. In terms of the politics we find ourselves, most of us rhetoricians, in, in our own departments—few of us are in departments of rhetoric; many of us are in departments of English—there's a politics that goes on there. And I find in much of the historiography that's going on there is a turn toward interpreting history through literary criticism. And I would like to know what your view is. Is this going to open up, or is this going to do something else?

JAMES BERLIN: What do you mean? I'm not sure what you mean by "interpreting through literary criticism." Do you mean using categories that are being used in literary theory now?

BOB JOHNSON: Well, using categories and also using the literary criticism as the basis for the theoretical interpretation of what we are doing now.

JAMES BERLIN: There's one good reason for that: They've discovered rhetoric. They're struggling for language that we have. Sometimes I feel like I live in a ghetto. I've lived in a ghetto for ten years and it's humble but at least it's *mine*, and now people in power have said, "This property's worth something." And so I'm going to be moved. It seems our terrain is being co-opted.

On the other hand, this can be very valuable to us politically within the English Department, it seems to me, as we attempt to merge the language of poststructuralism in its various forms—neo-Marxist, post-Marxist, psychoanalytical. Beyond that it seems to me that this literary theory is useful because of its inherently rhetorical nature. By rhetoric, I mean language in its service of power. Whatever else a rhetoric does, it always has some notion of the way in which language is going to become accommodated with power. So I think it's useful in that perspective.

One of the problems, of course, is that now that we see this convergence of literature and rhetoric—look at some of the advertisements for conferences or look at Jonathan

Culler's work. Since rhetorical texts and literary texts both use rhetorical strategies, they're all literature. Isn't that interesting? They use rhetorical strategies, they're all rhetoric? No, they're all literature. And I understand that that's a possibility. I'm sure that that's the charge that's made against Victor, that he is trying to propose a notion of history that is purely contemplative. How would you respond to that?

VICTOR VITANZA: Nes; yo.

ROBERT CONNORS: To try to place us in the historical context once again, at least one of the reasons this is happening now is because for 35, 40 years, we have had an institutional inferiority complex, and we looked beyond our own discipline for something that would validate what we do. Literary criticism is the contemporary version of what linguistics was in the 1950s, what cognitive psychology has at times been. We're looking for something sexy to marry.

RICHARD ENOS: I'd like to respond to your well-formed question. I thought it was a very good one. I think that departments, English Departments for example, have both a normative and a corrective function.

And the norm has been conventional literature. I think recently there is a healthy corrective function going on, to call attention to other ways of viewing things. And that's, from my perspective, mostly come through rhetoric. I think you could probably say critical theory as well. But I think that the point is that what's going on in our *polis* here is being extended to this larger body politic where good reasons for looking at things, other ways than the norm, conventional literary ways, are being adjudicated, and I think that it's coming through quite positively. That's my perspective.

VICTOR VITANZA: I don't think that we have to validate what we're doing. *We are 25 hundred years old or more.* When I was in the research network preconvention meeting, people were saying, "Well we're about 20 years old," and occasionally someone would say, "the modern profession." "Composition is cut off from rhetoric." I would hear occasionally, "and it has nothing to do with the history of rhetoric anymore." *We are 25 hundred years old. We are not a discipline. We are a meta-discipline.* If we teach writing across the curriculum, doesn't that tell us, isn't that a self-evident experience, that we are a meta-discipline. *We inform all the other disciplines. They don't inform us.*

SUSAN JARRATT: I'd like to second that and also respond to Janice and to this person [Bob Johnson]. In response to Janice, I think that a history which is self-conscious and reflexive and tries to locate itself in time and place is not automatically a good history; but I would say any history that does that is better than history that doesn't do that. And I think that there are ways to validate histories which do that.

Some of the ways we've already talked about, they're ways that we're very secure and familiar with, that have to do with kind of evidence and proof and so on. There're other ways of proof that are being explored. There's a whole body of work by Walter Fischer who is working with narrative—and he's, to my mind, unfortunately dependent upon Aristotelian logic in coming up with these reasons—but he talks about coherence and fidelity as validating features of narratives, all kinds of narratives, histories as well as fictions.

And finally, I would really like to second Victor's assertion that, yes we've been defensive, and, yes we've looked in other places, but why don't we recast ourselves? Why don't we recast ourselves instead of looking for somebody sexy to marry, to say, "We're in control, we're the master discipline over these other disciplines" and that literary critical methods are a part of what we do. Not that we're borrowing them just because they're sexy or interesting but because they are innately, inherently, powerfully rhetorical and we can define them for themselves. We aren't just borrowing them because of their glitz.

Unidentified male voice: But isn't there going to be resistance to that?

Unidentified female voice: From whom?

Unidentified male voice: Isn't there already resistance?

VICTOR VITANZA: Yes, there is. Yes, absolutely.

JAMES J. MURPHY: [as Vitanza continues] Let the record show . . .

VICTOR VITANZA: Look at the field of cognitive psychology, how it wants to resist what some of us are doing, how it makes us *persona non grata,* because "we" are "non-scientific," because "we" have a different "language game." But that's inevitable, right? And that's okay. That's part of the contest in the academy as Ong says. That's to be expected.

Unidentified male voice: Victor, you'd say it's necessary . . .

VICTOR VITANZA: Necessary, yes. But the worst thing is "being ignored."

LINDA FLOWER: I want to ask a question that kind of picks up on Janice Lauer's question and it has to do with the parallel I'm seeing between the argument going here and the one that was going on in the preconvention workshop on research. I think there are some of the political strains behind this. The question is this: When I hear the weak version of the "left" position, it seems like a position that I think we would all agree with, that it's good to be reflexive and to locate what you're doing in time and place. But the strong version seems to be something like, "it is important to avoid closure" and "history is more story than fact" and "to play the role of critic deconstructionist as opposed to constructor, digger, and so forth, is moving in a beneficial direction." And that seems to be a strong version. I think my question is: Is there evidence that that's true? And if it's just possible that that strong version *isn't* beneficial, and that systematically avoiding closure is *not* the best thing to do, how would we ever get evidence that that is perhaps not as valid as the claims being made for it. Because I don't hear in that posture any attempt to validate those strong claims.

JAMES BERLIN: Do you think I speak for the strong version, avoiding closure?

LINDA FLOWER: No. I didn't really hear you saying that.

JAMES BERLIN: Ok. Because I don't. I think closure is inevitable. Versions of history that are inscribed with political notions are inevitable. What I'm arguing for is that we make the closure—we have to. We have to explain ourselves. This is why rhetoric was invented. As Robert Scott said in formulating epistemic rhetoric, if there were something such as objective truth that we could agree on, we wouldn't need rhetoric. Why we need rhetoric is that we disagree, a probabilistic realm. But on the other hand, we still have to act. We have to make laws, we have to protect ourselves from people who violate laws, violate *us*. So closure is necessary; but, it seems to me, we must make it with a consciousness that we are not arriving at some universal truth, some eternal truth. We are arriving at a rhetorical solution, a stay against chaos, against confusion, against disorder, a tentative position. And history is the story of it.

JAMES J. MURPHY: I'm sorry but our contract says that we have to vacate this [room] in a couple of minutes. You can appreciate how much of a torture this is for me.

I would like to point out something that might not occur to you. Look at the age of the people up here as compared to my age. When I first sent an article—it happened to be about medieval rhetoric—to *PMLA*, the only game in town, in 1960—some of you were not here yet in 1960—the response, of rejection, of course, came in two parts. One, rhetoric is not a subject; and if it were, there would be no history of it.

ROBERT CONNORS: That's *still* the reaction you get from *PMLA*.

JAN SWEARINGEN: That's right.

Unidentified male voice: Yeah.

JAMES J. MURPHY: That is *not* the reaction you now get from *PMLA*. I have been named to the advisory board *specifically* to encourage people to submit rhetorical manuscripts and I should have announced that at the beginning. That's a good point. The person who wrote that review, about 15 years later out of the blue—in fact, after *Rhetoric in the Middle Ages* came out—wrote me a letter and said he realized how wrong those statements were. I thought it was grand; he's a grand man you'd recognize if I told you who it was.

Now, 28 years later, look at the age of the people who are starting to work hard on this. They may disagree, but they certainly agree on a general direction and a general objective and the disagreement about methodology and particular points is probably valuable. I say *probably* as an Aristotelean, of course.

But I think the very fact that 200 people came in here to talk about what is potentially a very abstract, dry, arcane, sophomore-level subject, and you virtually all stayed. I mean, the two ladies that fainted were the only ones that left. But look at the ages. When I started in this business, this conversation over coffee would have been difficult. There wouldn't have been enough people to fit around a round table in the cafeteria here. Literally. Nobody cared. And there was no way to get at it. And now, almost three decades later, we're on the verge of an explosion of knowledge. We're even beginning to find out how Americans got themselves into the mess they're in now, by ignoring their own rhetorical history. (That's out of a book I edited lately that some of you will recognize.) Our own American history, as some of these people have been trying to tell you, is so critical of what we are doing. That history in general is critical of what we're doing. If nothing else it'll show us that we're brighter than the people who failed doing it a hundred years ago. So I would hope to end this on an extremely positive note.

Let me remind you, if you didn't get a handout to see what these people alleged before they came up here, if you want to sign your name, I'll send them to you. Alas, we do have to vacate, but I think I and we owe these people a tremendous round of applause.

Reflections

James Berlin

I will take up a practice I encountered while participating in the recent *PRE/TEXT* discussion on historiography, responding to the roundtable by reconsidering my position across the materials generated.

I am interested in subversive histories of rhetoric, histories that force us to re-examine our understanding of the relation of language to power. It is understandable then that I never leave an encounter with the work of Victor Vitanza without seeing my own position in a fresh way. Victor is to my mind the most revolutionary figure working in rhetoric today, our foremost poststructuralist rhetorician. Counter to my collectivist orientation, Victor pursues a micropolitics of power, seeing problems and solutions in terms of the individual, intent on freeing each of us through deconstructing our ordinary experience, disrupting the conceptions of our discursively forged manacles. Despite his insensitivity to the communal, Victor continually reminds me to think of the solitary as well as the social.

I am committed to histories of rhetoric that seek the silenced voices, the defeated remnants in the battles of language and power. Susan Jarratt inspires me with her work, expanding the exploration of rhetoric beyond the formal rules found in schoolbooks, displaying the formulations of rhetoric inscribed in a variety of texts, texts that have been omitted from privileged canons. Jan Swearingen too has taken up this search for the excluded other, looking for the texts of women and exploring the devices used to silence their voices, devices she has determined are parts of larger cultural structures designed to privilege the masculine and the chirographic. Susan and Jan are exploring the margins, examining the supplement—the excluded and silenced—and giving it voice. Theirs is a project in exposing the mystifications of the powerful, the appropriations undertaken in the name of transcendental truths.

In a different way, Richard Enos is also traveling the margins, intent on identifying the concrete material conditions that nurtured classical rhetorics. Embroiled in the conflict over competing interpretive strategies now at the center of classical studies, Richard is concerned with hermeneutic theory, with the relations between interpretation and evidence. He now needs a concept of mediation, of the intercessions that are enacted between theory and practice, concept and event, subject and object. Nan Johnson is now moving in this direction, acknowledging the narrativity of her historical writing, seeing it as an act of appropriation and interpretation in the service of necessary fictions, accounts true only in a provisional sense yet powerfully determinative of human action just the same.

Bob Connors and Sharon Crowley remain the most conservative members of this group, the farthest removed from my position, but, I must admit, rich contributors to the larger discussion. Bob continually reminds us of the intractability of certain cultural facts—the power of textbooks and classroom practices, for example. On the other hand, the terms of his position—notably, the quest for "closure" and the worry over "inductive research and deductive research"—suggest his hope that the facts of history, when studied long and hard, will recite their own story, confessing their significance in unequivocal terms. Still, he is beginning to realize the ideological functions performed by the historian of rhetoric, seeing the political dimensions of his project. Sharon Crowley seems to me torn between two irreconcilable efforts—a hermeneutical and dialectical historiography on the one hand, and an uncomplicated historiography of heroes and origins on the other. The first is seen in her theoretical pronouncements, the second in her practice. Thus she admits the complex narrativity of historical accounts, the historian's role as constructor rather than stenographer, responding to an elaborate web of interconnected practices. Yet she simultaneously asserts with confidence that she will eventually find the very day and time in the seventeenth century when a particular intellectual method was formulated. She can even claim for Isaac Watts the origination of the ubiquitous notions of unity, coherence, and emphasis. This is history as treasure hunt, a determination to find the origin, the presence and plenitude of meaning informing contemporary practices, in some uncomplicated, univocal event and agent. In a similar vein, Sharon charges composition teachers with the heresy of awarding the "facts" she discovers a "quasi-metaphysical status," with reifying them, making them actualities rather than constructions. In this she overlooks the same gesture in her own project, her method itself reifying the bourgeois notions of history as the work of great persons thinking great ideas.

The roundtable articulated issues that will constitute the debates in historiographies of rhetorics for the near future. The discipline is richer for it, closer to serving its role as cultural critic in a society that has devised devious rhetorical schemes for concealing its failures.

Robert Connors

Reading over all we said that fateful day, I can't help feeling that most of us seemed to be acting out a kind of intellectual multiple-personality disorder. On the one hand, no one, not even Rich Enos down at the right-hand side of the table, seemed willing to make the direct claim that they wrote the truth when they wrote history. It's all stories, we say over and over, no real objectivity is possible, we're all products of our heredity and culture and are determined by class and other interests and we can't be objective in any sense. Right. Then nearly all of us go on to talk about how we write to convince, to persuade, to recover this or that figure or idea or tradition. How, in other words, we all take certain stands and *write* as if we knew the truth and wanted only to share and promulgate it. (Victor is the only holdout, but modest though he is, I suspect him of believing he's smart and right as strongly as the rest of us preterites believe we're smart and right.) We don't—we *can't*—act on the basis of the theories we seem to hold.

Similarly, the position that all research must be deductive, that there can be no such thing as truly inductive research, mirrors the theoretical position that all we have are *doxa* and stories. If all historical research is *a priori*, if we simply decide something exists and then go out to find it in sources, then radical relativism must reign. But all of us know that that's not really what happens when we approach those dusty shelves of books that no one but us has touched for a hundred years. Whatever *a priori* ideas experienced historians approach our sources with (and I would argue that there *have* been times, especially during the first few years of my historical researches, when I did *not* necessarily approach sources with any powerful ideas about what I'd find), those sources themselves act as controls on us and our galloping prejudices. Whatever ideas I may have about Edwin Woolley's conception of the comma splice, how it was constrained by previous books, or Edwardian grammatical theory, or the socioculture of teachers in 1907, I'm finally gonna have to *see what Woolley says* about this thing. My preconceptions don't control *that* at all. They may have led me to Woolley, but what I find there will lead me someplace else. Way leads on to way in historical research, as we all know, and neither induction nor deduction can by themselves explain all of history's cunning passages.

Finally, facts. Although theoretically we seem not much to defend it, I think we all tacitly accept the following startling claim: there are facts out there that historians attempt to find and explain. We do order them into meanings, but on a pragmatic level, a level of action, evidence exists. It exists in books and journals, in paper records of all kinds, in the sorts of archaeological data that Rich Enos is so ably introducing to us. Only the blankest kind of epistemic agnosticism—which none of us here, I think, would profess—would try to deny the pragmatic reality of this evidence, of these data. Out of these semiotic data we induce facts. Fact: Lindley Murray's *Grammar* was more widely used than any other grammar text in the first half of the nineteenth century. Fact: Women were not allowed into college rhetoric courses in America until after 1855. Fact: Edwin Woolley published his *Handbook of Composition* in 1907. The people on this panel might disagree on whether these claims are *interesting*, but I don't think any of them would deny that they are *true.*

We know this in our bones: To have any reasonable discourse at all, there are simply some ideas we must agree to hold in common. The most basic such idea is that there are facts we agree exist. The Woolley book is there, on my shelf. You may or may not accept my judgment that Woolley was the first handbook, but if we are to talk at all you have to accept the idea that I've held the book in my hands and that I'm telling you the truth about what I saw.

You agree to trust us. From there we start. You trust us not to make things up. You trust us to look carefully at the books we talk about. You trust us to try for corroborating evidence for claims. You trust us to sift evidence intelligently, not to deliberately exclude important items, not to reach closure and certainty too early. You trust us to try not to bore you when we write things up. And we try to earn your trust by doing the best job we can. Because all of us are trying, in our perhaps naive ways, to do good for you, to do good with you.

What it comes down to in the end is a kind of resolute—and, I believe, admirable—unwillingness on our parts to sit on our hands and theorize. Historiography cannot exist without our "doing" history. The glum relativism implied by the theoretical position that all we can create are stories, and that one story is as good as another, simply won't do for us. As Nan Johnson says, we all "tend to believe and subsequently proceed as if some stories are truer than others." This refusal to act out the paralysis implicit in any theoretical disbelief in epistemic closure results, I have been arguing, from a need we all feel to do some good in the world. It is no coincidence that the members of this panel, though our ages have some diversity, all come from a generation whose radical critique of the American status quo reshaped our culture. Jim's neo-Marxism, Jan's and Susan's feminism, even—though this is not always obvious—Victor's passionate and deeply idealistic poststructuralism, are all criticisms of life. Quietism and relativism are not enough. The ivory tower is not enough. There are problems out there, and willing hearts and able hands are needed to solve them.

Why do we care, why must we act? Because we are writing teachers. The writing courses we teach are unique in college curricula in that they were instituted to address the social issue of perceived illiteracy and not simply to carry on an intellectual enterprise. We are, as I have pointed out elsewhere, the heirs of those nineteenth-century composition teachers whose specific charge was to solve a problem in the culture, and we have been striving to do so ever since. Composition teachers and composition researchers from early on have felt a moral responsibility that goes far beyond mere aesthetics: instill the literacy, transfer the power, solve the problem. That we have not always succeeded in solving the problem set us does not minimize its reality or disparage our efforts.

So now we have had our panel in which we paid dutiful homage to historiography, to the theoretical relativism that none of us can quite argue away—being the devout secular humanists that we are. It's time to get back to work doing what we do: history: searching in good faith through records of human experience, offering our separate, hard-won little truths to one another, and trying to approach agreement on some greater truth we can all secretly believe in.

Sharon Crowley

What I wanted to say during the panel, and never quite said, was this: We rhetoricians who write history are amazingly complacent about our readers' sympathy with us. We expect that they will appreciate the labor, enjoyment, love, frustration, and anxiety with which we put histories together, and that they will take the published results with the necessary grains of salt. But I am not sure that this is always the case.

An audience for the history of rhetoric is out there (who would have expected, for example, that a bunch of historiographers, scrapping about the politics of history-writing, would draw an audience of two hundred listeners?). I suspect that many members of this audience are practicing teachers of rhetoric and composition, and that their interest in our histories is professional, in the sense that Bob Connors is interested in—"what does our history tell us about our teaching today?" If we, as a professional group, have arrived at the point where our histories are written only to "advance knowledge," that's news to me. (But then I live in the mountains of Arizona.)

As Jan Swearingen persisted in pointing out, there are so few histories of rhetoric and composition studies in print that those which have been written and published so far have become much more authoritative than I imagine their authors ever thought they might be. (If anyone doubts that our histories are authoritative, even among ourselves, he or she need only to remind him- or herself of the fact that we refer to each other's work by its author's name, rather than by its title.) Add to this the fact that texts get read in lots of unintended ways. (At least my own work has been read in ways that surprise me—as "Great Man" history, for example.) And when the potential for multiplicity of interpretation gets coupled with the dearth of histories of rhetoric that now exists, the responsibility laid on the first- or second-generation historian becomes heavy indeed.

It is this responsibility to readers, most of whom are working composition teachers, that stymies me as a writer of history. (I'm not so much deterred by theoretical squabbles over the impossibility of writing history, as I think the panelists may have inferred from my remarks. The difficulty of getting it right has been acknowledged by every practicing rhetorician since Gorgias.) Rather, I simply want us to acknowlege the rhetorical situation within which our work is read, and to think carefully about its potentially widespread effect.

By conservative estimate, there are 33,000 college composition teachers in this country; again, conservatively, each of these teaches upwards of 100 students every semester. About 80 percent of these teachers work in impossible conditions which dictate that they have little opportunity to do sustained scholarly work. So they must look to those of us who do have this opportunity for an understanding of their function within the academic community. If they do find time to read our work, they do so on their own hook, and they do it alone—their colleagues haven't the time, energy, or interest to engage them in the sort of conversation the panelists enjoyed at the session. If they are convinced by us, they are quite likely to borrow our insights to inform their teaching; and they may do so quite uncritically, since they have been systematically dis-equipped to be critical about rhetoric and composition theory.

All of these considerations ineluctably situate the writing of the history of rhetoric squarely within a rhetorical situation, an occasion, which is dictated by the institutional and ideological confines within which composition teachers work. Jim Berlin will say, of course, that this is what he has been arguing all along; but I don't think his neo-Marxist critique of history-writing goes quite far enough, or won't, as long as he continues to focus his very considerable analytical talents on the larger intellectual dialectics that have characterized our past, and away from the power relations that shaped the conditions in which today's composition proletariat finds itself. Nor will the work of traditional historians be very helpful to its audience if it loses itself in the minutiae of traditional scholarly debate over the relative claims of this or that piece of evidence. (I am not advocating sloppy scholarship here. I am simply adopting the very wise advice given by Jerry Murphy, that, in consideration of their readers, scholars ought to know a lot more detail than they put into their histories.)

The writing of history is a profoundly rhetorical art, as Tacitus knew, and as Gibbon knew, in their different ways. Thanks to the academic and intellectual isolation in which contemporary historians and scholars work, we are more inclined, I think, to forget that our work may have profound effects on our readers, and, through them, on a generation of students. Santayana's canard is inappropriate, as well as inaccurate, here; we historians of rhetoric need, rather, to take our cue from Gorgias, who knew that words affected the souls of their hearers like drugs affect the body.

Richard Enos

My reading of the transcript prompted me to reflect on the presuppositions of my comments and the remarks of others. My retrospective view was directed toward understanding if my view and the views of others were clearly stated and cogently argued to the readers of *Rhetoric Review*. In essence that act was, in microcosm, a central point of my comments: the cogency of accounts should be articulated with a sensitive understanding of the starting points and the process of gaining adherence to one's viewpoint. I believe that a parallel point holds true in the writing of history. That is, historiography is itself an argument, an effort to advance an interpretation and articulate reasons that will be shared by readers. From this perspective, both readers and historians share, and even co-create, meaning. It is the burden of the historian of rhetoric, however, to articulate views in a manner that enables readers to participate in, to share in, the making of meaning. In a sense, readers of *Rhetoric Review* are engaging in that activity while reading this work; that is, participating in the making of meaning about the events of that day last March. Will those statements in St. Louis withstand the test of time? Each generation of readers will again engage in that act as they read through the events and determine if they are "meaningful." That phenomenon is, as stated above, akin to writing "good" history; engaging the reader in sharing in the making of meaning about events completed but dynamically understood at the moment meaning is jointly created between reader and historian.

Victor Vitanza

[Dedicated to the memory of Jacques Yaché] . . .

As I studied our Polylogue, I initially thought of Papa KB's metaphor of "the human barnyard" and thought of my eight contesta(s)*tory* metaphors (or mis/representative antidotes) in my opening statement and how they are polylectical, *not* dialectical with a lustful eye on sin/thesis. Here in the same (but non-Hegelian) spirit, I offer more polylectical Third Sophistic fragments for those of us who wish "to dirty our minds" instead of our hands; after all, Rich, there are many ways to be an archaeologist! . . . as our mentor Foucault has taught us:

(1) My business . . . in this case . . . is *not* "circumference," or "closure," or "validity," or "cure"; instead, it's "counter"-themes to the tradition of dialectics . . . whether Socratic, Aristotelian, Hegelian, or Marxian. My business is not Rhetorik, but Third Sophistic Rhetorics, what I also call "Pararhetorics"; it's not (rational) *history,* but (non-rational, Desire-in-language) *hystery,* my business is not Aristotelian/Marxist tragedy, but post-Burkean comedy-*cum*-"Farce." *Hence,* my "counter"-themes ("counter"-attitudizings) are ironic/*dissoi-paralogoi*-modes of "resistance" (constructed semiotically) "across" all who have some terrible need to make the world "a better place" and who have only (incipiently through center-mental deflection) kept it The very Same. *Hence* (again), my business is not that of *medicina mentis!* What I offer is not "a cure." And why not? Because a cure is a form of domesticated violence; it would be the end of *dissoi paralogoi,* of difference, of juggling, of drifting! The cure would be Total philosophical Rhetorik/Polis/Good Reasons/Paideia/Parnoia. . . . Death itself! . . . My motto (at least, one of them) is *Better a Schizoid than a Fascoid*! (Fascoid = totalization and homogeneity.) My trope is not the Sin/thesis (of die/alectics), but an Anacoluthon (of radical troping). (Schizoid + Anacoluthon = heterogeneity or 1001 plateaus.)

(2) J. Kristeva writes: "we have [a] Platonistic acknowledgment on the eve of Stalinism and fascism: a (any) society may be stabilized *only* if it excludes poetic language" [or people who "represent" such language—Lacanian *lalangue*—such as gypsies, prostitutes, body-hysterics . . . all nomads]. And then: "The question is unavoidable: if we are not on the side of those whom society wastes in order to reproduce itself, where are we?" ("The Ethics of Linguistics"; italics mine).

(3) My "collig," Bob Connors, who is terribly upset with me, says: "I write history to try to make *my world* a better place" (italics mine). I ask him. "Do you really mean, as you say, 'my world'?"; or "Do you mean 'our world'?" I fear the latter, its totalization, its homogeneity; for we've been there before—always already—in history! Let's don't, through deflection, repeat the mistakes of the past, right? As Thoreau said . . . if I thought a man were coming to my house with the intention of making the world better for me . . . I would run from my house. H. Cixous says: Let us fly and steal away while we still can. "Let's get out of here!"

(4) The Stalinists say, . . . "Ah, comrades, we love and understand you. We want to make the world a better place for you, too." Both vulgar and especially polite Marxists, Utopian creatures that they are, say this, too! But M. Kundera writes: "Anyone who thinks that the communist regimes of Central Europe are exclusively the work of criminals is overlooking a basic truth: the criminal regimes were made not by criminals *but by enthusiasts convinced they had discovered the only road to paradise.* They defended that road so valiantly that they were forced to execute many people. Later it became clear that there was no paradise, that the enthusiasts were therefore murderers" (italics added). The desire to make the world a better place is what Kundera calls "the fantasy of the Grand March." (Please see his part six of *The Unbearable Lightness of Being*) . . .

So yes, Marx demanded that the world be not interpreted, *but changed;* he said that the State had been ill and consequently had made "Us" all ill; but the New State would "cure" all of Us. Such was his new covenant! As one of three major hermeneuts of suspicion, Marx, however, was not suspicious enough . . . about himself and about all of Us. The world, after all, *did not change!* The humanism of Marx's (at times, wonderfully) contra/dictory and para/doxical and almost para/rhetorical thinking was mixed with and then finally betrayed by the worst form of totalitarianism (and so, what was politically-ethically left . . . became Far Right). I believe such *betrayal* was and will ever be inevitable! especially for those involved, directly or indirectly, in "The Grand [utopian] March." The cause (if we can speak of "a cause") is not economics (or poor communication), which can therefore be "fixed" in yet another newer covenant. (Nor do I have faith in Habermasian Neo-Enlightenment thought as a "cure" based on "efficient and honest [!] communication." Such thought is a bad case of claptrap and is horribly europocentric and totalitarian; such thought slouches towards *homologia,* just as does "your" so-called "logic of good reasons.") The "cause," instead, is in The Maskuline, which is "disciplined and rotten with perfection." So . . . let's do get out of here! Let's hit the road and *disperse-like-rhizomes* so as to get beyond the walls of The polis and so as to avoid "The Grand March."

(5) *Whose* Reasons are Good Reasons? when fifty percent, or more, of the population (in the West) is systematically suppressed. For whom are these Reasons good? Be careful how you answer that trick-question: For you can easily slip into the "phallologocentricline." Understand that the "warrants" or "representative anecdotes" or "grand narratives," undergirding these so-called Good Reasons, are greatly eroded *for many of us.* Therefore, The Third Sophistic (Post-Modernism) has eternally returned with a vengeance. Such grand narratives, then, as "emancipation" and "consensus" have (in eroding) "become an outmoded and suspect value. But justice as a value is neither outmoded nor suspect. We must thus arrive at an idea and practice of justice that is not linked to that of consensus" (see J-F Lyotard, *The Postmodern Condition*).

(6) Linda Flower asks, "is there evidence" that the "strong version" of the far left—the version that she associates with deconstruction and "nonclosure"—is "beneficial"? (Is this the same question asked yet again by another person who needs "to make the world better"? If so, let's flee!) But Janice Lauer had asked earlier and more self-consciously if the words "valid" and "valuable" are "meaningful in this context," that is, in respect to "Victor's juggling act—the fact that one is doing that and not coming to closure and playing that role in historiography." Then finally, my Collig JB, being very nervous that he might be identified with the "lunatic fringe," quickly disassociated himself from the concept of "nonclosure"!

To Linda, I would "counter"-ask: "Is there any evidence for evidence?" "Is there any proof for proof?" The criterion for your own "language game," when reflexive, destroys such a game. This criterion has been attacked continuously by philosophers of science. Linda, my "language game" is very "contrary" (as Feyerabend would say, is "counter-inductive") to yours. You and I, then, are in some "accountable respects" very incommensurable: For ours is the difference between the "pragmatics of scientific knowledge" and "legitimation by paralogy." (Please see Lyotard). . . . To Janice, I would

[Octalog I:] The Politics of Historiography

say respectfully but pararhetorically, as Molly and Papa eternally say to us both and to all, "Nes/Yo!" ... And to some of my Colligs and especially to JB who wants to be a "laughing Marxist" (there's an oxymoron for you), I would dis/chant: "Let's cackle together and, unlike W. Benjamin's quasi-Marxist Angel of history, let's cackle neither horizontally nor vertically through history," but by getting out of here and dispersing like Deleuzeian rhizomes across the hysterical *lalangue*scape.

Susan Jarratt

In the terms of a question posed near the end of the discussion, none of the panelists appeared willing to speak out against the "weak" version of the "left" position on the nature of history-writing—to disagree that it requires *a degree of* awareness of historical contingency, that its arguments are *to a degree* provisional, that it is *to a degree* a literary construction. The discussion took shape and color from the warmth with which that position was embraced or the gingerliness around which it was danced. The two chief stages for these choreographies were the affective outcomes of acknowledging history as ideological construct and the problems of verifying the results of such histories.

Somehow, that afternoon, the emotional price of giving up history as a science was despair, paralysis, or at best boredom. Into that unhappy place reentered nostalgically the figures of a gendered empiricism. The taint of the "feminine" brushed histories akin to stories, suspected of stealing glamour from literary theory. Their creators sit impotently in armchairs while others dig manfully in the dirt and experience the pleasure of discovery—penetrating mysteries, lifting the veil, pushing forward into the unknown. A Baconian light will be cast by these other historians onto the dark corners of the world. But what strange memory lapse allows for an historian in one moment to endorse an ideological view of history-writing and in the next speak in the language of a system designed to mask the authority of a privileged group to determine what counts as "fact," to hide the processes of exclusion and oppression operating in its name?

I would argue that the histories written by *all* the panelists arise directly or indirectly out of the *disruption* of institutions built on the positivist epistemology whose language crept into our conversation—a system authorizing the barriers Professor Murphy experienced twenty-eight years ago with *PMLA*. Our reasons for participating in that disruption are both public and private. The desire to historicize the writing classroom is a direct and public motive—an admirable motive, one which has borne fruit. But that motive perhaps doesn't best describe how, for example, a classicist like Richard Enos, faced with the ubiquitousness of Aristotle, decides to look to the sophists—with such stunning results. Such decisions, I believe, move beyond the writing classroom, taking in a larger view of the field, of canon, of authority and power in teaching and publication. The process of forming questions, in both its personal and institutional moments, establishes the conditions of possibility for "facts" and remains a crucial area for ideological inquiry. The continuing process of exposing the cultural formations influencing (if not determining) such decisions, as well as our continuing attempts to describe the forms of historical research implicated in them, must be ongoing.

A demand for further investigation of our own socialization as academics, as researchers, as "truth-seekers" does not exclude going to Sicily, reading dusty textbooks, or getting pleasure from either of those things. Nor does it deny their great value. It *does* demand a continuing reexamination of the grounds on which we defend those enterprises, of the terms in which we describe our pleasure, of how we ourselves came to make the decisions we have made about our subjects and methods—methods which do *not* simply emerge on their own agency from our research.

On the question of verification, even the defense of the "weak" position seems to have found itself once again, as the first wave of "new rhetoricians" in the eighteenth century, having to reassert—against the system of hypothesis-making, data-searching, and verification—the emotional, affective grounds for granting assent to arguments. John Henry Newman a century ago eloquently explored the interior landscape of assent, describing an *organon* "more delicate, versatile, and elastic" than Aristotle's or Bacon's (*An Essay in Aid of a Grammar of Assent* [Notre Dame, 1979], 217). He sees certainty emerging from the "cumulation of probabilities . . . arising out of the nature and circumstances of the particular case" (230), gathering "substance and momentum" to win over a reader (233). Why do we, who are experts both at weaving and unweaving strands of language as they wind their way into and out of our minds and veins, ask for "methods of verification" for histories other than our own experiences of them? There is an exterior landscape of assent as well, though it looks more like a classroom than a garden. When a history changes the way writers behave in the classroom (both instructor and student) in ways that allow for the recognition of inequity and oppression; that give voice to silence; that create the means for just action, as well as open negotiation over what constitutes "justice"—then that history is a good one. These two methods of verification are better named "experience" than "fact." And our field's experiences and uses of the wide range of histories of rhetoric written by the panel members proclaim their success.

I got a sense from listening to the panel of a hesitancy to endorse further disruption, now that our field has gained a footing on the terms of the dominant epistemology and its institutional structures. The most frightening face of this resistance is the possibility that some histories would *not* be sanctioned—are not to be spoken. If such exclusions were enacted, dialectic of the sort that in recent years has changed "cognition" to "social cognition" would lose its sharp edge, tapering off into a flat ground of sameness. Because our fears, our language, our motives will be reproduced, they risk more danger of reification than the histories themselves. We must continue to ask: From where do they come? Whom do they serve? Whom do they exclude? If we, now, in support of a "weak" view of history as an ideological project of constructing multiple, provisional visions of the past, but suspicious of granting a voice to a "strong" attempt to avoid closure, to challenge "logic," to question "reason," to insist on the fictive, were to remain at home in the language of history as science; if we were to cease a conversation on the grounds of that agreement, believing ourselves to be done with the uncomfortable business of self-examination; if we were to rest complacently in the belief that we were lighting dark places and making progress without continuing to go "no place" (i.e., utopia) now that we have *some* place; then we would have gained little. Then our agreement would be only a superficial contract, not a continuing commitment to the history of rhetoric.

Nan Johnson

When I stood up during the panel exchange segment to make the point that different types of histories are motivated by different interests and contribute unique perspectives that are significant collectively, I was trying to redirect the energy of the discussion away from evaluative contrasts between various types of histories (traditional, revisionist, Marxist, etc.) toward a consideration of how our historical perspective on any aspect of the history of rhetoric is enhanced by depth of scholarly field. I don't think "depth of field" is a particularly original concept, but it is a useful term for defining that intense and dense intellectual space which is created when we struggle to react to the demands and implications of multiple interpretations. This means going further than simply acknowledging that multiplicity is inevitable; it means feeling obliged intellectually by multiplicity. If I had thought of it during the panel, "depth of field" is the notion that I would have thrown out as an important issue in any debate about historiography or about the relative merits of types of histories; depth of field is a scholarly value which insists that insight into the past comes only from a radiance of attention.

One of the issues which I felt we did not get to during the panel (and how could we have gotten to everything?) was exactly what a "traditional" history of rhetoric entailed other than a methodological respect for evidence. I would say that "traditional" histories of rhetoric focus overtly on the *disciplinary configuration of rhetoric* in specific historical periods and proceed on the governing assumption that the discipline of rhetoric in any era inevitably embodies a coalition of classical and innovative theoretical and pragmatic features. A traditional historian of rhetoric intends to account for the theoretical substance, the range of praxis, and the social and cultural function of the formal discipline of rhetoric as it existed in earlier eras. Such an intention requires the historian to offer an interpretive reconstruction or "true story" based on factual evidence (in so far as the archaeological and rhetorical nature of research allows) of what, in that time and place, for those people and that culture, constituted normative theory and practice. In pursuit of this "true story" about a particular discipline of rhetoric, the traditional historian also addresses questions such as: what intellectual developments shifted the content or emphasis of rhetorical theory? what economic, social, or cultural trends created new rhetorical genres and/or shifted attention away from others? how did educational aims and standards affect the configuration of the discipline of rhetoric and how it was regarded? These questions are part-and-parcel of the traditional historian's primary scholarly interest in "tracking" formal rhetoric as a kind of generic, cultural phenomenon.

In my view "traditional" histories of rhetoric make two significant contributions to rhetoric studies. (1) Traditional histories provide profiles of those theoretical assumptions and practices which have been promoted as "the study of rhetoric" in the past and which influenced educational practices and social and cultural attitudes regarding rhetorical behavior. The more such profiles we assemble, the more aware we become of the many permutations rhetoric has undergone; the more aware we are of this, the more sensitive we become to the dynamic nature and potential of our own discipline and to probable configurations of a future one. (2) Because what traditional histories record when describing the formal discipline of rhetoric in a given period is, in fact, the most conventional and institutionalized "main line" regarding rhetorical theory and practice, such profiles of the "norm" provide (have provided) a great deal of the material that historians seeking to revise or critique traditional understandings must scrutinize and subsequently re-read and re-write: for example, revisionist historians point to who and what fell into the shadow of the "main line" in a given period, and Marxist historians deconstruct the "main line" in terms of the "play of power" which allowed or compelled the direction and consequences of that line.

What type of perspective is created when *all* this is going on? Depth of field.

It occurs to me that looking at writing histories of rhetoric in terms of taking "stances" makes some sense too, e.g., taking a "traditional" stance on a first pass at the material to set up a "revisionist" pass which might be the larger point. This stance-switching could work a number of ways but "traditionalist" stance in the way I am using it here would still mean an initial willingness to "reconstruct" a disciplinary profile from artifactual evidence no matter what one moves on to do to/with that profile.

Jan Swearingen

Reflections in a Time of War: Some Afterthoughts

Why "in a time of war"? Because there have been too many lately, and because I believe our conceptualizations and praxis of historiography and theory sometimes contribute to them. Polarization and confrontation are a kind of dialectical argument. As historians of rhetoric and as theorists of rhetorical praxis we should examine our own academic agon in the contexts that we study. I think of Kenneth Burke's epigraph, *per bellum purificandum* and then I listen to polemics enjoining us to divorce ourselves from English departments, shun literary study, denounce naive history, stop deluding ourselves with outworn beliefs in facts, and launch neo-Marxist attacks on academic institutions and their discourse. I am not surprised when William Bennett perceives faculty as wanting to trash Plato and Aristotle. Polarization begets polarization; confrontation should be a last resort. No one wins wars—or revolutions—because when one *side* wins, everyone loses in the end.

I find it's the rhetoric rather than the substance of postmodernism, deconstructionism, and post-Enlightenment epistemologies that are problematic. Postmodernism has been around at least since Donne: "The new philosophie casts all in doubt." William Bennett versus the Stanford faculty provides an instructive caricature of an irony. Begin with all the best intentions and proper liberal post-Enlightenment thought in the world, deliver yourself of same using the rhetoric of confrontation, and observe how it is that in their manner of discourse the academic right and the left undermine their own positions much more than they succeed in subverting each other. Bully begets bully. Not that I don't understand the frustrations of our English Department wars, the sad partitioning within rhetoric/composition and between literature and rhetoric/composition. Now even "literature" is a house divided by wars among several deconstructionist and anti-deconstructionist dogmas. The rhetoric of assent hasn't been heard from in years.

These thoughts are roundaboutly in response to Janice Lauer's question regarding validity, evidence, and proof. Should we spend most of our time, and teach students to spend most of their time, exposing presuppositions, making them explicit, establishing their validity, or problematizing them? Or should we look out the window instead? Or should we look within for raw material for "self-expression" or "exposition"? I would like to think a balance is possible, that the history and critique of agonistic rhetoric might lead to insight, and teach us to minimize some forms of confrontational discourse. Nontraditional, nonmainstream, and particularly non-Western students come to our classrooms untutored in what Shakespeare called "the world's false subtleties," by which he meant the contrivances, arguments, and cunning imparted by training in rhetoric. Again and again I have faced the reality (yes, I said *reality*) of how far students have to be brought in order to even begin to comprehend the problematizing moves. To impose that move too early can be an invasion of self and values of the worst kind. But then, it is also an invasion of self and values to impart a rigid and traditional concept of fact, research, or exposition. In my most disgustingly optimistic moments I think all these views could be brought together in our scholarship and pedagogies, *per bellum purificandum.*

2.
DREAMS AND PLAY: HISTORICAL METHOD AND METHODOLOGY
Robert J. Connors

Historical research, until a decade ago only a minor part of the ongoing activity in composition studies, has recently been evolving into one of the recognized strands in our burgeoning field. Unlike certain other research strands, however, historical research uses methods more closely related to traditional humanities inquiry than to scientific or social-scientific paradigms What, exactly, does writing composition history presuppose and entail?

What Constitutes Data in Historical Studies?

It has been common until recently to think of data in historical research as composed of historical "facts." These facts would be uncovered by assiduous gleaning of sources pieced together like a jigsaw puzzle (which has, of course, only one possible correct solution), and presented to readers as "the historical truth." Historians and careful students of history, however, have always known that such an idealized view of their work with data was false. In reality, data in historical studies are made up of at least these three elements: the historian's perceptions of the present, her assemblage of claims based on study of materials from the past, and an ongoing internal dialogue about cultural preconceptions and prejudices and the historian's own. These three elements—present awareness, archival retrieval, and realization of prejudice—are the pieces of information that the historian brings to the attempted solution of the historical problem facing her. Let's look at these elements in more detail.

It may sound strange to say that among the most important data for the historical researcher in composition studies are perceptions of the present day, but every narrator knows it. Until we have some knowledge of the situation a posteriori, our ability to understand the prior situation is hopelessly lacking. Partially, of course, knowledge about the present is central data for the historian because causes can be clearly understood only in the light of their effects; each generation of economic historians since the New Deal has understood and analyzed Roosevelt's policies differently as more and more cause-effect data have come in. But I am also calling perceptions of the

---

Connors, Robert, J. "Dreams and Play: Historical Method and Methodology." *Methods and Methodology in Composition Research*. Eds. Gesa Kirsch and Patricia Sullivan. Carbondale: Southern Illinois UP, 1992. Print.

present central data because they stimulate questioning, excitement, and curiosity, without which history of any sort is a dead compiling of facts without affect. Without intellectual curiosity, without the wish to discover and explain something about life, history *is* a dust bin.

Knowledge of the present is important data for any historian, but it is particularly fundamental to the history of composition studies, because that history is relatively short. Historians of classical rhetoric, for instance, use their knowledge of the present day primarily in a general way; they examine claims and written sources from ancient Greece with their own perceptions of rhetorical action and their own knowledge of human and institutional behavior in mind. The knowledge of the present they bring to the task is of general human nature and of the slow evolution of large institutions. This is how historians of the remote past must operate, since the "causes" seen at a remove of two millennia must have relatively broad and general effects today. But the historian of composition studies, an essentially modern discipline, sees all around her the direct and specific effects of the activities whose genesis she studies. There, in that classroom next door, is the new edition of the *Heath Handbook*; not even D. C. Heath knows it's really the fourteenth, not the twelfth edition—but the historian knows it was the first handbook, born in 1907. Here, in this curriculum meeting, someone is arguing for the "old four mode from classical rhetoric," and the historian knows that the modes were made up by Alexander Bain in 1866. A news magazine rends the welkin with warnings about "the new illiteracy," and the historian knows this is the fourth great American literacy crisis. All around us are the data of the present, and they constantly press on us the immediate question, "What shall we do?" The historian tries to help answer this by looking into less immediate but essential questions, "What have people done in the past?" and "How did things come to be this way?"

From these observational data we begin. All around the composition historian are phenomena that need to be explained. Why is freshman English the only course required for every student? Where does the paragraph come from? Why do students at many colleges fold their papers in half lengthwise before passing them in, without being instructed to do so? Why are there instructors? Why do many literature specialists despise composition? When did the grading system begin? Is student writing worse now than it was in 1900? In my own case, the vital question often used to be, "How did things get this bad?" History nearly always begins as simple curiosity about how we got here.

The next kind of data must be uncovered by painstaking research. We take our questions and our perceptional data, as all historians must, into the Archive, the storehouse of data about the past. The Archive must be explored, analyzed, cross-checked, deconstructed, reconstructed, made meaning of, be stripped, checked, and polished. Here, for the composition historian, is the world of the written word, the printed word, the picture, the table, the diagram, the voice on the tape. The Archive is where storage meets dreams, and the result is history.

The overwhelming bulk of data from the past that the historian of composition studies must deal with is in written and printed form, and what I am calling the Archive actually consists of two discrete kinds of sources, library and archival. Libraries are repositories for printed and published materials generally, while institutional archives deal in more specific primary sources, many of which exist nowhere else and were never meant to be published. A great deal of the material for composition history is available in good research libraries, since most records having to do with teaching writing in general—as opposed to composition teaching at a specific school—were printed and distributed in either books or journals and magazines. From the 1820s on, rhetoric and writing instruction were important issues in American education, and there is a great deal of information to be sifted through in library sources.

When doing library research, the historian must initially determine whether secondary sources exist, how complete they are, and whether they must be consulted. Only a decade ago, this was much less of an issue, but recently the list of creditable secondary sources in composition history has grown markedly. We now have five or six good short books on composition history, and fifty or sixty respectable journal articles. About even the best of these works, most historians have mixed feelings. On the one hand, it is important to know who has been doing work in the area and what they have found out. No one wants to reinvent the cotton gin. Sharing sources and methods is not just collegial, it is good sense. On the other hand, as the field has grown, so too has a healthy tendency grown to disregard secondary sources, to go directly to the primary sources. Some historians refuse to read secondary sources, especially the better-known works by such authors as Kitzhaber and Berlin, because they want to approach the primary works without preconceptions they could have avoided. Too much reliance on secondary sources may result in historians' efforts being relegated to "normal science," cleaning up small-scale problems within the larger paradigm of the existing source's conception. Perhaps the best answer is to read many secondary sources voraciously, seeking for methods, style, coherence, looking for models to pattern your own history on—in any specific area but your own. There, go to the primary sources. See what *they* say to you.

And what are those primary sources? Composition textbooks since the beginning of composition history have been obvious sources, able to tell us much about both the theory and the practice of writing pedagogy. From John Walker's *Teacher's Assistant in English Composition* of 1795 onward, they were used as the theoretical matrices of courses. Soon after 1810, questions to be asked in classes became part of textbook apparatus, thus providing classroom organization. Beginning in the 1830s, rhetorics also came to include written exercises, devices which organized homework activities for students. These "do-everything" books could be used by less-experienced teachers as the pedagogical organizing tools for entire courses, and with them the "modern" form of the rhetoric text was set. We can learn about theory, questions, exercises, advice, and assignments from these books. Historians argue about the degree to which we should assume that textbook organization really informed classroom practice, but no one claims that older textbooks do not constitute important data.

Specialized journals and even general magazines also represent important primary sources. From the 1840s onward, education journals like *Barnard's* dealt with pedagogical and even more specialized language and rhetoric issues. With the *Educational Review, PMLA, School Review,* and *Journal of Education* in the late nineteenth century, a recognizably modern literature on educational issues was created, and the researcher can find in them many articles on composition teaching. Finally, in 1912 comes *English Journal*, the first English-pedagogy journal, and throughout the rest of the century this journal and its eventual spinoffs, *College English* and *College Composition and Communication*, constitute the central fora for professional discussion. In addition, there have been periods—especially the late nineteenth and early twentieth centuries—when composition issues have been seen as so important that general-interest magazines such as *Harper's* and *Atlantic Monthly* would discuss them, and so traditional bibliographic tools like the *Poole's Index* of nineteenth-century magazines can be called into play.

The final primary source likely to be found in libraries is the "professional book" written for teachers or practitioners. Professional books about the teaching of writing go back to the 1890s, when the first media-driven literacy crisis had produced the freshman composition course as one of its answers. That course created its own methodological problems for curriculum planners, and specialized books for teachers have existed since then. There are descriptions of programs, tips for teachers, various forms of braggadocio and apologia among these books. Biographies and memoirs of various figures can be helpful, although few full-scale biographies of central figures in composition history have yet been done, and memoirs are about as rare.

With textbooks, journal and magazine articles, and professional books, the primary sources available at general scholarly libraries have probably been covered. Archives are specialized kinds of libraries that usually contain materials specific to one institution or activity. The archival record contains those rarest and most valuable of data, actual student writings, teacher records, unprinted notes and pedagogical materials, and ephemera that writing courses have always generated but rarely kept. Unlike printed sources, by nature meant for distribution and multiple copies, these notes, papers, and ephemera existed in only a single copy (or sometimes carbon-copy form). As a result, such important data are much more difficult for historians to get hold of than are printed sources. Unlike books and journals, which are cataloged by circulation in libraries and can thus be accessed through bibliographic search and interlibrary loan, archival papers and notes tend to be cataloged separately. Usually researchers have no way to know what college archives contain without hands-on examination, and that can be expensive and difficult for many scholars. There is to this point no central clearinghouse or depository for this sort of archival material. Harvard University's collection is the largest and most detailed, but it refers only to one school's work. The Richard S. Beal Collection at the University of New Hampshire was begun in 1989 as a central depository for composition archives, and over the next decade it should develop into a diverse collection in composition studies.

These are, then, what I call the Archive, those written and printed materials that most people think of as the only real historical sources. But finally, along with the historian's current perceptions and the inert archival material that can be worked with or discarded, there is one more source of data that the conscientious historian must keep in mind: his or her own prejudices. No person exists without prejudice. Our entire life experience functions to predispose us favorably toward some ideas or practices and less favorably toward others. Constitutional affinities and ideological positions form what Kenneth Burke calls *terministic screens* through which we view both current reality and archival materials. The question we face is how we work with our prejudices. No historian is free from prejudiced ideas, but no historian wishes to try for anything less than fair presentation of her findings. So the only way of dealing with our always already being prejudiced is to study the prejudices *as data*. Why do we admire Fred N. Scott and despise Adams S. Hill? Why do we dismiss the terms *clearness, force,* and *elegance* while we accept *unity, coherence,* and *emphasis*? Why do we find a sneer in our voices when we say the word "workbook"? We may not always be able to see all of our own terministic screens, certainly, but then again we cannot claim to know all of current reality or to have found all the possible archival sources. We work with what we can find of all three kinds of data.

All of historical work, then, is provisional, partial—fragments we shore against our ruin. We are trying to make sense of things. It is always a construction. It is always tottering.

How Are Data Used in Producing Knowledge, Generating Theories, and Building Models?

We always start with a hypothesis or a question. In some historical research, this question may be abstract, or prompted by other historians' assertions, or based on newly discovered archival material. In composition history, however, it is much more common for the motivating question to arise out of simple curiosity about one or both of two general situations: (1) Why are things around me as they are? or (2) Why do I see and judge things around me as I do?

Why, for instance, does every teacher know the four "modes of discourse" when they are so little treated in modern textbooks? That was the vague curiosity that began the research that ended in my essay "The Rise and Fall of the Modes of Discourse." In another case, the question arose in my mind, "Why do many teachers mark only the mechanical errors in papers?" That was a reasonable perception-data question. If that had been the only question I had considered, the result might have been a straight historical narrative that took no strong position on the phenomenon of journal marking. I had to admit, however, that I found superadded a more complex and interesting corollary question based on my own prejudices: "Why do I condemn formal-criterion grading when I consider it?" With this question, you see, we plunge into the complex world of the historian's own training, context, personality, ideology, and experience. And only from there do we go to the Archive for confirmation or denial.

So how do data first interact in historical research? Most historical writers, if they are honest, will admit that perceptions and prejudices always must come first in shaping a research question. Seldom does anyone plunge cold into the Archive without something to look for, something they're hoping to find, hoping to see proof of. To try to approach the Archive without even a general hypothesis would go against the human instinct to make sense of things. We gravitate toward organizing ideas. Old composition materials are seldom fascinating or enjoyable to read as art-prose, and we enter that jungle because we think something is there for us to track.

So theory generation is never really *ab ovo*. We start from theory, at least from a theory about building challenging, supportable hypotheses, and historians seldom work through serious archival research unless they have a hypothesis that they tacitly think is supportable. My hypothesis about formal-criteria marking went, at the beginning, something like this. "Paper-marking for mechanical correctives began sometime in the middle of the nineteenth century, probably as a result of handbook use, and it's a bad, a-rhetorical way to mark papers, used then, as now, by lazy, untrained teachers." Now I'm not claiming this is a good hypothesis. It's shot through, as early historical hypotheses often are, with vague assumptions, unsupported assertions, huge gaps in knowledge. It is, in fact, largely false. But it was a place to start. From that questionable but real starting place, built on perception and prejudice, I could go to the Archive with the initial distinctions I needed to begin work there.

What do historians do in the Archive, when they confront that inert, dusty mass of past records? Though it would be neat to be able to say that they sift through everything with hypothesis in hand, "keeping up a running fire of exclamations, groans, whistles, and little cries," drawing scientific deductions Holmes-like, t'aint true. What historians really do in the Archive—and really need to do—is play. Search is play.

How can I describe the work of historians in the Archive? It is not, cannot be, a forced march from hypothesis to support to further support to thesis, since more than half of all sources examined with hypothesis in mind turn out to have little or nothing to do with the question at hand. I might leaf through three or four volumes of early *English Journal*, as I did for a recent essay on the status and salaries of composition teachers, without seeing a single article on the topic. But neither is my examination of archival data ever a random stroll, turning pages without purpose. Historians seldom conduct basic research of that sort. Archival reading is, instead, a kind of directed ramble, something like an August mushroom hunt. There are various concurrent intentions in it: I am looking for information on my specific question; I am looking to increase my own general knowledge of various periods and persons; I am seeking, to be better acquainted with the sources themselves; I am looking for fascinating anomalies; I am hoping for unexpected treasures; and of course I am seeking those conjunctions of historical evidence with sudden perception or understanding that occasionally light up the skies for the lucky historian and reveal a whole world whose genesis and current realities have been subtly reshaped—the "Ah!" of realization that is always the historian's true payoff.

To shift down a step, what we do is browse with directed intention. There is a track, constraint exercised by the developing hypothesis, but we may and must dart off the track to follow a likely scent, a fascinating claim, a mysterious author, a curious fact. I wander about the library with a stack of five-by-eight notecards and a legal pad—the cards for bibliography and citations, and the legal pad for the slowly accumulating "brainstorming" insights that accrue from gradual mental conjunction of the materials examined. The path is always circuitous. Following up one lead may take all afternoon, forcing me to chase through an early *College English* volume, then to the *National Union Catalog*, then to the library circulation computer and the Online Catalog for the Library of Congress computers, then over to my own office to check my database program, then back to the stacks, and finally—oh, frustration!—to the interlibrary loan office, which means a two-week wait before the chase can be taken up again.

As Nan Johnson once put it at a historians' "octolog," or symposium, we often seem unwilling to admit that our research can be exciting, can satisfy curiosity, can be fun. But it can. Historical research at its best is detective work, with all the intellectual rewards of problem and puzzle solving. Of course, for every moment when "the game is afoot," there will always be hours of careful slogging through quotidian facts, deadly educational statistics, dreadfully written accounts of how writing is taught. But we must come out and say it—much archival research is fascinating, and much of the challenge of history is the challenge of puzzle solving.

What, specifically, do historians do as they read, browse, sift, write notes and cards? There are three primary parts to traditional historical analysis: external criticism, internal criticism, and synthesis of materials. These are not "stages" that must take place only in linear order; they are recursive steps that can take place in various orders. Let me, however, go through them one at a time.

External criticism has primarily to do with the choice of sources the historian will read. Given a hypothesis, she must first establish what sources are available that might support (or disprove) it, and then determine whether those available sources are indeed appropriate to the task or able to handle it effectively. It is here, at this primary stage, that researchers really need to know their Archives. What books, journals, paper, ephemera do they have access to? Which are the most likely to serve the needs of the project? For my recent essay, "The Creation of an Underclass," dealing with the status and labor of writing teachers, I was forced to a whole new level of external criticism, one not demanded by earlier projects. For previous work on textbooks, for instance, I had become familiar and comfortable with the University of New Hampshire Library holdings in old textbooks. But a complex sociocultural inquiry about the conditions surrounding composition teaching required very different sources. I had to acquaint myself with economic studies of college teaching, with educational reports and statistics, with histories of individual colleges and universities, with the few reports English professors ever wrote concerning their own status. I had to go to new journals; I had to explore new sections of the library stacks; I had to examine novel secondary sources; and I had to make extensive use of interlibrary loan. Poring over all this new material was quite a departure from the simpler history-of-ideas research that informed much of my early work, and possible sources seemed to ramify in countless directions. But I had to get as many sources as possible into my hands, and after a search of some months, I was confident that I had at least the rudiments of the map, if not a complete vision of the territory.

At the same time that she searches for and judges sources, the historian must also engage in the next stage of analysis—internal criticism. Internal criticism examines the sources found with the intent of making sure they are judged correctly. Historians check the language and usage of their sources, examine them for obvious or subtle biases, try to eliminate glosses or corruptions. Most importantly, internal criticism implies a search for corroborative support of claims made by sources. If thoughtful, defensible history has a methodological nexus, it must be in this search for corroboration. All records we have are written by human, all-too-human, agents. They are necessarily filled with self-justification optimistic delusion, pessimistic distortion, partisan argument. Not a one can stand as the complete and trusty truth—not even the statistics. And so a process of comparison and corroboration is central work for the historian.

This internal criticism is especially important when studying the history of composition, because for the last century and a half, teaching writing has been an arena echoing with claims and counterclaims—a genuine rhetorical situation. As I have argued elsewhere, freshman composition is the only college-level course that was instituted to solve a perceived social problem rather than to investigate a branch of knowledge, so claims about its methods, necessity, and usefulness have always been as argumentative as they were expository. Composition historians must dig through this mass of claims and rejoinders. If we cannot always make judgments about whose arguments were right, we can at least try to determine certain factual realities. Barrett Wendell, for example, claims to have invented the "daily theme" at Harvard in the 1880s. Did he? This was the question that my colleague Tom Newkirk faced recently. Was this a claim that Tom, as a historian, wished to endorse? Through a process of internal criticism, he had to test this claim. What did Wendell's students say? What do the Harvard records and memoirs say? What did Wendell's colleagues think? What, if Tom could find evidence in the Harvard archives, do Wendell's teaching notes or student essays show? Only after a thorough cross-check of all these sources could the historian really support the claim.

As you can see, it is never possible to separate internal criticism from external criticism completely, because one often sends a historian out into a round of the other. To understand and accept any claim internal to a document, it must be compared to claims in other documents. When I was searching for information on instructors' salaries in 1920, I could not be certain about the figures I found until I had a second source that gave me approximately the same figures—a second source I had to get from interlibrary loan. Barbara Tuchman, in *Practicing History,* says that she never accepts a single primary source as effective evidence, but always contrasts at least two different accounts. This is not always possible in composition history, but enough different kinds of evidence exist to give a careful historian a sense of whether the archival fact will support a developing hypothesis.

The depth of corroboration needed for a historical claim has a direct relationship to the novelty and current acceptance of that claim. (This is why we cannot completely dispense with reading secondary sources.) What is the researcher's discourse community likely to know already, likely to accept as given? If I claim, for instance, that composition teaching burgeoned after the Civil War because of the growth of universities and the needs of a capitalist economy, I will hardly have to do more than cite one or two secondary sources. No one disagrees with those claims, and they need little corroboration today. But if I claim, as I have been doing lately, that composition burgeoned in America because of the demand of women to be taught rhetoric, the corresponding responses of men, and the general educational changes forced on colleges by coeducation after 1840, I will need to provide considerable evidence and extensive corroboration for that claim.

It is a novel claim, and one that must be strenuously supported if it is to be accepted. My internal criticism of sources, given the intensely polemical nature of most of the nineteenth-century debates on coeducation and rhetorical training for women, will need to be deep. That is why I am currently four years into this project and have thus far published little about it.

When external and internal criticism have been brought forcibly to an end—and it is nearly always necessary to bring the research period to an end forcibly, since by its nature research is never "done," and investigation always seems more comfortable than conclusions—the final stage of analysis is synthesis of materials. This step corresponds in some ways to *dispositio* in classical rhetoric. The historian structures the scattered and disparate sources she has located and compared, bringing into play ideas of cause and effect, inductive generalizations, patterns of influence, taxonomic groupings, and all of the other various systems of connection by which we make sense of the world. Of course, since the research has itself been guided by a hypothesis, the synthesis of materials has in a sense been going on since the inception of the project. But even as the index cards mount up, even as the legal pad fills with hastily scrawled connections and insights, the shape of the final thesis-and-support often cannot be seen until the organizing and actual composing begin.

The way this usually happens for me is that the archival sources build up and interinanimate until they produce a subhypothesis that then generates further search. In the case of my "Creation of an Underclass" piece, which had as its general hypothesis the low pay and status of composition teachers, this subhypothesis developed as I struggled to understand why rhetoric came to be so despised at nineteenth-century American universities when it had been so respected at American colleges. What differentiated universities from colleges? Lawrence Veysey's *Emergence of the American University* told me that the answer was specialized schools. What were the most obvious kind? Graduate schools. What did graduate schools produce? Ph.D.'s. So that was one line of evidence.

Then I turned to biographies of English professors and teachers active from 1880–1900—Adams Hill, Fred Newton Scott, Barrett Wendell, John Genung, Henry Frink. What I found there—what I had always vaguely known but had never really brought together in my mind—was that there *were* no Ph.D.'s in rhetoric. Where Ph.D's existed, they were in philology or literature. Except at Michigan between 1896 and 1927, no American university had ever granted rhetoric Ph.D.'s until speech departments took rhetoric over and separated it from written discourse. Why had this been the case? For the answer to that I had to go to the history of international graduate study, especially to the country after whose higher learning nineteenth-century Americans patterned their own: Germany. And there I found my answer, in sources on the German university system that I had never seen before: there was no German intellectual tradition of rhetoric after 1810, and no German rhetoric Ph.D.'s. So by synthesizing my study of American universities and colleges, the development of English departments and their associated literary and compositional luminaries, and the German intellectual condemnation of rhetoric, I was able to come up with a working subhypothesis that composition teachers were marginalized because they had no Ph.D. licensure and no way to advance in the university hierarchy that licensure had created.

This subhypothesis existed through much of my research, of course, and when time came actually to draft the essay, the synthesis of materials was done on a much smaller scale. The questions involved in *writing* history are stylistic, presentational, small-scale. What order should the stack of note cards take? Which of these juicy quotes must be discarded as redundant? Of the two major modes of presentation available, thematic and chronological, which should be chosen where? How much general explanation does the background of the intended audience require? These are synthetic questions that have more to do with presentation than with research, yet that does not make them unimportant; many times a perceived need for better support during composing has sent me back (grudgingly, and sometimes frantically) to external and internal criticism.

So that is how developing data build theories in historical research. Occasionally a beautiful hypothesis is supported for a while only to be killed by a cruel counterfact, but more often hypotheses start as vague suppositions that are sharpened and directed by accumulating archival evidence.

What Kind of Questions Can and Can't Be Answered by Historical Research?

Obviously historical research can give fairly solid answers to discrete factual questions about the past. I can tell you what the first composition workbook was, and who invented the methods of exposition. David Russell can run down for you the first programs to use writing across the curriculum. Donald Stewart can name all of Fred Newton Scott's publications. And if we don't have the facts at our fingertips, we know where to get them, or at least whether they are likely to be had.

But these discrete historical facts hang in a vacuum, useless, without the interpretations that order them in all historical writing. And so the two questions that are continually argued about in historical writing are these: (1) Does this interpretation of the historical data seem coherent, reliable, interesting, useful? and (2) What can this interpretation of the past show us about the present and the future?

For the first question, there are criteria that can be applied to allow us at least provisional answers. We can make informed judgments about any historian's basic knowledge, depth of research, imaginative facility, ideological predispositions, and writing ability, to determine who writes history we will call "good." How original is the thesis? How broad is the explanatory power?

How many primary sources were consulted? Were any important sources missed or scanted? Are there careless generalizations? Are the assertions backed up with enough proof? Is there any attempt at explaining alternative interpretations, or is it a presentation of only one single strong side? Is the narrative written in a way that draws the reader along? Are the issues explored important or involving to the readership? These and other questions can clarify for us the "quality" of the history being presented.

For the second question, however, the one that historians are always being asked, the answer is much less clear. *Can* we learn about the present or the future from the past? On some levels, obviously, we can be advised by the lessons of the past. But can we learn enough, in enough systematic ways, to make any historian's view of the past an accurate guide to the present and future? The answer to this question must be, sadly, no.

Historical research cannot tell us what we should and should not do in any given set of circumstances. It cannot even give us the plausible "certainties" provided by statistical analysis. History is always written from probabilistic, and therefore rhetorical, points of view. All it can do is tell us stories, stories that may move us to actions but that in themselves cannot guide our actions according to any system. If history were, or could be, systematic, things might be different. But history is not, and never has been, systematic or scientific. Any attempt to make history predictive would have to assume that there are dependable recurring circumstances, which is simply not the case. In fact, history is narrative, and every attempt to create a system to give that narrative a predictive meaning is fraught with peril.

This is not to say that we cannot learn *anything* from history. If history does not allow us to predict or anticipate what is coming on the basis of what has been, it certainly does paint pictures of the past for us from which we can draw lessons. For example, the great literacy crisis of 1885 was followed by fifteen years of frantic attempts to solve it, and these attempts were then followed by thirty years of dogmatic torpor. I would appear foolish if I were to say that the great literacy crisis of 1976 would have to be followed by exactly the same scenario. History has too many cunning passages for that to be simply the case.

But what can I say, with any confidence, on the basis of knowing about the literacy crisis of 1885? Surely I can compare the social and cultural conditions of the time. Surely the economic reasons for and the pedagogic results of the 1885 crisis might tell me something about our own era. Surely the student papers of the time could give me insight into today's basic writing students and their papers. The point is that although what we face as teachers and scholars every day is always new, it is never completely new. Others have been here before, facing similar problems and choices. The story of their hopes, ideas, struggles, disappointments, and triumphs can tell us about our own stories. We may not learn how ours will end from how theirs ended, but we can gain valuable insight into people and their conditions, their motives, and their responses to problems.

So we cannot learn what to do from history. All we can learn is what others have done, perhaps a little about what not to do, and, perhaps, a little about who we are.

What Problems Emerge in the Process of Inquiry, and What Issues Are Raised by Historical Methodology?

The most obvious problem we face as historical researchers and writers is how to make our narratives reliable and persuasive. Practically, this issue comes down to the way in which induction balances deduction during the research process itself. How much do our preexisting ideas about what we will look for in the Archive create the data paths we then actually follow, rendering our narratives self-creating? The Chicago formalist critics used to castigate New Criticism as "a priori" criticism because New Critics would often choose some literary element a priori—an element like irony or ambiguity—and simply chase it down through a text or texts, ignoring other important formal elements at work there. Historians can always be pronounced guilty of this same offense, of course, because we hardly ever step into the archival forest without an existing hypothesis. We are always looking for something. The sticky point remains how the hypothesis we are using may constrain our search and make us less sensitive to other important elements in the historical equation. If an a priori hypothesis is too strong, too neat, it may take over the entire work of seeking archival data. The historian may end up searching through the stacks with blinders on, seeking only confirmation of the hypothesis. Similarly, if a historian depends too much on secondary sources and received wisdom, her hypotheses are apt to be constrained by those sources, and her research is apt to present no threat to standard ideas. That way lies orthodoxy, and bad history.

Again, the case of Barrett Wendell can illustrate this danger. The grandfather of composition history, Albert R. Kitzhaber, pronounced the verdict in his seminal 1953 dissertation, *Rhetoric in American Colleges, 1850–1900*: Barrett Wendell was an interesting eccentric but a dogmatic, retrograde rhetorician whose Harvard department put composition teaching on the road to ruin in the 1890s. Since Kitzhaber's 1953 pronunciamento, nearly all other historians have taken his damnation of Wendell and Harvard as accurate. Donald Stewart and James Berlin in particular, in works they wrote extolling Fred N. Scott and contrasting Scott's University of Michigan department with Harvard, continued Kitzhaber's dismissal of Wendell. The hypotheses historians evolved about Wendell grew out of the Kitzhaber legacy of received wisdom, and the research line followed the hypotheses, which—surprise!—were supported by the research.

Not until 1987, when newer historians such as David Jolliffe and Thomas Newkirk began to investigate the Harvard archives, were a new Barrett Wendell and a new *fin de siècle* Harvard writing program revealed. When historians looked carefully at the heretofore despised Harvard program, they found that under Wendell the Harvard writing courses had been taught almost like contemporary "process writing" courses, with student topic choice, revision, and individual conferences. The myth of the error-obsessed, mechanistic Harvard course that became the freshman composition prototype was exploded.

What's the lesson here? Not, certainly, that all received wisdom is wrong, but that all received wisdom is partial, incomplete. It must be examined again and again, not merely accepted. That, finally, is why there are, and why we need, multiple histories. There can never be any history so magisterial that it precludes the need for other histories. The scholar who claims, as does a classicist I know, that his intention is to write *the* book on Protagoras—one that would render any other book on Protagoras forever unnecessary—is living in an epistemological time warp. We should, of course, always strive to write the most reliable, valid, thorough, coherent, and fair-minded narratives we can, but no one narrative can ever, or should ever, shut down the narrative enterprise. There are too many interesting perspectives for that to be desirable.

This necessity for multiple histories can, of course, be taken on a theoretical level all the way to a claim about the validity of any history—to epistemological atheism, as it were. Victor Vitanza, that loving gadfly of rhetorical historians, is fond of asking "What's the proof for proof? What's the evidence for evidence?" Against so thoroughgoing a critique of any belief system as Victor mounts, historians can only continue to proffer their hard-won narratives and say to readers with A. E. Housman's Terence, "I will friend you, if I may." Simply, we hope to do some good. If we cannot really controvert the deconstruction of all epistemic certainties, we can at least keep the voices going, keep talking to one another, keep telling the stories that finally are all that can ever body us forth one to another.

Because that is what history is: the telling of stories about the tribe that make the tribe real. That is why the recovery of composition history after it had been lost for 150 years is so important. Finally, we are telling the stories of our fathers and our mothers, and we are legitimating ourselves through legitimating them. Yes, the story is sometimes discouraging; yes, many false paths and useless methods were tried; yes, there were long periods of dogma and desuetude. But we in composition studies have a history. It's murky in places so far, and much of it has not been well explored. But it exists. We are part of a discipline that is twenty-five hundred years old, and our continuity from Aristotle and the earliest rhetoricians cannot now be doubted by anyone. Our history is its own justification, and if our methods can grow more solid and sophisticated our motives should not. The methods are not new, nor can they be; the effort there is to wield them with more control, more self-awareness. But our motives for writing our history are what such motives have always been: we write histories to define ourselves on the stage of time.

Works Cited

Bain, Alexander. *English Composition and Rhetoric: A Manual.* New York: D Appleton, 1866.

Berlin, James. *Rhetoric and Reality: Writing Instruction in American Colleges 1900–1985.* Carbondale: Southern Illinois UP, 1987.

Berlin, James. *Writing Instruction in Nineteenth-Century American Colleges.* Carbondale: Southern Illinois UP, 1984.

Connors, Robert J. "Rhetoric in the Modern University: The Creation of An Underclass." *The Politics of Writing Instruction, Postsecondary.* Ed. Richard Bullock and John Trimbur. Portsmouth, NH: Boynton/Cook, 1991: 55–84.

Connors, Robert J. "The Rhetoric of Mechanical Correctness." *Only Connect: Uniting Reading and Writing.* Ed. Thomas Newkirk. Upper Montclair, NJ: Boynton/Cook, 1986: 27–58.

Connors, Robert J. "The Rise and Fall of the Modes of Discourse." *College Composition and Communication* 32 (1981): 444–55.

Horner, Winifred, ed. *Historical Rhetoric: An Associated Bibliography of Selected Sources in English.* Boston: C. K. Hall, 1980.

Horner, Winifred, ed. *The Present State of Scholarship in Historical and Contemporary Rhetoric.* Columbia: U of Missouri P, 1983.

Jolliffe, David. "The Moral Subject in College Composition: A Conceptual Framework and the Case of Harvard, 1865–1900" *College English* 51 (1989): 163–73.

Kitzhaber, Albert R. *Rhetoric in American Colleges 1850–1900.* Dallas: Southern Methodist UP, 1990.

Newkirk, Thomas. "Barrett Wendell and the Birth of Freshman Composition." Paper read at CCCC, Chicago, IL, March 1990.

Newkirk, Thomas. "Octolog: The Politics of Historiography." *Rhetoric Review* 7(1988): 5–57.

Tuchman, Barbara. *Practicing History: Selected Essays.* New York: Knopf, 1981.

Veysey, Lawrence R. *The Emergence of the American University.* Chicago: U of Chicago P, 1965.

Vitanza, Victor J. "'Notes' Towards Historiographics of Rhetorics." PRE/TEXT 8 (1987): 63–125.

Wendell, Barrett. *English Composition.* New York: Scribner's, 1891.

3.
REMAPPING RHETORICAL TERRITORY
Cheryl Glenn

Until recently, we could pull a neatly folded history of rhetoric out of our glove compartment, unfold it, and navigate our course through the web of lines that connected the principal centers of rhetoric. Whether using Corbett's, Kennedy's, Kinneavy's, or Murphy's map, we followed an aristocratic blue line, a master narrative that started with Corax and Tisias and led directly to Plato and Aristotle, then Cicero, Quintilian, and St. Augustine, and eventually to Weaver, Richards, Perelman, and Burke—each rhetorician preparing us for the next, like Burma Shave signs. For years, we ignored the borders of our map, the shadowy regions where roads run off the edge of the paper and drop away at sharp angles. Were we assuming that those were barren territories devoid of scenic routes, historic events, influential people? Yes. Did we think they were off limits, like those murky territories on Renaissance charts that bore warnings of monsters beyond the sea? Perhaps.[1]

The map we were using did exactly what we wanted it to do: it met our professional, intellectual, and social needs. That canonized map embodied and reflected our institutional focus on great, powerful men whose texts, lives, and actions transcended the particularities of history and circumstance. Resonating with the rest of our intellectual traditions—literary, poetic, scientific, historical, political—all of which focused on masculine power, that map both "expresse[d] and transcend[ed] the values, conventions, and circumstances of a discipline at a particular moment (Atwill 91). But most importantly, perhaps, that map served us well "at a time when rhetoric's legitimacy as a field of scholarly inquiry was contested." In addition, Takis Poulakos goes on to tell us, "A narrative account of rhetoric's stable subject matter across time proved to be an effective response to charges of illegitimacy . . . [as well as] a successful way of resisting pressures . . . to turn the study of rhetoric into a positivistic investigation" (1).

Now, we are turning to a new map, or rather, to new, often partially completed maps that reflect and coordinate our current institutional, intellectual, political, and personal values, all of which have become markedly more diverse and elastic in terms of gender, race, and class. Over the past ten years alone, the cartographic achievements of James Berlin, Patricia Bizzell, William Covino, Sharon Crowley, Richard Enos, Bruce Herzberg, Susan Jarratt, Nan Johnson, Susan Miller, Jasper Neel, Edward Schiappa, C. Jan Swearingen, Victor Vitanza, Kathleen Welch, Ross Winterowd, and many others have encouraged (and sometimes intimidated) those of us just getting started in our map-making. We all seem to agree that our new maps are "doing" differently what

---

Glenn, Cheryl. "Remapping Rhetorical Territory." *Rhetoric Review* 12.2 (1995): 287–303. Print.

maps do: they are taking us more places, introducing us to more people, complicating our understanding in more ways than did the previous map.

The Heritage Turnpike featured no communities of women, the places many of us want to visit. So, for several years, my own work as an historian of rhetoric has been to trace the routes to those settlements and to resurvey the territory in order to locate and position women rhetoricians on the map—rarely an easy task. My most satisfying historical research so far might well have to do with Aspasia's rhetorical community, which I'll discuss below, and the most all-round useful research essay has been Patricia Bizzell's "Opportunities for Feminist Research in the History of Rhetoric." Anticipating and accounting for disruptions and realignments of the rhetorical map, Bizzell provides three specific feminist projects and methodologies that those of us just getting established can use as a reference point as we plot our own scholarly projects: (1) resistant readings by both women as well as men of the Paternal Narrative; (2) consideration of female-authored rhetorical works comparable to male-authored works; and (3) broad definitions of *rhetoric* that move it from an exclusionary to an inclusionary enterprise.

It is beyond the scope of this essay to provide a thorough overview of Bizzell's suggested methodologies, but I want to call to mind the broad scope of their application in the light of three angles: *historiography* (which informs the entire enterprise of feminist remappings), *feminism* (which specifically works to situate female rhetorical figures), and *gender studies* (which refigure gender as a category for historiographical analysis). I've viewed the terrain from these three angles in order to illustrate how they have informed my own work on Aspasia of Miletus, the intellectual, sexual, and political partner of Pericles—a woman who was also his teacher of rhetoric (Glenn). Of course, any such set of methodological categories overlap when used purposefully to advance a feminist project like mine, and such categories also take a postmodern slant when used deliberately to reveal multiple and different *angles* from which to map rhetorical terrain.

Lines and Angles on the Rhetorical Map

Postmodernism influences our resistant readings of the Paternal Narrative, particularly since it demands our awareness of situatedness, our angle (in my case, reading as a woman). And postmodern angles help us identify previously unseen and unconsidered problems of "foundational" knowledge, in this case, the tradition of rhetorical history. Therefore, "*The* History of Rhetoric" is quickly displaced by questions of *Whose* history? *Whose* rhetoric? *Which* rhetoric?—necessary challenges to a canon that is so "unrelentingly white, elite, and male (Bizzell, "Opportunities" 51). Postmodernism forces us to admit that we each have an "angle," and it has made us skeptical about the procedures that legitimized and mapped out "the" history of rhetoric in the first place. No wonder, then, that historians of rhetoric no longer rely exclusively on *linear* plotting to connect one rhetorician to the "next." Instead, we have taken to measuring and charting territory by means of *angles*. And by constructing our map by means of angular as well as linear measurements, we can chart and account for previously unseen and unmeasured contours of the landscape. Through angular lenses we catch fragmentary glimpses of the previously unconsidered variations that had been smoothed over by the flat surface of received knowledge.

I began writing about Aspasia, for instance, only when I began resisting the Paternal Narrative that assured me she was either apocryphal or a glorified prostitute, that she could not be legitimized because her words appeared only in "secondary" sources, and that she could not and did not represent an entire community of rhetorical women in classical Greece. How could I write a map of rhetorical history if I didn't have "proof"? if I had only an angle instead? if Aspasia provided only a fragmentary view rather than a panoramic vision of rhetoric? Before I could publish anything, I had to come to an understanding of what I wanted my map, my history, *to do*. I wanted to challenge the male-dominated story of rhetoric by telling a story of Aspasia that illustrated just how the various renditions or uses of Aspasia configure an emblem of Woman in rhetorical history.

Those of us charting historical maps know that we cannot tell the "truth," that no one map can ever tell the truth, that our traditional foundations are shaky, that maps are neither stable nor coherent, and that the notion of capturing any "reality" rings of empiricism, positivism, and naïveté. Yet we cannot completely separate ourselves from writing or from reading these histories, these stories. Carroll Smith-Rosenberg insists that despite any postmodern complications, we just continue to read and write such stories, for if we "relinquish our grasp on the world behind words," if we "deny the knowability of the world, we lose that aspect of the world we are . . . committed to knowing" (32). In my case, women's use of rhetoric. Besides, as Hans Kellner so forcefully writes. "It is the power of story . . . that can make people change, and . . . such stories will be single authored and feature heroes" ("Afterword" 249).

Maybe the story of fifth-century Aspasia will make some people change their view of rhetorical history, their opinion of women's participation in the theory and practice of rhetoric, even their research agendas. Maybe the story of a heroic Aspasia will open the door, just a crack, to a fuller understanding of the intellectual, non-Athenian, noncitizen woman during Periclean Athens, of how Periclean Athens might look when it includes a woman. And maybe the resistances inherent in the postmodern critique (especially those resistances that play out in current historiography, feminism, and gender studies) can influence and interrogate our traditional historiographic projects—our mappings—so that they survey many more women's settlements.

Historiography and Feminist Remappings

As we write our histories of rhetoric, especially as we write women into the tradition, we, like historians in other fields, must continue to resist received notions both of history and of writing history, what Michel de Certeau calls "scriptural construction" (309). In *The Writing of History,* he tells us that "history" connotes both a science and that which it studies—the explication which is *stated,* and the reality of *what has taken place* or what takes place (21). And because that connotation of history is "our myth," Certeau goes on to tell us that "historiography (that is, 'history' and 'writing') bears within its own name the paradox . . . of a relation established between two antinomic terms, between the real and discourse" (xxvii). The task of historiography, then, is one of connecting the real and the discourse, and at the point where this link cannot be imagined, historiography must work *as if* the real and discourse were actually being joined (xxvii). Certeau is right: that's what we're all doing. As we resist the Paternal Narrative of rhetorical history, we're all working as if the real and discourse were actually being joined in our texts, on our maps. We have no choice, for how can we know the world except through the words it constructs?

The text of history writing, then, initiates a play between the object under study and the discourse performing the analysis. And even the most conscientious history writers play the game. Fredric Jameson defines "history" as an "ideologeme," a construct that is susceptible to both a conceptual description and a narrative manifestation all at once (87). Hayden White writes that "a historical narrative is . . . at once a representation that is an interpretation and an interpretation that passes for an explanation of the whole process mirrored in the narrative" (51), echoing Richard Rorty, who nearly twenty years ago rotated the argument of Thomas Kuhn and convinced us that we simply cannot "mirror" any reality in any narrative—scientific, historical, or otherwise. And in her compelling "Making Up Lost Time: Writing on the Writing of History," Nancy Partner describes history as "the definitive human audacity imposed on formless time and meaningless event" and calls history-writing "the silent shared conspiracy of all historians (who otherwise agree on nothing these days)" who "talk about the past as though it were really 'there'" (97).

Why, then, should we continue to write histories of rhetoric when both writing and history are suspect? when the past wasn't really "there"? or when we agree that there was a past but not what the past really was? Well, it's too late to do otherwise.

Historiographic practices are now so firmly situated in the postmodern critique of rhetoric that we already take for granted that histories "do" (or should do) something, that they fulfill our needs at a particular time and place. But even before that critique, Douglas Ehninger's 1967 "On Rhetoric and Rhetorics" inaugurated the call for revisionary histories of rhetoric (see also Scott's "Necessary Pluralism of Any Future History of Rhetoric" and Berlin's "Revisionary History"). Since then, the proliferation of new rhetorical maps as well as new ways of interpreting any rhetorical map—often conflicting, necessarily fragmented, never final—have allowed us to see that historiographic rhetorical maps never reflect a neutral reality. In choosing what to show and how to represent it, these maps "do" something: they subtly shape our perceptions of a rhetoric englobed.

Because these mappings "do" something, Kellner encourages us to keep on mapping. In "After the Fall," he tells us that learning to write new histories, histories worthy of the remarkable revival of rhetorical consciousness at the present moment, means, above all, *to devise new ways of reading* that will look at the texts as texts, that will look for the "other" sources of historical discourse in constant tension with the evidence (32). We must risk, then, "getting the story crooked." We must *look* crookedly, a bit out of focus, into the various strands of meaning in a text in such a way as to make the categories, trends, and reliable identities of history a little less inevitable, less familiar. In short, we need to see what is familiar in a different way, in many different ways, as well as to see beyond the familiar to the unfamiliar, to the unseen (32–33).

Narratives are no longer unquestioned or overarching; therefore, historiographers study the shape of each narrative to determine how "form outlines the contour of a loss, an absence, a voice, a silence, which in turn is assumed to be the ground of history" (Conley 8). And those contours have become more prevalent on our maps, as we continue to explore and chart those once-murky regions on the edges of our maps, particularly those regions occupied by women and other disenfranchised groups. The recent prominence of the sophists is a case in point.

As soon as the sophists were determined a conspicuous absence on our rhetorical map, historiographers began practicing the crafts of resurrection, animation, and even ventriloquism to re-present them. Following the influential work of G. B. Kerford, recent books (see Barrett, R. Enos, Jarratt) and recent issues of *PRE/TEXT, Rhetoric Review,* and *The Rhetoric Society Quarterly,* for example, have featured various rehabilitations and promotions of the sophists—specifically of Gorgias, Protagoras, and Isocrates. Such historiographic work enables us to move toward a broader understanding of the sophists. For instance, we now realize the sophists' role in preparing "young men for public life in the *polis*" (Jarratt, *Rereading* xv); we now understand the influence of Sicilian sophists on establishing what would become the rhetorical tradition (R. Enos passim); and we have come to believe in the "theoretical coherence and practical validity" of sophistic rhetoric (McComisky 79). And as Edward Schiappa cautions us in "Sophistic Rhetoric: Oasis or Mirage," the idea of "sophistic rhetoric" has become so familiar (and therefore acceptable) in the works of Crowley, Roger Moss, Neel, and John Poulakos, for instance, that he has to "make the case that 'sophistic rhetoric' is, for the most part, a mirage—something we see because we want and need to see it" (5).

So far as my own work is concerned, I wanted and needed to see sophistic rhetoric in order to see beyond it, beyond the sophists, beyond the scraps of texts that have insufficiently represented them. Until I read crooked, to see how sophistic texts connected with other sources of historical discourse, I could not make my way past the configurations of Aspasia as intellectual joke or harlot. When I realized how closely connected Aspasia of Miletus was with the sophists, both in proximity and ideology (a connection Jarratt, Ong, and Swearingen were also making), I could write about how that connection contributed to her erasure from rhetorical history.

Just because she was erased was no reason to stop looking for her trace. I could make the unfamiliar familiar and the familiar unfamiliar. After all, she was effaced in much the same way as Socrates, for none of their words exist in primary sources. Although the rhetorical tradition has readily accepted those secondary accounts of Socrates' influence, teaching, and beliefs, the same cannot be said about any female counterpart. But with Bizzell's encouragement, I could consider her female-authored words and ideas comparable to his, and I could read Aspasia through the palimpsest of her thoughts, knowing that her words and actions have been inscribed and reinscribed by those of men. We could know Aspasia the same way we know about Socrates—from secondary sources. The surviving fragments and references to Aspasia's intellect in the work of male authors compelled me to piece those fragments together to see what and who appeared, what was present, what was missing. Historiography, reading it crooked and telling it slant, could help me shape—re-member—a female rhetorical presence.

Feminist Research and Situating Female Rhetorical Figures

In concert with historiography, feminist research has also worked to resist the Western Paternal Narrative of rhetoric—a narrative Edward P.J. Corbett describes as "one of the most patriarchal of all the academic disciplines"—by recovering and recuperating women's contributions in the broad history of culture-making. In 1990 Corbett could only hope for the recovery of names of women rhetors (377). In the last five years, we have recovered such names. In 1989 Karlyn Kohrs Campbell published *Man Cannot Speak for Her: A Critical Study of Early Feminist Rhetoric*, which catalogues successful rhetorical women such as Sojourner Truth, Elizabeth Cady Stanton, and Lucretia Coffin Mott, who spoke from the often-controversial traditions of temperance, suffrage, and abolition work. In their 1990 *Rhetorical Tradition*, Bizzell and Herzberg include the rhetorical discourse of a number of women, starting in the Renaissance: Christine de Pizan, Laura Cereta, Martha Fell, Sarah Grimké, Hélène Cixous, and Julia Kristeva. And in *Reclaiming Rhetorica*, Andrea Lunsford offers us a collection of women's rhetorical endeavors that includes essays ranging from Swearingen on Diotima and Jenny Redfern on Christine de Pizan to Jamie Barlowe on Mary Wollstonecraft and Suzanne Clark on Kristeva. These three collections offer a number of recovered women as well as methodologies for recovering even more. At present, many other feminist scholars are employing these as well as Bizzell's methodologies (they often overlap, with Bizzell being the more explicit) for writing women into the history of rhetoric; the work of Vicki Collins, Drema Lipscomb, Roxanne Mountford, Catherine Peaden, Krista Ratcliffe, and Jacqueline Jones Royster immediately comes to mind.

And although many feminist scholars have been putting Bizzell's advice to use, the results have not led automatically to unanimously happy or harmonious results within feminist communities. For instance, in "Coming to Terms with Recent Attempts to Write Women into the History of Rhetoric," Barbara Biesecker refers to the kinds of projects I've just mentioned as the "mere inclusion of women's texts in the rhetorical canon" (142). Drawing her representative generalizations from the much-celebrated work of Campbell, Biesecker warns that a collection of cameo appearances by extraordinary women resolidifies rather than undoes the ideology of the received history of Rhetoric (144). Biesecker's charges of "female tokenism" and "affirmative action" in current feminist scholarship (a point concurrent with Michelle Ballif's argument) provoked an immediate and strong response from Campbell, titled "Biesecker Cannot Speak for Her Either," in which Campbell countercharges that one scholar's "female tokenism" is another scholar's incipient analysis of women's rhetoric" (154).

Given what we know about the writing of any intellectual history, given what we know about the limits of any one methodology, particularly an inchoate one, we cannot simply measure out the distance between women, chart their place on the rhetorical map, and travel. Remapping rhetoric will demand much more of us. Even though our feminist historiography points to a different set of subjects (in this case, women) for historical inquiry, our studies will not be merely compensatory or additive histories of women rhetoricians. Instead, any remapping must locate female rhetorical accomplishments within the male-dominated and male-documented rhetorical tradition that it interrogates. And when Biesecker moves us beyond an argument of Bizzell's plan or Campbell's scholarship, she moves us even closer to those necessary demands. In "Coming to Terms," she asks us to push the envelope of our (feminist) research to do more than add women to the canon: "the *radical* contextualization of all rhetorical acts can enable us to forge a new storying of our tradition that circumvents the veiled cultural supremacy operative in mainstream histories of Rhetoric" (147). As Carole Blair and Mary Kahl demonstrate in their "Revising the History of Rhetorical Theory," such restorying (on whatever grounds—gender, class, or race, for example) can take place only within a reevaluation of rhetorical theories in general.

Therefore, whatever theoretical, practical, or political challenges—whatever agreements or disagreements—feminist rhetoricians bring to the map of rhetoric, their contributions are moving us beyond the restoration of women to rhetorical history; they are revitalizing rhetorical theory by shaking the conceptual foundations of rhetorical study itself. In the broadest sense, then, feminist historiography is performative—it *does* something. Toward that end of bringing feminism to rhetoric and rhetoric to feminism, recent issues of both *Rhetoric Society Quarterly* and *The Southern Communication Journal* have been devoted to feminist research: Susan Jarratt guest edited the special issue of *RSQ*, titled "Feminist Rereadings in the History of Rhetoric," and Janice Hocker Rushing edited the *SCJ* issue titled "Feminist Criticism." Yet despite all the established and ongoing feminist historiographic work, much feminist work remains to be done, for each time we face the rhetorical *woman*, we still see *terra nova*, barely perceptible on our horizon.

It was only by incorporating various feminist methodologies that I was able to move my own work forward. My initial, graduate-school work on Aspasia (which ran for merely seven pages in my dissertation) now seems to me a purely descriptive, somewhat solitary account. Only when I was able to broaden my definition of rhetoric and its practice, only when I was able to give Aspasia the kind of acceptance I had always given Socrates, did I realize that I'd discovered a pocket of rhetorical activity. Such small methodological steps, but what a rich payoff: I could write a fuller, relational account of Aspasia's place and participation in rhetorical history, as a woman, a foreigner, and as an intellectual and political force.

Gender Studies as a Category for Analysis

The last of the critiques I want to discuss, however briefly, is gender studies. Despite the feminist work of the past five years, the rhetorical map still most familiar to us, regardless of its contours, is one exclusive of women, a map featuring only agonistic, upper-class, public, privileged males. And because those rhetorical maps are always inscribed by the relation of language and power at a particular moment (including who may speak, who may listen, and what can be said), such maps have replicated the power politics of gender, with men in the highest social elevation and rank. It is no coincidence, now, that feminist scholarship has pressed us toward examining the social construction of gender and gendered power. Susan Bordo tells us that "gender theorists ... cleared a space, described a new territory, which radically altered the male-normative terms of discussion about reality and experience; they forced recognition of the difference gender makes" (137). And what a difference. Although gender and sex are often used interchangeably, gender theory is much more about power than genitalia.

Gender theory provides the newest and perhaps most scenic route into the wilderness of unexplored and unrecorded rhetorical theories and performances. Closely allied with feminism, gender theory investigates the politics of power and the relations of domination. And it works to understand the process by which some humans—males and females alike—have more power than others. As Jane Flax tells us, "the single most important advance in feminist theory is that the existence of gender relations has been problematized" (43).

Figuring gender denaturalizes the concept of sexual differences and investigates the cultural construction of men and women, revitalizing our thinking about the appropriate or inappropriate roles and opportunities for sexed bodies. Gender is nothing more or less, according to Joan Wallach Scott, than "a social category imposed on a sexed body" (32). For two thousand years, humans have been conditioned to accept the opinions of "thinkers from Aristotle and Rousseau to Talcott Parsons and Erik Erikson ... [who] have argued that women not only differ from men but are not as equipped mentally and physically to function in the spheres of society in which men *predominate*" (Epstein 2, emphasis added). Each of these men seems to have returned to the beliefs of Aristotle, who wrote that "between the sexes, the male is by nature superior and the female inferior, the male ruler and the female subject" (*Politics* I.ii.12) and "one quality or action is nobler than another if it is that of a naturally finer being: thus a man's will be nobler than a woman's" (*Rhetoric* 1.915). For Aristotle, then, the "natural" deficiencies of women rendered women naturally subordinate to those naturally finer beings, men, who were awarded the right and privilege of a public voice. The universally subordinate evaluation of women in relation to men has provided the tautology that women were closed out of the rhetorical tradition only because they were women. Nevertheless, once feminist historians began looking around, forward and backward, for intellectual and rhetorical sisters, they discovered traces of rhetorical women in the very places they were thought to be forbidden or nonexistent.

Putting gender studies on the rhetorical map problematizes the power politics of rhetoric itself in several provocative and related ways. First of all, gender studies is more about power, performance, and societal expectations than about male and female biology; therefore, gender studies successfully unsettles "the manner in which decidedly male experiences have been made to stand in for the history of Rhetoric" (Biesecker, "Coming" 141). Second, gender studies obstructs the master narrative mapped in the introduction of this essay, that "preservative, continuous history of rhetoric from ancient Greece to contemporary America" (Blair, "Refiguring" 181). Hence, even though the rhetorical power of the oppressed and marginalized (the sophists or Aspasia, for example) have yet to be in the mainstream (or what Mary O'Brien calls the "*male-stream*") of rhetoric, the influence of the oppressed and marginalized is no longer gendered as a space reserved to enhance the center. They are coming into their own rhetorically. Finally, gender studies complicates "the notion of classical rhetoric as a preferred archetype from which all departures are greater or lesser" (Ehninger, "On Systems" 140).

Because the archetypal rhetor of antiquity was a vocal, virile, public, privileged male, gender studies automatically moves us away from the belief in the exclusive validity of classical rhetoric and its male practitioners. Classical technique no longer delimits rhetoric, and masculine performance no longer delimits rhetoric either— particularly now that various rhetorical performances and performers are being considered in their own right. Although "the standards according to which any particular speech is assessed [have traditionally been] constructed on the basis of male attributes, capacities, and modes of activity" (Biesecker, "Towards" 88), we have broadened our conception of rhetorical activity and performance not only to be more inclusive (as Bizzell would have us do) but also to be more accurate.

Clearly, gender studies provides a different lens by which to survey rhetoric. Gone is the dualist lens of male/female biology; instead, we have a lens that regards gender as a social product, an institution of power relations learned through and perpetuated by culture. And even though gender studies is closely allied with feminist research, the two lenses continue to supply different views and different methodologies. Thus, scholars surveying the same rhetorical territory are seeing different shapes and contours and are discovering different absences. In their surveys historiographers, for instance, are locating pockets of uncharted rhetorical activity; feminists have discovered unappreciated female orators; and gender theorists are calibrating the rhetorical activity located along the fault line of gender. Naturally, such conflicting and complementary visions serve to arouse and enrich the various analyses of both marginalized and centralized rhetorics and rhetors.

Gender theory is an exceptionally useful analytical category for writing women into the history of rhetoric. Until I began to view Aspasia's intellectual context through the lens of gender studies, she first appeared in my view as an upper-class courtesan who successfully and perhaps wisely translated her sexual access to Pericles into access to his intellectual and political circle as well. But by contextualizing Aspasia within the gendered limits and expectations of her time, we are now able to explain her political and intellectual influence—and her rhetorical accomplishments—in terms other than erotic.

Aspasia emigrated from Miletus, a cultivated, far-Eastern Greek subject-ally (in what is now Turkey), renowned for its literacy and philosophies of moral thought and nature. And she arrived in Athens educated, fully conscious of civic rights and responsibilities, and linked with the great statesman Pericles (fl. 442 BCE). As a free woman brought up in Asia Minor, Aspasia was subject to Athenian law but without citizen rights. That combination freed her from the rigidity of traditional womanhood, from marriage, and from the gendered identity that arose from those fixed roles: The severe strictures of the aristocratic Athenian woman, whose activity, education, marriage, and rights as citizen and property-holder were circumscribed by male relatives.

When other women were systematically relegated to the domestic sphere, Aspasia seems to have been the only woman in classical Greece to have distinguished herself in the public domain, in the *polis*. Aspasia's intellectual participation in Athenian culture was unprecedented at a time when the construction of gender ensured that women would be praised only for such attributes as their inherent modesty, their inborn reluctance to join males (even kinsmen) for society or dining, and their absolute incapacity to participate as educated beings within the *polis*. A woman's only political contribution was serving as a nameless channel for the transmission of citizenship from her father to her son (Keuls 90). So it is difficult to emphasize how extraordinary the foreign-born Aspasia would have been in fifth-century BCE Athenian society.

But if we think of gender as a cultural role, a social rank, or as "a primary way of signifying relations of power" (Laqueur 12), then we can more easily trace Aspasia's movement across gendered boundaries of appropriate roles for both non-Athenian, citizen-class women and men during her historical moment. The story of Aspasia's gendering is about more than her being sexed-female; it is also about her being a foreigner, being educated, and being unacculturated as an Athenian. Considered as such, Aspasia appears as an intellectually forceful woman—not as a merely successful courtesan. And this learned woman seems to have profited by her excursion into the male domains of politics and intellect, for she left firmly and fully realized contributions to rhetoric. However, for those very same reasons (being female, being a foreigner), her contributions were later directed through a powerful, gendered lens to both refract and reflect Socrates and Pericles.

How could she have been a powerful force in Periclean Athens, an influence on Plato and Socrates? How could she have been a teacher, much less a rhetorician? After all, by the principle of *entelechy* (the vital force urging one toward fulfilling one's actual essence), she would have naturally followed her predetermined life course as a traditional wife and mother, her progress toward fulfillment distinctly marked off and limited to a degree of perfection less than that for a man. The power politics of gender, the social category imposed on each sexed body, establishes the social creation of ideas about appropriate roles for women and men. Denied the *telos* of perfect maleness, Athenian citizen-class women, such as Aspasia, were denied a passport into the male intellectual battlegrounds of politics, philosophy, and rhetoric. But somehow Aspasia had approached the border—and trespassed into the masculine territory of classical rhetoric.

Both historiographic and feminist research pointed me toward using gender studies to explore the societal gendering (power) inherent in the expectations, strictures, and possibilities for humans of different sex as well as the ways in which we think about the social order and hierarchy. And I've profited from what gender studies can reveal about power. But no one analytical category (historiography, feminism, or gender studies, for instance), no single route into rhetorical territory, can address all our divisions or questions as we rewrite rhetorical histories.

Gender studies, in particular, cannot be used alone, for "gender never exhibits itself in pure form but in the context of lives that are shaped by a multiplicity of influences, which cannot be neatly sorted out" (Bordo 147). After all, whatever we think we know about the sexed body is inevitably culturally produced anyway: anatomical sketches and biological explanations of the body throughout the ages have continually reflected and "proved" each society's beliefs about the body. In fact, during the time of Aspasia's excursions into rhetorical territory, her female body would have been considered that of an undeveloped male, for the Athenians believed Aristotle when he said that "the female body was a less hot, less perfect, and hence less potent version of the canonical body" (Laqueur 34–35). And in *Children of Athena,* Nicole Loraux tells us that "there is not, and never has been, a real female Athenian. The political process does not recognize a 'citizeness,' the language has no word for a woman from Athens" (10). Aspasia, then, spent her life with Athenians, and with women, for any person who could not meet the prestigious requirements of Athenian citizenship was automatically feminized, gendered "nonmale."

Whatever the reinterpretations of the body or whatever the model of gender(s), the point is that each model accounts for and prescribes the movement of females and males along and across the range of gendered performances. And if we understand the particular and contextually specific ways gender and society (or culture) interinanimate one another, we can more knowledgeably chart and account for those gendered limits and powers as we take a specific route along the borders of rhetorical history. But we must keep in mind that narratives of gender analysis can harbor the same grandiose and totalizing concepts as rhetoric's now-disputed Paternal Narrative, that grand narrative of masculinist display that many of us want to complicate, disrupt, interrupt— but finally enrich.

New Maps, New Directions

So what? So what if the traditional rhetorical map flattened the truth, leaving scarcely a ridge on the surface that could suggest all the disenfranchised rhetorics just off the main road? After all, Thomas P. Miller tells us that "the rhetorical tradition is a fiction that has just about outlived its usefulness" anyway ("Reinventing" 26). So why revisit the history of rhetoric? why challenge that dominant narrative? why find new points of interest? why bother to remap it? and why encourage any new mappings?

The recent collections of Theresa Enos, Enos and Stuart Brown, Takis Poulakos, and Vitanza demonstrate that now is the time to "take a good look at the wherefrom and whereto of our discipline, reconsider its tradition, and rethink its history" (T. Poulakos, "Introduction" 2–3) as well as "learn from our histories of rhetoric" (T. Enos, "Brand" 11). If historical narratives are primarily motivated actions to *do* something, as Kellner would have us believe, and if that something has to do with power ("Afterword" 242), then perhaps we should find ways to connect our current rhetorical inquiries, histories, and mappings with our contemporary academic and social concerns. After all, the only way we can displace the old map of rhetoric, that monolithic Heritage School[2] map of masculine performance, is to replace it with maps that *do* something else, that are immediately recognized as being better suited to our needs.

The study of rhetoric has taken root in various disciplines: philosophy, classics, history, speech, communication, English, and composition. And each of these disciplines taps rhetoric for maps of theory as well as pedagogy. By inviting our remapping activities into our institutions, we can—regardless of the discipline, regardless of the mapping—introduce new curricula, new syllabi, new research and mentoring projects, new readings, and new writings into our classrooms. For instance, Thomas Miller suggests that we use our courses in classical rhetoric to provide "opportunities for research on the rhetorical practices of more diverse groups [other than the intellectual gatekeepers or owners of intellectual production]" ("Teaching" 72). He goes on to suggest that we use our courses to analyze "the discursive formations that establish positions of authorship, condition how people read, and locate the purposes of writing and reading within the social relations of time" (74). Welch suggests that we foreground the frequently unseen problems of classical rhetoric—history, hierarchy, and gender—in ways that students can recognize and identify as problems, not with themselves as female or minority students, but with "the universalized reader—the white, male, middle class, bookish decoder whose values, ideologies, and desires underlie many of the assumptions of standard readings" ("Plato" 7). And Bizzell, of course, would have us remap by finding ways to resist the Paternal Narrative and reread the Heritage Trail; to search for lost voices, favorably comparing "other" works with "canonized" (i.e., male) works; and to reconceptualize the definition of rhetorical practice to challenge its traditional limitation to the dominant male discourse and include "others." Each time we encourage such remappings and reconceptualize basic assumptions, whether in our theories or our practices, we are redrawing the boundaries of rhetoric to include new practitioners and new practices.

Even if/because we don't "form any one school of historical-rhetorical thought" (Vitanza, "Preface" viii), we need to help one another and the new scholars with their own mappings, for remapping rhetorical territory is an important way we can locate ourselves or our students or our various rhetorical activities in the field we are studying. And we also need to support the classroom activities that result from such remappings. Those of us living in English departments should realize that some 3,500 college writing teachers are professionalizing themselves by learning the history, theory, and praxis—the maps—of rhetoric (T. Enos, "Brand" 7). And just a glance at a CCCC program will reveal the various mappings available to us all: in addition to the great male figures mentioned in my introduction, the CCCC offers analyses of male and female figures; minority groups (ethnic, religious, social); professional, religious, and popular discourse practices (including twelve-step programs); solitary and collaborative activities, all of which are being figured onto rhetorical maps. And intrinsic to each of these remappings is the necessary historical inquiry that empowers political action, whether social, academic, or religious, for historical inquiry helps people to situate problems in a broader context and to discover the available means of persuading their communities to act from their shared historical experiences and needs. Indeed, all of these rhetorics must *do* something new if they are to fulfill our present needs: our needs as citizens, researchers, teachers, students, and colleagues in the diverse and multidisciplinary professions of rhetorics.

Notes

1 I am grateful to Thomas Miller and Kathleen Welch, the two *Rhetoric Review* reviewers, for their careful readings and helpful responses to this essay. I am also thankful to Jon Olson, who read every draft of this essay, sometimes willingly.
2 *Heritage School* is Welch's term.

Works Cited

Aristotle. *Politics.* Trans. H. Rackham. Cambridge: Loeb-Harvard UP, 1977.

———. *The Rhetoric and the Poetics of Aristotle.* Trans. W. Rhys Roberts and Ingram Bywater. New York: Modern Library, 1984.

Atwill, Janet. "Instituting the Art of Rhetoric: Theory, Practice, and Productive Knowledge in Interpretations of Aristotle's *Rhetoric*." T. Poulakos. 91–118.

Ballif, Michelle. "Re/Dressing Histories; or, On Re/Covering Figures Who Have Been Laid by Our Gaze." *Rhetoric Society Quarterly* 22 (1992): 91–97.

Barrett, Harold. *The Sophists.* Novato: Chandler, 1987.

Berlin, James. "Revisionary Histories of Rhetoric: Politics, Power, and Plurality." Vitanza. 112–27.

———. *Rhetoric and Reality: Writing Instruction in American Colleges 1900–1985.* Carbondale: Southern Illinois UP, 1987.

———. *Writing Instruction in Nineteenth-Century American Colleges.* Carbondale: Southern Illinois UP, 1984.

Bizzell, Patricia. "Opportunities for Feminist Research in the History of Rhetoric." *Rhetoric Review* 11 (1992): 50–58.

Bizzell, Patricia, and Bruce Herzberg. *The Rhetorical Tradition: Readings from Classical Times to the Present.* Boston: Bedford-St. Martin's, 1990.

Biesecker, Barbara. "Coming to Terms with Recent Attempts to Write Women into the History of Rhetoric." *Philosophy and Rhetoric* 25 (1992): 140–61.

———. "Towards a Transactional View of Rhetorical and Feminist Theory: Rereading Hélène Cixous's *The Laugh of the Medusa*." *Southern Communication Journal* 57 (1992): 86–96.

Blair, Carole. "Contested Histories of Rhetoric: The Politics of Preservation, Progress, and Change." *Quarterly Journal of Speech* 78 (1992): 403–28.

———. "Refiguring Systems of Rhetoric." *PRE/TEXT* 12 (1991): 179–94.

Blair, Carole, and Mary L. Kahl. "Introduction: Revising the History of Rhetorical Theory." *Western Journal of Speech Communication* 54 (1990): 148–59.

Bordo, Susan. "Feminism, Postmodernism, and Gender-Scepticism." Nicholson. 133–56.

Campbell, Karlyn Kohrs. "Biesecker Cannot Speak for Her Either." *Philosophy and Rhetoric* 26 (1993): 153–59.

———. *Man Cannot Speak for Her: A Critical Study of Early Feminist Rhetoric.* 2 vols. New York: Greenwood, 1989.

Certeau, Michel de. *The Writing of History.* 1975, Trans. Tom Conley. New York: Columbia UP, 1988.

Collins, Vicki Tolar. "Perfecting a Woman's Life: Methodist Rhetoric and Politics in *The Account of Hester Ann Rogers*." Diss. Auburn U, 1993.

Conley, Tom. "Translator's Introduction: *For a Literary Historiography*." Certeau, vii–xxiv.

Corbett, Edward P.J. *Classical Rhetoric for the Modern Student.* 3d. ed. New York: Oxford UP, 1990.

Covino, William. *The Art of Wondering: A Revisionist Return to the History of Rhetoric.* Portsmouth: Boynton/Cook, 1988.

Crowley, Sharon. "A Plea for the Revival of Sophistry." *Rhetoric Review* 7 (1989): 318–34.

———. *The Methodical Memory: Invention in Current-Traditional Rhetoric.* Carbondale: Southern Illinois UP, 1990.

de Laurentis, Teresa, ed. *Feminist Studies/Critical Studies.* Bloomington: Indiana UP, 1986.

Ehninger, Douglas. "On Rhetoric and Rhetorics." *Western Speech* 31 (1967): 242–49.

———. "On Systems of Rhetoric." *Philosophy and Rhetoric* 1 (1968): 131–44.

Enos, Richard Leo. *Greek Rhetoric before Aristotle*. Prospect Heights, IL: Waveland, 1993.

Enos, Theresa. "'A Brand New World': Using Our Professional and Personal Histories of Rhetoric." T. Enos. 3–14.

———, ed. *Learning from the Histories of Rhetoric*. Carbondale: Southern Illinois UP, 1993.

Enos, Theresa, and Stuart Brown, eds. *Defining the New Rhetorics*. Newbury Park: Sage, 1993.

———, eds. *Professing the New Rhetorics*. Englewood Cliffs: Blair-Prentice Hall, 1994.

Epstein, Cynthia Fuchs. *Deceptive Distinctions: Sex, Gender, and the Social Order*. New Haven: Yale UP, 1988.

Flax, Jane, "Postmodernism and Gender Relations." Nicholson, 39–62.

Glenn, Cheryl, "sex, lies, and manuscript: Refiguring Aspasia in the History of Rhetoric." *College Composition and Communication* 45 (1994): 180–99.

Jameson, Fredric. *The Political Unconscious*. Ithaca, NY: Cornell UP, 1981.

Jarratt, Susan, and Rory Ong. "Aspasia: Rhetoric, Gender, and Colonial Ideology." Lunsford, 9–24.

Jarratt, Susan. *Rereading the Sophists*. Carbondale: Southern Illinois UP, 1991.

———. ed. *Rhetoric Society Quarterly* 22 (Winter 1992).

Johnson, Nan. *Nineteenth-Century Rhetoric in North America*. Carbondale: Southern Illinois UP, 1991.

Kellner, Hans. "After the Fall: Reflections on the History of Rhetoric." Vitanza, 20–37.

———. "Afterword: Reading Rhetorical Redescriptions." T. Poulakos, 24–56.

Kennedy, George A. *Classical Rhetoric and Its Christian and Secular Tradition from Ancient to Modern Times*. Chapel Hill: U of North Carolina P. 1980.

Kerferd, G. B. *The Sophistic Movement*. Cambridge: Cambridge UP, 1981.

Keuls, Eva C. *The Reign of the Phallus*. New York: Harper, 1985.

Kinneavy, James L. *Greek Rhetorical Origins of Christian Faith*. New York: Oxford UP, 1987.

Kuhn, Thomas. *The Structure of Scientific Revolutions*. 2nd. ed. Chicago: U of Chicago P. 1970.

Laqueur, Thomas. *Making Sex*. Cambridge, MA: Harvard UP, 1990.

Lipscomb, Drema. "Sojourner Truth: A Practical Public Discourse." Lunsford. 227–46.

Loraux, Nicole. *The Children of Athena*. Trans. Caroline Levine. 1984, Princeton, NJ: Princeton UP, 1993.

Lunsford, Andrea A., ed. *Reclaiming Rhetorica*. Pittsburgh: U of Pittsburgh P, forthcoming 1995.

McComiskey, Bruce. "Disassembling Plato's Critique of Rhetoric in the *Gorgias* (447a–466a)." *Rhetoric Review* 11 (1992); 79–90.

Miller, Susan. *Textual Carnivals: The Politics of Composition*. Carbondale: Southern Illinois UP, 1991.

Miller, Thomas P. "Reinventing Rhetorical Traditions." T. Enos. 26–41.

———. "Teaching the Histories of Rhetoric as a Social Praxis." *Rhetoric Review* 12 (1993): 70–82.

Moss, Roger. "The Case for Sophistry." *Rhetoric Revalued*. Ed. Brian Vickers. Binghamton: Center for Medieval and Early Renaissance Studies, 1982. 207–24.

Mountford, Roxanne. "The Feminization of the *Ars Praedicandi*. Diss. Ohio State U, 1991.

Murphy, James J. *Rhetoric in the Middle Ages*. Berkeley: U of California P, 1974.

Neel, Jasper. *Plato, Derrida, and Writing*. Carbondale: Southern Illinois UP, 1988.

Nicholson, Linda J., ed. *Feminism/Postmodernism*. New York: Routledge, 1990.

O'Brien, Mary. *The Politics of Reproduction*. London: Routledge, 1981.

Partner, Nancy F. "Making Up Lost Time: Writing on the Writing of History." *Speculum* 61 (1986): 90–117.

Peaden, Catherine Hobbs, ed. *Nineteenth-Century Women Learn to Write: Past Cultures and Practices of Literacy.* Charlottesville: U of Virginia P, 1994.

Poulakos, John. "Towards a Sophistic Definition of Rhetoric." *Philosophy and Rhetoric* 16 (1983): 35–48.

Poulakos, Takis. "Introduction: Alternative Approaches to the Rhetorical Tradition." T. Poulakos. 1–10.

———, ed. *Rethinking the History of Rhetoric.* Boulder: Westview, 1983.

Ratcliffe, Krista. *Anglo-American Challenges to the Rhetorical Tradition(s): Virginia Woolf, Mary Daly, and Adrienne Rich.* Carbondale: Southern Illinois UP, 1994.

Rorty, Richard. *Philosophy and the Mirror of Nature.* Princeton, NJ: Princeton UP, 1979.

Rushing, Janice Hocker, ed. *Southern Communication Journal* 57 (Winter 1992).

Royster, Jacqueline Jones. "To Call a Thing by Its True Name: The Rhetoric of Ida B. Wells." Lunsford 167–84.

Schiappa, Edward. "Neo-Sophistic Rhetorical Criticism or the Historical Reconstruction of Sophistic Doctrines?" *Philosophy and Rhetoric* 23 (1990): 192–217.

———. *Protagoras and Logos.* Columbia: U of South Carolina P. 1991.

———. "Sophistic Rhetoric: Oasis or Mirage?" *Rhetoric Review* 10 (1991): 5–18.

Scott, Joan Wallach. *Gender and the Politics of History.* New York: Columbia UP, 1988.

Scott, Robert L. "The Necessary Pluralism of Any Future History of Rhetoric." *PRE/TEXT* 12 (1991): 195–210.

Smith-Rosenberger, Carroll. "Writing History: Language, Class, and Gender." de Laurentis, 31–54.

Swearingen, C. Jan. "A Lover's Discourse: Diotima, [Aspasia,] Logos, and Desire." Lunsford.

———. *Rhetoric and Irony.* New York; Oxford UP, 1991, 25–52.

Vitanza, Victor. "Editor's Preface, Dedication, and Acknowledgments." Vitanza, vii–xii.

———, ed. *Writing Histories of Rhetoric.* Carbondale: Southern Illinois UP, 1994.

Welch, Kathleen. *The Contemporary Reception of Classical Rhetoric.* Hillsdale, NJ: Erlbaum, 1990.

———. "Plato, Diotima, and Teaching Discourse." Young Rhetoricians' Conference. Monterey, California. July 1994.

White, Hayden. *Tropics of Discourse.* Baltimore: Johns Hopkins UP, 1978.

Winterowd, W. Ross. *Rhetoric: A Synthesis.* New York: Holt, 1968.

4.
WHEN THE FIRST VOICE YOU HEAR IS NOT YOUR OWN
Jacqueline Jones Royster

This essay emerged from my desire to examine closely moments of personal challenge that seem to have import for cross-boundary discourse. These types of moments have constituted an ongoing source of curiosity for me in terms of my own need to understand human difference as a complex reality, a reality that I have found most intriguing within the context of the academic world. From a collectivity of such moments over the years, I have concluded that the most salient point to acknowledge is that "subject" position really is everything.

Using subject position as a terministic screen in cross-boundary discourse permits analysis to operate kaleidoscopically, thereby permitting interpretation to be richly informed by the converging of dialectical perspectives. Subjectivity as a defining value pays attention dynamically to context, ways of knowing, language abilities, and experience, and by doing so it has a consequent potential to deepen, broaden, and enrich our interpretive views in dynamic ways as well. Analytical lenses include the process, results, and impact of negotiating identity, establishing authority, developing strategies for action, carrying forth intent with a particular type of agency, and being compelled by external factors and internal sensibilities to adjust belief and action (or not). In a fundamental way, this enterprise supports the sense of rhetoric, composition, and literacy studies as a field of study that embraces the imperative to understand truths and consequences of language use more fully. This enterprise supports also the imperative to reconsider the beliefs and values which inevitably permit our attitudes and actions in discourse communities (including colleges, universities, and classrooms) to be systematic, even systemic.

Adopting subjectivity as a defining value, therefore, is instructive. However, the multidimensionality of the instruction also reveals the need for a shift in paradigms, a need that I find especially evident with regard to the notion of "voice," as a central manifestation of subjectivity. My task in this essay, therefore, is threefold. First, I present three scenes which serve as my personal testimony as "subject." These scenes are singular in terms of their being my own stories, but I believe that they are also plural, constituting experiential data that I share with many. My sense of things is that individual stories placed one against another against another build credibility and offer, as in

---

Royster, Jacqueline Jones. "When the First Voice You Hear is Not Your Own." *CCC* 47.1 (February 1996): 29–40. Print.

this case, a litany of evidence from which a call for transformation in theory and practice might rightfully begin. My intent is to suggest that my stories in the company of others demand thoughtful response.

Second, I draw from these scenes a specific direction for transformation, suggesting dimensions of the nature of voicing that remain problematic. My intent is to demonstrate that our critical approaches to voice, again as a central manifestation of subjectivity, are currently skewed toward voice as a spoken or written phenomenon. This intent merges the second task with the third in that I proceed to suggest that theories and practices should be transformed. The call for action in cross-boundary exchange is to refine theory and practice so that they include voicing as a phenomenon that is constructed and expressed visually and orally, *and* as a phenomenon that has import also in being a *thing* heard, perceived, and reconstructed.

Scene One

I have been compelled on too many occasions to count to sit as a well-mannered Other, silently, in a state of tolerance that requires me to be as expressionless as I can manage, while colleagues who occupy a place of entitlement different from my own talk about the history and achievements of people from my ethnic group, or even about their perceptions of our struggles. I have been compelled to listen as they have comfortably claimed the authority to engage in the construction of knowledge and meaning about me and mine, without paying even a passing nod to the fact that sometimes a substantive version of that knowledge might already exist, or to how it might have already been constructed, or to the meanings that might have already been assigned that might make me quite impatient with gaps in their understanding of my community, or to the fact that I, or somebody within my ethnic group, might have an opinion about what they are doing. I have been compelled to listen to speakers, well-meaning though they may think they are, who signal to me rather clearly that subject position is everything. I have come to recognize, however, that when the subject matter is me and the voice is not mine, my sense of order and rightness is disrupted. In metaphoric fashion, these "authorities" let me know, once again, that Columbus has discovered America and claims it now, claims it still for a European crown.

Such scenes bring me to the very edge of a principle that I value deeply as a teacher and a scholar, the principle of the right to inquiry and discovery. When the discovering hits so close to home, however, my response is visceral, not just intellectual, and I am made to look over a precipice. I have found it extremely difficult to allow the voices and experiences of people that I care about deeply to be taken and handled so carelessly and without accountability by strangers.

At the extreme, the African American community, as my personal example, has seen and continues to see its contributions and achievements called into question in grossly negative ways, as in the case of *The Bell Curve.* Such interpretations of who we are as a people open to general interrogation, once again, the innate capacities of "the race" as a whole. As has been the case throughout our history in this country, we are put in jeopardy and on trial in a way that should not exist but does. We are compelled to respond to a rendering of our potential that demands, not that we account for attitudes, actions, and conditions, but that we defend ourselves as human beings. Such interpretations of human potential create a type of discourse that serves as a distraction, as noise that drains off energy and sabotages the work of identifying substantive problems within and across cultural boundaries and the work also of finding solutions that have import, not simply for "a race," but for human beings whose living conditions, values, and preferences vary.

All such close encounters, the extraordinarily insidious ones and the ordinary ones, are definable through the lens of subjectivity, particularly in terms of the power and authority to speak and to make meaning. An analysis of subject position reveals that these interpretations by those outside of the community are not random acts of unkindness. Instead, they embody ways of seeing, knowing, being, and acting that probably suggest as much about the speaker and the context as they do about the targeted subject matter. The advantage with this type of analysis, of course, is that we see the obvious need to contextualize the stranger's perspective among other interpretations and to recognize that an interpretive view is just that—interpretive. A second advantage is that we also see that in our nation's practices these types of interpretations, regardless of how superficial or libelous they may actually be within the context of a more comprehensive view, tend to have considerable consequence in the lives of the targeted group, people in this case whose own voices and perspectives remain still largely under considered and uncredited.

Essentially, though, having a mechanism to see the under considered helps us see the extent to which we add continually to the pile of evidence in this country of cross-cultural misconduct. These types of close encounters that disregard dialectical views are a type of free touching of the powerless by the power-full. This analytical perspective encourages us to acknowledge that marginalized communities are not in a good position to ward off the intrusion of those authorized in mainstream communities to engage in willful action. Historically, such actions have included everything from the displacement of native people from their homelands, to the use of unknowing human subjects in dangerous experiments, to the appropriation and misappropriation of cultural artifacts—art, literature, music, and so on. An insight using the lens of subjectivity, however, is a recognition of the ways in which these moments are indeed moments of violation, perhaps even ultimate violation.

This record of misconduct means that for people like me, on an instinctive level, all outsiders are rightly perceived as suspect. I suspect the genuineness of their interest, the altruism of their actions, and the probability that whatever is being said or done is not to the ultimate benefit and understanding of the people who are subject matter but not subjects. People in the neighborhood where I grew up would say, "Where is their home training?" Imbedded in the question is the idea that when you visit other people's "home places," especially when you have not been invited, you simply can not go tramping around the house like you own the place, no matter how smart you are, or how much imagination you can muster, or how much authority and entitlement outside that home you may be privileged to hold. And you certainly can not go around name calling, saying things like, "You people are intellectually inferior and have a limited capacity to achieve," without taking into account who the family is, what its living has been like, and what its history and achievement have been about.

The concept of "home training" underscores the reality that point of view matters and that we must be trained to respect points of view other than our own. It acknowledges that when we are away from home, we need to know that what we think we see in places that we do not really know very well may not actually be what is there at all. So often, it really is a matter of time, place, resources, and our ability to perceive. Coming to judgment too quickly, drawing on information too narrowly, and saying hurtful, discrediting, dehumanizing things without undisputed proof are not appropriate. Such behavior is not good manners. What comes to mind for me is another saying that I heard constantly when I was growing up, "Do unto others as you would have them do unto you." In this case, we would be implored to draw conclusions about others with care and, when we do draw conclusions, to use the same type of sense and sensibility that we would ideally like for others to use in drawing conclusions about us.

This scene convinces me that what we need in a pressing way in this country and in our very own field is to articulate codes of behavior that can sustain more concretely notions of honor, respect, and good manners across boundaries, with cultural boundaries embodying the need most vividly. Turning the light back onto myself, though, at the same time that my sense of violation may indeed be real, there is the compelling reality that many communities in our nation need to be taken seriously. We all deserve to be taken seriously, which means that critical inquiry and discovery are absolutely necessary. Those of us who love our own communities, we think, most deeply, most uncompromisingly, without reservation for what they are and also are not, must set aside our misgivings about strangers in the interest of the possibility of deeper understanding (and for the more idealistic among us, the possibility of global peace). Those of us who hold these communities close to our hearts, protect them, and embrace them; those who want to preserve the goodness of the minds and souls in them; those who want to preserve consciously, critically, and also lovingly the record of good work within them must take high risk and give over the exclusivity of our rights to know.

It seems to me that the agreement for inquiry and discovery needs to be deliberately reciprocal. All of us, strangers and community members, need to find ways to sustain productivity in what Pratt calls contact zones (199), areas of engagement that in all likelihood will remain contentious. We need to get over our tendencies to be too possessive and to resist locking ourselves into the tunnels of our own visions and direct experience. As community members, we must learn to have new faith in the advantage of sharing. As strangers, we must learn to treat the loved people and places of Others with care and to understand that, when we do not act respectfully and responsibly, we leave ourselves rightly open to wrath. The challenge is not to work with a fear of abuse or a fear of retaliation, however. The challenge is to teach, to engage in research, to write, and to speak with Others with the determination to operate not only with professional and personal integrity, but also with the specific knowledge that communities and their ancestors are watching. If we can set aside our rights to exclusivity in our own home cultures, if we can set aside the tendencies that we all have to think too narrowly, we actually leave open an important possibility. In our nation, we have little idea of the potential that a variety of subjectivities—operating with honor, respect, and reasonable codes of conduct—can bring to critical inquiry or critical problems. What might happen if we treated differences in subject position as critical pieces of the whole, vital to thorough understanding, and central to both problem-finding and problem-solving? This society has not, as yet, really allowed that privilege in a substantial way.

Scene Two

As indicated in Scene One, I tend to be enraged at what Tillie Olsen has called the "trespass vision," a vision that comes from intellect and imagination (62), but typically not from lived experience, and sometimes not from the serious study of the subject matter. However, like W. E. B. Du Bois, I've chosen not to be distracted or consumed by my rage at voyeurs, tourists, and trespassers, but to look at what I can do. I see the critical importance of the role of negotiator, someone who can cross boundaries and serve as guide and translator for Others.

In 1903, Du Bois demonstrated this role in *The Souls of Black Folk*. In the "Forethought" of that book, he says: "Leaving, then, the world of the white man, I have stepped within the Veil, raising it that you may view faintly its deeper recesses—the meaning of its religion, the passion of its human sorrow, and the struggle of its greater souls" (1). He sets his rhetorical purpose to be to cross, or at least to straddle boundaries with the intent of shedding light, a light that has the potential of being useful to people on both sides of the veil. Like Du Bois, I've accepted the idea that what I call my "home place" is a cultural community that exists still quite significantly beyond the confines of a well-insulated community that we call the "mainstream," and that between this world and the one that I call home, systems of insulation impede the vision and narrow the ability to recognize human potential and to understand human history both microscopically and telescopically.

Like Du Bois, I've dedicated myself to raising this veil, to overriding these systems of insulation by raising another voice, my voice in the interest of clarity and accuracy. What I have found too often, however, is that, unlike those who have been entitled to talk about me and mine, when I talk about my own, I face what I call the power and function of deep disbelief, and what Du Bois described as, "the sense of always looking at one's self through the eyes of others, of measuring one's soul by the tape of a world that looks on in amused contempt and pity" (5).

An example comes to mind. When I talk about African-American women, especially those who were writing non-fiction prose in the nineteenth century, I can expect, even today after so much contemporary scholarship on such writers, to see people who are quite flabbergasted by anything that I share. Reflected on their faces and in their questions and comments, if anyone can manage to speak back to me, is a depth of surprise that is always discomforting. I sense that the surprise, or the silence, if there is little response, does not come from the simple ignorance of unfortunate souls who just happen not to know what I have spent years coming to know. What I suspect is that this type of surprise rather "naturally" emerges in a society that so obviously has the habit of expecting nothing of value, nothing of consequence, nothing of importance, nothing at all positive from its Others, so that anything is a surprise; everything is an exception; and nothing of substance can really be claimed as a result.

In identifying this phenomenon, Chandra Talpade Mohanty speaks powerfully about the ways in which this culture coopts, dissipates, and displaces voices. As demonstrated by my example, one method of absorption that has worked quite well has been essentially rhetorical. In discussing nineteenth century African American women's work, I bring tales of difference and adventure. I bring cultural proofs and instructive examples, all of which invariably must serve as rites of passage to credibility. I also bring the power of storytelling. These tales of adventure in odd places are the transitions by which to historicize and theorize anew with these writers re-inscribed in a rightful place. Such a process respects long-standing practices in African-based cultures of theorizing in narrative form. As Barbara Christian says, we theorize "in the stories we create, in riddles and proverbs, in the play with language, since dynamic rather than fixed ideas seem more to our liking" (336).

The problem is that in order to construct new histories and theories such stories must be perceived not just as "simple stories" to delight and entertain, but as vital layers of a transformative process. A reference point is Langston Hughes and his Simple stories, stories that are a model example of how apparent simplicity has the capacity to unmask truths in ways that are remarkably accessible—through metaphor, analogy, parable, and symbol. However, the problem of articulating new paradigms through stories becomes intractable, if those who are empowered to define impact and consequence decide that the stories are simply stories and that the record of achievement is perceived, as Audre Lorde has said, as "the random droppings of birds" (Foreword xi).

If I take my cue from the life of Ida Wells, and I am bold enough and defiant enough to go beyond the presentation of my stories as juicy tidbits for the delectation of audiences, to actually shift or even subvert a paradigm, I'm much more likely to receive a wide-eyed stare and to have the value and validity of my conceptual position held at a distance, in doubt, and wonderfully absorbed in the silence of appreciation. Through the systems of deep disbelief I become a storyteller, a performer. With such absorptive ability in the systems of interpretation, I have greater difficulty being perceived as a person who theorizes without the mediating voices of those from the inner sanctum, or as a person who might name myself a philosopher, a theorist, a historian who creates paradigms that allow the experiences and the insights of people like me to belong.

What I am compelled to ask when veils seem more like walls is who has the privilege of speaking first? How do we negotiate the privilege of interpretation? When I have tried to fulfill my role as negotiator, I have often walked away knowing that I have spoken, but also knowing, as Anna Julia Cooper knew in 1892, that my voice, like her voice, is still a muted one. I speak, but I can not be heard. Worse, I am heard but I am not believed. Worse yet, I speak but I am not deemed believable. These moments of deep disbelief have helped me to understand much more clearly the wisdom of Audre Lorde when she said: "I have come to believe over and over again that what is most important to me must be spoken, made verbal and shared, even at the risk of having it bruised or misunderstood" (*Sister* 40). Lorde teaches me that, despite whatever frustration and vulnerability I might feel, despite my fear that no one is listening to me or is curious enough to try to understand my voice, it is still better to speak (*Black* 31). I set aside the distractions and permeating noise outside of myself, and I listen, as Howard Thurman recommended, to the sound of the genuine within. I go to a place inside myself and, as Opal Palmer Adisa explains, I listen and learn to "speak without clenching my teeth" (56).

Scene Three

There have been occasions when I have indeed been heard and positively received. Even at these times, however, I sometimes can not escape responses that make me most weary. One case in point occurred after a presentation in which I had glossed a scene in a novel that required cultural understanding. When the characters spoke in the scene, I rendered their voices, speaking and explaining, speaking and explaining, trying to translate the experience, to share the sounds of my historical place and to connect those sounds with systems of belief so that deeper understanding of the scene might emerge, and so that those outside of the immediacy of my home culture, the one represented in the novel, might see and understand more and be able to make more useful connections to their own worlds and experiences.

One, very well-intentioned response to what I did that day was, "How wonderful it was that you were willing to share with us your 'authentic' voice!" I said, "My 'authentic' voice?" She said, "Oh yes! I've never heard you talk like that, you know, so relaxed. I mean, you're usually great, but this was really great! You weren't so formal. You didn't have to speak in an appropriated academic language. You sounded 'natural.' It was nice to hear you be yourself." I said, "Oh, I see. Yes, I do have a range of voices, and I take quite a bit of pleasure actually in being able to use any of them at will." Not understanding the point that I was trying to make gently, she said, "But this time, it was really you. Thank you."

The conversation continued, but I stopped paying attention. What I didn't feel like saying in a more direct way, a response that my friend surely would have perceived as angry, was that all my voices are authentic, and like bell hooks, I find it "a necessary aspect of self-affirmation not to feel compelled to choose one voice over another, not to claim one as more authentic, but rather to construct social realities that celebrate, acknowledge, and affirm differences, variety" (12). Like hooks, I claim all my voices as my own very much authentic voices, even when it's difficult for others to imagine a person like me having the capacity to do that.

From moments of challenge like this one, I realize that we do not have a paradigm that really allows for what scholars in cultural and postcolonial studies (Anzaldúa, Spivak, Mohanty, Bhaba) have called hybrid people—people who either have the capacity by right of history and development, or who might have created the capacity by right of history and development, to move with dexterity across cultural boundaries, to make themselves comfortable, and to make sense amid the chaos of difference.

As Cornel West points out, most African Americans, for example, dream in English, not in Yoruba, or Hausa, or Wolof. Hybrid people, as demonstrated by the history of Africans in the Western hemisphere, manage a fusion process that allows for survival, certainly. However, it also allows for the development of a peculiar expertise that extends one's range of abilities well beyond ordinary limits, and it supports the opportunity for the development of new and remarkable creative expression, like spirituals, jazz, blues, and what I suspect is happening also with the essay as genre in the hands of African American women. West notes that somebody gave Charlie Parker a saxophone, Miles Davis a trumpet, Hubert Laws a flute, and Les McCann a piano. I suggest that somebody also gave Maria Stewart, Gertrude Mossell, Frances Harper, Alice Walker, Audre Lorde, Toni Morrison, Patricia Williams, June Jordan, bell hooks, Angela Davis and a cadre of other African American women a pencil, a pen, a computer keyboard. In both instances, genius emerges from hybridity, from Africans who, over the course of time and circumstance, have come to dream in English, and I venture to say that all of their voices are authentic.

In sharing these three scenes, I emphasize that there is a pressing need to construct paradigms that permit us to engage in better practices in cross-boundary discourse, whether we are teaching, researching, writing, or talking with Others, whoever those Others happen to be. I would like to emphasize, again, that we look again at "voice" and situate it within a world of symbols, sound, and sense, recognizing that this world operates symphonically. Although the systems of voice production are indeed highly integrated and appear to have singularity in the ways that we come to sound, voicing actually sets in motion multiple systems, prominent among them are systems for speaking but present also are the systems for hearing. We speak within systems that we know significantly through our abilities to negotiate noise and to construct within that noise sense and sensibility.

Several questions come to mind. How can we teach, engage in research, write about, and talk across boundaries *with* others, instead of for, about, and around them? My experiences tell me that we need to do more than just talk and talk back. I believe that in this model we miss a critical moment. We need to talk, yes, and to talk back, yes, but when do we listen? How do we listen? How do we demonstrate that we honor and respect the person talking and what that person is saying, or what the person might say if we valued someone other than ourselves having a turn to speak? How do we translate listening into language and action, into the creation of an appropriate response? How do we really "talk back" rather than talk also? The goal is not, "You talk, I talk." The goal is better practices so that we can exchange perspectives, negotiate meaning, and create understanding with the intent of being in a good position to cooperate, when, like now, cooperation is absolutely necessary.

When I think about this goal, what stands out most is that these questions apply in so much of academic life right now. They certainly apply as we go into classrooms and insist that our students trust us and what we contend is in their best interest. In light of a record in classrooms that seriously questions the range of our abilities to recognize potential, or to appreciate students as non-generic human beings, or to appreciate that they bring with them, always, knowledge, we ask a lot when we ask them to trust. Too often, still, institutionalized equations for placement, positive matriculation, progress, and achievement name, categorize, rank, and file, while our true-to-life students fall between the cracks. I look again to Opal Palmer Adisa for an instructive example. She says:

> Presently, many academics advocate theories which, rather than illuminating the works under scrutiny, obfuscate and problematize these works so that students are rendered speechless. Consequently, the students constantly question what they know, and often, unfortunately, they conclude that they know nothing.
>
> (54)

Students may find what we do to be alienating and disheartening. Even when our intentions are quite honorable, silence can descend. Their experiences are not seen, and their voices are not heard. We can find ourselves participating, sometimes consciously, sometimes not, in what Patricia Williams calls "spirit murder" (55). I am reminded in a disconcerting way of a troubling scene from Alex Haley's *Roots*. We engage in practices that say quite insistently to a variety of students in a variety of ways, "Your name is Toby." Why wouldn't students wonder: Who can I trust here? Under what kinds of conditions? When? Why?

In addition to better practices in our classrooms, however, we can also question our ability to talk convincingly with deans, presidents, legislators, and the general public about what we do, how we do it, and why. We have not been conscientious about keeping lines of communication open, and we are now experiencing the consequences of talking primarily to ourselves as we watch funds being cut, programs being eliminated, and national agencies that are vital to our interests being bandied about as if they are post-it notes, randomly stuck on by some ill-informed spendthrift. We must learn to raise a politically active voice with a socially responsible mandate to make a rightful place for education in a country that seems always ready to place the needs of quality education on a sideboard instead of on the table. Seemingly, we have been forever content to let voices other than our own speak authoritatively about our areas of expertise and about us. It is time to speak for ourselves, in our own interests, in the interest of our work, and in the interest of our students.

Better practices are not limited, though, even to these concerns. Of more immediate concern to me this year, given my role as Chair of CCCC, is how to talk across boundaries within our own organization as teachers of English among other teachers of English and Language Arts from kindergarten through university with interests as varied as those implied by the sections, conferences, and committees of our parent organization, the National Council of Teachers of English (NCTE). Each of the groups within NCTE has its own set of needs, expectations, and concerns, multiplied across the amazing variety of institutional sites across which we work. In times of limited resources and a full slate of critical problems, we must find reasonable ways to negotiate so that we can all thrive reasonably well in the same place.

In our own case, for years now, CCCC has recognized changes in our relationships with NCTE. Since the mid-1980s we have grown exponentially. The field of rhetoric and composition has blossomed and diversified. The climate for higher education has increasingly degenerated, and we have struggled in the midst of change to forge a more satisfying identity and a more positive and productive working relationship with others in NCTE who are facing crises of their own. After 50 years in NCTE, we have grown up, and we have to figure out a new way of being and doing in making sure that we can face our challenges well. We are now in the second year of a concerted effort to engage in a multi-leveled conversation that we hope will leave CCCC well-positioned to face a new century and ongoing challenges. Much, however, depends on the ways in which we talk and listen and talk again in crossing boundaries and creating, or not, the common ground of engagement.

As I look at the lay of this land, I endorse Henry David Thoreau's statement when he said, "Only that day dawns to which we are awake" (267). So my appeal is to urge us all to be awake, awake and listening, awake and operating deliberately on codes of better conduct in the interest of keeping our boundaries fluid, our discourse invigorated with multiple perspectives, and our policies and practices well-tuned toward a clearer respect for human potential and achievement from whatever their source and a clearer understanding that voicing at its best is not just well-spoken but also well-heard.

Works Cited

Adisa, Opal Palmer. "I Must Write What I Know So I'll Know That I've Known It All Along." *Sage: A Scholarly Journal on Black Women* 9.2 (1995): 54–57.

Anzaldúa, Gloria. *Borderlands/La Frontera*. San Francisco: Aunt Lute, 1987.

Bhabha, Homi K. *The Location of Culture*. London: Routledge, 1994.

Christian, Barbara. "The Race for Theory." *Cultural Critique* 6 (1987): 335–45.

Cooper, Anna Julia. *A Voice from the South*. New York: Oxford UP, 1988.

Du Bois, W. E. B. *The Souls of Black Folk*. New York: Grammercy, 1994.

Haley, Alex. *Roots*. Garden City: Doubleday, 1976.

Hernstein, Richard J., and Charles Murray. *The Bell Curve: Intelligence and Class Structure in American Life*. New York: Free, 1994.

hooks, bell. *Talking Back: Thinking Feminist, Thinking Black*. Boston: South End, 1989.

Lorde, Audre. *The Black Unicorn*. New York: Norton, 1978.

———. Foreword. *Wild Women in the Whirlwind*. Ed. Joanne M. Braxton and Andree Nicola McLaughlin. New Brunswick: Rutgers UP, 1990. xi–xiii.

———. *Sister Outsider*. Freedom: The Crossing Press, 1984.

Mohanty, Chandra Talpade. "On Race and Voice: Challenges for Liberal Education in the 1990s." *Cultural Critique* 14 (Winter 1989–90): 179–208.

———. "Decolonizing Education: Feminisms and the Politics of Multiculturalism in the 'New' World Order." Ohio State University. Columbus, April 1994.

Olsen, Tillie. *Silences*. New York: Delta, 1978.

Pratt, Mary Louise. "Arts of the Contract Zone." *Profession 91* (1991): 33–40.

Spivak, Gayatri Chakravorty. *In Other Worlds: Essays in Cultural Politics*. New York: Routledge, 1988.

Thoreau, Henry David. *Walden*. New York: Vintage, 1991.

Thurman, Howard. "The Sound of the Genuine." Spelman College, Atlanta. April 1981.

West, Cornel. "Race Matters." Ohio State U, Columbus, OH, February 1995.

Williams, Patricia. *The Alchemy of Race and Rights*. Cambridge: Harvard UP, 1991.

SECTION 2

ACCESSING THE ARCHIVES

5.
OCTALOG II: THE (CONTINUING) POLITICS OF HISTORIOGRAPHY
(Dedicated to the Memory of James A. Berlin)
Panel Organized by Richard Leo Enos

Foreword

At the start of the fall 1995 term, I asked incoming graduate students in our English Department at Texas Christian University to read and comment on "Octalog: The Politics of Historiography" (*Rhetoric Review,* Fall 1988, 5–49). Many will recall that these published proceedings were first presented as a panel at the March 1988 CCCC in St. Louis. That panel was coordinated by Theresa Enos, chaired by James J. Murphy, and included the active and engaged participation of eight historians of rhetoric who each held positions on the nature, aims, and methods of doing research in the history of rhetoric, the nature of interpretation, and issues concerning the belief in objectivity. As I reread the Octalog, I not only recalled that wonderful experience but saw what an important historical event it was in its own right. I was not surprised to learn that permission to reproduce that piece has been one of the most requested of all contributions from *Rhetoric Review*.

Two items struck me as I reread the essay. First, we are fast approaching the tenth anniversary of that CCCC Octalog in St. Louis. Second, a great deal has happened to the study of rhetoric since then. In fact, I felt that so much had happened that I asked the class what they thought about my proposing another such Octalog. The class overwhelmingly agreed, and Theresa Enos was (again) supportive enough to agree that the statements would be published in *Rhetoric Review*. Armed with these two votes of confidence, we set about requesting panel members. Our effort was to attract a new set of voices, historians who hold strong, current, and sometimes rival views. The following members agreed to participate:

Janet Atwill, University of Tennessee
Linda Ferreira-Buckley, University of Texas
Cheryl Glenn, Pennsylvania State University
Janice Lauer, Purdue University
Roxanne Mountford, University of Arizona

Enos, Richard Leo. "Octalog II: The (Continuing) Politics of Historiography." *Rhetoric Review* 16.1 (Fall 1997): 22–44. Print.

Jasper Neel, Vanderbilt University
Edward Schiappa, University of Minnesota
Kathleen Welch, University of Oklahoma

In order to provide continuity, we asked three scholars to facilitate the interaction in various ways. Theresa Enos (University of Arizona) agreed to introduce the panel and to mention that it is dedicated to James Berlin. Edward P. J. Corbett (Ohio State University), whose work in the history of rhetoric provided much of the motivation for our present study, agreed to serve as chair. Thomas Miller (University of Arizona) agreed to serve as the respondent; his role was to provide the response printed here and to coordinate subsequent discussion between panel members and the audience.

Included in this collection are the statements of participants and the response by Thomas Miller. Lois Agnew, Mark James, and I edited this material with the intent of providing a coherent packet that could be used by readers for continued discussion and interaction. In this same spirit, Theresa Enos has encouraged Kevin Brooks (Iowa State University) to provide a "review" of the first Octalog, "Reviewing and Redescribing 'The Politics of Historiography': Octalog I, 1988." Brooks' essay, which appears in this issue, serves as a bridge for the two Octalog panels by reflecting on the assumptions of historiography made by the 1988 panelists and the perspectives that he argues ought to be addressed by our discipline.

Richard Leo Enos
Texas Christian University

CHANGING THE PUZZLE

Janet M. Atwill

University of Tennessee

Thomas Kuhn in his 1969 Postscript to *The Structure of Scientific Revolutions* describes disciplinary exemplars as "concrete puzzle solutions." According to Kuhn, professional communities solve these problems with methodologies—and their attendant values and assumptions—that are inculcated in the culture of these communities. Barbara Herrnstein Smith similarly describes a disciplinary community as a network of exemplars, methodologies, conditions, and subjects.

I begin with Kuhn's notion of the "puzzle solution" because that is how I view my work in rhetoric. I do not see myself writing history per se. I have made a book-length argument about classical rhetoric by sometimes challenging and other times submitting to the conventions of a number of disciplines: classics, history, anthropology, literary theory, and rhetoric. That book will function for a time as a contribution to the exemplars of our field to the extent it provides a temporary solution to the problems we presently confront.

Thus, in contrast to several members of the last Octalog, what has been at issue for me in this work is not the objective or subjective character of my "history." Instead, I have struggled with the demanding methodologies and unfriendly gatekeepers of the disciplines whose boundaries I have crossed. I have also tried not to leave my own shifting identities at home. I have tried to read texts, once safely protected by classics and history, as a woman, a mother, a writing teacher, and a citizen. I believe that difference "happens" in the university when new constituencies take hold of the exemplars of the humanist tradition.

I wrote these paragraphs close to a year ago, and though I still "believe" in the terms I used to describe my practice of history writing, those terms for me now raise as many questions as they solve. I will share, more than I will answer, two of these questions here. First, how does submitting to the conventions of other disciplines affect exemplar status of a text (in this case a "history") in one's "home" field? Second, does that submission obviate the critique that I have believed is embodied, literally, in reading canonical texts as a woman/mother/teacher/citizen?

My project of reexamining rhetoric and Aristotle's concept of productive knowledge in light of the tradition of *têchnê*, or art, was motivated by my interest in critical theory and classical rhetoric, but it was also guided by my desire to "reclaim" Greek rhetorical treatises for our field—to break or at least threaten the death grip classicists seemed to hold on these texts. I knew I was making some progress in this effort when several years ago, in response to a paper I had delivered, a scholar in a related field made the following comment to a mutual friend, "I disagree with everything she says; but she's done her homework, so you have to listen to her." I relay this comment because the idea of homework is so important to the question I explore here. What is at issue is who assigned the homework. I did not receive those assignments from people in my field, so whether or not that homework is meaningful in my own discipline is an open question. Moreover, I did not receive those assignments in polite classroom settings; they were issued in the form of criticism—indeed ridicule would not be too strong a word—by colleagues in classics. I came to approach these challenges in interdisciplinary research by remembering Protagoras's description of the political art of rhetoric as consisting of respect and justice. Lest I sound too pietistic, my paraphrase of this definition has been "I will show respect for the conventions of your discipline. In return, I expect a just reading." And the fact is that I have received just readings from outside the discipline. But two questions remain, one for myself and one for the field of rhetoric and composition. How does doing my homework for those outside my field affect the ability of my work to be an exemplar in my home territory? In terms of the field at large, how are we going to define our conventions of history-writing in relation to other disciplines in the humanities?

My second area of concern is closely related to the first and reducible to a relatively simple question: Does accepting the conventions of a traditional discipline mitigate meaningful critique? A year ago I maintained that I had tried to read canonical texts as a member of an alternative, if not new, constituency in the university. Herrnstein Smith (as well as Pierre Bourdieu) suggests that shifting constituencies have as much shaping force on a discipline as its exemplars—indeed, alternative constituencies will eventually create alternative exemplars. I don't see my own work as an alternative exemplar;

however, I think that it makes some difference that in my text a quotation from Deleuze and Guattari's *Thousand Plateaus* can be found on the same page as a quotation from Hesiod—that Tacitus is forced to share the first page with Laclau and Mouffe. Still, I could be accused of submitting to a patriarchal tradition by being willing to respect some of its conventions. In the end, readers of my book will make their own judgments on this point. What Herrnstein Smith and Bourdieu imply, however, is that different constituencies cannot do otherwise than value a discipline's conventions "differently." I read some of the same texts as Milton; clearly, they do not hold for me the same significance. This is not radical change, but small differences, I believe, can "matter." It is probably not by chance that my book is an argument for reclaiming rhetoric as an art of intervention in the world outside the classroom and the university. And now, having been fully persuaded by my own argument, I find myself far more interested in listening to those outside the university than repeating my own position inside it. I have submitted to the conventions of a patriarchal discipline, but I have tried to use those conventions to raise as much hell as possible. I like to imagine that I have been "willing" to be the stubborn product of my own circumstances; but, in the end, that is all that we can ever be.

SERVING TIME IN THE ARCHIVES

Linda Ferreira-Buckley

University of Texas at Austin

Decades ago, when scholars were composing histories of rhetoric and composition, their accounts seemed unproblematic, at least to professionals proud to discover that their discipline had a long history, a history predating that of a literature faculty contemptuous of oratorical and writing instruction. But the limitations of those early histories soon became visible. Where were the women? The people of color? We owe much to the panelists of Octalog I, who voiced concern about the apparent lack of self-critique of early historians and who presented theoretical perspectives too long ignored. So carefully was their counsel heeded that the place of theory in historical circles now seems secure, even as we disagree about which theories obtain. But in our enthusiasm for theorizing the writing of history, have we come to undervalue primary sources—the very stuff of history?

Primary materials should ground our projects, however slow and painstaking the work, however incomplete the records. My own research in the rhetoric of Victorian England led me to dozens of boxes of letters, notes, examinations stored in college archives. I endeavored to examine all extant materials from the period, not only those from "English" classes. Some proved relevant, a few central, but most irrelevant and even dull. In my account I offer lengthy excerpts from course materials to convey the nature of Victorian educational practices. No doubt some readers will find the details of my account tedious, for I have sacrificed the pleasures of style for historical depth.

I made the conscious choice to convey the texture of the times and allow readers to study the evidence. I do not intend nor will I pretend to offer a comprehensive defense of my claim that the rhetorical tradition was important in Victorian language studies. Instead, I focus on six "sites," which I argue are representative. These chapters will not form a narrative, much less a seamless one. My sense is that very often we impose narrative structures where they ought not be by smoothing over missing links. It may well be that we need to start not only with local histories *but with fragments of local histories.* Thus my questions: How ready are we as a field to accept such disconnected accounts? Will such accounts get published? Should they?

These details are not insignificant. I can argue with some confidence and a lot of "evidence" that rhetoric was formative not only in the creation of university-level English studies but also across the university curriculum. My claims challenge those literary historians such as Franklin Court who diminish the significance of rhetoric's contributions. You may well be thinking that my work would not have been undertaken without the trailblazing work of theorists. I agree. (How well I remember when as a graduate student at Penn State, I heard Jim Berlin announce—to the horror and disbelief of the department head at the time—that rhetorical studies far predated literary studies, itself a relative newcomer to the American college scene. When, during the question-and-answer period, the head, a literature scholar, quizzed Jim on his sources, Jim sent him to early issues *of PMLA*. The department head never again raised the issue.) And so, however "old-fashioned" my methodologies, my research leaves me more aware than ever of the inescapability of power, perspective, and exclusion.

Never before were such wide-ranging materials available to scholars, as the bibliographic quests of John Gage and Win Horner document. So too in *Nineteenth-Century Rhetoric: An Enumerative Bibliography,* Forrest Houlette lists 3,929 items written in English that directly address rhetoric, composition, and grammar published between 1800 and 1920; he predicts the next edition will list between 6,000 and 7,000 items.

What's more, technology offers tools for increasingly sophisticated analyses. In July 1992 I attended a meeting at Cambridge University that brought together scholars working on the History of the Book in Nineteenth-Century Britain project. Research librarians, university faculty, and independent scholars—representing a dozen fields and as many perspectives—shared information and argued about the scope of their common project. The weekend was *exhilarating* and frightening, exhilarating because new research tools (such as databases from publishing records) allow for historical recovery of a kind never before possible, frightening, *humbling* because no one researcher can process all that is relevant to her project. How many print runs were there of each edition of a text? To whom were these books sold and for how much? Were they available in school libraries? Working in the large and in many cases scattered records of publishing houses, booksellers, and school libraries—to name just three possibilities—is time-consuming work that may not yield results (little wonder that we prefer to rely on the more general conclusions of such works as Richard D. Altick's *Common Reader*).

With all these new resources, why has there been so little of the "thick description" that Thomas Miller, following Geertz, has called for? A few possible explanations:

(1) While many graduate programs in rhetoric insist that students immerse themselves in theory, few provide rigorous training in traditional research methods (itself the means by which to recover materials essential to the revisionist histories we take as our mission). Instead, we make do with the training offered by colleagues in literature or simply proceed by "the seat of our pants."

(2) Because of the rush to publish, scholars dare not engage in such painstakingly slow work.

(3) Seduced by narrative structures (even as we proclaim them false), we perhaps are less than patient with detailed records.

(4) Relatively few of us have serviceable educations in Latin, Greek, and Hebrew. (I don't.)

(5) Not all institutions fund extensive research travel and graduate assistants.

Even so, we must make archives our starting point, for failing to do so weakens both our historical accounts and our theorizing. Ten years ago our histories were undertheorized; today I fear they are underresearched. Despite the serious obstacles brought to our attention in the first Octalog, I believe in the possibility of writing accurate histories—histories in the plural, histories that are revised and updated through rhetorical negotiation and renegotiation.

REGENDERING THE RHETORICAL TRADITION

Cheryl Glenn

Pennsylvania State University

At Octalog I Jerry Murphy reminded us that an "historian's reason for writing his or her account of things will shape the way in which the task is undertaken" (5). An historian's perceptions of what "ought to be discovered for the good of the community ... lead inevitably to variations in focus, in choice of data, in mode of presentation." Rhetorical history has never been neutral territory; it has always done exactly what we wanted it to do—for the good of our community. Until recently, rhetorical history has embodied and reflected our institutional focus on powerful public men whose texts, lives, and actions surely transcended (or so we told ourselves) the particularities of history and circumstance. Our focus on masculine and rhetorical performance replicated the power politics of gender, with men in the highest cultural role and social rank. After all, rhetoric itself has always inscribed the relation of language and power at a particular moment, indicating who may speak, who may listen, and what may be said—and historical records indicate that males have participated in and controlled most public discourse.

Given the gendered power differentials implicit in traditional historical accounts, I have chosen to regender the rhetorical tradition—for the good of our ever-expanding intellectual community. Gender theory has proved to be an exceptionally useful analytical category for writing women into the history of rhetoric, for (to paraphrase Susan Bordo) it clears a space and describes a new territory, which radically alters the male-normative terms of discussion about reality and experience; it also forces recognition of the difference gender makes (137). And what a difference. Even though the term *gender* itself is merely a concept borrowed from grammar, it, nonetheless, connotes a "socially agreed upon system of distinction," a "primary way of signifying relations of power" (Scott 29; Laqueur 12).

To *re*gender rhetorical history, then, is to imagine gender as an inclusive and nonhierarchical category of analysis for: (1) examining a wide range of rhetorical performances by sexed bodies; (2) denaturalizing the concept of sexual differences; (3) investigating the sociocultural construction of male and female, of masculine and feminine; (4) revitalizing our thinking about the (in)appropriate roles and opportunities for sexed bodies, particularly in terms of rhetorical performance; and, finally, (5) writing both women's and men's contributions and participation into an expanded, inclusive rhetorical tradition. It is no coincidence that feminist scholarship has pressed us toward examining the social construction of gender and gendered power, a move that is the "single most important advance in feminist theory" (Flax 43).

Regendering rhetorical history is a feminist performative act, a commitment to the future of women, a promise that rhetorical histories and theories will eventually and naturally include women. Gender as a category of analysis contributes to this feminist project because it successfully unsettles the "manner in which decidedly male experiences have been made to stand in for the history of Rhetoric" (Biesecker 141). But gender theory also obstructs the master narrative, the "preservative, continuous history of rhetoric from ancient Greece to contemporary America" that Kathleen Welch refers to as the Heritage School of rhetoric (Blair 181; Welch 9). Finally, gender theory complicates the "notion of classical rhetoric as a preferred archetype from which all departures are greater or lesser" (Ehninger 140).

Gender studies is vital to our work, but it is the regendering that unsettles stable gender categories and enacts a promise that rhetorical history will be a continuous process of investigating the works of women and men rather than a final product that can be finally or universally represented. As soon as it is written, any historical interpretation—including my own—becomes an anachronism, for it immediately encodes its own investigative site as needing and deserving more attention: the past is, after all, "*necessarily* larger than the sum of even its entire output of documentation" (Belsey 2). Even though a regendered rhetorical history can never be completed or concluded, if we are to cultivate and invigorate rhetorical theory and practice, we scholars, male and female alike, still have much work to do.

Works Cited

Belsey, Catherine. *The Subject of Tragedy: Identity and Difference in Renaissance Drama*. New York: Methuen, 1985.
Biesecker, Barbara. "Coming to Terms with Recent Attempts to Write Women into the History of Rhetoric." *Philosophy and Rhetoric* 25 (1992): 140–61.

Blair, Carole. "Contested Histories of Rhetoric: The Politics of Preservation, Progress, and Change." *Quarterly Journal of Speech* 78 (Nov. 1992): 403–28.
Bordo, Susan. "Feminism, Postmodernism, and Gender-Scepticism." Nicholson 133–56.
Ehninger, Douglas. "On Systems of Rhetoric." *Philosophy and Rhetoric* 1 (1968): 131–44.
Flax, Jane. "Postmodernism and Gender Relations." Nicholson 39–62.
Laqueur, Thomas. *Making Sex.* Cambridge: Harvard UP, 1990.
Murphy, James J. "Prologue." "The Politics of Historiography." *Rhetoric Review* 7 (1988): 5–49.
Nicholson, Linda J., ed. *Feminism/Postmodernism.* New York: Routledge, 1990.
Scott, Joan Wallach. *Gender and the Politics of History.* New York: Columbia UP, 1988.
Welch, Kathleen. *The Contemporary Reception of Classical Rhetoric.* Hillsdale, NJ: Erlbaum, 1990.

STORIOGRAPHY AND RHETORIC AND COMPOSITION

Janice Lauer

Purdue University

In my seminar in rhetorical history, we talk about foregrounding ideology, confounding categories, using language as a source of power, recovering the marginalized, and paying attention to social differences of race, gender, and class. We speak of making a difference in society and pedagogy and of connecting history to social, economic, and political contexts. We mention intertextuality and different kinds of evidence and arguments. Yet there is an irony in all of these discussions because when we write the history of our own field, our storiography often runs counter to some of the above features. I will therefore couch my remarks about the politics of historiography in a discussion about histories of our field. As I read stories about the development of rhetoric and composition, I encounter those that try to stuff dynamic developments into static categories; that claim definitive status; that distort to promote a thesis, that puff hot air instead of arguing using evidence; and that ignore many voices as they whisper to a few within a limited strand of scholarship. Below are some examples of the result of such discrepancies between theory and practice.

Every year as new doctoral students enter our graduate program, they bring along a collection of names of composition theorists, positioned often as heroes or villains, collected from "histories" of the field they have read in previous courses. These names are pinned to categories, particular ideas or theories, seldom viewed as dynamic scholars, whose ideas change and develop. Their static map of the field positions all theorists' work, no matter the decade, as ahistorical, contemporaneous and open to the same evaluation. In addition, many students have read only secondary historical accounts or a few primary texts, but in any incoming group of students, there is little overlap in the texts they have read at previous levels. Missing from their maps are many voices whose ideas have enriched our field over the years.

A few histories of our field have also woven master narratives. One type of epic argues that the initiating forces in rhetoric and composition were major eastern universities in the 1950s and 1960s. Even though these accounts have been challenged by several people that helped develop the field in the sixties, the narrative continues to be told. Another type of narrative "definitively" confines formative factors in the field to major texts and their citation histories, overlooking factors like journal founding and editing, graduate program development, bibliographic efforts, conference and seminar construction, and informal networking and mentoring. Other stories narrow their version of the "true beginning" to cognitive or social-construction theory, relegating other work to "pre-disciplinary" tales. To what extent, we might ask, is our effort to foreground our own ideology complicitous with writing a "definitive" story imbued with this ideology?

A last example of a disjunctive between our theory and practice of storiography lurks in its intertextuality. Although our theory privileges multiple voices and heteroglossia, some stories of our field merely name drop and critique, setting up straw persons against which to authorize their own accounts instead of representing another's work in its own time and exigencies and acknowledging its contribution. But elaborating the ideas of another in an historical account entails taking this work seriously and articulating reasons for building on it or countering it. Too often, however, ideas are only labeled *postmodern, positivist, vitalist,* or *social-constructionist,* as if these terms were self-explanatory or self-warranting.

Stories about our field that better connect their practice with their historiographic principles round out other stories, let us in on the writer's interpretive practices, offer arguments and evidence, and draw on many sources: academic texts (students and professionals), and artifacts, interviews, journals, and logs from diverse (in many senses) individuals, textbooks, professional texts (public, workplace, disciplinary), oral genres, and so forth. These stories don't subjugate events, individuals and their contributions, and whole groups to a grand narrative. Their authors share their purposes for writing and situate their discussions of the field in economic, social, political, and social arrangements. Finally, such stories make connections between theory and pedagogy. As I struggle to write my own stories, however, I realize how challenging it is to emulate these kinds of histories and how admirable are those narrators that manage to do so.

LOOKING FOR RHETORIC WHERE IT HAS NOT BEEN FOUND: DEFINITIONS, BORDER DISPUTES, FUTURE DIRECTIONS

Roxanne Mountford

University of Arizona

I want to take up an issue posed by Richard Enos in the original Octalog on the politics of historiography, but in my view not fully engaged by that panel. Enos said:

> Heinrich Schliemann, the father of modem archaeology, was vilified because others believed that dirtying one's hands through actually going to see what was at Troy was something that scholars shouldn't do, but rather make armchair explanations based solely upon the *Iliad* and the *Odyssey.* But his innovation established new methods and new insights to the Homeric world. Unfortunately, many researchers in the history of rhetoric have taken

the prevailing disposition of the polis, our scholarly community, with tacit acceptance and have not learned from Schliemann and have been reluctant to "dirty their hands" in such a manner of research, but rather perpetuate and even glorify the armchair, venerable methods of analysis in the history of rhetoric.

(15)

Enos then called for the development of "new methods and new theories" beyond the textual to study problems in rhetoric (15).

A decade later, we have not gone very far in our search for new methods. Enos's call is being answered by a few young scholars, but they are looking outside the field of rhetoric and composition for examples. As well they should: Beyond our borders the study of rhetoric is robust. Rhetorical analysis is the basis for many cultural-studies projects. It is becoming the basis for the work of many anthropologists. For instance, medical anthropologist Emily Martin studies the rhetoric of obstetrics and gynecology through a textual- and ethnographic-based approach she calls "cultural analysis." Scholars such as Martin point to other ways to study rhetoric: through fieldwork *as well as* textual analysis; through interviews of informants *as well as* archival research. In a recent article, Nedra Reynolds and I point to this burgeoning scholarly work outside of rhetoric and composition and suggest that graduate courses should be changed to reflect the transdisciplinary nature of rhetoric studies.

I am watching and learning from the young scholars in the field who are ready to engage in boundary-crossing and in the development of new ways to study rhetoric. For instance, in a dissertation on law, rhetoric, and infertility titled, "Conceiving the American Dream: Ethnographic Interpretations of Law, Rhetoric, and Infertility," Beth Britt, a PhD candidate at Rensselaer Polytechnic Institute, has been exploring the cultural impact of a 1987 Massachusetts law requiring insurance policies that cover pregnancy to also cover infertility treatments. Located at multiple sites in the greater Boston area, including the legislature, law firms, clinics, and support groups, her fieldwork reveals assumptions about gender, race, class, and sexual orientation underlying the legislation; the rhetorical strategies used by insurance companies to minimize the impact of the legislation; and the discursive responses by individuals, clinics, and attorneys attempting to negotiate the changing legal terrain. In this project the object of historical work is the genealogy of a law; the research involves both ethnographic and archival methods. I am also inspired by the work of Scott Lyons and Malea Powell, whose fieldwork focuses on Native American rhetorics, and Ellen Cushman, whose fieldwork focused on African American women's attempts to overcome federal bureaucracies.

Despite the new methods and new opportunities for research these studies bring to the field, a familiar refrain in English department-based rhetoric and composition programs makes such work suspect: "What does this have to do with the teaching of writing?" "Will graduate students who do interdisciplinary work get jobs?" James Porter writes, "At the point where rhetoric informs and intersects with composing practice, we want to maintain the broadest notion of rhetoric possible"; yet for Porter, traveling beyond these borders risks "losing our identity" (213). He writes, "If rhetoric tries to encompass everything, it becomes nothing; rhetoric as a field disappears" (213).

I disagree. Our identity expands with new scholarship. This research has everything to do with writing—as long as the classroom is not our only vista. And these new scholars are not only getting jobs but also winning major grants and awards.

We must resist viewing interdisciplinarity as Alice's rabbit hole. Rhetoric already is a transdisciplinary subject, an "interdisciplinary matrix that touches on such fields as philosophy, linguistics, communication studies, psychoanalysis, cognitive science, sociology, anthropology, and political theory" (Bender and Wellbery vii–viii). We need to be talking about how our students, who come to us with transdisciplinary and cross-cultural interests, can be trained to study rhetoric in many cultural locations through the methods and theories of many fields. At a time when the polis is increasingly in need of rhetorical exploration, we must risk looking for rhetoric beyond narrow disciplinary interests—to look for rhetoric where it has not been found.

Works Cited

Bender, John, and David E. Wellbery. "Rhetoricality: On the Modernist Return of Rhetoric." *The Ends of Rhetoric: History, Theory, and Practice.* Ed. John Bender and David E. Wellbery. Stanford, CA: Stanford UP, 1990: 3–39.

Britt, Elizabeth C. "Conceiving the American Dream: Ethnographic Interpretations of Law, Rhetoric, and Infertility." Diss. Troy, NY: Rensselaer Polytechnic Institute, in progress.

Cushman, Ellen. "Rhetorician as Agent of Social Change." *College Composition and Communication* 47 (1996): 7–28.

Enos, Richard Leo. "Viewing the Dawns of Our Past Days Again: Classical Rhetoric as Reconstructive Literacy." *Defining the New Rhetorics.* Ed. Theresa Enos and Stuart C. Brown. Sage Series in Written Communication 7, Newbury Park, CA: Sage, 1993, 8–21.

Lyons, Scott. "Crying for Revision: Postmodern Indians and Rhetorics of Tradition." *Making and Unmaking the Prospects for Rhetoric.* Ed. Theresa Enos and Richard McNabb. Nahwah, NJ: Erlbaum, 1997. 123–31.

Martin, Emily. *The Woman in the Body: A Cultural Analysis of Reproduction.* Boston: Beacon, 1992.

Mountford, Roxanne, and Nedra Reynolds. "Rhetoric and Graduate Studies: Teaching in a Postmodern Age." *Rhetoric Review* 15 (1996): 192–214.

Octalog, "The Politics of Historiography." *Rhetoric Review* 7 (1988): 5–49.

Porter, James E. "Developing a Postmodern Ethics of Rhetoric and Composition." *Defining the New Rhetorics.* Ed. Theresa Enos and Stuart C. Brown. Sage Series in Written Communication 7, Newbury Porte. CA: Sage, 1993, 207–26.

WHAT "I" CAN DO TO SOCRATES: THE FICTIONS OF RHETORIC

Jasper Neel

Vanderbilt University

Let me remind you of the subtitle of this session: "The (Continuing) Politics of Historiography." "Historiography," as you know, ordinarily denotes two different grammatical functions—noun and verb. As noun, "historiography" signifies two different "bodies": not only "the body of literature dealing with historical matters" but also "the body of techniques, principles, and procedures of historical research." As verb, "historiography" signifies "the narrative presentation of history based on critical examination, evaluation, and selection of material from primary and secondary sources and subject to scholarly criteria" (*Random House* 907). As for "politics," well, "politics," as they say in Chicago, "is politics."

Of "politics" I am undeniably guilty. Of "historiography," by contrast, almost entirely innocent. I have participated neither in defining a body of literature dealing with historical matters nor in articulating a body of techniques, principles, or procedures for historical research. By like token, I have never rendered a narrative that would qualify as historiography. This leaves me with politics, an activity that takes me to Isocrates. "Old man eloquent," as Milton so famously described Isocrates, was my sort of "politician." He never held public office, never spoke in the Assembly, and rarely ventured outside his own domestic setting. He taught his students, published essays explaining how Athenian life in particular and human life in general ought to be lived, remained lucid and active for ninety-eight years, and grew very, *very* rich. Isocrates, in other words—far more than Plato or Aristotle, Cicero or Quintilian, Toulmin or Burke— is my hero. Let me be clear. When I say "Isocrates," I do not signify the ideas, the reputation, or the techniques. When I say, "Isocrates," I signify the material life itself, for if Isocrates taught us anything, he taught us the paramount importance of material life.

Thus, the politics of my choice are clear. I will let you decide whether the *histor* (whether *y, iography,* or some other suffix) is worthwhile. Here's what one can foreground as a result of just one (albeit perhaps the most important one) of Isocrates' texts. I refer, of course, to the *Antidosis*.

A rhetorician who operates in the (fictional) politics of the historical moment of the *Antidosis* (roughly 353 BCE) will be misunderstood, misrepresented, persecuted, and in constant need of a defender. Such a rhetorician will have to speak with a borrowed voice, in an artificial situation, through indirection, in constant violation of the rules of genre (even though the chosen genre itself is a falsification), and using a deceitful medium: deceitful both for the speaker, who will really be a writer, and for the listener, who will really be a reader. That's the bad news.

Here's the good news. A rhetorician who decides to speak/write politico/historiographically from this moment will be very popular with students, selling a product that nearly everyone with sufficient means will wish to buy, excused from normal time constraints, allowed wide intertextual leeway, exempt from the more onerous and horrific tasks sometimes required for employment, permitted to remain on the margins of life, not expected to master what s/he professes, and inordinately wealthy.

Such a rhetorician would, of course, need a title. Isocrates offers one: "logologist." A logologist uses the methods of "the logos" in the service of wisdom as a process of making all inquiry pertinent; a logologist operates only through inscription, soon only through electronic inscription. In logological speak/writing, education—both self- and other-directed—becomes a way of life, an end in itself. The logologist becomes both the "owner" and the "beneficiary" of the best, most comprehensive education available in the world. Though the language and the audience for the discourse suggest risk, little is really at stake. Enabled to seek out those with ability, to educate them in theory, and to guide them in practice, the logologist is then excused from responsibility for their behavior. Better yet, in a forever naïve, self-contradictory way, such a logologist is enabled to think that discourse makes the person, that the logologist makes the discourse, and that the very making is ameliorative. Best of all, the logologist is expected to be acutely self-conscious and highly sophisticated about discursive practices; discursive practices become, as Macbeth puts it, "the be-all and the end-all."

"For since it is not in the nature of man to attain a science," as Isocrates puts it in his most frequently quoted passage, through which "we can know positively what we should do or what we should say, in the next resort I hold that man to be wise who is able by his powers of conjecture to arrive generally at the best course, and I hold that man to be a philosopher who occupies himself with the studies from which he will most quickly gain that kind of insight" (335). Or even better, as Isocrates puts it a little later in a not-so-well-known passage, the logologist has the task of cultivating the mind, which "is the noblest and worthiest of pursuits" (353). All who have the ability, the means, and the leisure will inevitably seek such cultivation, one might even say such "culture."

Is such an historical moment really possible? Absolutely. Would it be, must it be political? Undeniably.

Works Cited

Isocrates. *Antidosis, Isocrates, Volume II.* Trans. George Norlin. Cambridge, MA: Harvard UP (Loeb), 1992, 185–365.
Random House Unabridged Dictionary. Second Edition, 1993.

THE HISTORIAN AS ARGUER

Edward Schiappa

University of Minnesota

My presentation will advance a series of claims about rhetorical historiography: my thesis is that the writing of history is a thoroughly rhetorical enterprise and can be evaluated with the traditional tools of rhetorical criticism, including the analysis and evaluation of the first, second, and third *personae* enacted through the text of the historian. That the writing of history is rhetorical is a commonly accepted premise, and now critics such as Ronald Carpenter are acting on this premise by producing detailed studies informed by the methods and assumptions of rhetorical criticism. It strikes me as unfortunate that most of the time, when we simply use the notion that "historical scholarship is rhetorical," we use it merely as a means to undercut points of view with which we disagree. Instead, as Carpenter's book illustrates, we can use the insights of rhetorical theory and criticism to understand how certain historical accounts succeed or fail, as well as better understand the cultural work that such accounts do.

Thinking of history-writing in a rhetorical vein also may be a productive route into addressing ongoing theoretical disputes about historiography. For example, I would suggest that the "Historian as Mere Subjective Interpreter" and the "Historian as Objective Observer" *personae* are both problematic rhetorics from an epistemological and ideological perspective (cf. Campbell 1975). We all know the charges against the myth of objectivity in history. But few theorists are willing to see history-writing as "merely" the idiosyncratic projections of the historian's own ego. Otherwise, to use a familiar example, we have trouble explaining why Stanley Karnow's account of the Vietnam War is better or worse than Ronald Reagan's. Once we move to seeing the writing of rhetoric as an *intersubjective* act of persuasion, as is encouraged by the perspective of rhetorical criticism, then we can begin to explain *why* one account succeeds over another in a way that avoids the extremes of there being only "one true account" of history on one side, and "all accounts are equally valid" on the other. The question needs to be reasked along the lines of "What historical accounts succeed given what purposes?"

Specifically, the "Historian as Arguer" *persona* acknowledges the rhetoricity and the constructedness of historical accounts without abandoning history as a distinct genre of writing. Even if written history is no more than the idiosyncratic projections of the historian's own ego, some are more persuasive accounts than others. Depending on our needs and interests, we find some accounts more useful and productive than others. Sometimes our primary interest is pedagogical, in which case we seek such accounts that best inform our need for useful teaching concepts and practices. Other times our primary interest is to enter a dialogue with an "Other" from history, in which case we seek accounts that respond to the Other's "uniqueness and singularity" (cf. Nealon 1997). Though our interests are always somewhat mixed, I still believe it is useful to acknowledge those needs by using such distinctions with such labels as *contemporary appropriation* and *historical reconstruction*.

We should take note of recent feminist accounts of argumentation to acknowledge that describing the historian as an "arguer" does not mean that the historian is necessarily masculine, aggressive, combative, and antagonistic (see the recent special issues on feminisms and argumentation in *Speaker and Gavel* and *Argumentation and Advocacy*). Arguers can be lovers, as Wayne Brockriede pointed out years ago. They do not have to be warriors out to exterminate competitors. They can argue in the spirit of cooperation and openness to the possibility of having their minds changed.

Finally, thinking about the second *persona* (the implied audience of a text) and the third *persona* (those marginalized by a text) can encourage historians to recognize the ideological and epistemological assumptions of their writings. Edwin Black (1970) illustrates the utility of the second *persona* as a critical tool with which to examine who a given text asks its audience to become. Does the historian ask us to treat their claims with certainty, or with tentativeness? How does the historian ask us to feel about the people, places, and events of the past? Phil Wander (1984) invites us to consider who our account leaves out and to what effect? What sort of subjectivities do our accounts produce for those we write about? Who is the "Other" constructed and performed in our texts?

Time does not permit an extended example of the use of these perspectives, although I can share with you that my students have produced wonderful, insightful papers using these tools to engage competing historical accounts of such events as Polk's Mexican War (1846–48), college campuses in the 1960s, the 1492 "discovery" of the "New World," and, of course, narratives of the origins of rhetoric. It is my hope that such exercises encourage us to recognize the rhetoricity of historical accounts while maintaining enthusiasm for producing our own contributions to the important genre of writing known as history.

Works Cited

Black, Edwin. "The Second Persona." *Quarterly Journal of Speech* 56 (1970): 109–19.
Campbell, Paul Newell. "The *Personae* of Scientific Discourse." *Quarterly Journal of Speech* 61 (1975): 391–405.
Carpenter, Ronald H. *History as Rhetoric: Style, Narrative, and Persuasion.* Columbia: U of South Carolina P, 1995.
Nealon, Jeffrey T. "The Ethics of Dialogue: Bakhtin and Levinas." *College English* 59 (1997): 129–48.
Special Issue: Argumentation and Feminisms. *Argumentation and Advocacy* 32 (1996): 161–217.
Special Symposium on Feminism and Argumentation. *Speaker and Gavel* 32 (1997): 1–70.
Wander, Philip. "The Third *Persona:* An Ideological Turn in Rhetorical Theory." *Communication Studies* 35 (1984): 197–216.

HISTORIOGRAPHY OF TECHNOLOGY AND GENDER IN RHETORIC: RHETORICAL "HUTS," LOGOS-USERS, AND NEOSOPHISTIC PERFORMANCE

Kathleen Ethel Welch

University of Oklahoma

As we rehistoricize rhetoric and composition studies, we must account for the ubiquity of HUTS, the demographic term for Households Using Televisions, because rhetoric and writing practices have been reprocessed in the last 45 years by the gradual immersion in television of almost all social classes, genders, and races and ethnicities in United States cultures. This ubiquitous literacy technology, which has been normalized for many people and so unnoticed (including by various intellectuals, many of whom continue to deny that they interact with television), has changed the way that we perform literacy in our households, our schools and universities, and other locations. This position paper calls for two major moves: (1) the historicizing of television as a dominant communication technology (as opposed to video, the form) that has been a radical transformer of rhetoric, writing, and literacy practices and the recognition of the inherent rhetoricity of television and (2) the acknowledgment of gender constructions in the historicizing of all literacy technologies. These moves depend on accounting for changes in how we construct rhetorical history, including previous communication technologies. In other words, all rhetorical histories—Western, Eastern, etc.—must be reperformed to understand the radical change in episteme brought about by the powerful forces of communication technologies and new understanding of gender construction, as well as race construction.

This call includes a plea for a move away from the inevitably dead-ended binary of form and content in favor of logos-performers. By logos here, I do not refer to the familiar "logic" frequently associated with logos; nor do I refer to the ubiquitous Aristotelian logos that has driven so much of Western rhetorical historicizing. Instead, I refer to an Isocratic logos of performance, situatedness, persuasion, ethics, and a measured relativism. This sophistic logos performance is also conditioned by Diotimic Sophism. To correct the traditional SPA tradition (Socrates-Plato-Aristotle), we must turn to the alternative EGI (Empedocles-Gorgias-Isocrates) and, then, to Diotima, the teacher-sophist of Socrates.

In this way, the still frequently unacknowledged privileging of mind over articulation (in writing, in speaking, in videotaping, etc.) can be overcome in favor of neosophistic logos performance. We would then revolutionize the direction of the humanities so that we would take leadership over the technological revolution, using rehistoricized rhetorical history and writing practices as one of many strategies. This move would lead us away from playing catchup with corporate-driven computer and television communication technologies and instead help us to position rhetoricians, compositionists, and other literacy/humanities/posthumanities people to lead this revolution.

Part of the enactment of these issues lies in a large-scale campaign of literacy education (using the technologies of television and the computer) that will include the complete replacement of the current-traditional paradigm that continues to poison the well of the teaching of writing throughout the United States. Part of this move will be to replace the divine term *humanities* with the divine term *literacies*. As the traditional humanities continue to decline, we must absorb their remaining importance into the Literacies and so enter the new millennium.

WHAT IS THE HISTORY OF RHETORIC AT CCCC?

Thomas P. Miller

University of Arizona

This panel has occurred at an interesting time in the history of historical scholarship at the Conference on College Composition and Communication. With the two Octalogs as points of reference, we could compose a couple of different histories for our work on the history of rhetoric and composition. I would like to sketch out two such histories in order to situate this discussion within the development of historical research at CCCC.

One history that we could compose for this discussion would be a story of decline. The first Octalog at the 1988 CCCC appeared on a program that included 276 concurrent sessions, with 20 of those indexed under "History of Rhetoric/History of Instructional Practices." Ten years later, the current CCCC program includes 484 concurrent sessions (excluding the featured speakers), with 18 panels indexed under "History of Rhetoric and Writing Instruction." These statistics could easily be used to argue that work on the history of rhetoric has declined at CCCC by almost half, from 7.2 percent to 4.1 percent of the concurrent sessions.

With these facts as points of reference, we could compose a history that looked back with nostalgia to a time when The Rhetorical Tradition was valued at CCCC. To deepen the nostalgia, this history would note events and individuals who have passed into memory. I remember the first Octalog as an exciting occasion where historians I respected gathered to debate the purposes and methods of work in rhetoric and composition. Along with the hundreds of others who attended the session, I assumed that reflections on our history would enable us to understand the development of the whole field of rhetoric and composition. Today, this second Octalog was held in part to remember James Berlin, but such formal acts of remembrance seem rather superfluous because nobody needs to be reminded of Professor Berlin. He is part of the work we do, sitting there with that wry smile of his every time we attend a prelim exam or pick up a scholarly journal. The histories he wrote for our work have served to explain the discipline to the legions who have entered it in the last decade, as has the work of the other participants in the first Octalog—Bob Connors. Sharon Crowley, Richard Enos, Susan Jarratt, Nan Johnson, Jan Swearingen, and Victor Vitanza. These are names we remember because they helped write the history of the work we do. Following upon the work of such scholars as James Murphy, who also participated in the first Octalog, these scholars helped establish rhetoric and composition as a scholarly discipline by writing a history for it. One could, in fact, argue that their work marks the end of the era in which historians played such a definitive role in the whole field of rhetoric and composition.

While the participants in the first Octalog argued over many aspects of the history of rhetoric and composition, they all assumed that one cannot understand the work of rhetoric and composition without knowing its history. While Professor Berlin published works arguing that Aristotle's rhetoric was based on a convoluted contradiction and that eighteenth-century rhetoric was based on a repressive epistemology, he spent much of his career arguing from the canonical texts of The Rhetorical Tradition. His works form part of the revisionary response to the earlier tendency to look to the masterworks of the classical tradition as canonical authorities. The first Octalog perhaps marks the end of the period when ancient authorities could be unproblematically invoked at CCCC to claim professional respect for the teaching of writing. At that time we were fond of reminding ourselves that rhetoric was the oldest as well as the newest of the humanities. Such historical lessons were often repeated when people went home from CCCC to argue for the creation of graduate programs in rhet/comp. The first Octalog came in the midst of a tremendous expansion in such programs, for the number of graduate students in rhetoric and composition more than doubled between

1985 and 1993 (see Brown, Meyer, and Enos). The 1988 Octalog can be situated at the center of that development in more than mere chronology.

To compose a history of decline from the first Octalog, we could point to the absence of panels on classical rhetoric at this year's program and note that only one paper invokes the work of an ancient master in its title. The absence of classical rhetoric from the CCCC program could be cited to argue that our rhetorical heritage has been forgotten as rhetoric and composition have fragmented into separate spheres of inquiry. We could then conclude our account with a sense of righteous indignation and perhaps a quotation from Santayana, or better yet Cicero.

An opposing history could also be composed for historical scholarship at CCCC since the first Octalog. This history would argue that the program actually includes more historical work than ever before. Our sense of history has simply expanded beyond The Rhetorical Tradition, in the traditional sense of the history of rhetorical theory. This history of our work would argue that we are looking beyond histories of ideas about rhetoric because we have become more broadly engaged with the rhetorical practices of groups who have been excluded by the dominant intellectual tradition, most notably women and people of color. At CCCC as elsewhere in rhetoric and composition, scholars are looking beyond the canon of rhetorical theorists to examine how other traditions have drawn on their shared values to speak against oppression. Our transition from rhetorical theory to rhetorical practice helped us to develop an historically informed awareness of the limitations of the work that we were doing; and the research on this program on the history of literacy, the experience of people of color and women, and education marks an important transition in how the field is historicizing its understanding of our work as teachers and scholars in rhetoric and composition.

This account of our historical research would argue that CCCC is composing a history for itself that is less clearly defined and more broadly inclusive, a history with an ambivalent relationship to a traditional sense of rhetoric. The history of rhetoric at CCCC has become a less distinct and more pervasive project because it is not confined within a separate set of panels on the history of The Rhetorical Tradition. Perhaps historical work just seemed more central at CCCC ten years ago simply because there was less going on at the conference. Not only were there fewer sessions, but we seemed to have a simpler and more unified sense of our field of work. For example, ten years ago the topical index to the program had but 24 categories, while this year's program has 157 categories organized into 15 separate areas. We have expanded our focus beyond composition courses to study broader aspects of literacy and the rhetoric of public discourse.

Despite the smorgasbord of sessions, we have, I think, maintained our shared concern for purposeful action. Unlike the historical scholarship presented at such conferences as the Rhetoric Society of America, the history of rhetoric at CCCC is not merely an academic project because it has always been defined by a guiding concern for making historical inquiries practically relevant, generally to teaching. This concern is evident in the fact that the topical indices for the 1988 and 1997 programs both pair the history of rhetoric with the history of composition teaching, a pairing that only seems natural to those working in rhetoric and composition at CCCC. The definition of historical scholarship as a resource for teaching was challenged by speakers at the first Octalog, but for all their differences, the panelists shared a concern for orienting historical inquiry to practical action. As rhetoricians who value teaching, those of us who do historical work at CCCC differ from historians in most fields because we assume that the purpose of historical inquiry is not just understanding but action.

As a rhetorician doing historical research at CCCC, I choose to identify with the latter history, though I feel the nostalgia of the former story as well. I came to CCCC through studies in classical rhetoric with James Kinneavy, and I respect the generation of scholars who have passed in the decade since the first Octalog. My respect for those who have come before is part of my civic sense of the work that lies before us. I value a civic philosophy of teaching that links critical understanding with collaborative action toward social justice. The challenge for us as historians of rhetoric at CCCC, I believe, is to follow through on the transition from rhetorical theory to rhetorical practice to help our community develop an historical sensibility that values the civic dimensions of the practical projects that are included on our program. There are few if any academic conferences that present such a challenging set of practical projects: service learning initiatives concerned with developing more organic relations with marginalized communities, research on writing across the curriculum that examines the social construction of shared beliefs and values, and work with the technologies that are creating whole new domains of deliberative discourse. Historically informed scholarship on these issues, along with historical research on the experiences of women, people of color, and the working classes, is central to our program of action. I hope that historians of rhetoric will take up the challenge of helping all who gather at CCCC to act upon these practical projects with an historical understanding of their possibilities and limitations.

This history of our work forms the context in which I respond to this Octalog. Every interpretation is an appropriation, and so I hope that you will excuse me for appropriating these papers into the history that I have sketched out for us. As we expand our frame of reference beyond The Rhetorical Tradition, Janet Atwill challenges us to consider how disciplinary paradigms define our sense of experience because she wants to make sure that our efforts to read like classicists or historians do not turn us into them. Linda Ferreira-Buckley reminds us of the values of archival work—work that takes on new value as we take up the project of reconstituting the experiences of those who have been erased from accounts of the dominant tradition. The experiences of women are engendered in the histories that Cheryl Glenn challenges us to write for rhetoric—histories that will help us to broaden our sense of the past and situate it in a dialectical relationship with the work that we are doing. Janice Lauer encourages us to realize the generative possibilities of the stories we tell ourselves by valuing the telling more than the told, and Roxanne Mountford invites us to follow through on our stories about rhetoric's interdisciplinary nature to investigate sites where civic discourse makes a difference. While professing his "innocence" of historiography, Jasper Neel enacts an historical sensibility that renames rhetoric to give new meaning to the practical wisdom of the civic rhetoric of Isocrates. Edward Schiappa directly questions how we rhetoricians compose histories, and Kathleen Welch takes up the broader project of rehistoricizing rhetoric and composition with a gendered awareness of meaning as performance that will enable us to make practical sense of the technologies that are changing what it means to be literate.

While I may be misappropriating these scholars' work, I believe that their work raises several questions that need to be addressed quite explicitly at this point in the history of historical research at CCCC. When we were working with texts that identified themselves as works on rhetoric, we could unproblematically call ourselves historians of rhetoric, but what sense of rhetoric is involved when we as rhetoricians turn to examine the broader historical developments of literacy, sociopolitical movements, and marginalized groups? What are the methods and assumptions that distinguish our historical work from the histories composed by other disciplines? And what purposes are served by this new sense of the history of rhetoric? These questions are important because the basic relationship of rhetoric and composition is becoming increasingly strained, and the two halves of our field are at risk of losing the cross-fertilization that has defined what it means to be a rhetorician working at CCCC, rather than at MLA or RSA. As we expand our frame of reference beyond the history of rhetorical theory, we need to ask ourselves if there is a characteristically rhetorical stance on history. I believe that there is and that it is characterized by the orientation of historical inquiry to practical action. This orientation has traditionally been understood in terms of studying history to learn how to teach better. I believe that historical scholarship can help us to speak to the broader practical projects that are included on our program if we reflect together on what it means to read history from a rhetorical stance. This reflection needs to be informed by an historical awareness of where we stand as rhetoricians working at CCCC. I hope this response helps you to make practical sense of the history of what we are doing together here and now.

Work Cited

Brown, Stuart C., Paul R. Meyer, and Theresa Enos. "Doctoral Programs in Rhetoric and Composition: A Catalog of the Profession." *Rhetoric Review* 12(1994): 240–51.

6.
RESCUING THE ARCHIVES FROM FOUCAULT
Linda Ferreira-Buckley

Historians of rhetoric need to return to the archives. In calling for this return, and for a tempering of our recent preoccupation with historiographic theory, I join other historians, including some of the Octolog II panelists at CCCC 1997 ("Octolog"). I am somewhat reluctant to push the point: I like theory and have learned a great deal from those in our field who have advanced it, I believe fully the truism that even historians who deny theory operate nonetheless from a theory, *and* I don't want to be labelled conservative.

There are past traditions worth preserving—foremost among them many nineteenth- and twentieth-century research methodologies. Most rhetoric and composition graduate programs require students to be conversant with histories of rhetoric and even theories about historical writing, but few require that students be expert at standard research methodologies. Literature students are often schooled in such methods, which has contributed to ever-richer histories. Of course, some graduate students in rhetoric also take those literary research methods courses, and are better for having taken them. But that training leaves out much that is necessary to the rhetorical projects our discipline most needs to undertake. I would argue that it is this neglect of methodological training that more than anything else prevents us from writing "better" histories of rhetoric. What we need is the kind of archival training graduate students in departments of history undergo, training tailored to recovering the history of rhetorical practice and instruction. Katherine Arens argues persuasively that requisite research skills vary according to the humanities discipline under study.

Conceptions of archives predating Foucault differ very little from those held by contemporary historians, and the theories of early historians and philosophers—including Friedrich Wilhelm Nietzsche, Thomas Macaulay, and Thomas Arnold—serve as an invisible foundation for current historians. My use of the term "archive" differs radically from Foucault's "first law of what can be said, the system that governs the appearance of statements as unique events" (*Archeology* 129). We can agree with much of what Foucault concludes about discursive practices but insist upon concomitant methodologies; the joining of the two is tricky but tenable.

Archives have long been understood as providing the stuff from which histories are constructed. Archives were maintained in the ancient world. But modern conceptions of archives and archival administration originated in revolutionary France: the National Archives were founded in 1789, the Archives Department in 1796, thus bringing together the management of all public repositories and agencies. The English Public Record Act followed in 1838 and systematized archives in England. Many private agencies and citizens emulated these record-keeping practices. True, restrictions did and do apply. Yet these changes are no small matter, for they institutionalized citizens' right to governmental records. Historical materials were open to competing interpretations as never before. Access to archives thus democratized, historical writing was irrevocably altered. (Thomas Arnold insisted upon the centrality of history to a democracy and urged that histories be revised to be more inclusive.)

Late-twentieth-century historians have rejected much of the past's exclusivity as they expand archives and reconsider what merits preservation. On the other hand, the bulk of materials from which recent progressive histories have been constituted had lain unexamined in private and public collections in America and in Britain. What was required was a radical shift in attitudes toward who counts and who was worth writing about—which is no small matter, of course.

The point I want to make concerns past historians' attitudes toward archives: that is, what historians thought ought to be done with materials and what they believed archives might reveal. We sometimes write as though only we (and the Sophists) recognize the contingencies of historical composition. To the contrary, historical scholarship has *always* been viewed with suspicion. In *Greek Skepticism: A Study in Epistemology*, Charlotte Stough points out that the word "skeptic" signified *inquiry* (3–4) and thus was often associated with historical invention. Of course, there were (and are) grades of skepticism, ranging from the radical assertion that no historical knowledge is possible to a recognition that our historical knowledge is necessarily limited in some way. Concerns may be merely about the reliability and availability of evidence—or about the limits inherent in the human mind and social being. The full range of positions is well represented through the centuries. The Greeks were appropriately skeptical of history; after all, their historical accounts were constructed largely from human memory and oral tradition, scarcely at all from written records. The so-called father of history, Herodotus, was deemed a liar (Momigliano 127). Cicero would later honor him as history's "primus inventor," even as he cautioned against many of his elder's claims and practices (*De Divinatione* II: 116, qtd. in Momigliano 127–28). To be sure, many Renaissance historians professed a healthy skepticism. Recall that history was a division of rhetoric, and as such, its primary office was *to persuade*. (In this, humanists did not look to Aristotle but to Cicero and the Sophists.) The historian, in Sir Philip Sidney's words, is "loden with old Mouse-eaten records, authorising himselfe (for the most part) upon other histories, whose greatest authorities are built upon the notable foundation of Hearesay, having much a-doe to accord differing Writers, and to pick trueth out of partiality" (15). In the century that followed, Descartes demoted history to the rank of "fiction" or "gossip," a reasonable attitude given his requirement that "knowledge" be mathematically certain.

We owe these skeptics gratitude. Not only have such challenges sharpened historians' insights into history-making, they have prodded historians to forge methods that somewhat mitigate criticisms. These skeptics thus prompted the rise of history as a discipline in the late eighteenth and nineteenth centuries.

True, nineteenth-century historians, deeming history a science, had too much faith in their methods. What's more, even if the nineteenth century is marked by its conservative intellectual and historiographical practices, many nineteenth-century historians recoiled from the narrow rationality of the Enlightenment and the French Revolution and developed more sophisticated theoretical positions. German intellectuals like Baron Wilhelm von Humboldt and Leopold von Ranke took the lead, but Karl Marx, who had faith that history might be an objective science, was not a leader among progressive historians. Railing against reigning historiographical orthodoxy, Nietzsche, whose *The Use and Abuse of History* was first published in 1874 with the title "Of the Advantage and Disadvantage of History for Life," asked

> Might not an illusion lurk in the highest interpretation of the word objectivity? We understand by it a certain standpoint in the historian who sees the procession of motive and consequence too clearly for it to have an effect on his own personality. We think of the aesthetic phenomenon of the detachment from all the personal concern with which the painter sees the picture and forgets himself, in a stormy landscape, amid thunder and lightning, or on a rough sea; and we require the same artistic vision and absorption in his object from the historian. But it is only superstition to say that the picture given to such a man by the object really shows the truth of things....
>
> But this would be a myth, and a bad one at that. One forgets that this moment is actually the powerful and spontaneous moment of creation in the artist, of "composition" in its highest form, of which the highest result will be an artistically, but not a historically, true picture.
>
> (44–45)

Nietzsche, despite his belief that humans needed knowledge of the past, adjudged history "mythic," a judgment that would profoundly influence Anglo-American theorists like Hayden White. To be sure, Nietzsche foreshadows poststructuralist critiques:

> How difficult it is to find a real historical talent, if we exclude all the disguised egoists and the partisans who pretend to take up an impartial attitude for the sake of their own unholy game! And we also exclude the thoughtless folk who write history in the naive faith that justice resides in the popular view of their time, and that to write in the spirit of the time is to be just.... The measurement of the opinions and deeds of the past by the universal opinions of the present is called "objectivity" by these simple people. They find the canon of all truth here: their work is to adapt the past to the present triviality. And they call all historical writing "subjective" that does not regard these popular opinions as canonical.
>
> (44)

British, American, and Continental intellectuals took note, and a few active historians like Karl Popper insisted that histories could not be disinterested.

Early twentieth-century historians reacted against the dogmatism that nonetheless prevailed among late nineteenth-century historians who believed their discipline an objective science. The first half our own century was marked by historical relativism as scholars acknowledged that new evidence might well require revising or even overturning standard historical accounts. According to Harry Ritter, by the middle of the twentieth century, "A measure of 'bias' in historical accounts was ... accepted as inevitable, and it was conceded that scholarship could not produce 'certain' knowledge; in this sense, a mild form of skepticism is integral to the present orthodoxy" (405). All this before Foucault and White.

For every skeptic I can summon from the past, there were many naïve traditionalists (objectivists). But is that not also the case in the last thirty years? I have been talking to historians at my school, where I am a member of the Harry Ransom Humanities Research Center's British Fellows seminar. This is an interdisciplinary group of two dozen faculty from History, Asian Studies, Women's Studies, Economics, Art History, Theatre, Comparative Literature, and English, among others. The study group was founded three years ago out of the concern of historian Roger Lewis (himself a member of the British Academy and Editor of Cambridge University Press's multi-volume history of British Imperialism) that the faculty who had been attending the weekly lectures tended to be traditionalists out of touch with, and disapproving of, recent critical trends. Participants are actively, insistently redrawing the boundaries of historical studies—and as a consequence they are just as insistently refiguring what had been *within* the boundaries. What has most surprised me in talking to these colleagues is their sophisticated and extensive use of primary sources and their considerable training in how to work in archives. Their skepticism is informed by this expertise.

Looking through professional journals, I surmise that such is also true of historians at large. While theory figures in these journals, historical construction using rather traditional methodologies thrives. Never before has such work been held to such rigorous standards, and well it should be, because never before has the historian had the tools and the resources now available. In addition to older methodologies, we have electronic databases, dating devices, archeological finds, and anthropological methods; these enable a more complex understanding of the past. Indeed, attacks on historians continue to give rise to more rigorous standards and refined methodologies.

All this has me thinking that although one's theory and one's guiding approach are linked, they are not coterminous and that methodological approaches per se do not indicate a political position—at least not in any simple way.

Let us turn briefly to historians of rhetoric, taking Thomas Miller's excellent 1997 book, *The Formation of College English Studies*, as a case in point. Subtitled *Rhetoric and Belles Lettres in the British Cultural Provinces*, it explores the emergence of the study of the vernacular in the eighteenth century. The introduction lays out Miller's theoretical frame, invoking such theorists as Foucault, Habermas, and especially Gramsci. This frame helps to determine what is included in the book and what is not. But when we look at subsequent chapters, the book seems rather traditional in its use of primary archival materials. What's more, the author draws upon scores of books whose authors drew upon primary materials and rendered them in rather conventional ways: E. P. Thompson's *The Making of the English Working Class* (1964), Robert Morell Schmitz's *Hugh Blair* (1948), Richard Sher's *Church and University in the Scottish Enlightenment* (1985), and even Garry Wills's *Explaining America* (1981) and *Inventing America:*

Jefferson's Declaration of Independence (1978). Indeed, much of the work we admire by historians of rhetoric and writing proceeds in much the same way.

Miller's commitments to civic rhetoric and his belief that history has something to teach us—evident from his book's dedication to its conclusion—follow from the tradition of Arnold, Collingwood, and Macaulay. Like Macaulay, he sees history as a narrative spun from rhetorical practices; like Collingwood, he is evolving views on the relationship of history and philosophy; and like Arnold, he sees history as a means of fostering civic humanism. Arnold wished to construct histories that were marked not only by factual accuracy but by astute narrative political analysis. He saw a period's oratory as key to historical understanding. I note this to make the point that our histories—including those published recently by scholars of rhetoric—are shaped by the practices and philosophies of British historians of the past century, even when our histories bear the imprimatur of continental theory. These historians have much to teach us, even as we reject many of their assumptions and conclusions. Of course, my comparisons elide significant epistemological differences among theorists whose work often turns on fine points. But I would argue nonetheless that studying such "traditional" accounts (accounts whose diversity and richness we tend to overlook) offers substantive opportunity for studying history-making.

Revisionist historians depend upon traditional archival practices. Elizabeth McHenry, for example, has reconsidered the literacy practices of nineteenth-century African Americans after a half-dozen years of working with the archival materials of literary societies. Jacqueline Jones Royster has edited the work of Ida B. Wells, a woman whose writing must be considered central to nineteenth-century rhetoric. And John Brereton's *Origins of Composition Studies in the American College, 1875–1925: A Documentary History* won the 1997 CCCC Outstanding Book Award. To be sure, some stimulating historical works operate from theoretical frames that are clearly antifoundational—Susan Jarratt's influential *Rereading the Sophists: Classical Rhetoric Refigured,* for instance, and Jasper P. Neel's *Plato, Derrida, and Writing.* Yet such books are few.

I want to insist that traditional methodology, far from being incompatible with a progressive politics, is in fact the best agent of change. There is a wealth of materials available to historians—materials that demand the attention of any historian who wants to understand the past. What is most required to look at these materials and to recover others is scholarly training. Of course, our perspective on what constitutes history and what materials are worthy of study has changed radically, and I do not underestimate the monumental nature of that shift. As we acknowledge the deep centrality of the lives of people of color, of women, and of members of the working classes, we cannot but look back with regret on historical works published in the past. As historians of rhetoric interested in rhetorical theory and practice, we know much work remains to be done, work that challenges and in some cases explodes old definitions of what counts as a worthy historical record. Archives were construed too narrowly, and we now know better. But our students—and some of us—are underprepared in the specialized research techniques necessary to revisionist histories. Theoretical sophistication does not obviate the need for practical training. We lack the tools of the historians' trade; familiar with only the most obvious granting agencies, we cannot secure the money needed to carry out research agendas that are both deep and broad. There are exceptions, of course, but they are too few. I urge all progressive historians to master traditional and emerging research methodologies—tools crucial to revising traditional accounts of history.

Works Cited

Arens, Katherine. "A Power Base of Our Own: A New Case for the Historiography of the Language Sciences." *Beitrage zur Geschichte der Sprachwissenschaft* 6 (1996): 19–52.

Brereton, John. *The Origins of Composition Studies in the American College, 1875–1925.* Pittsburgh: Pittsburgh UP, 1995.

Jarratt, Susan. *Rereading the Sophists: Classical Rhetoric Refigured,* Carbondale: Southern Illinois UP, 1991.

McHenry, Elizabeth. "'Dreaded Eloquence': The Origins and Rise of African American Literary Societies and Libraries." *Harvard Library Bulletin* 6 (Spring 1995):32–56.

Miller, Thomas P. *The Formation of College English Studies: Rhetoric and Belles Letters in the British Cultural Provinces.* Pittsburgh: U of Pittsburgh P, 1997.

Momigliano, Arnaldo. "The Place of Herodotus in the History of Historiography." *Studies in Historiography.* Ed. Arnaldo Momigliano. 1958. London: Weidenfeld and Nicolson, 1966. 127–42.

Neel, Jasper P. *Plato, Derrida, and Writing.* Carbondale: Southern Illinois UP, 1988.

Nietzsche, Friedrich. *The Use and Abuse of History.* Trans. Adrian Collins. New York: Liberal Arts P, 1949.

"Octolog II: The (Continuing) Politics of Historiography." *Rhetoric Review* 16.1 (Fall 1997): 22–44.

Ritter, Harry. *Dictionary of Concepts in History.* Westport, CN: Greenwood P, 1986.

Royster, Jacqueline Jones, ed. *Southern Horrors and Other Writings: The Anti-Lynching Campaign of Ida B. Wells, 1892–1900.* Boston: Bedford, 1996.

Sidney, Sir Philip. *An Apologie for Poetrie.* Ed. Evelyn S. Shuckburgh. Cambridge: Cambridge UP, 1905.

Stough, Charlotte L. *Greek Skepticism: A Study in Epistemology.* Berkeley: U of California P, 1969.

7.
RECOVERING THE LOST ART OF RESEARCHING THE HISTORY OF RHETORIC
Richard Leo Enos

Introduction: A Rhetorical *Faux Pas*

Perhaps by its very nature, rhetoric is a subject that attracts interdisciplinary interest. Departments in English, communication, philosophy, linguistics and classical studies have provided us with great scholars who have refined theories, contributed to a better understanding of our history, constructed research methodologies, and offered heuristics for sensitive criticism. As this century closes, we can look back with pride at our scholarly accomplishments and at how rhetoric has been integrated back into higher education. Yet, at one moment several years ago, I realized how fragile sustaining that momentum can be. In 1985 the then Speech Communication Association (now National Communication Association) awarded Wilbur Samuel Howell its highest honor, The Distinguished Service Award, in recognition of his career-long contribution to scholarship. I had known Professor Howell for many years; we participated together on panels, corresponded frequently and spoke to each other over the phone on a regular basis. When he learned of this award, Professor Howell called me, not just to share this news but to ask a favor. Travel had become a great burden for him in his later years and he asked if I would attend the convention and accept the award in his honor. I, of course, was delighted to share the moment, even as a bystander, and readily agreed. My obligations at the SCA Convention were relatively simple. I was to accept the award in Sam's behalf and say a few words of appreciation. This simple task, however, was, for me, fraught with anxiety. It is, after all, an intimidating task to speak for one of this century's great scholars of rhetoric and all the more so since I hold him in such personal esteem. All that is to say that I wanted my remarks to honor Professor Howell on that important occasion.

The point of this anecdote, however, is not what I said at that banquet but how the audience reacted to what I said. In the process of honoring Wilbur Samuel Howell I mentioned not only the word "rhetoric" but "oratory" as well. Having worked closely with and across the fields of Speech Communication and English for many years I know that "rhetoric" is a term shared by scholars both in communication and English. In fact, the history of scholars of rhetoric interacting across disciplines is long and fruitful. Thus,

---

Enos, Richard Leo. "Recovering the Lost Art of Researching the History of Rhetoric." *Rhetoric Society Quarterly* 29.4 (Fall 1999): 7–20. Print.

even though Howell and I had been in English Departments for several years, no one saw either of us as outsiders to SCA. The audience's discomfort was with the words "rhetoric" and "oratory." Evidently, I had selected *the* words that listeners wished to have left unspoken. Yet, as any oralist will tell you, there is no turning back in orality once the word, as Homer says, passes through the barrier of your teeth. I simply could not erase the winged word acoustically. As I look back on that moment, I realize that the issue that was revealed by the audience's reaction was that the terms "rhetoric" and "oratory" were politically incorrect. If I had used another synonym—perhaps communication—all would have been socially acceptable or at least tolerable. The safest of all terms was probably "discourse" but by that time the damage already had been done.

For several years I thought a great deal about that moment. Perhaps, I considered, this event was an aberration and, at the moment, I had committed an unwarranted generalization. I think not. I am convinced that this *faux pas* uncovered a serious problem that constrains the field today: the belief that research in rhetoric is retrospective or, at best, static. That night's audience associated the study of the history of rhetoric as an out-of-step phase of their march toward research excellence, and believed that the terms "oratory" and "rhetoric" conjured up methods and topics that the discipline had outgrown. NCA has a large and growing stake in research methods and topics associated with the social sciences. This perspective has been represented in ways that make it appear to be incompatible with the tradition of humanistic scholarship that characterizes much of the field's history. The growing intolerance toward the humanistic study of rhetoric has serious, detrimental consequences not only to the field in question but for the entire temperament about research and what it contributes. This essay is an effort to reveal those consequences and to argue for the benefits of a more inclusive attitude than the one exhibited by listeners on that night.

It is important to emphasize that while I am convinced that this attitude existed with many in the audience on that day, such a perspective is not shared by scholars in other disciplines. Let me demonstrate a different perspective on rhetoric and oratory, one that comes from outside Communication. I know that classicists such as Eric Havelock, anthropologists such as Claude Lévi-Strauss, sociologists such as Jack Goody and Ian Watt, and rhetoricians from English such as Walter Ong rushed to use such shared terms as "orality" and "oral" unabashedly (Havelock 1986, 24–29). Father Ong even dared to give it marquee status in his book, *Orality and Literacy: The Technologizing of the Word*. Since Father Ong's book had just recently been translated into its seventh language I felt that saying "oratory" would be tolerated with that night's SCA elite but it is clear that I had been the little boy who matter-of-factly told the King that he was wearing no clothes: I had reminded my immediate audience of a past that some apparently did not wish to recognize. An anachronism that some no longer wished to associate with as a part of their present discipline had been resurrected and exhumed for all.

This curious dissociation from the past preoccupies my thoughts. I wonder what those audience members back in 1985 would think about what I learned at our recent 1995 SCA Convention in San Antonio when the eminent classicist, Professor Michael Gagarin, told me over lunch that he recently had become the general editor of a multiple-volume series on the Attic orators for The University of Texas Press. I learned that The University of Texas Press was delighted to acquire this project, and that it was also heavily sought after by at least one other prestigious press. What a fascinating condition! "Oratory" was embraced by distinguished presses but I was at a conference composed of some members who wished the term to go away. On a personal level, I can tell you that there is no topic more engaging to graduate students in my English Department at TCU than orality and literacy and, in that respect, they mirror the interest emanating from both CCCC and MLA. In fact, a few years ago, I reviewed a manuscript for *PMLA* on orality and literacy in St. Augustine's work and was delighted that it was published in the October 1996 issue of *PMLA*. Oratory is alive and well everywhere but in its home discipline. It is now widely accepted in the field of English that one route to studying literature historically is to understand the relationship between oratorical practices and literary habits.

What does all this related interest in orality tell me about that audience's reaction fifteen years ago? I believe that the explanation is quite simple: a lack of education and understanding. In the space of a little more than one generation of scholars we have almost lost the knowledge of our discipline and the scholarly lessons they taught us. To paraphrase the words of Sir Kenneth Clarke, we are hanging on to our "civilization" by the skin of our teeth. I believe, however, that the discomfort felt by those audience members on that night was grounded in ignorance, that a recognition of the fine research for which scholars such as Wilbur Samuel Howell have been justly honored was lost to some members of that audience due to a lack of understanding. I feel that this lack of understanding led to a lack of appreciation which, in turn, prompted many to seek other academic communities. Some historians of rhetoric and oratory have responded with a conservative and even reactionary approach. Many have walked away from their critics by voting with their feet, establishing their own journals and associations. The Rhetoric Society of America and The International Society for the History of Rhetoric are two examples of associations that came into existence because of the need for an arena and a voice for research in rhetoric and oratory.

Those who anticipate that I will now launch into a tirade vilifying any sort of research that is non-humanistic research will be disappointed. No reactionary musings. No gloom and doom laments for pristine days now gone with the wind. Quite the opposite. I wish to engage in the most fundamental benefits of history: to learn lessons from the past. The saving grace in NCA's history of scholarship has been its multimodality, the willing disposition to make topics and methods inclusive. There was a time, in the history of American universities, when the opposite was true in other disciplines. Robert Scholes argues in his recent published book, *The Rise and Fall of English: Reconstructing English as a Discipline*, that one of the chief reasons leading to bitter arguments in literature over the last two decades can be traced back to the problem of having a canon based on authors rather than a canon based on methods. Unlike literature, Scholes argues, rhetoric's canon is grounded in invention and based on methods. Scholes believes that one reason that rhetoric has risen in this century is because modifications to its canon have sought to increase the sensitivite understanding of discourse rather than to replace one set of favored authors with another. Despite Scholes's praise for rhetoric, however, even a canon based on methods can have its own share of problems. In an effort to search for a disciplinary identity some rhetoricians have sought to define themselves by methods rather than problems. Like cancer, these educators sought to make all cells in the organism look like themselves and destroyed those that did not match. Following a German model of universities, departments became specialized and isolated. In that milieu of purity disciplines sought respect. Some in NCA are advocating such a path and I suspect that the reaction I experienced in 1985 was a manifestation of that "sweep under the rug" mentality. Today, the idea of a university is changing, moving away from Balkanized, autonomous departments, moving toward interacting and even collaborating. Universities are again becoming interdisciplinary in action and mentality. It is not that they are *returning* to interdisciplinarity but becoming so in a new and different way. I believe that the route to understanding the reaction of that night's audience, and the internal problems that led up to it, can best be found by examining the research methods and topics most currently practiced.

Basic Research and Primary Scholarship: Treading Up a Slippery Slope

One of the biggest problems in recovering the lost art of researching the history of rhetoric is an obvious one: so few of us are doing historical research in rhetoric. On the surface, this statement appears ludicrous. Our journals regularly publish a number of essays where the most appropriate descriptive adjective is "historical." In addition to articles, one could argue, a number of important books dealing with historical studies have been published. Finally, organizations such as the International Society for the History of Rhetoric and the American Society for the History of Rhetoric are thriving; in fact, at the 1997 NCA Convention in Chicago there were approximately twenty panels from ASHR appearing on the convention program. Yet, much of what is done in our discipline is not basic research, that is, new primary scholarship. Rather, what are presented as historical studies are critiques on secondary scholarship, speculative essays on meta-theory and point/counter-point debates over characterizations of ideologies. As I will discuss later, these approaches have value and deserve to be heard. They do not, however, equate with basic historical research. Specific illustrations will anchor my point. Over the last several years I have been involved in projects that require a re-examination of pioneering work in rhetoric and oratory. I contributed to the classical sections of Winifred Bryan Horner's *Historical Rhetoric* and both of her editions of *The Present State of Scholarship in Historical and Contemporary Rhetoric* as well as *Speech Communication in the 20th Century*. More recently, I was asked to write a commentary on the emergence of rhetoric journals over the last thirty years for *Philosophy and Rhetoric*. These projects obligated me to re-examine research that is now decades old. The reviews that I did over a sixteen-year period highlighted some amazing and demonstrable trends. One of the most dominant trends of earlier scholarship was that the typical research study done in rhetoric and oratory was primary; scholars would do archival work, field work, translate important primary material and make theoretical interpretations directed at explicating primary material not, as is often now the case, eliciting a reaction to secondary sources.

I also noted this trend in contrast with the occasional opposite—the Guru paper. In the early years of my graduate education—which I characterize here as the twilight period after these pioneering studies—I had noticed that much of the work published in journals was not research but rather commentary. At the time, I had little tolerance for published work based upon (what I thought was) idiosyncratic opinion. At the time, I thought that all research should be basic research; work that provides new evidence that directly contributes to the scholarship of our field. At the time, I yearned to know the "facts" and those essays that did not measure up to this standard seemed to me then only to have the outward form of scholarly research but not the substance. My fellow graduate students and I even developed a condescending term for such pieces. We called them "Guru papers," published essays written by (usually) prominent leaders of the field. These commentaries contained not a hint of research but a load of speculative, subjective critical remarks . . . or that is, at least, how we chose to characterize them.

I also was bothered by assumptions that (I thought) went unchallenged. For example, when I was a student, we were led to think that sophists were inferior thinkers about rhetoric when contrasted with Plato and Aristotle. We were also encouraged to believe that rhetoric thrived only in democracies such as Athens or republics such as Rome's. We were also encouraged to think that Athenian rhetoric equaled all Greek rhetoric and that Roman rhetoric was only a modified adaptation of Athenian rhetoric. We went from Greek to Roman rhetoric without questioning or understanding how Greek rhetoric came to influence Roman rhetoric . . . we just *somehow* knew that it did. Looking back now I see that I should have asked more basic questions and challenged more assumptions, although I am sure that my former professors will readily say that I did more than my share of "resisting" as a student. Perhaps a kinder and fairer answer would be for me to admit that these professors did not know the answer to such questions because we, as a profession, had not sought to find them out and supply them with such information. We had not directed our efforts at finding out answers as our founding fathers and mothers had done. Now that my beard is grayer and my hair is shorter and thinner I see the constraints my former teachers had much more clearly and I even see those Guru papers differently. I appreciate great scholars sharing the wisdom they acquired over a lifetime of research and teaching, the type of knowledge that is the consequence of talent, practice and experience over years. Yet, I also see that we as a profession fell short in giving our teachers the information they needed to enrich the knowledge of our discipline for our students.

I still feel that the need and importance of basic research that I first sensed as a graduate student is present. While my views about the worth of critical commentaries has modified, the concerns are still present, principally because there is a dark side to this brilliant coin. I am concerned because I see a genre emerging which is a variant of the sort of "Guru papers" that I once chided but now admire—particularly in the area of historical research—and I feel that it is a problem that affects the training and preparation of our students to do primary historical scholarship. Over the last decade I have seen basic research in the history of rhetoric replaced by critical posturing, speculative theory and meta-historiography. These enterprises, although varying from criticism to theory to method, all share a trait—interpretation often without advancing basic knowledge. In short, these are "Guru papers" but not advanced as the consequence of a career of careful historical research or years of classroom experience. Rather, such statements stand in as replacements for (and become) the research itself.

I would like, at this point, to nip some possible inferences in the bud. I am not against criticism; I am not opposed to advancing warranted interpretation; I am not opposed to self-reflection on our methods. I feel that these enterprises are valuable and deserve their place in our field. What I am concerned about is these enterprises operating independently from basic research and existing as ends in themselves. Our first and necessary obligation is to provide new information, new material evidence, new data. Then we can use the tools of criticism and interpretation to understand this evidence and, if needed, to develop new methods to refine our theories and analyses. When we understand this important perspective the agenda for educating students to engage in historical scholarship will become clearer.

In the April 1977 issue of the *Quarterly Journal of Speech*, Barnett Baskerville wrote an important essay, "Must We All Be 'Rhetorical Critics'?" The essay was important because it was itself a telling criticism about rhetorical criticism. Baskerville's concern was that the interest in critical work was so fashionable that it lured students away from the more laborious work of historical scholarship. Quoting Donald C. Bryant, Baskerville asserted that "rhetorical criticism must depend almost entirely upon historical knowledge for its effectiveness" (112). In his own words, Baskerville concluded his argument by stating that "In our field, as in most fields, there is a need for scholars who can record accurately and artistically the history of our art as it relates to more general history, to delineate its place in and contributions to the cultural history of the nation" (116).

Baskerville expressed his concern in 1977 and I believe that his voice responds to a problem we have today. In the May 1995 issue of the *Quarterly Journal of Speech* the editor, Robert L. Ivie, prefaced the issue with his introduction, "The Social Relevance of Rhetorical Scholarship" (138). Ivie expressed his concern over the current separation between rhetorical theory and social criticism. In much the same way that Baskerville argued for historical scholarship as a grounding for criticism, Ivie expressed his belief "that the language of rhetorical theory, which academic criticism subscribes to and attempts to refine, should prove of heuristic value to those who would engage in significant social criticism and that theory would benefit from its increased accountability as a social heuristic." The point is clear in both arguments. Sensitive criticism—whether it concerns historical or contemporary issues—must be grounded in basic research. Understanding what we criticize is as essential as how we analyze. This point is particularly evident in historical studies. Our students are being trained in the history of rhetoric as critics at the expense of, and not complementary with, training in historiography. Certainly the problem I pose is not a new one. In this century alone I can think of three such related situations. In the early decades of this century literary scholars expressed concern that literary history was being replaced by literary criticism. In the middle of this century, Communication scholars expressed concern that the history and criticism of public address was becoming less history and exclusively criticism. Lastly, our present condition in the history of rhetoric is such that the actual chronicling of rhetoric's history is being replaced by criticism content to comment upon and refine what has already been recorded rather than advancing any new historical information.

Baskerville's concerns remind me of the voice of another even earlier scholar, the seventeenth-century father of archaeology, Jacob Spon. Spon believed that the monopoly of classical philology as the sole route to understanding antiquity constrained unnecessarily advancements toward understanding ancient Greece. Spon believed that non-literary sources were also material evidence that should no longer be ignored and recommended expanding the research domain of philology to areas such as archaeology and epigraphy. Spon recommended that scholars arise from their arm chairs, actually go to Greece and engage in field work. He saw ancient remains as "books whose stone and marble pages have been written on with iron points and chisels" (Etienne 38). We too must expand our domain beyond the established canon of literary texts of rhetoric, for texts—including theoretical treatises—are only one form of material evidence. And that form, at best, is a transmitted one, corrupted necessarily by generations of well-intentioned scribes and the unsympathetic ravages of time.

The contributions made by this century's historians are remarkable and they must be acknowledged, but there are concerns with the present direction. We have many critics who have not demonstrated the talents or skills that they see lacking in others. This type of posturing and orientation—often done in the classroom—indirectly encourages students to passively respond to research rather than to actively produce it. The quality of such responses, moreover, is often judged by how telling the criticism is; that is, the quality of a student's performance is adjudicated by how well he or she can deconstruct the work of another rather than an orientation that encourages students to advance their own findings, to make their own contributions.

A second concern about current work in the history of rhetoric is an overemphasis on historiography as an abstract topic of discussion without the development of new, sensitive methods of historical research. In other words, a great deal of emphasis is spent not on the actual activity of *doing* history but abstract discussion about the notions and presuppositions *about doing* history. Certainly, both before and throughout the time that one engages in historical work serious concerns about method and analysis must always be asked. This process, however, is inextricably bound with the activity of research in the history of rhetoric; the epistemology of writing history is a process that is done during the act. Engaging in questions of historiography without eventually performing historical research, however, leaves historiography on the level of the speculative, work done that may only (and possibly) be effective. That determination of effectiveness, however, is only consequenced by actually writing history.

One manifestation of this trend in historiography is lap-top research that encourages students only to look at the exegesis of the text. Many would argue that "new criticism" or the analysis of text as an entity unto itself is no longer practiced. Yet, much of our current work in the history of rhetoric is based on the idea of "close readings" of works, confusing this act with the philological labor of textual criticism or the painstaking scholarship required to provide a careful translation. Analysis as "close readings" that presuppose the text to be the only source of knowledge has attractions. The work is facile, one does not need to go across the world seeking evidence, but only to slide one's chair over to the book case and reach for a volume. Most scholars agree, however, that works are best understood when viewed not as isolated and autonomous events but as intertextual, that even discrete texts are part of a diachronic chain of being. I am encouraging us to elaborate the notion of intertextuality to include not only the positioning of texts but also contextual methods that will help us to position them.

The orientation toward speculative historiography and passive criticism affects students in other ways. By default, such an orientation reduces the time and emphasis of basic research so that students do not have adequate exposure to the activity of historical work in progress during their education. There is a danger that we could unwittingly be encouraging our students to be dilettantes; that is, to dabble in historical study and commentary without method and without basic knowledge (Etienne 146). What traits will avoid these concerns in the preparation for historical research? Studying the social and political history of the period will provide knowledge of the context of the rhetoric. Attention to the nature and general orthography of the primary language will further inform our contextual knowledge, since language habits are often influenced by social and political forces as well as linguistic phenomena. Studying the material evidence of a culture by expanding our notion of "texts" to archaeological and epigraphical sources will further specify our understanding of the rhetoric and oratory that operated. Such an effort, however, will require students to learn techniques to assimilate data and procedures for field work. Since all such evidence must be interpreted, it is essential that we emphasize and learn how to argue for interpretations of evidence that account for verifiable explanations and are the source from which to advance theories.

Winning the Right to Research Rhetoric

Historians of rhetoric exist in a tacit community. The community participates in a dialectic in which research is offered and responded to primarily through journal essays, books and reviews. Not enough attention, however, is paid to the categories of evidence brought under analysis or to the creation of new methodologies. Some of us equate historical research with antiquated methods of scholarship. The two—topic and method—are not the same and do not have to coexist. For the sake of the pristine and the venerable, a conservative orientation to what constitutes valid evidence in historiography has promoted a closed system that risks limited acquisition of evidence, and ultimately an imprecise understanding that fails to account adequately for forces shaping the subject under study. Here is an analogy that applies to research in the history of rhetoric. Heinrich Schliemann, the father of *modern* archaeology, was vilified because others believed that dirtying one's hands through actually going to see what was at Troy was something scholars should not do. Rather, the accepted mode of scholarly operation was to make armchair explanations based solely upon the *Iliad* and the *Odyssey*. Schliemann had many faults, but one of them was not a lack of zeal for knowing. Dissatisfied with the wrangling and speculations of scholars whose weight of interpretation was often grounded more on personal authority than evidence,

Schliemann literally went right to the source and his innovative methods of archaeological research established new methods and insights into the Homeric world. Unfortunately, many researchers in the history of rhetoric and oratory have taken the prevailing disposition of our scholarly community with tacit acceptance. Our students are tempted to think that an argument is right based on the persona of the author and not the weight of the evidence. At the same time, non-experts outside our immediate community (but within the academy) are not swept away by ethos-posturing but await insights based on new discoveries that make sense to them. Many of us, however, have not learned from Schliemann and have been reluctant to "dirty our hands" in such a manner of research, but rather perpetuate and even glorify the armchair, venerated methods of analysis.

Would it be, for us, a question of "dirty hands," for example, to actually go to Sicily and examine artifacts that may tell us more about Corax, Tisias, and Gorgias, than what literary fragments alone would yield? Would it be unthinkable to immerse oneself in the study of Greek archaeology and history in order to learn about cultural forces shaping Greek rhetoric and oratory? Why would we not, for example, wish to journey to the Clements Library at The University of Michigan and examine first-hand the arguments of the British side of the Revolutionary War? And lastly, would it be unthinkable for us, like our colleagues who have done such a good job in the social sciences, to develop new methodologies and new theories to try to account for the evidence that they present in the formulation of their theories? The truth is that the reaction to the words "rhetoric" and "oratory" on the part of those members of that SCA audience was the response of closed minds who had made a knee-jerk reaction. They were inappropriate. From our side, the type of primary scholarship that earned Professor Howell such praise had lost its growth and trajectory. We are lacking on that count. Excellent research will make not only the merits of the observation obvious but will underscore the worth of the subject itself. Recovering the lost art of researching the history of rhetoric means not going back but progressing forward by providing new basic research and sensitive methods for acquiring and assessing that information.

The development of new methods is of obvious importance if we hope to continue making sensitive explanations but of shared, if not equally obvious importance, is the discipline's openness to receiving new methods. The benefits of developing new methods for research applies to rhetoric that is both written and oral. Seeing relationships between orality and literacy, however, can come at great personal cost, especially if a community is resistant. The importance of seeing the relationship between orality and literacy is no better illustrated than in Kevin Robb's *Literacy & Paideia in Ancient Greece* (1994). Robb, often a critic of Eric Havelock's pioneering work, is nonetheless convinced of the relationship of oral and written discourse. It may sound odd to say this, but arguing for the relationship of orality and literacy has taken considerable personal courage. The opposition that Eric Havelock received when he made the study of oral literature "scholarly" is known to us. Robb, however, shows how the initial scorn that Havelock received for his *Preface to Plato* is mild by comparison with another scholar who advanced similar claims a century earlier, Frank Byron Jevons.

According to Robb, Frank Byron Jevons, a little-known Greek historian, published *A History of Greek Literature from the Earliest Period to the Death of Demosthenes* in 1886. Jevons committed academic suicide when he argued, from inscriptional evidence and not conventional literary sources, that the development of Greek literacy was closely related with oralism. To his Victorian readership, who judged eloquence by the standards of what has been called white essayist prose and poetics, Jevons challenged the questionable dates inferred from "proper" literary sources, opting to examine the archaeological evidence of epigraphy or writing that came directly from such primary sources as marble inscriptions and pottery engravings. From the evidence, Jevons claimed that orality and literacy had a long and sustained relationship. In fact, Jevons asserted that Greek literature remained "classical" as long as it remained oral. That is, the Greek literature of the Fifth Century B.C. was oral. Unwilling to tolerate his politically incorrect claims, and waving away the primary evidence Jevons presented, Victorian scholars snubbed his research. They refused to give it a fair hearing. For Jevons, the route to understanding Greek literature was through Greek culture, and understanding that culture meant understanding the development of writing and its relationship to orality. Blinded by their own social views, scholars of Jevons' era categorized "literature" in either-or terms: as something written rather than spoken, aesthetic rather than functional, and (above all) never in any way related to rhetoric. Because of such resistance, Jevons died unheralded for his achievements. Almost a century lapsed before the prejudice against orality and literacy, and rhetoric itself, began to dissolve.

In 1948 a work of scholarship too stellar to be ignored argued for the centrality of rhetoric in ancient Greece: H. I. Marrou's *A History of Education in Antiquity.* Through exhaustive basic research from primary material, Marrou was able to claim that not only were orality and literacy related but that rhetoric was the dominant discipline shaping Greek education. In fact, Marrou believed that rhetoric had such a pervasive influence on Greek culture that much of our confusion over Greek culture would be clarified if we more fully understood the nature of rhetoric and its impact Ancient Greeks never separated reading and writing from speech; even when Greece was literate that "literature" was performed orally. Ancient Greeks, Marrou argued, believed that if one could speak and write properly, one could think properly and even live properly; rhetoric helped people learn how to argue well and make cogent judgments. For ancient Greeks this quest for intellectual excellence that would improve society was called *paideia,* for Romans it was called *humanitas,* for us it is called "culture." While such ideas sound quaint they were nonetheless firmly believed in antiquity and it is impossible to understand sensitively Hellenic culture without grasping that mentality. It is no wonder, as Marrou asserted, that the rhetorical culture of Isocrates actually won out over the ontological culture of Plato. Thus, it is important both to retrieve this culture and to recognize its mentality in seeing an inseparable bonding of orality and literacy, as well as recognizing that cognitive processes affect society because they are the operations by which people make judgments. The route to such understanding, and the necessary starting point for any criticism, is basic historical research and a community of scholars open to non-conventional findings.

Conclusion

I would like to end by mentioning recent incidents which I find personally uplifting because they address the needs I have outlined. First, three scholars whom I respect very much—Lisa Ede, Cheryl Glenn, and Andrea Lunsford—sent me a manuscript that they had submitted to *Rhetorica* and asked for my opinion. Their essay is an insightful argument for detailed basic research on women theoreticians and practitioners of rhetoric and oratory; they illustrate perspectives that would contribute to a more representative accounting of the roles women played in our history. I found very little to suggest or modify; the essay was cogent and I am delighted that it was published in *Rhetorica*. Similarly, projects such as *Reclaiming Rhetorica: Women in the Rhetorical Tradition* (ed. Andrea Lunsford) and Cheryl Glenn's *Rhetoric Retold: Regendering the Tradition from Antiquity Through the Renaissance* (1997) are encouraging signs of historical research. Both of these works demonstrate how the rhetorical tradition is expanding. Yet, both works share the concern presented here, that our expanded view of the rhetorical tradition also creates the need for more primary research and advances in research methods that are sensitive to the new growth. I did recommend to these scholars that in their next project, however, they branch out to include women who taught rhetoric and oratory from the 1930–1970 era. In addition to Marie Hochmuth Nichols, I mentioned Laura Crowell, principally because I was so impressed by her work on British rhetoric and oratory when I was an undergraduate. I told Lunsford, Ede and Glenn that Crowell was an especially poignant example because in 1988 the CCCC at Seattle sponsored a panel on women in the history of rhetoric. The irony was that Laura Crowell was in a rest home only a few miles away and would have been delighted to attend the event. She was not invited only because she was not known by the panel members.

When I told these three colleagues my story they mutually agreed to the need and even volunteered to contact Professor Crowell in an effort to reclaim part of our living history. I agreed to call Professor Crowell (I had not spoken with her for several years) and let her know of this renewed interest. When I spoke with her in September 1995, she not only could not remember me but told me she could not remember what she had done as a professor of rhetoric and oratory at the University of Washington for so many years! I did not know what to say. I told this story to my former student, Barbara Warnick, who is a professor at Washington, at the SCA Convention in November 1995. Barbara told me (her eyes moist with tears) that Laura had just died in the last two weeks. I can think of no better or more personal illustration of the fragility of our collective memory, and the need for recovering historical study, than that instance.

I would like to mention another example of the importance of such historical work. Harold Barrett, my former and first professor of the history of rhetoric, also has convinced me of the value of reconstructing and preserving primary work, in this case an important address by an exemplar of The Cornell School of Rhetoric, one of our greatest scholars of this century, Harry Caplan. In 1968 Caplan gave a public lecture called "The Classical Tradition: Rhetoric and Oratory" at the Annual Conference on Rhetorical Criticism hosted by California State University, Hayward. Barrett was wise enough to record the address but Caplan did not wish to have the manuscript published at the time since (he believed) it required further polishing. Those who heard the address considered it to be invaluable, the product of wisdom acquired only after a lifetime of scholarship on rhetoric and oratory. Caplan died some years later and the lecture was left unpublished. For many years, Barrett and I have spoken of the loss of this treasure. Recently, Barrett was able to secure permission from Harry Caplan's literary executor to publish the lecture. He went to the rare book and manuscript collection at Cornell University and copied the text. Barrett sent the tape and manuscript to me at TCU. With the aid of research associates Mark James and Lois Agnew, we were able to have the text—heavily edited with handwritten changes—computer-scanned and formatted for reconstruction. We worked for months with the audio tape, the computer scan and some good old-fashioned textual criticism and have reproduced Caplan's lost speech, which is approximately sixty typed pages in length. This work can be found in the Spring 1997 issue of *Rhetoric Society Quarterly*. We are using this project as an argument for why our journals should consider publishing such primary evidence that does not fit into book or monograph-length format.

I believe that these two examples are positive illustrations of the importance of reclaiming the lost art of researching the history of rhetoric. The fragility of what we do should be apparent if scholars as recent as Professors Crowell and Caplan were almost lost to us, let alone those who existed centuries before, as I have been discussing for most of this essay. Edmund Burke, the prominent eighteenth-century British statesman, once wrote that "The only thing necessary for the triumph of evil is for good men to do nothing." For our purposes, we might well take the spirit of Burke's statement and paraphrase it to say that all that is necessary for ignorance to prevail in our discipline is for historians of rhetoric to forget their primary job of doing history.

Professor and Radford Chair of Rhetoric and Composition
Texas-Christian University

Works Cited

Baskerville, Barnett. "Must We All Be 'Rhetorical Critics'?" *Quarterly Journal of Speech* 63 (April 1977): 107–16.

Brigance, William Norwood and Marie Hochmuth [Nichols] (eds.) *A History and Criticism of American Public Address*. Three volumes. New York: Russell & Russell, 1943 (vols. I and II), 1955 (vol. III).

Ede, Lisa, Cheryl Glenn, and Andrea Lunsford. "Border Crossings: Intersections of Rhetoric and Feminism." *Rhetorica* 13 (Autumn 1995): 401–41.

Enos, Richard Leo. "The History of Rhetoric: The Reconstruction of Progress." *Speech Communication in the 20th Century*. Ed. Thomas W. Benson. Carbondale and Edwardsville: Southern Illinois University Press, 1985: pp. 28–40.

———. "How Rhetoric Journals Are Shaping Our Community." *Philosophy and Rhetoric* 28 (4, 1995): 431–36.

———. Mark James, Harold Barrett and Lois Agnew (eds). "Harry Caplan, 'Classical Traditions: Rhetoric and Oratory.'" *Rhetoric Society Quarterly* 27 (Spring 1997): 7–38.

Etienne, Roland and Francoise. *The Search for Ancient Greece.* Trans. Anthony Zielonka, New York and London: Harry N. Abrams, Inc., 1992.

Glenn, Cheryl. *Rhetoric Retold: Regendering the Tradition from Antiquity Through the Renaissance.* Carbondale and Edwardsville: Southern Illinois University Press, 1997.

Havelock, Eric A. *The Muse Learns to Write: Reflections on Orality and Literacy from Antiquity to the Present.* New Haven and London: Yale University Press, 1986.

——. *Preface to Plato.* Cambridge MA and London: The Belknap Press of Harvard University Press, 1963 (reprinted in 1982).

Horner, Winifred Bryan (ed.). *Historical Rhetoric: An Annotated Bibliography of Selected Sources in English.* Boston: G. K. Hall & Co., 1980.

—— (ed.). *The Present State of Scholarship in Historical and Contemporary Rhetoric.* Columbia and London: University of Missouri Press, 1983, revised 1990.

Howell, Wilbur S. *Logic and Rhetoric in England: 1500–1700.* New York: Russell & Russell, Inc., 1961.

Ivie, Robert L. "The Social Relevance of Rhetorical Scholarship." *Quarterly Journal of Speech* 81 (May 1995): 138.

Jevons, Frank Byron. *A History of Greek Literature from the Earliest Period to the Death of Demosthenes.* London: 1886. Cited in: Kevin Robb, *Literacy & Paideia in Ancient Greece.* New York and Oxford: Oxford University Press, 1994.

Lunsford, Andrea (ed.). *Reclaiming Rhetorica: Women in the Rhetorical Tradition.* Pitt Series in Composition, Literacy, and Culture. Pittsburgh and London: The University of Pittsburgh Press, 1995.

Marrou, H. I. *A History of Education in Antiquity.* Trans. George Lamb. Madison WI: The University of Wisconsin Press, 1982 (reprinted from the 1956 edition).

Matlon, Ronald J. and Sylvia P. Ortiz (eds.) *Index to Journals in Communication Studies Through 1990.* Two volumes. Annandale VA: Speech Communication Association, 1992.

Ong, Walter J., S. J. *Orality &. Literacy: The Technologizing of the Word.* London and New York: Methuen, 1982. Reprinted: London and New York: Routledge, 1993.

Robb, Kevin. *Literacy & Paideia in Ancient Greece.* New York and Oxford: Oxford University Press, 1994.

Schaeffer, John D. "The Dialectic of Orality and Literacy: The Case of Book 4 of Augustine's *De doctrina christiana.*" *PMLA III* (October 1996): 1133–44.

Scholes, Robert. *The Rise and Fall of English: Reconstructing English as a Discipline.* New Haven and London: Yale University Press, 1998.

Wallace, Karl R. (ed.). *History of Speech Education in America.* New York: Appleton-Century-Crofts, Inc., 1954.

8.
HISTORICAL STUDIES OF RHETORICAL WOMEN HERE AND THERE: METHODOLOGICAL CHALLENGES TO DOMINANT INTERPRETIVE FRAMEWORKS[1]
Hui Wu

Writing women into history is not new; writing rhetorical women into history, however, is fairly new. Feminist rhetorical historiography is going through a transitional period when the issues of methodology are intertwined with ideology and politics. On the one hand, feminist historiography of rhetoric in the Euro-American tradition has made tremendous progress, as exemplified by the work of Karlyn Campbell, Cheryl Glenn, Susan Jarratt, Andrea Lunsford, Krista Ratcliffe, C. Jan Swearingen, and Molly Meijer Wertheimer. More important, historiographies of the rhetoric dealing with color and class are emerging. The works of Shirley Logan and Jacqueline Jones Royster are notable examples. On the other hand, however, there are still skeptics about these methodologies. For example, in the debate publicized in the January and September 2000 issues of *College English*, (Gale, "Historical Studies and Postmodernism"; "Response," Glenn; "Response," Jarratt; "Response," Wu),[2] doubts about feminist methods kept resurfacing, and disputes about methodology loomed large. Feminist history writing was merely reduced to research techniques and was confusingly paralleled with postmodernism. The positive trend of feminist historiography has had little, if any, impact on women's rhetoric in non-Euro-American traditions. Feminist ethno-rhetorical historiography, particularly that of Third World women, remains largely an uncharted territory. Take Chinese women's history of rhetoric for example. In a situation where "most of the studies in feminist rhetoric do not talk about Chinese women, and those in Chinese rhetoric do not take up the issue of gender" (Lee 284), the historiography of Chinese women's rhetoric is even more marginalized. Those who do feminist historiography of rhetoric and support the historical study of Chinese women's rhetoric do not do ethnographic research themselves. Those who study Chinese women do not do rhetorical research.[3]

These controversies and problems cannot be solved unless we develop a theoretical framework that defines the nature and principles of a methodology for historical studies of rhetorical women. The following questions may help us re-articulate our understanding. For example, what is behind the skepticism toward women's historical

---

Wu, Hui. "Historical Studies of Rhetorical Women Here and There: Methodological Challenges to Dominant Interpretive Frameworks." *Rhetoric Society Quarterly* 32.1 (Winter 2002): 81–96. Print.

presence in rhetoric? If we agree that women do have a rhetorical history of their own, what materials do we document and analyze? What are the key concerns in documenting primary sources and gathering evidence? Is the historical study of rhetorical women similar to postmodernism as both supposedly deal with discourse and knowledge construction? These questions are crucial to understanding and assessing feminist rhetorical historiography and will serve as the theoretical parameters of this essay.

I will, first, clarify theoretical premises of women's history writing by defining the purpose and meanings of its methodology. Many feminist historians of rhetoric have repeatedly explained their purposes and methods (Bizzell, Jarratt, Ratcliffe, Glenn, and Royster, for example). In consideration of the existing problematics, however, it is not redundant, but compelling and worthwhile, to highlight the ethical and political concerns in feminist methodology in order to assess it accurately. Second, feminist studies of rhetorical history should be distinguished from postmodernism, which has become an overwhelmingly dominant theoretical framework in rhetoric/composition. Some misconceptions stem largely from the confusion of feminist rhetorical historiography with postmodernist paradigms based on the belief that both deal with language and discourse. This confusion is a major obstacle to understanding feminist methodology. Finally, I will draw attention to the theoretical significance of the historical research on black and Third World rhetorical women by discussing its challenges to the established criteria of selecting subjects and evaluating archival materials. This essay points out that the present difficulties in accepting discursive feminist methodologies in the study of rhetorical history are the direct results of a continued adherence to certain established interpretive frameworks dominating knowledge inquiry and construction.

My discussion addresses diverse rhetorical history writing about women here in the West and there in the East—from Euro-American, to African-American, and to Third World (in my case, Chinese) women. In this, I do not assume homogeneity among women's diverse rhetorics and histories, nor do I want to reduce the complexity of feminist methodology of historiography. The strategy allows me to address some neglect of the theoretical significance of the rhetorical history writing of women in marginalized groups, due to divisions and even conflicts of identity among scholars and their research priorities. There seems to be a hidden but ironclad contract that a scholar's racial, sexual, or ethnic identity determines his/her research area and interest. Writing about women in China within the U.S. academy, I aim to dispel the mystery of the minority Other who is supposed to cling to marginality and the majority Other who is supposed to stick to mainstream. If I am supposed only to speak for post-Mao Chinese women whose identity and history I share, then my points and theories would be safely and naturally ignored by everybody else. If those who are said to represent mainstream Euro-American culture only spoke for their own people, they would be considered as observers who look at the challenges that minority poses to mainstream theories with indifference. I prefer the "reciprocity" Royster sees connecting academic and racial/ethnic/sexual communities together (254). In spite of the difference in our identities and in the cultures we come from, we all share the wisdom of the rhetorical community and appreciate scholarship that is "theoretically sound, systematic, and generative" (Royster 254). As feminist researchers, we also believe that gender hierarchy exists across cultures, no matter what forms it takes. Hence my strategy suggests that my configurations of feminist methodology of rhetorical historiography represent some common concerns of the community. Finally, this strategy strengthens the purpose of the essay—to draw scholars' attention to alternative feminist research practices that challenge ethically and politically the dominant theoretical frameworks standing in the way of understanding and developing the historical study of rhetorical women.

Challenges to Traditional Methodology

Richard Enos's "Recovering the Lost Art of Researching the History of Rhetoric" synthesizes well the techniques necessary for historical research, such as archive work, field work, examination of historical traces and records, translation of important primary material, and theoretical analysis of primary material (11). The techniques of tracing the details of accurate chronology, genealogy, and historical geography remain the best tools for documenting the past and probably "the best agency for change" (Ferreira-Buckley 582). The application of these techniques enables researchers, including feminists, to provide new evidence that enriches rhetorical history. However, feminist researchers have two major reasons to transform traditional assumptions of methods. First, discussions centered on techniques alone cannot bring to light the principles of feminist methodology because "preoccupation with method mystifies the most interesting aspects of feminist research process" (Harding 1). Second, the craft of "how-to" does not illustrate the ethical and political concerns that distinguish feminist methodology from that of traditional history writing. For example, why was Gale still skeptical of their research findings, even after Glenn and Jarratt and Ong had applied all the traditional techniques? Why, for centuries after the establishment of traditional methods, didn't we find women rhetors in the canonized tradition? Why doesn't the rhetorical canon recognize that Aspasia had the same influence on rhetorical tradition as Socrates did, even though both of them appear in Plato's works and other independent primary sources? Why were Margaret Cavendish's notes on persuasion and her eloquence for imaginary political and social situations excluded from the canon of rhetoric? Were these women nonexistent? If so, how about Socrates? Were their works of inferior quality? If so, what criteria do we base our judgments on? Obviously, these questions are not merely about methods. Methods, to feminist researchers, are techniques of evidence-gathering in the research process. When feminists ask questions about methods, they are talking about concrete techniques of evidence-gathering that raise ethical and political questions about methodologies.

The traditional explanation of methodology is that it is a theory and analysis of how research does or should proceed (Harding 3); it includes theoretical explanations of the general structure and applications of methods in a particular discipline. For historians, methodology means the theorization of the goal of research, the selection of subjects in a particular period (the research topic and focus), and the categories for evaluating historical evidence and analyzing it in relation to sociopolitical changes. From a feminist viewpoint, these methodological issues are not value-free. Behind them are judgment calls: is the subject worth investigating and writing about? What criteria are these categories built on? It is evident that the seemingly "neutral," androcentric theoretical definition of methodology has erased women's historical experiences and researchers' standpoints in the research process (Harding 3–4). Traditional rhetorical history asks only questions about rhetoric that appear interesting to men from within the rhetorical experiences that are characteristic for men. The disinterested methodology reveals severe biases toward women's rhetorical experiences that seem irrelevant to the "big" civic events drawing men only. Even when women made an appearance in rhetorical history, they were apparently forgotten, for instance, Aspasia and Diotima. We can put traditional methodology to the test by asking further questions with women's experiences in mind. Given the fact that classical evidence is sporadic and fragmentary, how can traditional methodology answer the question, "If Socrates's Diotima, as written by Plato, is 'merely literary,' then what of Socrates, Protagoras, or Gorgias?" (Swearingen 27). How can tradition accommodate women's eloquence on sex roles in Margaret Cavendish's orations that sound irrelevant to the civic affairs defined by men (225–232)?[4] How can traditional methodology justify feminist researchers' emotional attachment to the subjects of their research (Bizzell 15)? How can traditional methodology justify the enlightenment of the historical writing of black and Third World rhetorical women to the larger, predominant model of historical analysis? Similar questions about rhetorics must be applied to other cultures as well. For thousands of years, the Chinese essay has been male-dominated and addressed themes defined by men as honorable and lofty. But how do these essays generate gender identity for men and women? How are women writers positioned in the history of essay writing? What are driving forces behind women's essays? Can traditional methodology provide answers? No. To explain why the answer is "no," I turn to an examination of the purpose and ethics behind feminist methodology.

From a gendered point of view, feminist methodology of rhetorical history does not refer to an innocent research activity for research's sake, but rather an intentionally radical effort to exert transformative power over research methods (Bizzell, Harding, Scott). The purpose of feminist history writing is "to restore women to history and to restore history to women," as Joan Kelly-Gadol articulates (15). To this end, feminist inquiry is linked avowedly to a political concern, that is, to "denounce sexism and discrimination against women, to expose the origins, foundations, and workings of patriarchy, and subsequently to formulate and implement strategies for its eventual demolition" (Thurner 122). This goal denominated clearly by the term "women's history" throws open questions about who owns history and what counts as "real" history. Semantically, "women" as the possessive case added to "history" subverts patriarchal possession of rhetoric and history. "Women's history" in its linguistic form opens up the possibility for women to share history with men. In its political sense, returning history to women is returning the rights of property ownership to women who traditionally had no rights to material and intellectual inheritance, thus returning their human rights to them. From both semantic and political viewpoints, women's history inevitably challenges the way the content of history has been constructed, which in turn demands a renewed standpoint to scrutinize who has produced and can produce history. This concern of "subject-producer of history," in Michel de Certeau's term (17), further shakes the notion of objectivity on which theories of methodology of history writing are built. It challenges the traditional categories of history writing, such as periodization, social analysis, and theories of social change (Kelly-Gadol 16). Women's social status and lived experiences as the index to general historical progress transform our understanding of historicity. We discover that rhetorical history has been written from the point of view of men and only records male theories and speeches. History has forgotten the other half of the population that has co-existed along with men but has been silenced. Put differently, women's rhetorical history writing indicates that rhetorical history as it has been is not only incomplete but also unfair because it has left out the other half of mankind from civilization by telling a partial story. Therefore, feminist rhetorical historiography requires us to become research agents who bring transformations to dominant research practices and interpretive frameworks. It must not only emphasize women as an additional historical subject but also pose methodological challenges to predominant theoretical models.

Challenges to Postmodernism

In the field of rhetoric/composition, postmodernist theories dominate critiques of rhetorical works and pedagogy.[5] The authority comes whenever one draws upon Foucault, Derrida, and Rorty, among others, as in Xin Liu Gale's article criticizing feminist historical studies of rhetorical women. Gale draws upon Rorty to measure the validity of the historical studies of Aspasia (364–365). Her paraphrase of Rorty's evaluation of feminism is that "one of the best things about contemporary feminism and feminist writing is its abandonment of notions of objectivity and reality" (Gale 364).[6] It is, however, the "abandonment" that makes postmodernism incompatible with feminist historical knowledge inquiry and construction. True, as an alternative interpretive framework, postmodernism offers a critical edge to diagnose problematics of universalized claims for gender, reason, science, language, progress, identity, self, and power. Some feminist historians, such as Joan Scott,[7] endorse poststructuralism and believe that postmodernism provides tools for negotiating accepted meanings and established practices in knowledge inquiry and power structures. But the general postmodernist belief in undecidability and relativity does not do justice to nor is appropriate for feminist studies of rhetorical history. "The abandonment of notions of objectivity and reality" negates the gendered standpoint in feminist methodology that requires researchers to be responsible for historicity, committed to collective civic actions, and conscious of the transformations the research may bring to society and to academic communities.

Historians, including feminist researchers, all understand the fundamental principle of history writing: the subject matter and the events of the past must be traceable as historical facts. In practice, "conceptions of archives predating Foucault differ very little from those held by contemporary historians" (Ferreira-Buckley 577). Feminist historians rely on many of these traditional tools of research (Bizzell 16). Like traditional historians, they recognize subjectivity in historical studies but at the same time remember that they are not allowed to rehearse the historical product as "literary texts" or "ideas." Historians are not entitled to create history but to reconstruct it from available and affirmable sources. Their attitude is "what historians thought ought to be done with materials and what they believed archive might reveal" (Ferreira-Buckley 578). However biased, prejudiced, incomplete, and inadequate that product may be, it embodies an account of events that happened quite independent of the existence of the researcher, who is not a free agent (Elton 54). In other words, historical facts are knowable only by the evidence they have left behind. Historical studies are not a question of interpreting fact, but of establishing it (Elton 57). Historians must be responsible for the stories they tell and primary sources they scrutinize and document. Their stories and documentation must contain truths, truths to be shared by the public and must be acknowledged by the public as such. Bizzell notices Royster's recognition that her scholarship must be "rigorous in the traditional sense and at the same time 'accountable to our various publics'" (15). For this reason, feminist history writing defines itself as adding what has been left out to present more complete and fair truths of the past than traditional historical accounts.

In contrast, postmodernism emphasizes an individual's meditations that are private and self-conscious. The postmodernist is a free agent who progresses toward the end of exploration along the path paved by his/her own rationalization. This process emphasizes the individual's satisfaction with the exploration itself and does not require the result to be accountable to the public. Though the findings from the contemplation may be creditable, they merely point to multi-faceted realities, relative and open to further interpretations with no way of justifying. But woman and women's history cannot be read as undecidable and relative. If the analytical category "woman" is fundamentally undecidable, Alcoff posits, then "we can offer no positive conception of it that is immune to deconstruction and, thus, nominalist once again" (421). As a result, women's history would turn out to be an idea, or a notion, rather than a distinct past containing real stories of women.

A personal case can further explain this point. I served as the Associate Chair of a department at a university in China[8] but was ordered by one of my male colleagues, the Chair, to clean the office for him. When asked "why?" he simply said, "this is a woman's job." Marked by this kind of gender politics is my history as a woman who has the same lived experience as my subjects and is my writing of post-Mao women's rhetorical history. How can I leave these facts and realities open to interpretation? How can I just play with the idea of "woman" or "history" without the commitment to telling true stories? My history does not allow me to read Chinese women's history as some literary works with undecidable meanings. I must read women's rhetorical history in and after the Maoist period (1949–1976) as facts and record it as facts, because any contingency in my methods would result in historical distortions.

The researcher's consciousness of engagement is vital in historical studies of rhetorical women. It represents a feminist standpoint, which is "not simply an interested position (interpreted as bias) but is interested in the sense of being engaged" (Hartsock 159). It is "not something anyone can have by claiming it, but an achievement through feminist struggles against male domination that women's experience can be made to yield up a truer social reality than that available only from the perspective of the social experience of men" (Harding 185). Postmodernism, however, is a perspective based on the promise that the autonomous use of reason will make us free (Tanesini 238). Rorty hopes that "feminists will continue to consider the possibility of dropping realism and universalism, dropping the notion that the subordination of women is *intrinsically* abominable, dropping the claim that there is something called 'right' or 'justice' or 'humanity' that has always been on their side, making their claims true" (210, emphasis original). The postmodernist beliefs in a masterful, self-conscious, and universal subject and in the segregation of justification and reason from power and force, as Alessandra Tanesini generalizes, do not agree with the goal of feminist research, for empowering women means engaging oneself in competing with the dominant force. Criticizing Foucault's *History of Sexuality* for diminishing women's sexuality from theoretical analysis and Derrida's critique of Nietzsche's construction of the female for undecidable meanings of texts, Linda Alcoff points out that postmodernism undercuts feminist ability to oppose the dominant trend in mainstream intellectual thought that insists on a universal, neutral, perspectiveless epistemology and ethics (420). The "resigned acceptance," writes Tanesini, is not the right attitude that feminists should take in their situation (239).

Associated with postmodernist relativism and "quietism" (Tanesini 239) is the dominant Western hermeneutics that center on "the self as the ideal knower and on the individual as isolated and separate from the negative influence of outers" (Ryan and Natalle 74). This self-centered thinking has been perpetuated in Anglo-American feminist epistemology. In consequence, feminist theoretical frameworks espouse two principles: "immanent value (all humans have inherent worth) and self-determination (all humans have the autonomous capacity to direct themselves)" (Ryan and Natalle 72). These principles no doubt acknowledge gender equality and women's human rights. However, if the purpose of feminists is achieving self and self-determination, then feminist rhetorical historiography would lose its vision of its particular functions in social justice and its goal of research that stresses social changes for the oppressed and collective efforts of women in the civic process. Thomas Miller and Melody Bowdon advocate a rhetorical stance on historical inquiry built on five methodological concerns: dialectical transaction between the rhetor and audiences, situational aspects of the transaction, rhetorical purpose, collective orientation, and productive engagement with political action (592). No matter how fundamental their message is, significant to historical inquiry is their emphasis on the historian's rhetorical awareness of the subject's collective civic action and transformative power in society through effective communication with target audiences. The subject is not indulged in self-mediation but actively interacts with the audience. This "collectivist orientation" (Miller and Bowden), when complemented with a gendered standpoint, is methodologically illustrative to feminist historiography, for many historians of rhetorical women combine their analyses with a conceptual frame that is rooted in traditions of rhetorical criticism, for example, Campbell, Jarratt, Royster, and Ratcliffe.

The centrality of collectivity becomes quite a primary value in selecting subjects and materials as well as in considerations of transformative powers of feminist research. For example, Royster's selections of her subjects are based on their strong sense of the communities they lived in and attempted to change (6). Her effort is "to document and account for what was accomplished by elite nineteenth-century women as a cadre of educated professional women, and to suggest how their activities might connect . . . to the practices of others both before and after them in the making of various traditions" (8). The rhetorical women in Campbell's books are all women's rights advocates or suffragists working to improve the conditions of women. Swearingen's comparison of Diotima, Jane Harrison, Virginia Woolf, and Ruth Benedict leads to the discovery of collective consciousness as a common thread in women's rhetoric (48). Feminists analyze their materials as rhetorical pieces: nonfiction prose/essays, speeches, or dialogues addressing ethical and sociopolitical concerns of and to the public, rather than as literary texts that are arts for art's sake.

The feminist historian is also keenly conscious of the political benefits that result from research. Glenn believes that "regendering rhetorical history is a feminist performative act [and] a commitment to the future of women" (174). In working on post-Mao Chinese women's rhetorical history and collaboratively anthologizing their essays on gender, I am increasingly aware of the potential enlightenment Chinese rhetorical women may bring to feminist theories and women's movements in the West. All the women writers included in the anthology experienced Maoist "women's liberation" from 1949 to the late 1970s when gender equality was approached through mandating women to work outside home for "socialist construction" and to eliminate signs of femininity. Mao's liberation of women, however, was not intended to subvert the traditional gender hierarchy. A woman took nontraditional tasks in the workplace, but the husband's career and domestic needs dominated hers. The government even encouraged women to take care of all housework, so men could be entirely engaged in socialist construction. As a consequence, the traditional gender ideology prevails in both public and domestic spheres. Since the economic reform beginning in the early 1980s, women writers have worried that the traditional Chinese gender hierarchy reinforced by commercialization has brought new problems to women. Their essays function as public discourse and document post-Mao writers' reflection upon gender politics in the wake of these sociopolitical changes. Their thoughts can serve as an orientation point from which to navigate the trajectory of China's progress on gender equality and can shed light on some questions common to both Western and Eastern women. For instance, why are women still suffering from institutionalized sexual exploitation even after women's equal rights have been written into law? Must gender equality be reached through androgyny? Is working outside the home the end of women's liberation or its means? What role does the form of labor play in liberating women? If abolishing labor division is supposed to bring forth gender equality, why do Chinese women who have "been there, done that" still find themselves subordinate to the other sex?

Royster expresses the feminist historiographer's commitment to social responsibility and social action:

> Knowledge does indeed have the capacity to empower and disempower, to be used for good and for ill. As researchers and scholars, we are responsible for its uses and, therefore, should

think consciously about the momentum we create when we produce knowledge or engage in knowledge-making processes. Our intellectual work has consequences. I believe the inevitability of these consequences should bring us pause as we think not just about what others do but about what we are obliged to do or not to do.

(281)

In subtle ways, postmodernism has created "epistemological troubles," to borrow Harding's words, for feminism and the understanding of the methodology of historical studies of rhetorical women. In light of ethics and political benefits to women (especially women of marginal status), which have accrued from producing a more accurate, less biased history, historians of rhetorical women may thank postmodernism for its alternative perspectives that enable them to question the traditional historical content. But these perspectives are not grounded on undecidability and relativity. Instead, they serve as microscopes for detecting concealed realities of women in rhetorical history. Moreover, researchers may respond to postmodernists that they cannot stay disassociated from their subjects and sociopolitical activism significant to women in the past, present as well as future. Civic activism symbolizes the rhetorical momentum that feminist historians want to establish collectively with their subjects to enlighten men and to improve material reality for women across the boundaries of culture, race, ethnicity, and gender.

Challenges from Women of Marginal Status

The recent development of feminist historiography has seen many innovative research designs in the historical work on rhetorical women in marginalized cultures. Landscaping mostly uncharted territories, these works challenge the standard notion of what merits historical documentation at a more profound level than the historical writing of rhetorical women in mainstream Euro-American cultures. Feminist theories from the Third World demonstrate that historical studies of rhetorical women should not be limited to the study of the deceased; living women should also be included as historical subjects as long as the study contributes to history building. To global feminists, this type of research engages in translations of primary texts and theoretical critiques of feminist thoughts and movements across cultures. The recognition of the importance of historicizing and preserving rhetorical women of marginal status, be it within or outside the U.S., demands us to acknowledge that this kind of research is informative, consequential, and indispensable to women's rhetorical history construction in general and to larger interpretive frameworks.

Recent history is as valuable as "old" history in terms of archival work. Since primary historical research has become disturbingly a "lost art" in rhetorical scholarship in general (R. Enos), it is imperative for historians of women's rhetoric to take precautions against potential losses of primary sources. For example, *Living Rhetoric and Composition: Stories of the Discipline* anthologizes the personal histories of Edward P.J. Corbett, Janice Lauer, Win Horner, and others about their becoming rhetoricians and compositionists (Roen et al.). Had the editors not worked out this project, where in the world could we have found out why and how Corbett transformed himself from a literary critic to a rhetorical theorist and composition teacher? We would have missed an important part of the history of our discipline. Richard Enos expresses a deep regret at the loss of Professor Laura Crowell's thoughts on rhetorical teaching and describes the hard process of recovering Professor Harry Caplan's public lectures (18–19). Enos's point is: why did we not record their rhetorical discourse and activities when the subjects were alive? Once lost, rhetorical treasures are almost impossible to recover. These incidents are poignant memories to people who care about the history of rhetoric and composition.

The same argument applies to documenting primary sources for building rhetorical women's history. Female scholars' personal accounts about their growth and roles as women faculty offer a new angle to look at the history of our profession (Roen et al.). Casting a gaze from the American terrain to a global landscape, we can now access leading Brazilian feminist Rosiska Darcy de Oliveira's thoughts since the early 1970s. Her translated book formulates the concept of the feminine as a paradigm of the twentieth century in favor of women's search for their identity through, or as a result of, their difference. We owe gratitude to a researcher for the English version of de Oliveira's milestone work in global feminist theory and for a historical analysis of her works. But all feminists from other cultures do not have the same luck.

Interestingly, and also ironically, when the subject is alive, often times she or he may not be deemed as valuable as she or he should be. Writing the history of living figures and their rhetoric is often more controversial and complicated than that of people in the past. In documenting living women's rhetoric, one is often tempted to make judgments based on an ideology derived from dominant academic research models. This tendency is more obvious when subjects and materials come from the Third World which some Euro-American feminists naturally assume the authority to judge, or even colonize. De Oliveira's praise of sexual differences and criticism of Western feminists' emphasis on androgyny as a way to achieve equal rights could be easily criticized as essentialism, if the judgment is merely based on the standard Euro-American feminist standpoint. The translator makes great tactical efforts to explain why de Oliveira should be introduced to the Anglophone world and why her thoughts are significant and illuminative to Euro-American feminist theory construction.

In the case of de Oliveira, her standpoint is actually almost identical to, though more systematic than, that of several Chinese women writers I am writing on, some of whom, however, are accused of "essentialism," the most-ready-to-kill word in feminist research. Zhang Kangkang and Lu Xing'er, prominent writers of Chinese women's issues, have been criticized for presenting "female stereotypes and essentialized view on gender."[9] This and other dismissals of women's discursive viewpoints put archival work at risk. Feminists may suppress the very women and the very voices they claim to support. Undoubtedly, disagreements could be attributed to differences of individual opinion, taste, or theoretical perspective, but the attitude is damagingly dangerous. The suppression could stop Anglophone readers from encountering some of the leading contemporary Chinese feminist thoughts, the thoughts that many Anglophone feminists are dying to know. In consequence, Chinese women writers might suffer the same misfortune as Frank Byron Jevons did because of their discursive routes to knowledge inquiry.[10] In China, many women's essays have encountered severe censorship, to the extent that no publisher dares to venture an anthology focusing on gender issues which the government may suppress. And in the U.S., there is an unwillingness to tolerate their different thoughts. This intolerance often represents structured hierarchy that is largely built on cultural bias. As Scott observes, "dominant styles and standards work to include some and exclude others . . . 'Mastery' and 'excellence' can be both explicit judgements of ability *and* implicit excuses for bias" (47, emphasis original). Resulting from the sense of a privileged class in the West vis-à-vis the oppressed and marginalized, biased scrutiny embodies "a fundamentalist confirmation of traditional attitudes toward 'history' and 'knowledge'" (Chow 110), ironically in the name of feminist research that is supposedly for the marginalized.

Ferreira-Buckley observes, "[a]s we acknowledge the deep centrality of the lives of people of color, of women, and members of the working class, we cannot but look back with regret on historical works published in the past" (582). To recover what has been missing and to prevent what may become missing requires the recognition that historical work on rhetorical women of marginal status has broader relevance. Like the transformations mainstream feminist works have brought to traditional knowledge making, historical writing of marginalized rhetorical women, in the forms of systematic critique of the subject's thoughts and deeds, documentation of primary sources, and translation, can provide more fresh perspectives on established definitions of who and what is worth rendering as history. Feminist works have demonstrated contributions of discursive feminist discourse from other countries (Scott et al., Mohanity et al., and Offen et al., for instance). Feminist theories from African and Latin American countries illustrate why women in the Third World persist in theorizing their histories from their own lived experiences (Arndt; de Oliveira). Their theories shed light on many unsolved dilemmas faced by Anglo-American feminists in their efforts to empower women, for example, causing them to realize that the Western feminist redefinition of gender dichotomies may not be an applicable category in the analysis of gender politics in the Third World (Bock). In the same way, black feminists' theories and the historical writing of black rhetorical women are informative to the research on women's rhetorics in other cultures. bell hooks's historical analysis of black men's humiliation under racial discrimination and black women's desire to have the luxury of being "ladies" provided for by men (*Ain't I a Woman*, 177–196) demonstrates some flaws in the dominant feminist conceptual framework, which tends to theorize gender politics from the departure point of upper- and middle-class white women. Royster's and Logan's analyses of black rhetorical women's appeals for self-improvement to develop moral and intellectual resources for women and the community can illuminate theoretically the similar tendencies in some historical European women and post-Mao Chinese women.[11] Some contemporary Anglo-American feminists have once rejected these appeals as criticism of sisters. The Afrafeminists' (in their own term) revelation of the double oppressions of black women by the institution in the form of racial discrimination and by male dominance indicate that the Euro-American feminist identification of male dominance as the oppressive institution[12] may reduce the complex nature of oppressions of women.

Third World feminists and Afrafeminists remind researchers that historical research on rhetorical women requires substantial sensitivity to the particular sociopolitical conditions that have affected the subject's rhetorical performance. The specific materiality and gender politics in the particular period and culture of the subject demand that the researcher revise the established categories of selecting and analyzing subjects and archival materials. The accommodation of discursive feminist approaches to history is necessary if the goal of research is to construct human history as honestly, truthfully, and completely as possible. This goal has triggered feminist rhetorical historiography and renewed the definition of its methodology. Thus, cultural, racial, ethnic, or gender identities may not separate us from our common agenda to better society and our common identity rooted in rhetoric and rhetorical history that have formed and strengthened the discipline of rhetoric/composition. What may separate us and jeopardize historical works on rhetoric is rejecting unconventional research practices due to the affiliation with predominant, mainstream theoretical frameworks and methodologies. If progressive scholars can carefully acknowledge and come to understand the purposes and meanings of feminist methodology necessitated by the complexities of women's rhetorics and histories, then a fair and accurate assessment of historical studies of rhetorical women can be made.

Notes

1 I am heavily indebted to Professor C. Jan Swearingen for her careful reading of the draft and insightful comments. Special thanks go to Professor Xiaoming Li and Professor Stephanie Vanderslice for their critiques.
2 For a detailed analysis of the debate, see Patricia Bizzell.
3 I constantly struggle with a question that may be too simple to other scholars: what kind of specialists would be appropriate reviewers for my projects? For instance, my current project on post-Mao (since 1976) Chinese women documents only nonfiction prose most properly categorized as public discourse from a rhetorical point of view. But reviewers from Asian studies have misunderstood it as a documentation of literature. I am fortunate to have received much support from the community of women scholars in rhetoric, but these scholars are often excluded as "non-specialists," whose primary research specialties are considered different from mine. In effect, I have struggled alone to try to make China studies specialists understand the methodology of rhetorical historiography.
4 See Christine Mason Sutherland for the historical positioning of Margaret Cavendish's *Orations of Divers Sorts Accommodated to Divers Places*.
5 To a large degree, it is conveniently forgotten that "as a theoretical position about the self, language, knowledge, truth, and power, postmodernism has been developed in the United States" (Tanesini 238) and that "as a discursive practice it is dominated primarily by the voices of white male intellectuals and/or academic elites who speak to and about one another with coded familiarity" (hooks, *Yearning*, 24). The geographic origin and cultural exclusiveness tell much about limitations postmodernism may impose upon historical studies of women across cultural, racial, and ethnic boundaries. I am also aware that postmodernist positions are incompatible in many ways, but my discussion is based on the general features.
6 In this discussion, I am following the common recognition of Rorty as a postmodernist as in Gale (and presumably others), though he is not fond of the term "postmodernism" (Rorty, note 18, 210).
7 The critiques and defenses of Joan W. Scott's application of poststructuralism as a philosophy in feminist historiography can be found in Kathleen Canning (417–432), Judith Evans (128–132), Martin Bunzl, Judith P. Zinsser, and others.

8   There were only two women out of forty-some departmental heads in that university. Both of us held the position of "Associate Chair" in our respective departments. At least at the time during my service (1987–1993), women faculty seemed to be qualified only for an "associate" or a "vice" position.
9   A reviewer of my grant proposal made this accusation.
10 For what happened to Jevons, see R. Enos, 15–16.
11 Chinese female writer Zhang Kangkang urges women to improve themselves intellectually and morally to confront male supremacy.
12 Black and post-Mao Chinese women's histories both challenge the mainstream feminist assumption that patriarchy is the social and political institution oppressing women. To post-Mao women, patriarchy and institution, though intertwined, must be coped with separately. The institution stands largely for the Maoist sociopolitical system (1949–1976) oppressive of both genders, while patriarchy refers to traditional gender hierarchy since Confucius (551–479 B.C.E.), which the Chinese government under and after Mao has supposedly subverted. Therefore, women's oppressions under Mao reinforced by traditional gender ideology demand a careful delineation of analytical categories (see the discussions in the previous section of this essay). The ongoing controversies about Chinese women's social standing within different historical eras actually demonstrate the concerns of how the categories of patriarchy and institution are used. See, for example, William Jankowiak's "Chinese Women, Gender, and Sexuality" and Jude Howell et al.'s "Responses." *Bulletin of Concerned Asian Scholars* 31.1 (1999): 31–58.

Works Cited

Alcoff, Linda. "Cultural Feminism versus Post-Structuralism: The Identity Crisis in Feminist Theory." *Signs* 13 (1988): 405–436.

Arndt, Susan. "African Gender Trouble and African Womanism: An Interview with Chikwenye Ogunyemi and Wanjira Muthoni." *Signs* 25 (2000): 709–726.

bell, hooks. *Ain't I a Woman?: Black Women and Feminism.* Boston: South End, 1981.

—. *Yearning: Race, Gender, and Cultural Politics.* Boston: South End, 1990.

Bizzell, Patricia. "Feminist Methods of Research in the History of Rhetoric: What Difference Do They Make?" *Rhetoric Society Quarterly* 30 (Fall 2000): 5–17.

Bock, Gisela. "Challenging Dichotomies: Perspectives on Women's History." *Writing Women's History: International Perspectives.* Eds. Karen Offen, Ruth Roach Pierson, and Jane Rendall. Bloomington: Indiana University Press, 1991. 1–24.

Bunzl, Martin. *Real History: Reflections on Historical Practice.* New York: Routledge, 1998.

Campbell, Karlyn. *Man Cannot Speak for Her: A Critical Study of Early Feminist Rhetoric.* Vol. 1. Westport, CT: Praeger, 1989.

—. Ed. *Man Cannot Speak for Her: Key Texts of the Early Feminists.* Vol. 2. New York: Greenwood, 1989.

Canning, Kathleen. "Feminist History after the Linguistic Turn: Historicizing Discourse and Experience." *History and Theory: Feminist Research, Debates, and Contestations.* Eds. Barbara Laslett, et al. Chicago: University of Chicago Press, 1997. 416–452.

Cavendish, Margaret. *Orations of Divers Sorts Accommodated to Divers Places: Written by the Thrice Noble, Illustrious and Excellent Princess, the Lady of Marchioness of Newcastle.* London: Anno Dom, 1662.

Chow, Ray. *Writing Diaspora: Tactics of Intervention in the Contemporary Cultural Studies.* Bloomington: Indiana University Press, 1993.

de Certeau, Michel. *Heterologies: Discourse on the Other.* Trans. Brian Massumi. Minneapolis: University of Minneapolis, 1986.

de Oliveira, Rosiska Darcy. *In Praise of Difference: The Emergence of a Global Feminism*. Trans. Peggy Sharpe. Rutgers University Press, 1999.

Elton, G.R. *The Practice of History*. New York: Thomas Y. Crowell, 1967.

Enos, Richard. "Recovering the Lost Art of Researching the History of Rhetoric." *Rhetoric Society Quarterly* 29 (Fall 1999): 7–20.

Evans, Judith. *Feminist Theory Today*. London: Sage, 1995.

Ferreira-Buckley, Linda. "Rescuing the Archives from Foucault." *College English* 61 (May 1999): 577–583.

Gale, Xin Liu. "Historical Studies and Postmodernism: Re-reading Aspasia of Miletus." *College English* 62 (January 2000): 361–386.

—. "Xin Liu Gale Responds." *College English* 63 (September 2000): 105–107.

Glenn, Cheryl. *Rhetoric Retold: Regendering the Tradition from Antiquity through the Renaissance*. Carbondale: Southern Illinois University Press, 1997.

—. "Comment: Truth, Lies, and Method: Revisiting Feminist Historiography." *College English* 62 (January 2000): 387–389.

Harding, Sandra, ed. *Feminism and Methodology*. Bloomington: Indiana University Press, 1987.

Hartsock, Nancy C. "The Feminist Standpoint: Developing the Ground for a Specifically Feminist Historical Materialism." *Feminism and Methodology*. Ed. Sandra Harding. Bloomington: Indiana University Press, 1987.

Jarratt, Susan C. *Rereading the Sophists: Classical Rhetoric Refigured*. Carbondale: Southern Illinois University Press, 1991.

—. "Comment: Rhetoric and Feminism: Together Again." *College English* 62 (January 2000): 390–393.

Kelly-Gadol, Joan. "The Social Relation of the Sexes: Methodological Implications of Women's History." *Feminism and Methodology*. Ed. Sandra Harding. Bloomington: Indiana University Press, 1987. 15–28.

Lee, Wen Shu. "In the Name of Chinese Women." *Quarterly Journal of Speech* 84 (1998): 283–302.

Logan, Shirley W. Ed. *With Pen and Voice: A Critical Anthology of Nineteenth-Century African-American Women*. Carbondale: Southern Illinois University Press. 1995.

—. *We Are Coming: The Persuasive Discourse of Nineteenth-Century Black Women*. Carbondale: Southern Illinois University Press, 1999.

Lunsford, Andrea, ed. *Reclaiming Rhetorica: Women in the Rhetorical Tradition*. Pittsburgh: University of Pittsburgh Press, 1995.

Miller, Thomas, and Melody Bowdon. "A Rhetorical Stance on the Archives of Civic Action." *College English* 61 (May 1999): 591–98.

Mohanty, Chandra Talpade, Ann Russo, and Lourdes Torres, eds. *Third World Women and the Politics of Feminism*. Bloomington: Indiana University Press, 1991.

Offen, Karen, Ruth Roach Pierson, and Jane Rendall, eds. *Writing Women's History: International Perspectives*. Bloomington: Indiana University Press, 1991.

Ratcliffe, Krista. *Anglo-American Feminist Challenges to the Rhetorical Tradition: Virginia Woolf, Mary Daly, Adrienne Rich*. Carbondale: Southern Illinois University Press, 1995.

Roen, Duane, H. Stuart C. Brown, and Theresa Enos, eds. *Living Rhetoric and Composition: Stories of the Discipline*. Mahwah, NJ: Lawrence Erlbaum, 1999.

Rorty, Richard. "Feminism and Pragmatism." *Truth and Progress*. New York: Cambridge University Press, 1998. 202–227.

Royster, Jacqueline Jones. *Traces of a Stream: Literacy and Social Change among African American Women*. Pittsburgh: University of Pittsburgh Press, 2000.

Ryan, Kathleen, and Elizabeth J. Natalle. "Fusing Horizons: Standpoint Hermeneutics and Invitational Rhetoric." *Rhetoric Society Quarterly* 31 (Spring 2001): 69–90.

Scott, Joan. "Women's History." *New Perspectives on Historical Writing*. Ed. Peter Burke. University Park: Pennsylvania State University Press, 1991. 42–66.

Scott, Joan, Cora Kaplan, and Debra Keates, eds. *Transitions, Environments, Translations: Feminists in International Politics*. New York: Routledge, 1997.

Sutherland, Christine M. "Aspiring to the Rhetorical Tradition: A Study of Margaret Cavendish." *Listening to Their Voices: The Rhetorical Activities of Historical Women*. Ed. Molly Meijer Wertheimer. Columbia: University of South Carolina Press. 1997. 255–271.

Swearingen, C. Jan. "A Lover's Discourse: Diotima, Logos, and Desire." *Reclaiming Rhetorica*. Ed. Andrea Lunsford. Pittsburgh: University of Pittsburgh Press, 1995. 25–51.

Tanesini, Alessandra. *An Introduction to Feminist Epistemologies*. Malden, Mass: Blackwell, 1999.

Thurner, Manuela. "Subject to Change: Theories and Paradigms of U.S. Feminist History." *Journal of Women's History* 9 (Summer 1997): 122–146.

Wertheimer, Molly Meijer, ed. *Listening to Their Voices: The Rhetorical Activities of Historical Women*. Columbia: University of South Carolina Press, 1997.

Wu, Hui. "A Comment on 'Historical Studies and Postmodernism: Rereading Aspasia of Miletus'." *College English* 63 (September 2000): 102–105.

Zhang, Kangkang. *ni dui ming yun shuo "bu"* (*Say "No" to Your Fate*). Shanghai: Shanghai Knowledge Press, 1994.

Zinsser, Judith, P. "Much More is at Stake Here: A Response to 'The Construction of History'." *Journal of Women's History* 9.3 (1997): 132–139.

9.
THE WPA AS RESEARCHER AND ARCHIVIST
Shirley K. Rose and Irwin Weiser

When writing program administrators (WPAs) describe their work, what do they say it entails? Certainly, most WPAs would include curriculum development, staffing and staff development, and assessment. Many would include budgeting, establishing interdisciplinary relationships, and representing the writing program on various committees. All would mention the day-to-day troubleshooting and problem solving that makes it often impossible to anticipate what one will accomplish at the office on a particular day. But too often programmatic research and the development of program archives are not activities that WPAs consider as integral to their positions. We believe that WPAs who do not include these activities as conscious parts of their jobs are underestimating the value of their work and perhaps making that work harder and less satisfying than it might otherwise be.

We understand why some WPAs may not think of program research and the development of program archives as essential. After all, writing program administration is very much a job based on dealing with the immediate: the immediate need to hire someone to teach, the immediate need to complete a required report or a budget request, the immediate need to address a student complaint or an instructor's problem. Research, on the other hand, is often thought to be a contemplative activity, demanding, above all, large chunks of time that WPAs typically can't find. And research is not typically as schedule-bound as other work WPAs do. If a report isn't submitted on time, problems may arise. If, on the other hand, the WPA lets work on an article about her program sit ignored for two months, the consequences are less immediately apparent. Similarly, archiving does not impose its own schedule; instead, archiving requires a long view, one that anticipates the future of the writing program—and the program's future administrators.

In this chapter we will argue that writing program research *and writing program records management are essential and interdependent responsibilities* of every WPA. WPAs may feel that they don't have the time to do either or that neither is appropriate to their administrative roles. Systematic research may seem impossible for a WPA immersed in the daily flow of program administration. Managing program records

---

Rose, Shirley K., and Irwin Weiser. "The WPA as Researcher and Archivist." *The Writing Program Administrator's Resource: A Guide to Reflective Institutional Practice*. Eds. Stuart C. Brown, Theresa Enos, and Catherine Chaput. Lawrence Erlbaum, 2002. 275–290. Print.

may be seen as a clerical task, and a program archive may seem like a luxury appropriate only to programs with excess staff and space. Yet we believe that the WPA who develops a strategy for establishing program archives and for thinking about those archives as the sources of data for research makes significant contributions to her ability to administer her program effectively, adds to the field's knowledge of administrative practices, and establishes a rich source of data for future research. Equally important, the research conducted by and the archives established by WPAs document their work in ways that transcend their programs or their discipline. Such documentation is often valuable in presenting the accomplishments and needs of the writing program to administrators who are unlikely to have detailed knowledge of it, but who may have a great deal to say about its funding, growth, and status.

The Researcher/Archivist Mind-Set

WPAs who assume the researcher/archivist mind-set do so in addition to their other ways of thinking about themselves and their work. They must think of themselves not only as administrators, curriculum designers, and preparers of teachers of writing but also as researchers and archivists. To assume the researcher/archivist mind-set, WPAs must consciously conceive of their administrative work and their programs as generative of data. Such a mind-set requires a different orientation to the work of program administration. WPAs define their work relationally whereas conventional conceptions of "researcher" and "archivist" construct these professionals as relatively autonomous and independent. WPAs who develop a researcher/archivist frame of mind have, for example, a different orientation to time. We must step out of the immediacy of the daily administrative flow, where the time we devote to an issue is often dictated by the situation and, for the purposes of research and archival work, take a longer view. Researchers and archivists plan their work and impose their schedules; they exercise control over the time they spend on such activities.

Not only does the research/archivist mind-set require a different orientation to time, it also has a different orientation to information. WPAs who include research and archiving in their conception of their work think about the information they generate or that crosses their desks not simply in terms of its immediate purpose, but also as data to be systematically collected, reviewed, and interpreted. Further, the researcher/archivist mind-set allows WPAs to pose and define problems and questions for themselves in addition to solving problems identified or created by others. It relies on abstract, studied, contemplative, even meditative thinking rather than the adept, expeditious, multitasking that is also required to administer a writing program successfully.

The researcher/archivist mind-set is thus purposeful, requiring planning. It requires the WPA to look into the future and speculate about what information will be needed and how it might be used before making decisions about what documents or data need to be generated, collected, or retained. Writing program records do not become an archive or data simply because they are old or they have not been discarded. Records become an archive and thus a potential resource for research when intellectual control has been exercised over them; that is, they must be organized and accessible to use. Thus, archiving, like research, is a deliberate activity, one requiring the exercise of agency.

Why WPAs Should Be Researchers[1]

In the past several years, composition studies has begun to give increasing attention to acknowledging, describing, and valuing/evaluating the intellectual work of writing program administration, recognizing that WPAs play a critical role in the development as well as application of knowledge in the field. This attention is reflected in the reception the profession has given the Council of Writing Program Administrators' document describing the intellectual work of program administration. Yet, WPAs' work as researchers is not well understood outside the profession or by new WPAs, and even experienced WPAs need to learn additional ways to identify the opportunities for doing significant intellectual work in the context of their programs.

Several shared features and qualities characterize WPA research. First, the *purpose* of WPAs' research is to understand program practices in order to improve or retain them. Thus, the *site of this inquiry* is those writing program practices—curriculum development, faculty development, and program evaluation. The *participant-subjects* in the research projects at these sites are the program stakeholders—instructional staff, writing students, other faculty and administrators, as well as the WPA himself or herself. Because these program practices, sites, and stakeholders are diverse, *the inquiry is multimethodological*, drawing on historical/archival, theoretical, empirical, and hermeneutic inquiry processes.

These features suggest that WPA research is guided by the following values: It is motivated by a desire to improve writing program practices; it is responsible to the field of writing program administration by answering or contributing to answers for shared questions; and it is ethical in its involvement of participants. Thus good research in writing program administration has the following qualities:

- It is informed by current theory and previous research in composition and rhetoric, literacy studies, education, and other related and contributing fields and in turn has a potential to inform future theorizing and research in these fields.
- It invokes, corresponds to, and acknowledges values shared by the professional community of WPAs at the same time it shapes, constructs, or calls into question these values.
- It is worthwhile and ethical.
- It is rigorous and systematic and does not squander human or material resources of time, energy, and money.
- It responds to or answers the questions that prompted it or generates new, better questions.
- It can withstand review by peers (even if not subjected to their review).
- It is documented in program records.
- It is circulated at the institutional site through documents and presentations to administrators and teachers and through application of its conclusions in

program practices, and it may be circulated beyond the immediate institutional context through electronic or print publication to WPAs and other composition studies researchers in other contexts.
- Its conclusions enable WPAs to justify strategic plans to implement program change where appropriate or to justify decisions to preserve program practices where appropriate.

These nine features together suggest an overarching criterion for WPA research: It must require and develop the WPA's agency by deploying his or her expertise and energies in responsive and responsible ways and by satisfying his or her need to gain understanding and insight into the culture and practices of the writing program and the broader institutional context.

As we hope is clear, the ways in which WPAs conduct research and the kinds of expertise their research requires are not categorically different from other research in rhetoric and writing studies. WPA research differs because of the institutional role of the WPA. Because the WPA is held responsible for the writing program, research on that program is in the WPA's own interest.

Thus, the WPA cannot pose as a seeker of knowledge for its own sake but must acknowledge that the outcome of her inquiry may have an immediate, obvious impact on many teachers and students. Her interested-ness does not, however, diminish the WPA's desire to understand, her intellectual engagement with the issues her research projects address, or her obligation and commitment to conduct principled inquiry and circulate its conclusions.

These characteristics, features, and criteria suggest the following definition of WPAs' research: *Research in writing program administration is theoretically-informed, systematic, principled inquiry for the purpose of developing, sustaining, and leading a sound, yet dynamic, writing program.*[2]

Why WPAs Should Be Archivists

The research that WPAs conduct generally depends on the collection, organization, and interpretation of documents found in program records, and those records, when managed and maintained deliberately, constitute the program archive. Thus program research and program archiving are interdependent activities with the former ensuring the generation of records that will constitute a useable archive of documents and the latter ensuring that the product of the research will not be lost. As Duane Roen has pointed out and as all WPAs know, WPAs and writing programs generate and receive enormous volumes of documents—program descriptions, syllabi, instructors' applications and files, course evaluations, reports, and a myriad of correspondence, memos, and so forth. Though it may be tempting, particularly in the age of electronic communication, to simply save everything, such unreflective saving cannot provide a *useful* archive.[3] Establishing an archive is not merely an act of accumulating and filing documents; they must also be evaluated. Determining the value of program records requires informed and careful analysis, for archivists must be able to evaluate the significance of the records' source, their informational content, uniqueness, usability, and relationship to other records (Schellenberg, "Appraisal" 61). Thus, making judgments about the archival significance of writing program records draws on WPAs' professional expertise. Even if the WPA is not directly managing the archive, she must be involved in developing the documentation strategy on which it is based.

Evaluating the archival significance of writing program records requires an understanding of rhetorical principles and writing theory, an understanding of administrative practices and principles gained through experience as WPAs, and an understanding of the research interests of the field of composition studies in general. This expertise is necessary to determine both the primary values of archives (the values for the originating agency, for administrative, fiscal, legal, and operating purposes) and the secondary values of archival materials, including evidential value (evidence of the organization and functioning of the agency that produced the records) and informational value (their value for information on persons, places, subjects, and things other than the organization that created them).[4]

Elliott lists several "understandings" necessary to archivists that are shared by writing theorists and researchers: understanding of document–event relations (360), understanding that a document can have different functions at different times for different audiences (362), and understanding that the form of a text is determined by the conversant's need to express something *within a particular situation* (363). WPAs' immersion in writing theory disposes them to agree that, as Samuels explains, "the integrated nature of society's institutions and its recorded documentation must be reflected in archivists' efforts to document those institutions" (112). WPAs need to work with professional archivists in their institutions in order to coordinate efforts and benefit from their expertise in such areas as archival principles and standard practices. Professional archivists can advise us on when and how to apply traditional archival principles and concepts such as original order, provenance, the life cycle of a document, and authority control. Professional archivists also can help us understand and apply relevant information systems theory and assist us in applying organization theory to development of our records management and archival practices for our writing programs.

But we can't depend on already overburdened and underfunded professional archivists at our institutions. Even in the most ideal of circumstances for qualified staffing and funding of program archives, WPAs need to participate actively in critical decision making about developing and maintaining their programs' archives. The extent to which we are involved in creating, developing, and maintaining our own archives determines the degree of intellectual control (as well as physical control) we will have over the record of our work. As archivists for our own programs, our knowledge of what records are in our collection, where they came from, and how they relate to one another gives us intellectual control of our program archives. Our knowledge of the location of materials and of how they can be retrieved gives us physical control. Given our intimate knowledge of our writing programs, we are optimally situated to meet the three primary objectives of archival programs identified by Kesner: identifying and selecting or collecting records for preservation, arranging and preserving these records, and ensuring the records' accessibility by providing finding aids and reference services (101).

As O'Toole has suggested, anyone who works as an archivist must understand the reasons for recording information in the first place, the reasons for saving information for long periods, the technology that supports records creation, and the characteristics and uses of recorded information (10). Given our overview of most of the activities of our programs, WPAs are well situated to become archivists for the writing programs. As the original creators of many of our programs' records, we know why and how they were developed, why they took the form they did, and what their continuing significance is likely to be. As creators and users of our programs' records, we can make informed judgments about the strengths, weaknesses, and potential future uses of records and analyze their long-term value (Schellenberg, "Appraisal" 59). In these ways, the work of establishing and maintaining a writing program archive is an intellectual task that draws on a WPA's professional experience and engagement in disciplinary practices.

Documentation Strategies For Developing Archives

The term *documentation strategy* refers to a proactive approach to records management and creating an archive, one that is particularly appropriate for writing programs. Originally developed by Helen Willa Samuels, a theorist of archive practices, a documentation strategy is a plan for establishing a usable archive of an aspect of society or culture that is of significance and interest. In the specific case of a writing program, a documentation strategy is a plan for archiving the program's practices: its development, its procedures, and its participants. The strategy is designed, promoted, and implemented by the mutual efforts of document creators, record managers, archivists, users, other experts, and beneficiaries and other interested parties. It is regularly refined or revised in response to changing conditions. Following are specific characteristics of a documentation strategy:

1. **How is a documentation strategy different from a conventional archival program?** Documentation strategies depend on cooperation between records creators and records managers in a variety of institutional positions; a conventional archival program, focusing on the activities of a single institution or unit, operates more independently and autonomously. Documentation strategies focus on *interactions* among individuals and organizations; collections typically focus on actions of central figures of importance whose papers have been preserved. A conventional archival program *collects*; implementers of a documentation strategy do not necessarily collect—that is, assume physical custody—of all records, but *take steps to ensure retention of records* in various institutions and departments. A traditional archival program only collects records already generated and saved; a documentation strategy plans for creation and retention of some records that might not otherwise have existed.
2. **How are documentation strategies developed?** The first step in developing a documentation strategy for a writing program is to *draft a statement of the strategy*—that is, to create a document. To do this, participants, including representatives from as many of the program's constituents or stakeholders as

possible, draw on a variety of information. They develop a profile of the way in which records are created, used, and administered by the groups and individuals participating in the program or project being documented; they develop data on records already included in the program's active records and archive; and they develop data on the use of archival and related documentation by persons other than the records creators.

This information is analyzed in order to address the following questions: What kinds of records are archival quality because they are vital to the future needs of the creators? What kinds of records are archival because they are important to the interests of others? What types of archival records lend themselves to sampling, through the selection either of certain records or of certain records creators, and what selection approaches seem most feasible, effective, and efficient? Who are the key groups and individuals who can most persuasively convince records creators, administrators, archival repositories, and others to consider the recommendations of the documentation strategy statement? How can these groups and individuals be persuaded to assist in implementing the strategy? What information is needed to improve future analysis of documentation conditions and needs and how might this be obtained? What needs of records creators and others presently are not being met because certain types of records are not being created at all? How might records creators be persuaded to create such records?

To *implement the documentation strategy,* records creators and records managers take measures to ensure that the appropriate documents are generated, circulated to the appropriate audience, and retained in an efficient filing system. Records creators take measures to adequately format and identify the records they generate.

The focus of *the documentation strategy is regularly reviewed and reconsidered* to determine whether its scope is clear and appropriate, and what revisions might be needed.

3. **Why are documentation strategies needed for writing programs?** As must be clear from the outline of the steps involved in a documentation strategy, developing, implementing, and reviewing a writing program's documentation strategy is a complex intellectual task that requires (a) an intimate knowledge of a writing program's practices and those of the larger institution in which it is located, (b) a sophisticated theoretical understanding of written discourse, and (c) considerable rhetorical skill, in addition to a significant amount of time and energy—and it uses a lot of paper and space.

Documentation Strategies and WPA Research

Writing program research and writing program documentation strategies can be strategically integrated. A well-designed and maintained documentation strategy for a specific element or activity of a writing program can develop a data bank for research projects related to that aspect of the program. For example, at Purdue we have developed a documentation strategy for a revision of the first-year composition curriculum, and we are developing a documentation strategy for our nationally recognized teaching assistant mentoring program. A more general documentation strategy for a writing program can ensure that basic program data such as enrollment and staffing profiles and program policies and procedures are available in anticipation of a variety of possible future uses of the information. The individual WPA can use the data to make strategic decisions for program development. The data can also be useful beyond the program for what it can contribute to research that develops our collective understanding of writing program administration. The data also have traditional historical research value for their potential contribution to the construction of narratives of writing program development, evolution of administrative practices, and the development of composition studies more generally.

In each of these integrations of documentation strategies and research, the WPA-archivist anticipates the interpretive work the WPA-researcher will do in the future. Recognizing that program records are not transparent, but rather wholly rhetorical representations of information, the WPA-archivist acknowledges and speculates about their potential strategic use. The WPA-archivist also recognizes that her or his choices about what records to generate will determine which aspects of the writing program are made visible and which are erased over time, what is remembered and what is forgotten. In addition, the archives a WPA establishes provide the opportunity for program continuity because they establish a history for subsequent WPAs to refer to. In this way the WPA-archivist makes decisions about what can be known to researchers.

Guidelines for Integrating Documentation Strategies and Program Research

The integration of documentation strategies and program research requires that the WPA think of archival development as a multiple-step process:

1. First the WPA needs to develop a general documentation strategy for the writing program that will ensure the development and maintenance of basic, general information about the status of program activities and practices. This "information" is not, of course, transparent; the documents that comprise it are, as we have indicated earlier, collected based on principles developed by the WPA and other stakeholders in the writing program and serve as the source of specific data about the program for research—principles that are ideologically, culturally, and politically determined.
2. Reviewing and interpreting this general information will enable the WPA to identify specific areas of the program that may require systematic research—either to determine whether a problem exists or to explore possible solutions to an acknowledged problem or aspect of the program in need of change. Thus this information can generate research questions or enable the WPA to refine research questions that may initially be quite broad. For each specific research project, the WPA develops an appropriate documentation strategy to collect relevant data. For these documentation strategies, choices made about types of

documents to generate and collect are critical because they will determine the outcome of the research project.
3. If the outcome of such a research project leads the WPA to undertake a change in program practices, a strategy for documenting that change should be developed as well in order to provide a record of the processes and decisions underlying the change. The specific focus of this documentation strategy will be determined in part by the WPA's particular interests and expertise, and it may evolve as the WPA reviews and reflects on the information gathered. In developing this documentation strategy, the WPA anticipates possible future research projects that will draw on the information. These documentation strategies may not immediately or directly affect the writing program's daily practices; that is, they yield archives that are records of a particular development in the program that may become research sources for the longer term.

Once the research questions are articulated, the WPA can determine what records/data are needed to adequately document the program area's activities and practices in order to answer them. At this stage of research, then, WPAs need to answer the following three questions:

1. What records are already routinely generated?
2. Which of these records need to be preserved?
3. What additional records need to be created?

Archival records may thus play a recursive role in WPA research: An examination of records may yield research questions, and the records may also provide partial answers to those questions.

At the outset, and throughout the implementation of the documentation strategy, it is important to establish consistent practices for identifying, collecting, and organizing the records/data. The following guidelines should be observed:

1. Establish consistent formats for created documents (indicating names of originators, dates, titles, page numbers, etc.).
2. Add the aforementioned information on documents generated by others if it does not appear.
3. Establish one collection point for records, to avoid duplication or efforts.
4. Determine a system for filing/organizing records, and follow it consistently.
5. Document all of the above decisions and provide a rationale for them.

Throughout the implementation of the documentation strategy, it is necessary to analyze and interpret the records and data generated and collected in order to determine whether and how well they address the research questions. A documentation strategy is not static. Though it is important to plan for the collection of documents as carefully as possible prior to beginning research, to anticipate as much as possible what kinds of documents will need to be collected, created, or located, it is also important to realize that during the course of research, it may be necessary to revise the documentation strategy to include additional kinds of records.

Conclusion

These guidelines for integrating writing program research and documentation strategies may seem obvious; but what is not self-evident is that WPAs need to adopt the researcher/archivist mind-set so they consciously view the documents they generate and review as data for program research. As we indicated earlier, it is easy for busy WPAs to focus on the immediate demands of their work. But in doing so, they may limit themselves to the managerial aspects of program administration. We want to urge WPAs to take as comprehensive a view of program administration as possible, to see their administrative work as consistent with and contributing to their work as researchers and scholars. And we believe that thinking of themselves as archivists and researchers who produce work that merits documentation, preservation and subsequent investigation enables them to do so.

Notes

1 This section is based on the introductory chapter of our collection *The Writing Program Administrator as Researcher*.
2 This is an elaboration of Christine Hult's definition in "The Scholarship of Administration."
3 And we caution against relying on digitally stored documents because the long-term stability of disks and other media is questionable, and the format of data storage media change rapidly: How many of us can read documents stored on 5¼" floppy disks or created on computers using CPM as their operating system?
4 These definitions of *primary, secondary, evidential,* and *informational values* for archives have been taken from Schellenberg (*Management*).

Works Cited

Council of Writing Program Administrators. "Evaluating the Intellectual Work of Writing Program Administration." *WPA: Writing Program Administration* 22.1/2 (1998): 85–104.

Elliott, Clark, "Communications and Events in History: Toward a Theory for Documenting the Past." *American Archivist* 48 (1985): 357–68.

Hult, Christine. "The Scholarship of Administration." *Resituating Writing: Constructing and Administering Writing Programs*. Ed. Joseph Janangelo and Kristine Hansen. Portsmouth, NH: Boynton/Cook, 1995. 119–31.

Kesner, Richard M. "Archival Collection Development: Building a Successful Acquisitions Program." *Midwestern Archivist* 5.2 (1981): 101–12.

O'Toole, James M. *Understanding Archives and Manuscripts*. Archival Fundamentals Series. Chicago: Society of American Archivists, 1990.

Roen, Duane H. "Writing Administration as Scholarship and Teaching." *Scholarship, Promotion, and Tenure in Composition Studies*. Ed. Richard C. Gebhardt and Barbara Gebhardt, Mahwah, NJ: Erlbaum, 1996. 43–55.

Rose, Shirley K, and Irwin Weiser. "Introduction." *The Writing Program Administrator as Researcher: Inquiry in Action and Reflection*. Portsmouth, NH: Heinemann-Boynton/Cook, 1999. v–xi.

Samuels, Helen W. "Who Controls the Past?" *American Archivist* 49 (1986): 109–24.
Schellenberg, T. R. "The Appraisal of Modern Public Records." National Archive: Bulletin No. 8. Washington, DC: National Archives Records Services, 1956.
——. *The Management of Archives.* New York: Columbia UP, 1965.

10.
OF HISTORICITY, RHETORIC: THE ARCHIVE AS SCENE OF INVENTION
Barbara A. Biesecker

First, an assertion: Whatever else the archive may be—say, an historical space, a political space, or a sacred space; a site of preservation, interpretation, or commemoration—it always already is the provisionally settled scene of our collective invention, of our collective invention of us and of it. To assert this much is, of course, to refuse absolutely the substantial constitution of any "us" or "we" as well as the evidentiary status of any archive, its inherent (by virtue of its "realness") capacity to guarantee in advance or serve as ultimate arbiter of identity, history, practice, criticism, and theory. To assert this much is also to open the way toward writing a different kind of rhetorical history that will not be governed by the notion of referential plentitude and the motif of truth. I am quite aware that in claiming that the archive may best be understood as the scene of a doubled invention rather than as the site of a singular discovery, I am challenging a whole set of presumptions that underwrite the lion's share of critical *and* theoretical work in the field at the present time. I am also quite aware that it is a good deal more likely that historians of rhetoric will take strong exception to my insisting on the *historicity* of the archive (its merely appearing to be present in an ontic sense, as material proof of the past) than my insisting upon the *historicity* of "us" (subjectivity as process rather than subjectivity as presence). Of course the reasons why this is so are multiple, and although a nuanced accounting of them no doubt would deepen our appreciation of the stakes and entailments of our recent return—nearly *en masse*—to archives of all kinds, for the purposes of this short essay suffice it to note only two. The first reason is the transformation into common sense of the deconstruction of the subject and, more specifically, of all the familiar concepts on which any sense of stable subjects depends: amongst others, origins, autogenesis, presence or consciousness as the self's being present to itself, and the immediacy of sensation and experience. The second reason, which is actually closely related to the first, is the widespread sense among academics that History—a certain idea of history, the Idea of history or history as the unfolding of the Idea—has come to an end.[1] History as a metaphysically animated and unilinear narrative of progress and overcoming is, well, history, and "this also consequently means," as Jean-Luc Nancy passionately put it, "that history can no longer be presented as—to use Lyotard's term—a 'grand narrative,' the narrative of some grand, collective destiny of mankind (of Humanity, of Liberty, etc.), a narrative that was grand because it was great, and that was great, because its ultimate destination was considered good."[2] Indeed, with the awareness of the resolutely discursive character of ourselves and the radically precarious character of history came the frenzied production of micrological analyses of the past that, at their best, ostensibly delivered a minimally mediated account of a "moment" whose value was understood to be predicated on the presumed stability, materiality, or "givenness" of the archival object and on the researcher's ability to allow it to speak on its own behalf.

To be sure, I am not alone in worrying our investment in, unbridled enthusiasm for, indeed under-interrogated relationship to the archive. Back in 1985 historiographer Dominick LaCapra admonished against the new archivism's tendency toward the misrecognition of words as things:

> The archive as fetish is a literal substitute for the "reality" of the past which is "always already" lost for the historian. When it is fetishized, the archive is more than the repository of traces of the past which may be used in its inferential reconstruction. It is a stand-in for the past that brings the mystified experience of the thing itself—an experience that is always open to question when one deals with writing or other inscriptions.[3]

Nearly 20 years later, in a special 2003 issue of *Poetics Today* in which theorists and critics who routinely work in archives meditate on the conceptual as well as physical transformations of the archive from antiquity to postmodernity, Renaissance scholar James A. Knapp looks again with suspicion on the revival of archival, material, or ocular proof in cultural history. More specifically, he questions its practitioners' tendency to bracket suddenly and altogether the problem of mediation, to "retreat into the safety of what Merleau-Ponty termed 'the perceptual faith,' a *belief* in the existence of the material world" and to grant archival discoveries the evidentiary status of fact.[4] As Knapp astutely observes,

> [l]ike Sinfield's tangible *stuff* ("it doesn't get any more material than that"), in the present cultural context it seems that "seeing is believing...." If a return to the things contained in the archive promises relief from the interminable difficulties of interpretive debate, it does so by suggesting that the material artifacts still visible to the historical observer can somehow offer a less-mediated interaction with the past.... Plenty has been said about the dangers of overlooking the role of the observer (the subject) in the formation of the historical account at both the moment of its writing and that of its reception. Similarly, poststructuralist theory has highlighted the radical instability of all objects of study by pointing out the necessity of mediation at every level of understanding. But while the historical contingency of subjecthood and objecthood may be widely acknowledged, the notion that historical study might yield—or at least approximate—a glimpse of the past *as it was* remains oddly compelling.[5]

Oddly compelling, indeed, as what Knapp alludes to here but does not elaborate explicitly on is the suggestion that historical work today follows the formula of festishistic disavowal: "I know very well that the archive is not the space of referential plentitude, but still..."

It is precisely what we, following Slavoj Žižek,[6] would identify as the sublime appeal of the archive that Helen Freshwater addresses in an essay that expresses her considerable unease with the new archivists' "myth of the fixed historical record" and the "beguiling fantasy of self-effacement, which seems to promise the recovery of lost time, the possibility of being reunited with the lost past, and the fulfillment of our deepest desires for wholeness and completion."[7] Drawing upon archaeological theorist Michael Shanks's book-length inquiry into the "antiquarian" absorption in the archival object that has superceded an archaeological investigation of the past, Freshwater reads "the academic fascination with the seemingly recoverable past contained within the archive" as "symptomatic of a more recent societal obsession" with archives of all sorts (from the once forgotten and now fading multigenerational family photo album in the attic to the meticulously managed collections housed in state sponsored and privately funded institutions).[8] Freshwater urges us to resist the dangerous "allure of the archive" by persistently reminding ourselves that the archival object is, as Jacques Derrida explained some time ago, given to us as a trace:

> Here the archive's inherently textual nature must interrupt our blissful encounter with its contents. During our investigation, we cannot avoid experiencing the familiar problem of all [textual] analysis: the indeterminacy of interpretation that haunts every text.... When digging up the details of the past hidden in the archive, we must remember that we are dealing with the dead. As Derrida notes, "the structure of the archive is *spectral*. It is spectral *a priori*: neither present nor absent 'in the flesh,' neither visible nor invisible, a trace always referring to another whose eyes can never be met." Any figures we encounter in the archive are ghosts, mere shadows of the past. Their actions are complete, and their original significance will remain undetermined, open to interpretation.[9]

Neither simply absent nor present, but both. For an elaborate explanation of Freshwater's judicious invocation of the rather recent Derrida of *Archive Fever* who writes of ghosts, I have time only to point the reader in the direction of the much earlier Derrida of *Margins of Philosophy* whose sustained mediation on *différence* would serve as a rigorous explication of why the archive as instituted trace anchors nothing absolutely, and to summarily state that it is in this sense that history is what is *not* in the archive, *not* in any archive, *not* even in all the archives added together.[10] But if history is what can neither be found in nor authenticated absolutely by the archive, where does that leave us? On the way toward (im)posing one answer to this question, I want briefly to revisit the *Enola Gay* controversy, reading in that now infamous "history war" an object lesson in the radical indeterminacy of the archive as the opening onto the vicissitudes of rhetoric, here taken not only or even primarily as the irreducibly tropological nature of all historical work but, rather, in its strict sense as the art of persuasion.

On January 30, 1995, and at the behest of 81 members of Congress, the Air Force Association, and the American Legion, Smithsonian secretary I. Michael Heyman canceled the National Air and Space Museum's planned 50th-anniversary exhibit of the historic flight of the *Enola Gay*. Coupled with the cancellation of "The Last Act: The Atomic Bomb and the End of World War II," conceptualized under Martin Harwit's directorship, was the promise that another exhibit would take its place. In less than six months Heyman's display, titled simply "The *Enola Gay*," opened to the public.

For all their differences there was one point on which both parties to the controversy over how to display the *Enola Gay* in the nation's most frequented museum could agree: namely, that "The *Enola Gay*"'s near-complete absenting of the devastation at ground zero was a difference between the two exhibits that mattered. For Harwit and his team, who understood themselves to be "responsible for portraying [the historic flight of the *Enola Gay*] accurately and truthfully" as well as champions of the exhibit who would enter the fray several years later and speak publicly on its behalf, photographs of the already dead or dying were the key archival evidence on which the balance of the exhibit hinged.[11] Without them, there would be nothing to counter the *Enola Gay's* sublime effects. However, to the opposition the matter looked altogether different. According to veterans, military historians, members of Congress, and journalists who pushed for the cancellation of "The Last Act," the supposed "shock and awe" effect of the sheer presence of Superfortress and, thus, the need to provide "balance" by incorporating photographs of what took place beneath the mushroom cloud was a ruse. First, as Colonel Paul Tibbets emphatically argued, because its size and weight prohibited display of the fully assembled B-29 in the National Air and Space Museum (NASM), the presentation of the forward fuselage—"without wings, engines and propellers, landing gear and tail assembly"—would not pay due homage to the historic aircraft but, instead, enhance "the aura of evil in which [it was] being cast."[12] Second, in light of the literal and figurative mutilation of the plane that Tibbets and other veterans took as a sacrilege of the sacred icon, the incorporation of photographic images taken of ground zero promised to deliver one thing only: a gross distortion of history that would inevitably provoke a crisis of national conscience and, thus, promote anti-American sentiment. Unlike the director and the curators for whom the photographs would *undoubtedly* lend "balance" to the exhibit, those opposing it were deeply troubled by their *irreducibly* obfuscating and ideological effects.[13]

But exactly what made all those involved so certain that the truth of the historical exhibition hinged on the inclusion or exclusion of those photographic images? What guaranteed that those bodies or, more precisely, their material traces were, to turn Judith Butler's phrase, bodies that would always already matter to patrons of the exhibit? Counter-intuitively, perhaps, I want to suggest that they were not. Indeed, I want to call into question the presumption on *both sides* of the debate that the incorporation into the exhibit of these bits of the archive would inevitably prompt patrons to question—rightly or wrongly—the official historical narrative sanctioning the dropping of the bombs.

That archival photographs or footage of the human suffering caused by the dropping of the bombs need not *necessarily* produce a crisis of American collective consciousness and conscience is, in fact, borne out by recent U.S. cultural history itself. On Memorial Day 2002, little more than ten years after the *Enola Gay* controversy began, NBC aired *Price for Peace*. Although the cultural cottage industry about World War II that emerged out of its golden anniversary had attended almost exclusively to the European campaigns, what was most striking about this prime-time two-hour special was not its singular focus on the Pacific theater. Even more remarkable was its unabashed inclusion of the kind of images that had caused so much trouble for Harwitt and his team at NASM a decade before and the kind of images that Heyman's surrogate exhibit avoided altogether. Indeed, *Price for Peace* did not leave the human cost of the blasts at Hiroshima and Nagasaki to the imagination of its viewers but brought it squarely into the living room of thousands of U.S. households. In a full segment of the program (seventh out of eight) on the atomic bomb and "the end of the war," audiences not only saw iconic footage of the mushroom clouds rising over both cities from above (not incidentally, with corresponding text at the bottom of the screen indicating the date of the drop and approximate casualty figures, 140,000 for the former and 74,000 for the latter), they also got a graphic look at what had taken place from below. Following sustained panoramic footage of the leveled landscape come five vivid and lingering close-ups of Japanese civilians maimed by the blast. Moreover, in this segment of the film the representation of the five women and children whose mutilated bodies metonymically stand in for thousands of others is prefaced by the inclusion of yet another civilian, Mr. Sakita, a Japanese eyewitness and survivor of the drop on Nagasaki, who gives voice to human suffering as the mushroom cloud begins to take shape on the screen.

More might be said about Mr. Sakita's return in the final segment of the documentary wherein he speaks passionately about his suffering from radiation poisoning, multiple surgeries, and a compulsion toward suicide that is checked only by a commitment "to abolish nuclear weapons," a "cause" that "gives [him] a reason to live." And more might also be said about the inclusion of competing views—albeit strictly bifurcated along American and Japanese lines—on whether a Japanese surrender would have come sooner or later had the bombs never been dropped or dropped in an unpopulated area so as to issue a warning without killing tens of thousands of Japanese civilians. And even more might be said about how this film, in striking contrast to Harwit's canceled exhibit, not only does not address Japanese aggression and brutality between 1930 and 1945 at length but also only mentions the Bataan death march once, never raised the ire of veterans. Indeed, despite candid admissions by World War II vets who testify over the course of the film that "the only thing that we wanted to see the Japanese was dead," that "It was very easy to shoot a Jap, believe me," that "I don't care if it had been a woman, child, baby, I could shoot," that "we didn't mind shooting them in the back either," *Price for Peace* is never charged with having sought, wittingly or otherwise, to produce anti-American sentiment. By Memorial Day 2002 it appears to be the case that those images of ground zero no longer signify in the same way as they did a decade before. That the visual and verbal representation of the carnage created by the dropping of the bombs will not necessarily cast a dark shadow on the national self-image finds additional support in the recent use to which *Price for Peace* has been put. On the 56th anniversary of the Normandy invasion (June 6, 2000), the 70,500-square-foot D-Day Museum opened its doors to the public. Founded by Stephen Ambrose in 1991 and located in New Orleans in honor of Andrew Higgins, the museum's exhibit space is organized into two main installations. Not coincidentally, *Price for Peace* is shown at regular intervals each day and serves as the preface to patrons' self-guided tour through the exhibit on the war in the Pacific.

Now the point of tracking this intertextual chain is not only to document the extent to which things changed between July 23, 1992, when World War II veteran W. Burr Bennett Jr. began his letter-writing campaign on behalf of "the proud display of the *Enola Gay*,"[14] and May 27, 2002, when Tom Brokaw hosted the Memorial Day prime-time network presentation of *Price for Peace*. More important than noticing that the archival "evidence" of Japanese civilian casualties that had aroused partisan passions in the early nineties did not do so a decade later is to understand why. That is to say, the detection of this significant shift need not be taken as the terminal point of an historical inquiry but may instead be read as pointing the way toward the critical analysis of the processes by which that difference has been produced: What happened over the course of a single decade such that the photographs whose "referential plentitude" had provoked a public controversy of near epic proportion (resulting in the unprecedented cancelation of an exhibit, the resignation of the director of the most frequented museum in the country, and U.S. Senate hearings on future management guidelines for the Smithsonian Institution) appear since then to have lost their power of counter-hegemonic address? To what are we to attribute the dramatic alteration of their effects?

Given the limited space allotted to me, answers to these specific questions will have to wait for another day. In the place of a demonstration, then, an assertion, not unlike the one with which I began. As I see it from here, which is to say, from within an intimate relation to one archive, scholars of persuasive speech have not yet begun robustly to engage the entailments of the archive's irreducible undecidability even though we are *uniquely* positioned to do so, given that the deconstruction of "fact" or of referential plentitude does not reduce the contents of the archive to "mere" literature or fiction (this is the most common and silliest of mistakes) but delivers that content over to us as the elements of rhetoric. Indeed, from the *historicity* of the archive, rhetorics; out of the deconstruction of the material presence of the past and, thus, in relation to what the archive cannot *authenticate* absolutely but can (be made to) *authorize* nonetheless, issues an invitation to write rhetorical histories of archives, which is to say, critical histories of the situated and strategic uses to which archives have been put.

Notes

1 This argument is to be distinguished rigorously from Francis Fukuyama's "end of history" thesis in *The End of History and the Last Man* (New York: Free Press, 1992) wherein the author advances the Hegelian thesis that the end of the Cold War marks the closure of history. Readers are encouraged to take a look at Jacques Derrida's critique of Fukuyama's eschatological Christian metaphorics of "good news" in *Specters of Marx: The State of the Debt, the Work of Mourning, and the New International,* trans. Peggy Kamuf (New York: Routledge, 1994), 56–65.
2 Jean-Luc Nancy, "Finite History," in *The States of 'Theory': History, Art, and Critical Discourse,* ed. David Carroll (Stanford, CA: Stanford University Press, 1990), 150.
3 Dominick LaCapra, *History and Criticism* (Ithaca, NY: Cornell University Press, 1985), 92, n. 17.
4 James A. Knapp, "Ocular Proof: Archival Revelations and Aesthetic Response," *Poetics Today* 24 (2003): 696.
5 Knapp, "Ocular Proof," 699–702.
6 See Slavoj Žižek, *The Sublime Object of Ideology* (New York: Verso, 1989), especially pages 55–84.
7 Helen Freshwater, "The Allure of the Archive," *Poetics Today* 24 (2003): 738.

8 Freshwater, "The Allure of the Archive," 731.
9 Freshwater, "The Allure of the Archive," 738.
10 Jacques Derrida, "Différance," in *Margins of Philosophy,* trans. Alan Bass (Chicago: University of Chicago Press, 1982), 1–28.
11 Marlin Harwit, *An Exhibit Denied: Lobbying the History of the* Enola Gay (New York: Copernicus, 1996), 52.
12 Cited in John W. Dower, "Three Narratives of Our Humanity," in *History Wars: The* Enola Gay *and Other Battles for the American Past,* ed. Edward T. Linenthal and Tom Englehardt (New York: Henry Holt and Company, 1996), 89.
13 See, for example, air force historian and Director of the Center for Air Force History Richard Hallion's letter to Harwit in which he writes, "Unit (400) of the exhibit, [dealing with the aftermath of the bombings at Hiroshima and Nagasaki], strikes me as possibly tasteless. I am not opposed to selective photographs that show graphic injury or damage—but the power of a broken person is overwhelming, and may leave visitors with the mistaken impression that nearly all victims of the Pacific were Japanese." Quoted in Harwit, *An Exhibit Denied,* 203.
14 Cited in Harwit, *An Exhibit Denied,* 129.

SECTION 3

DOING ARCHIVAL RESEARCH

11.
"I SEE DEAD PEOPLE": ARCHIVE, CRYPT, AND AN ARGUMENT FOR THE RESEARCHER'S SIXTH SENSE
Elizabeth (Betsy) Birmingham

In M. Night Shyamalan's 1999 movie *The Sixth Sense*, the child-protagonist, Cole Sear, communicates—against his will and with some horror—with spirits of the dead. The movie's plot becomes increasingly complex when the child whispers to his psychologist, Malcolm Crowe, that the spirits "don't know they're dead." They don't haunt us, it seems, out of malevolence; they don't even know they haunt. My experience of research as a lived experience has involved inhabiting the cool archival spaces occupied by spirits, listening to their stories whispered in historical traces, and having them not just tolerate my presence but befriend me and shape my research.

Architect Marion Mahony Griffin (1871–1961) doesn't know that she is dead. And then again, perhaps she is not—she's quite hot right now, though I hardly know what she would think of that. The first monograph devoted solely to her work, *Marion Mahony: Drawing the Form of Nature*, was published in 2005; she had her first solo exhibition (at Northwestern's Block Museum, on the shore of Lake Michigan, near where she grew up in Winnetka, Illinois); and I recently opened the *Chronicle of Higher Education* to see her architectural work splashing the whole of the back page. Since 2005, my own published research is a tiny fraction of the scholarly activity surrounding Mahony Griffin's life and work: the Art Institute of Chicago has gone live with a beautiful Web version of her manuscript "The Magic of America"; a well-known Australian biographer has a book project under contract; and Australian and American scholars have begun the early work on a collaborative project concerning transdisciplinary approaches to understanding the cultural impact of Mahony Griffin's work. She is hot.

It is difficult to say a woman like that is dead, as she helps me shape my tenure case, write this article, teach my graduate research methods class, and secure funding to work with others for whom she is equally alive, in Australia. As scholars who work with historical figures, we always know that we owe those figures some sort of debt, as we mine their lives (and deaths) to build our careers. But sometimes, when we are very lucky, we see dead people—people whose will won't be ignored—the relationship

---

Birmingham, Elizabeth (Betsy). "'I See Dead People': Archive, Crypt, and an Argument for the Researcher's Sixth Sense." *Beyond the Archives: Research as a Lived Process*. Eds. Elizabeth Rohan and Gesa Kirsch. Carbondale: Southern Illinois UP, 2008. 139–146. Print.

becomes reciprocal, and the work we do together leads to friendship and collaboration. That is the story that I have to tell.

I first learned of Marion Mahony Griffin in 1989 through my interest in her husband, Walter Burley Griffin, who was, at that time, the object of my intellectual longing. He was a turn-of-the-century architect possessed of the clean-shaven, Hollywood good looks not common during that mustached, mutton-chopped historical moment. I wrote my undergraduate honors thesis (for my art history degree) on his midwestern architecture, visiting nearly all of the thirty-some buildings still standing that he had designed between 1902 and 1913. My work was the traditional work of an architectural historian: I was studying a body of work, this group of buildings; attempting to determine contemporary addresses for each; using building records, city phone books, and architectural magazines to accurately date the buildings; and upon developing an accurate chronology, making some claims about the aesthetic development of the architect.

Because I was an undergraduate, much of this work really had been done some years before; there existed a solid history of secondary scholarship on the subject of Walter Burley Griffin's architecture extending back to 1964, including several references from the 1950s. Nonetheless, I undertook my charge diligently, revisiting the primary sources: I visited the Cook County records office and the Chicago Historical Society and dug through hundreds of mildewed issues of *Construction News* and *Western Architect* and ancient telephone books. My goal, as I understood it, was to suggest that Griffin's architectural skills developed in a way that made his work diverge from that of his mentor, Frank Lloyd Wright. I compiled note cards, created chronologies, and tried to understand what happened after 1910–11 that so changed his architectural style that he moved from being a follower of Wright to being an innovator in his own right.

I never met Mahony Griffin in these places, nor in the secondary scholarship written about her husband as I absorbed that scholarship unquestioningly. I knew that Walter married, at thirty-four, a woman six years older, who was, as a contemporary wrote, "Frank Lloyd Wright's most talented assistant." I found traces of her, though much of the information in secondary sources was contradictory (or wrong): her name was usually misspelled (Marian, or Mahoney, or both); her dates of birth, death, graduation, and marriage varied by source. Although many sources mention both Griffins and even include Mahony Griffin in their indices, she receives mention only because of her marriage to Walter. She is characterized as a pupil, a wife, and a draftsman—but not as a highly educated and competent architect in her own right. In all the secondary scholarship I read, written from 1947 to 1989, that one piece of information remained consistent. Though she may have designed a few buildings, though she graduated from MIT with a degree in architecture, though she was the first woman in the country licensed to practice architecture, she wasn't really an architect. She was a "draftsman," something lesser and dismissible. And I believed it, dismissing her. Those telling me so were scholars, scholars whose published credibility was intoxicating to me because I wanted to be one of them.

I first met Mahony Griffin herself through her 1,000-page manuscript, "The Magic of America," housed in the Burnham Library of Chicago's Art Institute. As an undergraduate in 1989, I carried to the archive a note from my art history professor, who had arranged this meeting, who had vouched for my integrity. I sat in the fluorescent archives, wearing white cotton gloves, leafing through Mahony Griffin's musty typescript, breathing her in, unable to read more than bits in the two days I had allowed for my research. Her typescript was a baffling puzzle of things—at my first glance perhaps more a huge scrapbook than a manuscript. It hid more of her than it revealed to me, a labyrinthine catacomb of stuff never quite catalogued or described by an archivist, just artifacts arranged by Mahony Griffin herself: architectural drawings, newspaper clippings, postcards, letters, lists of the native plants of Australia, texts of speeches delivered by her and by Walter—all wrapped a strange story of the entwined lives of two architects, lives that she described as a series of four "battles." I found both an unreadable text and a text that haunted me—by the time I left, I was convinced that the text, described in the card catalogue only as "a biography of architect Walter Burley Griffin," was something other than that. My note cards and chronologies helped me piece together a story of parallel paths that suddenly crossed, leading to architectural work such as neither had previously produced: the 1912 winning design for the international competition to build an entire city, the Australian national capital at Canberra.

Yet nothing that I had read in the secondary scholarship I obsessively consumed had described the text, or Mahony Griffin herself, in any but the most dismissive terms. The top scholars in my field described her variously as "coldly intellectual" (Birrell 14), "bitter and critical" (132), and lacking "the imaginative mind to create" (Brooks 164). Her work was easily labeled "derivative" (Van Zanten 21), and her architecture was "inconsistent, lacked restraint, and was not architecturally rationalized" (Johnson 12). Her text was dismissed much more thoroughly by scholars as the ranting of a senile and bitter old woman. These traces, the only discussion of her available to me through secondary sources in 1989, worked to erase any interpretation of her life or work as interesting or important. It is not surprising that I became certain that my engagement with and interest in the text and its author suggested something lax about my scholarship—a lack of discernment that would mark me naive and unsophisticated. Although "The Magic of America" was the richest document I found in my research, and my guesses about it were the only original conclusions that came from my research, I did not mention or cite the text in my undergraduate thesis, perhaps out of fear that my interest in a thing so dismissible would reveal that I really wasn't a scholar, that I was easily sidetracked by the unimportant. So I became possessed by a secret, a secret whispered by a text, written by a dead woman, misidentified by archivists, ignored by scholars. The text was not a biography of one architect but an autobiography of a joined career and a collaboration, two lives, and a shared love for architecture.

Architectural theorist Mark Wigley, citing Jacques Derrida, suggests that the crypt is the secret itself, formed by the not telling, "the act of vomiting to the inside" constructed of the tension of the "internal resistance of the vault like pillars, beams, studs, and retaining walls, leaning the powers of intolerable pain against an ineffable, forbidden pleasure" (qtd. in Bloomer 155). The pain was the haunting knowledge that in order to become an architectural historian, I had to give up the work I found interesting, the excavation of texts for those minute traces that documented the contributions of people long dead, long dismissed, and thoroughly discredited. The pleasure was of being possessed of and by a secret knowledge—evidence, clear evidence, I thought, that joined fortunes led two architects to produce better work than either had been capable of alone. When I hinted at this knowledge, later, while in my architectutal history master's program, a professor, a very smart professor, suggested that to tell such secrets would be "academic suicide." Historians never speculate, he offered. I am not the first student to have felt this tension among secret, crypt, pain, and pleasure, a tension that I would now identify as "discipline." But at the time, I knew only that when faced with a difference between what published scholars knew and what I guessed, I had to follow published scholars—that is how "we" build knowledge, and to do otherwise is "suicide."

More than fifteen years later, I still cringe at the real secret: that I so wanted to be an architectural historian that I refused to tell the story I was beginning to understand, that my note cards and chronologies did add up to something—an intellectual collaboration that enabled these two minor architects to produce work that would win an international competition. Discipline instead required me to tell a sideways story that maintained the fragile architecture of those histories I knew, the ones that described a male genius and a talented assistant whose skill as an artist helped her husband become successful. When I wrote about Mahony Griffin in 1991, in my aborted attempt to finish my master's degree in architectural studies, I even spelled her name Mahoney, as had the scholars I cited, even though I had seen her name, Mahony, typed by her own hand on the title page of her typescript when I read it in the archive.

This is my secret. I did not simply succumb to some perceived disciplinary pressure (I did that when I agreed to write about her husband's architectural work rather than about her text as my master's thesis). I talked myself into believing (with the help of the many scholars who claimed it) that perhaps Mahony Griffin herself had been senile, or perverse, or mistaken about many things. About the spelling of her own name? The weight of discipline made it seem more reasonable that she be mistaken about the spelling of her own name than that many scholars, one of whom sat on my thesis committee, could all be wrong. Mistaken.

If historians don't even speculate, I assumed they also did not misspell. I still struggle to understand who I was that I could have been made to doubt so easily. As a scholar, I had to make up an implausible story so that I could be wrong in good company. My discipline itself kept me distanced from the subject of my research, but not so that I might objectively evaluate the information I had collected. Rather, my discipline sought to narrow potential interpretations and to enforce, rigidly, the notion that my work must build on that of other scholars—even those who were mistaken—and that any other interpretation was speculation. And my professors, who walked me through this process, were smart and generous and careful scholars, as were the scholars whose work I was reading and parroting and internalizing and rebelling against, and I wanted to be like them. And I couldn't.

I wish I could say that Marion compelled me, or enabled me, or inspired me, or haunted me until I abandoned my dysfunctional relationship with my first academic love, architectural history. And perhaps she did, but mostly I just left, not for her but for me, abandoning a degree into which I had invested thousands of dollars and hundreds of hours of research. When I tried to explain to my thesis director, I could only say, "I can't do this. I think it's methodological." And perhaps it always is, but I think that I just didn't see *her*—I saw only the person that my disciplined vision allowed me to see.

If I met Marion Mahony in 1989, I befriended her in 1999, after I became a rhetorician (and no longer worried about being in the good company of architectural historians) and felt empowered to tell, finally, the most interesting story I knew. For the first time, I sat with her text. In that same fluorescent archive, she emerged as I read her letters. I read them as if they had been written to me, as if she were entrusting me with her story, her life, her love, and her career. I sat and cried. She wrote of falling in love at forty:

> But when I encountered W.B.G. I was swept off my feet by my delight in his achievements in my profession, then through the common bond of interests in nature and intellectual pursuits and then with the man himself. It was by no means a case of love at first sight, but it was a madness when it struck.
>
> ("Magic of America" IV 157)

But it was her letter to Walter's sister and brother-in-law describing her presence at Walter's death, so far from home together in India in 1937, that caused my crying:

> Then as his breath began to fail, I talked to him, told him what a wonderful life I had had with him, how he was beloved by everybody and suddenly he turned and fastened his eyes wide open and round on mine, startled and intense as if it had never occurred to him that he could die and they never left mine till he ceased breathing and I closed them.
>
> (I 305)

She never forgave Walter for dying too young, for leaving her alone for so many years. She never had another design built. There is no question that for nearly ten years, I had had a professional relationship with this talented woman—a relationship that had allowed me to study her life and puzzle about her work. Why then, on that day, did I first see her? What was it that made me cry, that made her befriend me?

The researcher's sixth sense isn't the ability to see the dead but our potential to help the dead, who do not know they are dead, finish their stories, and we do this in the moment in which we realize that their stories are ours. For many years, I found myself frustrated by those scholarly representations that subsumed Mahony Griffin's architectural work within that of her husband's, those representations that refused to describe a collaborative, mutually nourishing relationship at the heart of an exceptionally creative architectural practice. Is this the story that keeps me awake at night? The story my fellow scholars have told that seems most deeply false, mean-spirited, and unjust to my friend? No, not even close.

It has taken me more than fifteen years to understand the promise that has grown from my friendship with a woman who died before I was born. That promise, which has become my responsibility as a researcher, has led to my interest not in teasing apart some truth of her life, not in seeing it as a life that needs me to ride in like the cavalry to recover its importance, but to ask why it is a life that should need recovering at all. Mahony

Griffin's is a well-documented life. There are buildings, publications, letters, treatises, postcards, architectural drawings, blueprints, manifestos; a 1,000-page autobiography; mentions of her work by contemporaries, in manuscript memoirs, and in varied publications; records of her birth, her death, her college graduation, her senior thesis, her career as a professional, her passion for the theater, her public speeches, and her parties. There exist, with her name always correctly spelled, pages and pages and pages of primary records, nearly all unconsulted—in fact, nearly all dismissed—by a generation a highly trained scholars and historians who have in turn been almost exclusively consulted by a second generation of highly trained scholars and historians.

I became a rhetorician, and not a historian, so that my research could span the questions imposed by discipline. My research shifted from the attempt to pin down architectural influences, chronologies, and construction histories to attempting to pin down scholars—to examine our questions, our methods, and our preoccupations—noting the things we value and how those values shape the knowledge they claim to benignly reflect. My promise to my friend Marion has been to make visible the ways in which the language of architectural history has shaped her rich life into one that is dismissible, and has done so despite shelves of evidence to the contrary. And this was done so easily, and nearly accidentally and without malice, to a woman who did everything within her power to document the life she wanted remembered, a woman whose signature is everywhere and whose marks and traces cover three continents and shape major cities. If this can happen to her, not because of some grand conspiracy or international scholarly plot but rather because of uninterrogated habits of scholarship ingrained in us through an education of strict discipline, should it surprise us that we know so little of so few women in art, architecture, music, science, engineering? My argument for the researcher's sixth sense is not that it will enable us to recover and converse with the lost dead, to understand them in a way that is definitive and true, but that they will help us recover ourselves, help us discover that we did not know that we were the dead, inhabiting the crypt, repeating dead histories in dead languages.

Works Cited

Biemiller, Lawrence. "The Artist behind the Architect." *Chronicle of Higher Education,* Dec. 2, 2005.
Birrell, James. *Walter Burley Griffin.* Brisbane: U of Queensland P, 1964.
Bloomer, Jennifer. *Architecture and the Text: The (S)crypts of Joyce and Piranesi.* New Haven: Yale UP, 1993.
Brooks, H. Allen. *The Prairie School: Frank Lloyd Wright and His Midwest Contemporaries.* New York: Norton, 1972.
Griffin, Marion Mahony. "The Magic of America." Unpublished typescript. New-York Historical Society, c. 1949.
Johnson, Donald Leslie. *The Architecture of Walter Burley Griffin.* Melbourne: Macmillan Co. of Australia, 1977.
Van Zanten, David. "The Early Work of Marion Mahony Griffin." *Prairie School Review* 3.2 (1969): 5–23.
Wood, Debora, ed. *Marion Mahony Griffin: Drawing the Form of Nature.* Evanston: Northwestern UP, 2005.

12.
AN ARGUMENT FOR ARCHIVAL RESEARCH METHODS: THINKING BEYOND METHODOLOGY
Barbara E. L'Eplattenier

For as long as I have been a historian of composition and rhetoric, I have heard stories about archival work floating around conferences: books and rhetorical theories developed around two or three hours spent in the archives; archival documents consulted for "supporting quotes" after the arguments have been developed, completed, and written; semi-blatant plagiarism from other historians' archival work that made it appear as if the writer had spent more time in the archives than he or she actually had; newer histories that unquestioningly presented statements from seminal texts, ignoring works that contradicted said seminal texts or pointed out alternative practices that refuted previously published blanket assumptions about pedagogy or practice. These incidents were interesting gossip, items to be clucked over in coffee shops at various conferences or at publishers' parties. They worried me, to be sure, but I didn't think much could be done about them.[1]

Then, Lisa Mastrangelo and I were asked to be guest lecturers in an online class about research methodologies—we were "the archivist historians." Asked to supply supplemental class readings, we poked around our files, reread some articles, and reviewed the contents of various journals. We quickly came to realize that, with few exceptions, what we were looking for—practical articles to orient and guide people new to archival work, articles that described the methods of historical research—didn't exist. Aside from short descriptions of how the researcher found or stumbled upon a topic, the doing of history was rarely discussed.

We punted in the online class, and I began to think seriously about archival methods.[2,3] Why do we not have articles about finding aids? About searching databases? About organizing and using sources? About verifying information? Why do we as a discipline rarely talk about the methods we use to access our information? How might we incorporate such information into our research?

My concern is not a new one to the field. In 1997 and 1999 articles, Linda Ferreira-Buckley worried about our lack of practical training in archival research methods, our unawareness of basic resources, finding aids, and grants. Richard Enos decried our lack of

---

L'Eplattenier, Barbara E.. "An Argument for Archival Research Methods: Thinking Beyond Methodology." *College English* 72.1 (September 2009): 67–79. Print.

primary research in his 1999 "Recovering the Lost Art." Thomas Miller raised similar concerns even earlier in his 1993 "Teaching Histories," which describes his graduate classes and how he incorporates historical work into them. All of these authors concluded that we don't do enough work in, training in, and teaching of primary research methods.[4]

There are a number of reasons for this. Historians are a small subgroup within rhetoric and composition and tend to research a wide range of time periods and rhetorical activities.[5] We identify ourselves as rhetoric and composition historians, rather than historians who research writing practices and discourse during time period X. As a result, rhetoric and composition historians do not have a critical mass within departments, and we have not yet been able to recognize our common research methods, finding aids, or resources in the same way that other types of researchers do.[6] Additionally, because we don't yet have canonical historical methods articles, as teachers we may find it difficult to address the topic in our research methods classes, which leads to students who become teachers who don't address the topic, and so on and so forth. Finally, because archival historical work is often so unique—each archive, each situation, each study is different, with different resources, different access, different constraints— generalizing about archival work can be difficult, especially for the individual researcher.

However, I believe we can and should begin incorporating more explicit discussions of our primary research methods into our historical research. We can do this in a systematic and incremental way that both highlights the uniqueness of archival study and creates the depth and breadth of knowledge required to begin generalizing about the tools our discipline needs and uses.

Some readers will say that we do talk about methods, and they point to works that theorize the researcher's stance, ideological bias, and definitions of rhetoric; the non-neutrality of historical presentations; the plurality of histories; or the theoretical constructs that inform our work.[7] Such research addresses why we study *what* we study, why we study *who* we study, and how the theories we have read influence our writing and our perception of the world. In her excellent article, "Historical Studies of Rhetorical Women," Hui Wu pointed out that

> a traditional explanation of methodology [or historiography] is that it is a theory and analysis of how research does or should proceed. [...] For historians, methodology means the theorization of the goal of research, the selection of subjects in a particular period (the research topic and focus), and the categories for evaluation of historical evidence.
>
> (84)[8]

Such work, which often draws from postmodernism and/or feminism, solidly locates us within the fluidity of truth and allows for the expansion of "appropriate" rhetorical activity to study. As Sharon Crowley reminds us, the previous dominant model of rhetorical history gave historical scholars a narrow and specific arena in which to work—one that limited rhetorical activity to the white, male-dominated *polis* ("Let Me"). Our philosophical and theoretical arguments grant us the credibility, expertise, and awareness of our own biases to explore the rhetorical activity and impact not only of the classical rhetors, the Scottish rhetors/philosophers, and the polis, but also of women's groups, African American groups, labor groups, and religious groups, as well as various sites of literacy, civic discourse, and propaganda.[9] This gives us a rich, multidisciplinary, multifaceted body of history.

As important as it is, this work does not give us a "systematic method of gathering evidence" (Kirsch and Sullivan 2), nor does it give us Ferreira-Buckley's "tools of the historian's trade" ("Octalog" 28) needed by novice archival researchers to begin their work. *Methods,* as Kirsch and Sullivan note, means something very different than *methodology.* Vitally important to the development and construction of any research project, methods are the means by which we conduct our research, how we locate and use primary materials, and for historians, how we recover materials for our histories. Methods are about achieving access to information, about finding aids, about reference materials, about archive locations and restrictions, about the condition of the materials, about the existence of evidence or the lack of evidence, and about the triangulation of information—all the factors that impact our "systematic method of gathering evidence" and our interpretation of that evidence, our presentation of our revisionist histories (à la Miller). Just as methodology allows us to theorize the goals of our research, methods allow us to contextualize the research process or the researched subject and materials. Methods make the invisible work of historical research visible.

The few articles on methods available to new researchers either lament the lack of methods in our field or offer overly simplistic advice—read widely in your field, have a good time, formulate a research question, or something of that nature.[10] The contributors to the May 1999 special section of *College English* on "Archivists with an Attitude" (Brereton; Ferreira-Buckley; Mailloux; Miller and Bowdon) discussed archival work, but not the pragmatics of such work; rather, they argued for training and a theoretical understanding of archival work—an important requirement for doing archival research. The engaging and charming 2002 issue of *Rhetoric Society Quarterly* on feminist historiography (Bizzell and Clark) does not necessarily help someone enter the archives for the first time, but it does raise important issues: what can and should be used as archival materials, where might we find them, how might we use them, and what about them might our ideologies cause us to overlook. Wendy B. Sharer's "Disintegrating Bodies of Knowledge" reminded us of the materiality of our archives and argued for more archival training to both improve our research abilities and draw attention to disappearing resources, but it didn't address how to implement such archival training.

More recently, Gesa Kirsch and Liz Rohan's *Beyond the Archives* looks at the personal connections researchers have with their topics or subjects, and ways in which they go about developing the stories about their research subjects. *Beyond the Archives* articulates beautifully the lure and fascination archives have for many researchers and the serendipity often involved in archival work, but accessing archival information in a systematic fashion is not its main focus. Patricia Donahue and Gretchen Flesher Moon's edited collection *Reading Local Histories* incorporates a short methods paragraph in each chapter. Each essay in the collection includes a brief description of how and where the researcher located her documents. Some go into further detail about how the researcher came to her topic. Each essay also includes a note at the beginning to identify the archives and collections visited, and a specific bibliography at the end, identifying only archival sources, separated from other primary or secondary sources.

Such descriptions and bibliographies, especially if they were more fully developed, may suggest to novice archival researchers a beginning point or offer inspiration for their own work.

Finally, in part because of the questions raised by the online class and in this article, Alexis Ramsey, Lisa Mastrangelo, Wendy Sharer, and I have co-edited *Working in the Archives: Practical Research Methods for Rhetoric and Composition*.[11] *Working in the Archives* will offer some answers to the pragmatic realities of archival work—the where, who, what, why, and how of getting information. How to approach archivists, how to find materials of all types, how to handle the collection and maintenance of archival materials, how to organize and access archival material—all of these are vital questions for our field that are only now being addressed.

For me, working on *Working in the Archives* made it even more apparent that we are at the beginning stages of thinking and writing about specific methods in the way that Ferreira-Buckley envisioned. During the editing process, our constant refrain to contributors became "Our audience includes scholars new to the archival process; what practical, pragmatic piece of advice would you give them? What is their take-away from this piece when they are actually, physically working in the archives?" This refrain helped both the authors and the editors move beyond local and archive-specific issues while still grounding ourselves in specific archival work. We all pushed ourselves to think explicitly about transferability of information, in part because we as a field do not have enough "here's what I did in the archive" stories—enough lore, if you will—to generalize about archival methods that are not content/archive specific.

The question, then, is how to start talking about methods—how to begin to develop the literature, the "must read" articles that become the basis for the archival research unit in our research methods classes. How do we begin to develop an extended body of literature that will help us train ourselves and our students, to introduce our students (and other scholars interested in such work) to accessing the archives and what to do once you are there?

One obvious starting place is the discipline of history.[12] Stephen Fisher's *Archival Information*, for example, is a "broad strokes" finding aid that offers an overview introduction to various archives and their finding aids. It reviews and describes ten different subject areas' archives, such as federal, state, and local government archives; genealogical archives; sciences archives; various religious groups' archives; and business companies' archives. Because each chapter is written by an expert in that specific archival area, it lists a wide variety of holdings, details the strengths and weaknesses in them, and suggests other possible resources. *Archival Information* should act as a starting point for our own, more specific archival/finding aid searches. Another useful resource for those trying to incorporate archival methods into the classroom is Robert C. Williams's *The Historian's Toolbox*, which is an excellent introduction to what history is; different types of sources, such as official documents or movies, or material artifacts, and their strengths and weaknesses; the argumentative and narrative structures of historical texts; and the relevance of historical information.[13] Using previously published examples, *The Historian's Toolbox* walks novice historical researchers through finding and using sources.[14] Another text that does this, although in a bit more theoretical fashion, is the short and charming *History:*

A Very Short Introduction by John H. Arnold, which explores the questions history asks, how those questions might be answered, and the impact of answering said questions.[15]

Within our own discipline, an incremental way of developing such literature is to begin including methods sections in our histories that function in the same way as our methodological sections. Just as methodological sections theorize the goals of our research, our methods sections should describe the pragmatic goals, issues, and actions of our archival research. A methods section should present to the reader information such as data location, collection, material conditions, analysis—the pragmatic components involved in obtaining the materials that are the foundation for the stories historians of rhetoric and composition tell. A strong methods section tells us what occurred, how this information was developed, and where it was found.

A methods section might include the name and location of the archives; the finding aids used to locate information; the amount of time spent in the archives; the number of linear feet in a collection; the amount of the collection examined; the *provenance* of the artifacts; the physical state of the artifacts; problems, issues or difficulties with the materials; interesting facts about the materials; missing articles from the archives; and the specific types of materials examined. A good methods section will give readers a sense of what was examined, how it was examined, and where it is currently located.[16] A good methods section, however we construct it, offers us details regarding the circumstances of the research and pulls back the curtain on work done. It lets us see the man behind the curtain, so to speak. It is a pedagogical model to show our students—a way to familiarize ourselves with how to "do" histories.

Perhaps a methods section doesn't have to be an explicit section of the document or extensive footnotes. Perhaps it's enough to throw the documents themselves into stark relief. In "'Is it the Pleasure of this Conference to Have Another?'" Lisa Mastrangelo and I described our experience with the archival documents with which we were working. We told the story of how writing teachers from the Seven Sisters Colleges had come together to discuss the administrative aspects of writing programs, and then we explicitly described the document(s) used and its quirks in our research. Lisa's discovery of the archival documents had raised questions for both of us. As a result, we wanted to make clear to our readers that these pieces of documentation were puzzling to us, and thus should be examined and used with these limitations in mind. We wrote

> The primary pieces of archival evidence that we are relying on in this chapter are the conference programs from 1919, 1922, and 1924 and a transcript of the 1919 conference proceedings; other archival documents include memorandums and faculty meeting minutes. [...] Unlike other events or incidents, we found little reference to this gathering in the various official minutia that accompanies the administration of a department. The 1919 transcript led us to the documents referring to the conferences of 1920, 1922, and 1924; departmental annual reports also offered occasional references. These archival documents, however, are the only representation we have found thus far of these conferences.
>
> (118)

In other words, we wanted our readers to recognize that, although we were fairly certain of the importance of these documents, we didn't want to mislead them into thinking that such conferences were a common occurrence, or that they were occurring all over New England, or even that they were events within the normal work of these women. We wanted to make it explicit to our readers that these documents seemed to stand alone among the plethora of documents that have turned up in relation to the writing programs at various women's colleges. Their uniqueness, ironically, contributes to their instability as pieces of evidence. The problem with a historical "smoking gun" piece of evidence is that you need additional circumstantial evidence to orient the smoking gun; for these specific documents, that circumstantial evidence is minimal.

We went on to write about the actual document as well:

> The largest piece of archival evidence, the 1919 transcript, remains somewhat of a puzzle to us. The transcript is approximately forty-seven pages long, with an inconsistent typeset, two pages numbered eighteen and an inconsistent format. Equally puzzling—and unfortunate—is that the transcript ends on page forty-six—right in the middle of a discussion on the types of debating questions used in English classrooms. Thankfully, the conference program indicates that this subject was the eleventh out of twelve discussed at the conference. While frustrating, it is heartening to know that we have a record of the majority of the discussions which occurred. [...]
>
> Other aspects of the document also remain a mystery to us. The initial conference took place at Mount Holyoke, which has a copy of the conference program. It was Wellesley's archives, however, that possesses the actual transcript. This transcript is annotated by "C.F.S."—Mount Holyoke's Clara Frances Stevens, who often changed a word or two throughout the manuscript and initialed the entries. How the transcript made its way into the Wellesley archives, and why it is still held there, remains unknown.
>
> Despite its idiosyncrasies, we feel that the transcript's value as a document overrides its difficulties as a historical text.
>
> (119)

This description of the archival documents helps destabilize the story presented—it also explicitly limits what the research tells us about programmatic evaluation at the Seven Sisters Schools, but at the same time offers other areas of potential research. We felt that any discussion of the texts should be read against this backdrop of uncertainty, incompleteness, and *provenance.* By positioning the transcript with other documents and stating the difficulties with it, we did not accidentally misrepresent it or what we learned from it. Our description of the conference transcript contributes to the gaps and fissures in history, allowing future researchers a place to poke around in and explore for other possibilities. Perhaps some future researcher will learn how the document moved from Mount Holyoke to Wellesley, and in doing so, discover a new aspect of the connections between the Seven Sister Colleges that was unknown before. Perhaps some researcher, knowing about the conference, might discover another similar conference held somewhere and be able to recognize the conference for what it is. It is such information that can help us read crooked, as Cheryl Glenn advocated so long ago ("Remapping").

A fundamental question is why have a methods section at all? Aside from modeling archival strategies for other researchers, what does a methods section bring to rhetoric and composition's history? It's a reasonable question, especially because it places additional burdens on the researcher.

In part, a methods section will allow us, the reader, to develop a greater sense of trust in the history. As Crowley noted in the 1988 *Rhetoric Review* "Octalog: The Politics of Historiography," we read histories because of the ethos of the historian (21). At that time, this ethos, however, was built upon the other scholarship produced by the historian: James Berlin was trusted, in part, because of the soundness of his other scholarship. And, as we all know, historical studies are difficult to replicate—the time, money, and access to archival texts (our primary sources) are difficult to come by, and readers must rely on the (unstated) historical methods of the researcher. As readers, we are dependent on accepting the version or analysis presented to us. While incidents such as the Triangle Shirtwaist Fire have been the subject of much research by more mainstream historians, the fields of rhetoric and composition often do not have multiple histories on a topic. Instead, we have one excellent text that now serves as *the* text; the ethos of the researcher is paramount in our acceptance of that text and our use of it as a foundational text. As a result, readers must trust that the historian has represented the documents ethically and expertly, has reviewed significant materials to be able to make the claims made, has accessed appropriate resources and other research, and has tread that fine line discussed in the *College English* debate between Xin Gale, Cheryl Glenn, and Susan Jarratt—projection versus "reality." Because we often have no evidence of how this history was created and with what materials, we have no way—or few ways—to question our suspension of disbelief as we read the narrative and analysis.

A methods section allows us to decide whether we can trust this history and how much we want to trust it. Is an archival history that was developed with the researcher spending only three hours in the archives with 1.5 linear feet as valid as one where the researcher spent thirty hours with 5.5 linear feet? If a researcher never actually looks at primary sources, how should we read that history? Shouldn't we, the readers and users of those histories, know about what went into their construction? If all documents were drawn from online collections, is that an important fact to know? If a researcher used only secondary sources to develop an argument, should that be made explicit in more than just the Works Cited page? A methods section gives researchers a sense of the archival provenance of the documents used, and gives a clearer sense of the archival materials available to the researcher.

An actual methods section shows us the cracks, fissures, and gaps to allow us to see the construction. It allows us to more clearly point out our blind spots, our areas we didn't realize we could research, our awareness of the fragmentary nature of archival work. If all histories are constructions, then a methods section allows us to see the building blocks of that construction. We can see which section of the foundation is strong or weak, where we can build a wing, where we can add a door.

Similarly, a methods section lets us respond to the concerns of what counts as evidence raised by Carol Mattingly and Richard Leo Enos in their articles in the 2002 *Rhetoric Society Quarterly*. A methods section allows us to see what a wider range of sources might look like, and what a rich, detailed narrative and discussion might develop from. For example, if a researcher were using newspaper articles as a source, a methods section might address which specific newspapers were examined. Which were not? What influenced the researcher's choices about which newspapers to examine—availability? access? How might journals or broadsheet descriptions have informed the researcher's discussion for the readers of her histories? What else is available out there? Knowing such information can help us, as well as later researchers, review the blind spots in our research. We can envision new areas that build upon our previous work while knowing in a little greater detail what already exists. A methods section makes explicit for both the researcher and the reader the self-reflection of the researcher position in the writing of our histories. Similarly, a methods section and more explicit discussion of our sources allows us to know what we will never know—what information has been lost and cannot be retrieved.[17] Our methods section should remind us that we often work with a significantly limited palette of information. A methods section helps us question our suspension of disbelief in the histories we are reading.

Conclusion

I am not arguing for a right-or-wrong Truth stance. I don't think that including a methods section in our histories will do that. Rather, a methods section is a way of evaluating the interpretation against the sources. We're able to evaluate against the method and sources used—the amount and type of materials used—in terms of linear feet and accessibility, the ability or inability to triangulate sources, the status of the materials, and/or the location. Instead of presenting closed construction and a firm narrative, methods allows us to recognize the instability of our narrative and perhaps begin to write more destabilized historical narratives. Through a methods section, researchers can develop a methodological ethos, one that comes from the explicit presentation of their research. Such an ethos values admitting to failure—admires the historian's ability and willingness to say "I don't know" and "my tale is incomplete." In short, a methods section in a history helps us create a self-aware, self-reflective, self-representational description of not only how information was found, but also the time and care used to put that information together.

I've thought long and hard about the metaphors we use to describe our historical work.[18] After much deliberation, it seems to me that our understanding of the past is similar to the collages of photos that make up a larger photo. Using small images, we are able to create a much larger image. We see small pictures—individuals or groups or specific moments in time—and then, stepping back and looking at many small pictures, we can see a larger picture—trends, movements, ideologies. A methods section helps us complicate our collage, making it perhaps even more fragmented, but more layered and textured. A methods section helps us fill in our collage.

Notes

1 As always, I am grateful to my colleague, Lisa Mastrangelo, for her assistance and patience with this article. I also thank the two anonymous reviewers and John Schilb, who gave such thoughtful and generous responses.
2 For a revised version of the "lecture" we gave, see "Stumbling."

3 As I explain later, this realization has also resulted in an edited collection, *Working in the Archives* (Ramsey et al.).
4 One notable exception is the Winter 2002 issue of *Rhetoric Society Quarterly* (Bizzell and Clark), which focuses on reexamining archival methodologies in a variety of ways. But even this issue does not deal with practical, day-to-day, pragmatic issues of archival work.
5 For a long time, I could list on one hand the historians who were interested in the same topic I was. Only recently has that expanded to *two* hands.
6 At one point, Ohio State University was the only Rhetoric and Composition department with more than one researcher who explicitly made rhetoric and composition histories, or histories that focused on rhetorical activities, the main topic of research. Certainly many researchers have done historical projects or dissertations, but historical work, for one reason or another, tends not to be the main focus of their research.
7 Examples of such texts include Royster, "When"; Connors, "Dreams"; Gale, "Historical"; Jarratt, "Speaking"; "Xin Liu Gale Responds"; Berlin, "Revisionary History"; Glenn, "Truth" and "Remapping"; Bizzell; the collection edited by Royster and Simpkins; Vitanza, "Rudiments" and "'Notes'"; Enoch; and Royster and Williams.
8 Wu, of course, notes that for feminist theorists—and I would argue for most all rhetoric and composition historians—these are not value-free issues. Almost all of our seminal texts argue for the validity of composition and pedagogy as a subject worthy of study.
9 For example, one of the shelves in my bookshelf houses—in no particular order—the following books: Crowley; Sharer; Mattingly; Glenn; Kates; Paine; Connors; Clark and Halloran; L'Eplattenier and Mastrangelo; Royster; Miller; Buchanan; Schultz; Jarratt; Johnson; and Berlin, *Rhetoric and Writing Instruction*. I didn't bother to look at the other two or three similarly packed shelves.
10 My personal favorite is Robert Connor's advice in "Dreams and Play" about the August mushroom hunt with the Archives (note the capital "A"), described as a place where "storage meets dreams" (17). I appreciate and understand the sentiment—I am, after all, the feverish person who staggered out of the archives into the twenty-first century (*Beyond the Archives*)—but Connors's August mushroom hunt imagery left me asking, "Yes, but what do I *do*?"
11 Forthcoming from Southern Illinois University Press.
12 Of course, as one of the reviewers reminded me, literary scholars have done significant historical work: writing about time periods, literary movements, recovering primary texts. All of this is vitally important, and we should draw on this work as well. History, on the other hand, often uses sources and finding aids that we aren't readily aware of and that might help rhetoric and composition historians.
13 Although I think this is an excellent introductory text, Williams's views on how history uses postmodernism strike me as unfair and a misrepresentation of postmodernism. He subsumes postmodernism into anti-history, and argues that some postmodern thinkers believe that the past does not exist, reality does not exist, truth does not exist, and "one story is as good as another" (30). The blame for unethical research should not be placed at the feet of postmodernism; historical denial is not ethical research.
14 Books such as *Doing History: Research And Writing in the Digital Age* (Galgano, Arndt, and Hyser) or *Writing History: A Guide for Students* (Storey) lead students through similar points, although they tend to be much more like generic "how to do research" texts, with entire sections devoted to how to cite sources. *The Methods and Skills of History: A Practical Guide* (Furay and Salevouris) is essentially a workbook for studying sources; although I am skeptical of workbooks in general, it does provide inspiration for people incorporating more methods into their research course.
15 Although these texts are aimed at undergraduates, much of their research strategies and resource information should be very helpful to our discipline.
16 Some of these "location" questions might be mitigated if our field adopted the *Chicago Manual of Style* practice of separating primary sources consulted versus secondary sources consulted versus a Works Cited page. Additionally, the Works Cited pages should have more specific methods of tracking down specific pieces of data. *The Chicago Manual of Style* requires only that the collection be named (for example, Report on the English Department, 1916. Vassar College Special Collections.), and MLA does not have an adequate method for dealing with archival texts. They do

not, for example, require a researcher to give a box or folder number for the specific location of documents. If part of the function of a Works Cited page is to allow for the duplication of research, an entry without this information is sorely lacking.

17 Shirley K. Rose and I once had a conversation about the archival documents available to her when she was researching George Wykoff. Rose told me that Wykoff's housekeeper had thrown out all his personal papers shortly before Rose contacted her. It is important to know such things, so that we as researchers also know when something is *probably* no longer attainable.

18 See, for example, my piece "Questioning our Methodological Metaphors."

Works Cited

Arnold, John H. *History: A Very Short Introduction.* New York: Oxford UP, 2000. Print.

Berlin, James A. "Revisionary Histories of Rhetoric: Politics, Power, and Plurality." Vitanza. 112–27.

——. "Revisionary History: The Dialectical Method." *PRE/TEXT* 8.1–2 (1987): 47–61. Print.

——. *Rhetoric and Reality: Writing Instruction in American Colleges, 1900–1985.* Carbondale: Southern Illinois UP, 1987. Print.

——. *Writing Instruction in Nineteenth-Century American Colleges.* Carbondale: Southern Illinois UP, 1984. Print.

Bizzell, Patricia. "Feminist Methods of Research in the History of Rhetoric: What Difference Do They Make?" *Rhetoric Society Quarterly* 30.4 (2000): 5–18. Print.

Bizzell, Patricia, and Gregory Clark, eds. Spec. issue of *Rhetoric Society Quarterly* 32.1 (2002): 7–122. Print.

Brereton, John C. "Rethinking our Archive: A Beginning." *College English* 61.5 (1999): 574–76. Print.

Buchanan, Lindal. *Regendering Delivery: The Fifth Canon and Antebellum Women Rhetors.* Carbondale: Southern Illinois UP, 2005. Print.

Clark, Gregory and S. Michael Halloran, eds. *Oratorical Culture in Nineteenth-Century America: Transformations in the Theory and Practice of Rhetoric.* Carbondale: Southern Illinois UP, 1993. Print.

Connors, Robert J. *Composition-Rhetoric: Backgrounds, Theory, and Pedagogy.* Pittsburgh; U of Pittsburgh P, 1997. Print.

——. "Dreams and Play: Historical Method and Methodology." Kirsch and Sullivan 15–36.

Crowley, Sharon. "Let Me Get This Straight." Vitanza. 1–19.

——. *The Methodical Memory: Invention in Current-Traditional Rhetoric.* Carbondale: Southern Illinois UP, 1990. Print.

Donahue, Patricia, and Gretchen Flesher Moon, eds. *Local Histories: Reading the Archives of Composition.* Pittsburgh: U of Pittsburgh P, 2007. Print.

Enoch, Jessica. "Survival Stories: Feminist Historiographic Approaches to Chicana Rhetorics of Sterilization Abuse." *Rhetoric Society Quarterly* 35.3 (2005): 5–30. Print.

Enos, Richard Leo. "Recovering the Lost Art of Researching the History of Rhetoric." *Rhetoric Society Quarterly* 29.4 (1999): 7–20. Print.

Ferreira-Buckley, Linda. "Rescuing the Archives from Foucault." *College English* 61.5 (1999): 577–83. Print.

——. "Serving Time in the Archives." *Rhetoric Review* 16.1(1997): 26–28. Print.

Fisher, Steven, ed. *Archival Information: Haw to Find It, How to Use It.* Westport: Greenwood, 2004. Print.

Furay, Conal, and Michael J. Salevouris. *The Methods and Skills of History: A Practical Guide*. 2nd ed. Wheeling: Harlan Davidson, 2000. Print.

Gale, Xin Liu. "Historical Studies and Postmodernism: Rereading Aspasia of Miletus." *College English* 62.3 (2000): 361–86. Print.

——. "Xin Lu Gale Responds." *College English* 63.1 (Sep. 2000): 105–07. Print. Galgano, Michael J., Christopher Arndt, and Raymond M. Hyser. *Doing History: Research and Writing in the Digital Age*. Boston: Thomson Wadsworth, 2008. Print.

Galgano, Michael J., Christopher Arndt, and Raymond M. Hyser. *Doing History: Research and Writing in the Digital Age*. Boston: Thomson Wadsworth, 2008. Print.

Glenn, Cheryl. "Remapping Rhetorical Territory." *Rhetoric Review* 13.2 (1995): 287–303. Print.

——. *Rhetoric Retold: Regendering the Tradition from Antiquity Through the Renaissance*. Carbondale: Southern Illinois UP, 1997. Print.

——. "Truth, Lies, and Method: Revisiting Feminist Historiography." *College English* 62.3 (2000): 387–89. Print.

Jarratt, Susan C. *Rereading the Sophists: Classical Rhetoric Refigured*. Carbondale: Southern Illinois UP, 1998. Print.

——. "Speaking to the Past: Feminist Historiography in Rhetoric." *PRE/TEXT* 11.3-4 (1990): 190–209. Print.

Johnson, Nan. *Gender and Rhetorical Space in American Life, 1866–1910*. Carbondale: Southern Illinois UP, 2002. Print.

Kates, Susan. *Activist Rhetorics and American Higher Education, 1885–1937*. Carbondale: Southern Illinois UP, 2001. Print.

Kirsch, Gesa, and Liz Rohan, eds. *Beyond the Archives: Research as a Lived Process*. Carbondale: Southern Illinois UP, 2008. Print.

Kirsch, Gesa, and Patricia A. Sullivan, eds. *Methods and Methodology in Composition Research*. Carbondale: Southern Illinois UP, 1992. Print.

L'Eplattenier, Barbara. "Questioning our Methodological Metaphors." Royster and Simpkins 133–46.

L'Eplattenier, Barbara, and Lisa Mastrangelo, eds., *Historical Studies of Writing Program Administration: Individuals, Communities, and the Formation of a Discipline*. West Lafayette: Parlor Press, 2004. Print.

Mailloux, Steven. "Reading Typos, Reading Archives." *College English* 61.5 (1999): 584–90. Print.

Mastrangelo, Lisa, and Barbara L'Eplattenier, "'Is It the Pleasure of This Conference to Have Another?'" L'Eplattenier and Mastrangelo 117–44.

——. "Stumbling in the Archives: A Tale of Two Novices." Kirsch and Rohan 161–70.

Mattingly, Carol. *Well-Tempered Women: Nineteenth-Century Temperance Rhetoric*. Carbondale: Southern Illinois UP, 2001. Print.

Miller, Thomas P. *The Formation of College English: Rhetoric and Belles Letters in the British Cultural Provinces*. Pittsburgh: U Pittsburgh P, 1997. Print.

——. "Teaching Histories of Rhetoric as a Social Praxis." *Rhetoric Review* 12.1 (1993): 70–82. Print.

Miller, Thomas P., and Melody Bowdon. "A Rhetorical Stance on the Archives of Civic Action." *College English* 61.5 (1999): 591–98. Print.

"Octalog: The Politics of Historiography." *Rhetoric Review* 6.2 (1988): 5–49. Print.

Paine, Charles. *The Resistant Writer: Rhetoric as Immunity, 1850 to the Present*. Albany: State U of New York P, 1999. Print.

Ramsey, Alexis E., et al. *Working in the Archives: Practical Research Methods Rhetoric and Composition*. Carbondale: Southern Illinois UP, forthcoming. Print.

Royster, Jacqueline Jones. *Traces of a Stream: Literacy and Social Change Among African American Women*. Pittsburgh: U of Pittsburgh P, 2000. Print.

——. "When the First Voice You Hear Is Not Your Own." *CCC* 47.1 (1996): 29–40. Print.

Royster, Jacqueline Jones, and Ann Marie Mann Simpkins, eds. *Calling Cards: Theory and Practice in the Study of Race, Gender, and Culture*. Albany: State U of New York P, 2005. Print.

Royster, Jacqueline Jones, and Jean C. Williams. "History in the Spaces Left: African American Presence and Narratives of Composition Studies." *CCC* 50.4 (1999): 563–84. Print.

Schultz, Lucille M. *The Young Composers: Composition's Beginnings in Nineteenth-Century Schools*. Carbondale: Southern Illinois UP, 1999. Print.

Sharer, Wendy B. "Disintegrating Bodies of Knowledge: Historical Material and Revisionary Histories of Rhetoric." *Rhetorical Bodies*. Eds. Jack Selzer and Sharon Crowley. Madison: U of Wisconsin P, 1999. 120–39. Print.

——. *Vote and Voice: Women's Organizations and Political Literacy, 1915–1930*. Carbondale: Southern Illinois UP, 2007. Print.

Storey, William Kelleher. *Writing History: A Guide for Students*. 2nd ed. New York: Oxford UP, 2004. Print.

Vitanza, Victor J. "'Notes' Towards Historiographies of Rhetorics; or, The Rhetorics of the Histories of Rhetorics: Traditional, Revisionary, and Sub/Versive." *PRE/TEXT* 8/1-2 (1987): 63–125. Print.

——. "The Rudiments of the History of Rhetoric and the Rhetorics of History." *Rethinking the Rhetorical Tradition: Multidisciplinary Essays* on *the Rhetorical Tradition*. Ed. Takis Poulakos. Boulder: Westview, 1993. 193–239. Print.

——, ed. *Writing Histories of Rhetoric*. Carbondale: Southern Illinois UP, 1994. Print.

Williams, Robert C. *The Historian's Toolbox: A Student's Guide to the Theory and Craft of History*. 2nd ed. Armonk: M. E. Sharpe, 2007. Print.

Wu, Hui. "Historical Studies of Rhetorical Women Here and There: Methodological Challenges to Dominant Interpretive Frameworks." *Rhetoric Society Quarterly* 32.1 (2002): 81–98. Print.

13.
DRAMA IN THE ARCHIVES: REREADING METHODS, REWRITING HISTORY
Cheryl Glenn and Jessica Enoch

History, gathered slowly, slowly falls apart (James). It always has, it always will, and it should. After all, if historians of any stripe (rhetoric, composition, literature, politics, philosophy, history, and so on) were content with the way history was being told, if historians accepted the past as a set of determining factors that once and for all prefigure the present, or if any of us believed that history could tell us about a past that was really "there," then history, once gathered and written, would *never* change—and neither would we.[1] But histories do change—in response to the dominant values of institutions, cultures, and historiographers (history writers) themselves. Histories of rhetoric and composition are a case in point.

Our goal in this article is to examine the historiographic trajectory of rhetoric and composition studies by analyzing archival practices (our own and others), using Kenneth Burke's dramatistic pentad as our analytical tool. In the process, we hope to demonstrate how a Burkean framework of "scenes, acts, agents, agencies, purposes, and attitudes" can invigorate our understanding of historiographic methods and open up new possibilities for future histories of rhetoric and composition.[2]

The time is auspicious for such an analysis, especially given the drama in the archives over the past fifty years. The landmark histories of our field were established by the archival work of such respected researchers as Albert R. Kitzhaber, James Berlin, and John Brereton.[3] Their archival scholarship sparked the historiographic work that would soon follow, including such transformative historiographies as those by Jacqueline Jones Royster and Jean C. Williams, Anne Ruggles Gere, Nan Johnson, David Russell, and many others.[4] Thus, ever since Kitzhaber returned from the archives with a usable past that propelled us forward, these and countless other historians of rhetoric and composition have been rereading the archives, revising research practices, and rewriting histories, always relying on the elements of the Burkean pentad.[5] The resulting historiographies motivated actions. Whether they showcased traditionally valued people and practices or shed light on the "ways that underrepresented groups have acquired and exercised the arts of rhetoric to garner historical agency," these writings

---

Glenn, Cheryl and Jessica Enoch. "Drama in the Archives: Rereading Methods, Rewriting History." *CCC* 61.2 (Dec. 2009): 321–342. Print.

demonstrate just how rhetoric and composition history, once gathered and written, falls apart, only to be regathered and rewritten, regularly—and purposefully (Miller and Jones 436).

"Act, Scene, Agent, Agency, Purpose"—Burke tells us that although "men have shown great enterprise and inventiveness in pondering matters of human motivation," "one can simplify [that] subject by this pentad of key terms" (*Grammar* xv), which is what we do in this article. His dramatistic pentad provides familiar guides for us as we explore the "drama in the archives."[6] Within the archive (the scene), the researcher (agent) engages (agency) in a variety of recovery and recuperative practices (acts) directed toward a specific end (purpose). And the familiar ratio between those key pentadic terms (scene:act, scene:agent, agent:agency, and so on) provides purchase for an even closer examination.

We have chosen to use the elements of the dramatistic pentad to mark the sections of our essay not only because of their enthymematic familiarity but also to emphasize their mutually heuristic (and thus sometimes overlapping) nature in revealing human motives. Our framework, however, entails certain limitations. First is the limitation of this linear format, which demands that we explain consecutively a process that is overlapping, interactional, and (to use Burke's term) "compellingly corresponding"— even when illuminated by the dramatistic "ratios" ("Dramatism" 446). Second, we are limited by what Burke refers to as our "trained incapacities," our orientations and worldviews that give rise to a partial perspective, whereby our "very abilities can function as blindnesses" (*Permanence* 7).[7] Nonetheless, we think the pentad with its inherent ratios is a useful way to explore the drama in the archives. To that end, we have strived to overcome our own incapacities by leveraging a Burkean perspective by incongruity during the writing of this essay. After all, it is through a perspective by incongruity that researchers make some of their most important discoveries.

We pose a Burkean challenge to traditional historiographic research methods and invigorate conventional practices by drawing on our archival research that "troubled" histories of rhetoric and composition.[8] Much of our argument arises from our own acts, agency, scenes, purpose—and ourselves as actors (or agents) with attitudes—yet we hope that our argument reveals how the interrogation of various features of the archival drama can create opportunities for all of us researchers to continue to enrich contemporary understanding of researching and writing histories of our field.

Act I: Searching for Archival Materials with a Purpose

We begin our analysis with a focus on the ratio between "act" and "purpose." Burke tells us that the dramatistic approach is implicit in the key term *act*: "'Act' is thus a terministic center from which many related considerations can be shown to 'radiate,' as though it were a 'god-term' from which a whole universe of terms is" ("Dramatism" 445). This "act" implies an agent or "actor" (the researcher) and must have an "end," or a purpose, "a future state of affairs toward which the process of action is oriented" (447). As the initial dramatistic element, "act" is the formulation of the project and research agenda. The researcher rarely identifies an archive containing a ready-made research project.

More frequently, he or she begins with a broad research question and then reads (widely and deeply, across genres and subjects) until he or she ascertains an outline of significance for the project at hand. Once the researcher has a handle on the topic, he or she considers the kind of archival documents that might further the project.

The question then becomes one of selecting relevant materials. For years now, historians of rhetoric and composition have studied the history of university-level writing practices by turning their attention toward archival and primary documents such as "actual student writings, teacher records, unprinted notes, and pedagogical materials, and ephemera that writing courses have always generated but never kept" (Connors 225). These are the documents that provide insight into the material practices of English 101 and its iterations. These are the "stories about the tribe that make the tribe real" (234).

Scholars in our field curious about the contributions of women or other marginalized groups to the teaching of rhetoric and writing, figures who are not (yet) recognized as members of the rhetoric and composition community, might face setbacks in terms of this particular historiographic expectation concerning primary documents. In fact, just the purpose-act ratio of wondering about such figures can trigger a trained incapacity that "blinds" the researcher from quickly locating whatever resources might fuel this line of inquiry. Jess worked to overcome such trained incapacity during her dissertation research. Interested in how teachers may have participated in the rhetorical education of nonwhite students, Jess found herself reading widely about Mexican education in Texas during the period of the Mexican Revolution (1910–1920), a historical moment marked by shifting national identities, economic growth and disparity, wartime strife, and changing educational practices. When she searched for what Robert J. Connors identifies as field-specific archival materials (textbooks, student writing, teacher notes, pedagogical materials), she came up empty-handed, her search seemingly reifying the "myth of Mexican indifference toward public education": "Mexican Americans have not really cared for education or else they have failed to appreciate its importance and benefit to their community in particular and to the society at large" (San Miguel xvi).

To challenge this myth of indifference, Jess returned to secondary sources, purposefully reading beyond the myth, beyond her trained incapacity to consider what other kinds of materials (other than textbooks, pedagogical materials, student papers) might reflect educational initiatives inside the Mexican community. In a moment of serendipity, she came across José Limón's 1974 essay. "El Primer Congreso Mexicanista de 1911: A Precursor to Contemporary Chicanismo," which mentions *La Crónico*, a Laredo, Texas, Spanish-language newspaper that focused on a number of prominent issues, one of which was the discrimination of Mexican students in Texas public schools (86). Finally, Jess had the foothold she needed, proving Jean Ferguson Carr's point: "the tension between planned rigor and the luck of the moment is a valuable insight for archival researchers: it encourages them to return to their archives with competing questions, with refreshed eyes and interests, to pay attention to the remnant or the out of place" (239–40). "Refreshed," Jess redirected her search for viable historiographic resources from that of teachers' notes and textbooks to *La Crónica*.

The turn was pivotal, for Jess uncovered a wealth of information concerning Mexican teachers Jovita Idar, Marta Peña, and Leonor Villegas de Magnón, who used *La Crónica* as an alternative site to educate their Mexican students, thereby sidestepping the discrimination of Texas public schools. Had Jess not worked past her frustrations when she could not locate traditionally valued primary materials, had she not let go of the disciplinary ideal of such materials, and had she not rethought the language teachers might use, she never would have located *La Crónica*, let alone the valuable rhetorical educations inspired by these teachers. In retrospect, it makes sense that a Mexican newspaper might serve as a pedagogical resource and that Mexican teachers might use Spanish! But the trained incapacity of our discipline too often prompts us to imagine that our field's historical documents are defined by a specific list (students writing, textbooks, class notes) and that these materials are written in English only.

As Jess's experience demonstrates, rethinking what constitutes primary and archival materials can enrich the histories of rhetoric and composition with new perspectives and voices. Rethinking methods of research can as well. When Cheryl was conducting research for *Rhetoric Retold: Regendering the Tradition from Antiquity through the Renaissance,* she found herself moving from the materials she was "supposed" to read and translate at the Newberry Library to those she found simply interesting. In making this move, she hit pay dirt. The easy-to-read and gorgeously illustrated second-century gynecological guides of Galen of Pergamum fortuitously illuminated the one-sex model of humanity that dominated thinking from antiquity through the Renaissance. With his detailed gynecological and anatomical drawings of males and females, Galen persuaded early thinkers that women were, in essence, imperfect, undeveloped men, who lacked one vital and superior characteristic: heat. "Now just as mankind is the most perfect of all animals, so within mankind the man is more perfect than the woman, and the reason for his perfection is his excess of heat, for heat is Nature's primary instrument" (2: 630). The cultural construction of women as inferior had been "proved" by science.

Thus, by questioning the trained incapacity that conditions the first and most basic act of the drama—identifying potential resources—we can see how all scholars might invigorate the field's history in new ways. Indeed, "Much of the pleasure and skill of archival work is the ability to be open to illumination, to what a document can frame or call into question" (Carr 239). Considering archival work in terms of act and purpose and realizing how the two elements interanimate help researchers like the two of us remain open to new materials as well as new methods and new readings.

Scene I: The Archives

"Obviously," Burke tells us, "the concept of scene can be widened or narrowed" ("Dramatism" 446). But "insofar as men's actions are to be interpreted in terms of the circumstances in which they are acting, their behavior would fall under the heading of a 'scene-act ratio'" (446). In this section, we discuss the "scene" of the archives, a scene essential to this exploration because of the acts that can take place within it, the agents that work there, their agency, and their purpose.

It is difficult to tease apart the acts of researching, writing, and reading, for the scholar is simultaneously refining a research question, looking for sources, and evaluating each archive, that "revered place of pilgrimage.... Mecca" (Phelps 1). Even though traveling to "Mecca" "requires temporal and financial sacrifice ..., the traveler is sustained by the prospect of discovery ..., the perpetual hope that the next box, the next folder, the next file, will contain the elusive find that will afford a window to the past" (1). Connors confirms this description of the archives, defining the uppercase-A Archives as containing those "rarest and most valuable of data" that usually exist in "only a single copy," what most scholars believe to be the "only *real* historical sources" (225; emphasis added).

Given that traveling to the archive can be expensive, time-consuming, and risky, many scholars initiate archival work at rare books libraries at prominent institutions, sites that are likely to hold relevant materials. Rhetoric and composition scholars (Brereton, Berlin, Sharon Crowley, Robin Varnum and Karyn Hollis, for instance) excavate archives at Harvard, Yale, Michigan, Iowa, Amherst, and Bryn Mawr—sites that have proved to be abundant sources of student writing, rhetoric and composition documents, and textbook collections. Such archives have enabled scholars working on a wide variety of historiographic projects to reread archival materials and rewrite the history of our field.

Not all archival research in rhetoric and composition begins—or ends—on a university campus or at a great research library, however. With increasing regularity, many researchers in rhetoric and composition have looked beyond Connors's Archive to consider what other, lowercase-A archives might hold, archives that don't immediately promise insights into the practices or histories of our field. Surprisingly, some of the most exciting research of late has even begun at home. Wendy Sharer, for instance, opens *Vote and Voice: Women's Organizations and Political Literacy, 1915–1930* by describing how her project came into being: with a discovery of political materials in her grandmother's attic, where Sharer found material evidence of her grandmother's involvement in a women's club, the Y-Dames of Bethlehem (Pennsylvania). This archive was full of "records of meetings and collaborative projects that were devoted to, among other things, reforming internal affairs, studying political history, and advancing career opportunities for women" (2). Such a finding made Sharer realize that her own "understanding of 'citizenship' and 'politics' was severely limited and, as a result, so was [her] knowledge of women's discursive practices of civic and political engagement" (3). This realization led to more archival research, more writing, and the publication of *Vote and Voice*.

Charlotte Hogg's discovery of her grandmother's unpublished writings set in motion the intellectual project on women's literacy practices that was to become *From the Garden Club: Rural Women Writing Community*. In her examination, Hogg studies "Early Paxton," a leather-bound collection of remembrances of pre-1925 Paxton, Nebraska, written by local women. One of the most prolific and talented in the group was Hogg's grandmother: "While most women who contributed to the book wrote less than ten pages ..., my grandma wrote forty-four pages" (20). Not surprisingly, "Early Paxton" was not archived in a great research library on a college campus: it was shelved at the local library, which, years ago, Hogg's grandmother urged her eleven-year-old granddaughter to visit upon moving to Paxton. Hogg would later return to this unpublished book manuscript to read it under the lens of rhetoric and composition studies. In addition to tapping "Early Paxton," she fortified her study by examining newspaper clippings, short essays, cards, letters, funeral programs, and notes that her grandmother had saved over the years in her roles as mother, grandmother, library president, Methodist Church historian, and Paxton correspondent of the *Keith County News*.

Both Sharer and Hogg compel us to look beyond the university setting to consider places such as the attic and community library as viable sites for archival work. But even if scholars are interested in learning about institutionalized writing practices and programs, they can rethink the scene of the archive. For example. Sharer joined another nontraditional archival project when she, Brent Henze, and Jack Selzer decided to focus on the history of Penn State's writing program. In their research, these scholars could not access catalogued materials that had been archived by professional librarians at the university library. Instead, they leveraged the collections of their "pack-rat" colleagues. "The institutional and personal familiarity," they write, "enabled us to access the 'hidden' archives—the old file boxes in the attic; the yellowed, hand-written essays in the bottom drawers; the textbooks thankfully overlooked during the last office cleanings; the records of forgotten meetings; and the indispensable memories of departmental personalities upon which this history could be built" (Henze, Selzer, and Sharer 2).

Hogg, Sharer, Henze, and Selzer all demonstrate ways to widen the scope for the "scene" of historical research in rhetoric and composition. Widening the scene of our research creates new opportunities for archival recovery, archival methods, and historiographic intervention, for, as Burke would argue, when one shifts or broadens the scene, the agents, agency, purpose, and act will also change accordingly. Thus, even when we don't have the good fortune to find archives in our relative's attic or bureaus or in our colleague's bottom drawer, there are smaller, local archives that call us to reconsider what the archive is and what purpose this archive can serve. These smaller collections or accidental discoveries also expand our notions of what counts as a primary resource, as an archive, and especially what counts as a contribution to rhetorical theory and composition practice as well as to the history of our discipline.

Scene II: Agents in the Archive

According to Burke, we cannot discuss the "agent" without considering his or her "scene" or "act": "Insofar as men's actions are to be interpreted in terms of the circumstances in which they are acting, their behavior would fall under the heading of a 'scene-act ratio'. But insofar as their acts reveal their different characters, their behavior would fall under the heading of an 'agent-act ratio'" ("Dramatism" 446). In *A Grammar of Motives,* Burke goes further to say "both act and agent require scenes that 'contain' them" (15).

So far in this article, we have defined researchers such as ourselves (scholars in rhetoric and composition) as Burkean agents in the research project: ideally, we pose the research question, identify an archive, travel to it, and then "act on" and activate the materials we locate. From this perspective, folks like us are the primary agents in the archival scene. In the following section, we focus attention on the work of the researcher-agent by considering agency and purpose. Here, we consider the other "agents" on the scene—the other people who contribute to the work that gets done in and through the archive.

Other Researcher-Agents

First among the group of other agents are the scholars in the field of rhetoric and composition whose work enables their fellow researchers to ask new and different historiographic questions. In "Rethinking Our Archive: A Beginning," Brereton writes that "historians depend on the work of their forebears, on the collecting that forms libraries and repositories great and small and on the interpretations and narratives that shape consciousnesses" (575). In the opening of this article, we alluded to the scene of archival work in our field and the agents who have worked inside it. Where would our discipline be if Kitzhaber had not created that extensive bibliography? How would we know where to go if Brereton had not laid out in his acknowledgments all of his primary and archival sources (*Origins* xix)?[9] The work of our "forebears" and our contemporaries provides us researchers with guideposts for locating materials, inspiration for considering both long-established and informal archives, and ideas for how best to employ archived materials for our own purposes.

Although it is true that many of us researchers share archival information in the acknowledgments and bibliographies of our texts, we can more actively collaborate on research methods, archival potential, and findings. Jane Donawerth and Lisa Zimmerelli stress "networking" as the "shortest route to [archival] discovery": "Whenever I meet a feminist scholar, I [Donawerth] ask her whether she has come across any pre-1900 women's writing on communication. Eleanor Kerkham remembered Sei Shonagon's *Pillow Book,* and there I found sections on letter writing, conversation, and preaching" (6). Donawerth's story exemplifies the rich luck of off-the-cuff conversations that deliver the initial inspiration of a research project. Luck, to be sure, but important luck. It is the luck of "finding a particular document, following a stray recommendation, opening the right box on the right day to discover something powerful or illuminating" (Carr 239).

Casual revelations are exciting, but systematic public networking could be even more reliably productive for established researchers and graduate students alike. To that end, researchers in our field might consider formalizing collaboration about archival research, starting with the membership of the Special Interest Groups on Archival Work at the Conference on College Composition and Communication and ending, perhaps, with a collaborative archival database, an online publication in which scholars report on the archives they have visited, the work they have conducted there, and available summaries of archived sources. This kind of work would not only enable new scholars in the field to see the range and variety of our archival work but also help them envision new possibilities for historiographic recovery.

Archivist Agents

In addition to creating stronger disciplinary networks among researcher-agents, it is also important to acknowledge the archivists themselves as vital agents in the archival scene. Archivists catalogue the materials, decide what to preserve, and determine how to catalogue it, thereby controlling the materials we can access and the processes we take to get to them. In addition, archivists see the archive collections purposefully, as a whole, while we researchers often limit our vision to the small part of the archive we intend to use. As Sharer writes, it is as important that scholars of rhetoric and composition be knowledgeable in research "acts" (the methods and methodologies of historical scholarship in our field) as well as in the acts of the archivist: "We cannot afford to ignore the various materials processes—acquisition, appraisal, collection management, description, indexing, preservation, oxidation, and deaccession—that affect the corpus of records on which we may be able to construct diverse and subversive narratives to challenge previous, exclusionary historical accounts of rhetoric" ("Disintegrating" 124).

Sharer calls scholars to gain a sense of the archivists' work and then to establish lines of communication with them about the kinds of primary and archival materials valuable to our field. One excellent example of such a practice is the collaboration between rhetoric and composition scholars Cinthia Gannett, Kate Tirabassi, Amy Zenger, and Brereton with archivist Elizabeth Slomba, who together created the Archives on the History of Writing and Writing Instruction at the University of New Hampshire (UNH). Through the process of building the archive, the four scholars in rhetoric and composition "learned a great deal about how archives are constructed and participated directly in the composition and collection of the archive itself," while Slomba "came to value a variety of artifacts related to writing pedagogy and writing program administration" (Gannett et al. 115). Gannet, Tirabassi, Zenger, Brereton, and Slomba are not the only ones who will reap the benefits of this project. This archive invites the writing community at UNH and the discipline at large to enter a detailed scene of writing at a specific university setting; it serves as material evidence for the ways agents in rhetoric and composition can work with archivist agents to preserve the important and valued documents in our field; and the archive itself widens the possibilities for even further archival investigation. If more scholars and archivists follow the lead of those who built the UNH archive, all of us in our discipline would gain a more detailed understanding of how writing has been taught across time and institutions.

Act II: Agent, Agency, Purpose, and More Agents

Burke tells us that all the dramatistic terms correspond, using the "purpose-agency" ratio to show the relation of means to ends ("Dramatism" 446). Any drama in the archives must account for both the means and purpose the researcher employs to achieve an end. Traditional histories and research agendas strived to demonstrate their objectivity in a reach toward the truth: "to repair the damage done by those who in past ages have falsified, distorted, or destroyed the written record" (Altick 2). We contemporary researchers also strive toward the truth at the same time that we readily admit the interestedness of our research stance and theoretical grounding. Archival records may be, as Connors writes, an "inert dusty mass of past records," but they are real sources of data, inert until they are animated (whether worked with or discarded) by the researcher himself or herself, who is another, equally "real" source of data.

In this section, we want to consider what this interestedness and theoretical grounding mean to both the archival project and the project of writing history. We acknowledge that written histories are always partial and always interested—*partial* in the sense that they remain incomplete with respect to the reality they presume to depict and *interested* in the sense that they are interpretive renderings of evidence (Howard; emphasis added). Archival acts of reading, then, are tethered to the researcher's perceptions and prejudices as well as the theoretical frame used to approach his or her work. As we make these considerations about our own interestedness and theoretical grounding, though, we also consider how these two ideas prompt scholars to acknowledge other important agents in the archival scene besides the researcher and the archivist.

Interestedness

In the field of rhetoric and composition, it has become almost commonplace for researchers to devote space in their manuscripts to revealing their standpoint and interestedness in their project. In the opening paragraphs of *Unspoken: A Rhetoric of Silence*, Cheryl makes this commentary: "I am white, female, heterosexual, feminine, feminist, hearing, well-educated at a Big Ten school, fully employed at another Big Ten school. Thus it is that this volume bears the ideological weight of my own perspective, and while I cannot reduce it, I can acknowledge it" (xix). Jess makes a similar move as she articulates her relationship to her historical subjects in the introduction to *Refiguring Rhetorical Education: Women Teaching African American, Native American, and Chicano/a Students, 1865–1911*: "I am a white, middle-class woman teaching students from various cultured and classed backgrounds in the twenty-first century. Time, age, race, culture, and language are all factors that separate me from [the teachers in this study].... [Yet] it is in recognizing these differences that I continue to connect myself to these women because I see them doing the work I want to do—the work I think we should do in this discipline" (32–33). In both cases, there is more to our declarations than "merely" situating ourselves and our experiences: We are also declaring our (multiple) identities, the ways we make sense of our lived and researched experiences. Even though we may be underestimating the real epistemic and political complexities of these proclaimed identities, we are, nonetheless, cognizant of their interpretive power and limitations.[10]

In *Traces of a Stream: Literacy and Social Change among African American Women*, Jacqueline Jones Royster argues for the importance of articulating one's positionality in relation to one's research:

> I note the need for researchers and scholars to articulate their own ideological standpoints systematically, not simply as a personal or professional flag to wave at a convenient moment but in support of ideological clarity; in recognition of how our viewpoints are implicated in scholarly presentation and representation; and also in the support of humility, as we locate ourselves within the text as scholars, and thereby as people who have interpretive power.
> (281)

Royster's words serve to remind us that our descriptions of who we are and how we come to the research and our research subjects resonate with significance, if for no other reason than they continuously oblige us to consider how and why we read and write as we do.

Taking responsibility for our scholarly stance (or interestedness), though, extends far beyond the printed page in which the scholar acknowledges his or her positionality. This understanding of one's position inside and approach to the final text must accompany the scholar from the initial stages of archival inquiry through the completion of the writing, steadily interanimating the multiple acts that comprise the writing process. Moreover, such statements help the reader understand where the researcher thinks he or she stands in terms of the project and the ways that interestedness informs both the researcher's overarching agenda and the final text.

Often, it is one's positionality that creates a fruitful dissonance, a Burkean perspective by incongruity, which inspires the initial question-cum-research agenda. As a graduate student, Cheryl, like nearly everyone else in her academic generation, studied *the* history of rhetoric, a history of public, political, persuasive men. Jess's graduate curriculum included the study of rhetorical education, whose rare female figures were usually portrayed as either innocuous mother-teachers or spinster-disciplinarians. Both of us felt dissonance in our intellectual and pedagogical lives. Cheryl wanted to find a way to participate in a rhetorical tradition that had, for nearly 2,500 years, systematically excluded the likes of her (women) as well as "workers, people of color, and other outsiders" (Miller and Jones 422). Jess wanted to challenge the belief that the female educators were as absent and ineffective as public memory reported her to be. Our field of study, received-at-the-time history, did not contribute a positive value to our daily life. So, we each worked to "break up and dissolve those parts of the past" that conflicted with our contemporary living and ideologies (Nietzsche 75), tapped the resources of the archives, and embarked on revisionist and critical historiographies. As we entered the archive with these interests in mind, we also worked to understand how these motivations as well as our personal and professional backgrounds might inflect our work.

Naturally, any research stance leads to accentuating some materials and passing over others; we simply cannot tell everything and move in every direction. Akin to Burke's terministic screen, our research narrative is a "*reflection* of reality; but by its very nature, it must be a *selection* of reality; and to this extent, it must function also as a *deflection* of reality" (*Language* 45; emphasis in original). What is important is that we do our best to try to uncover the ways our positionality operates and to consider, throughout the research and writing process, how this stance "channels" us to write one kind of history and directs us away from other possibilities.

Theoretical Grounding

Along with many other scholars, we have worked to interrogate those parts of the past that conflicted with our contemporary ideologies, consciously reading the primary materials we accessed in the archive through an interested, theoretical framework. As we engaged in this two-part process, we soon realized that this relationship between archival reading and theoretical grounding creates a generative tension that opens up possibilities for what we see, value, and then leverage.

As we entered the archive and read certain archival materials, we found that we needed to relinquish the conceptual apparatus that produced a male-only tradition of rhetoric (Cheryl) and a gendered model of rhetorical education (Jess). Not surprisingly, feminist theory enabled us (and many others) to resist traditional histories and historiographic practices inside the field as a means to create new kinds of historical inquiry and archival reading practices. Cheryl's initial, graduate-student work on Aspasia (seven pages of historical description that could only be described as "thin") eventually moved forward, but only after she was able to use feminism as a way to broaden her definition of rhetoric, its practice in the private sphere, and the requirements for being a rhetor (figures whose contributions appear only in secondary sources, like Socrates—and Aspasia). Slow in coming, these small adjustments led to rich payoffs. Years later, Jess could take advantage of feminist theories and methodologies to question disciplinary narratives of rhetorical education that focused only on the achievements of canonical rhetorician-teachers. If she shifted the definition of rhetorical education from teaching *about* rhetors and traditional rhetorical theories to teaching students to *become* rhetors themselves (to be active participants in cultural and civic conversations), she instantly expanded the range of archived texts, teachers, and students she could study.

Thus, feminist theory enabled us to use a different lens for reading in the archives. Although every scholar will not and should not use feminist theory as a primary theoretical lens, we should remain conscious of the ways in which any theoretical frame we choose (like our positionality) enhances and limits our work. For instance, Carol Mattingly warns that the feminist perspective scholars bring to the archives can lead them to study only certain kinds of historical women, thereby misreading or overlooking the rhetorical work of women they might not immediately gravitate toward, such as socially conservative nineteenth-century women (103). As a way to address Mattingly's concern, scholars must continually put their archival reading in conversation with their theoretical frame. Rather than simply applying theory to what they find in the archive, researchers should allow for a reciprocal process—one that lets the archives speak back to the theory and allows the findings there to push against, open up, question, extend, constrict, or even disregard the theoretical frame altogether. Neither the theoretical approach nor the archival reading is predominant: the reading and theory work together, informing each other as well as the researcher.

More Agents in the Archive

Finally, in addition to reflecting on positionality inside the research project and the theoretical approach we bring to it, we must consciously broaden the archival scene to include who else, beyond the researcher and archivist, might be affected by our scholarly conversation. When Royster sets out her afrafeminist methodological approach in *Traces of a Stream,* she explains that her approach should prompt a paradigm shift in the ways scholars conceive of both their subjects and their audiences. Scholars should develop more discerning understandings of *"who* the primary and secondary audiences are and *who,* even, the *agents* of research and scholarship include" (*Traces* 274: emphasis in original). In other words, researchers must keep in mind the members of the community they are writing about: "Whatever the knowledge accrued, it [sh]ould be both presented and represented with this community, and at least its potential for participation and response, in mind" (274).

Royster is not alone in this perception, as researchers using various methodologies are expected to account for how their own positionalities and ways of asking, seeing, interpreting, speaking, and writing influence their production of "partial representations of engagement in the field" (Jacobs-Huey 792). Increasingly, rhetoric and composition scholars are, like Royster, identifying agencies and audiences, and "operating ethnographically" (Royster, *Traces* 282). When Cheryl embarked on the research that would become *Unspoken,* she spent several weeks working in the Center for Southwest Research, an archive located on the University of New Mexico campus. Her purpose was to uncover materials that could explain the stereotype of the "silent Indian" that circulated so widely in sociolinguistic and cultural anthropological research. Cheryl soon discovered that if she were to make any sense of the archival materials in terms of that research, she needed to speak with Native American people herself, asking for their comments on the materials she had uncovered. During a series of interviews and meetings, Cheryl realized that all the Native people knew about the stereotype and welcomed the opportunity to get the story straight—to speak for their individual selves (never for everyone in their tribe, let alone for *all* Native people) on tape, in person, over the telephone, or through email. And when Cheryl shared her word-for-word transcripts with them, they sometimes improved them, always for the purpose of talking back to researchers and research, of speaking for themselves.

"The goal," Royster writes, "is better practices so that we can exchange perspectives, negotiate meaning, and create understanding with the intent of being in a good position to cooperate," benefit, and understand the people who are "*subject matter* but not *subjects*" ("When" 38, 32; emphasis added). Even with this goal in mind, the dialogic ethnography that Cheryl undertook (and many other researchers in our field continue to employ) remains a genre involving the art of interpretation. It is not an exact science—and carries with it many of the same tensions of historiography: the task of connecting the "real" and the discourse. Even the most collaborative and dialogic ethnography or archival inquiry, even the most ethically admirable, is an intervention into a world that has been lived and narrated by the person who has experienced it and then is once again recorded, interpreted, and circulated by the researcher. In other words, historiographers, like ethnographers, concentrate on connecting the experiences of *some one* to the representation of those experiences by *someone else*. Thus, the issue is not so much *why* we approach various groups of people or archival collections but *how* we work to understand and honor their perspective, their experience. The *goal* of accurate interpretation is never enough. When we engage in research, we need to know what our self-interest is, as well as how that interest might enrich our disciplinary field and how it might affect others (perhaps even bridging the gap between academia and other communities). We also need to resolve to participate in a reciprocal cross-boundary exchange in which we talk *with* and listen *to* others, whether they are speaking to us in person or via archival materials.

Conclusion: Rereading Archival Dramas, Rewriting History

As we hope we have demonstrated, the drama in the archives is an ongoing one—much to our delight. Each new generation of rhetoric and composition scholars invigorates the archival drama by producing a version of history that, in turn, prompts new questions and concerns about the historiographic process and product. Our dramatistic analysis aims to help scholars continue to consider how we might open up even more possibilities for archival recovery. A concerted attention to the "act" of choosing archival documents and locations ("scenes") can enrich our sense of the kind of texts that can contribute to our historical understandings as well as the places where these texts might be found. A greater consciousness of the "agents" in the archive can prompt us to initiate better networks among scholars and to collaborate with archivists as a means to broaden our historiographic vision and deepen our knowledge of what an archive is and can be. And, finally, a consistent reflection on who we are as researchers can call us to think more critically about our "purpose" as we work to interrogate our "agency"— our interestedness in our research agendas, our choice of theoretical frames, and our attention to and regard for the *other* agents in the archive.

Furthermore, in taking this *excursus* among the ratios of Burke's pentadic terms, we have also been especially conscious of our central metaphor: the drama in the archives. For us, this metaphor has been most powerful in its quiet reminder that the ratios of the pentad shift and overlap; their tensions inevitably weaken and collapse before rising again in a different iteration. Despite our attempts to keep the ratios separate, such categories always overlap and sometimes leak. Such leakage reminds us that any categories or ratios that we have set out (pentadic ratios, un/traditional research, histories and historiographies) continue to be sites of theoretical struggle.

We highlight this theoretical struggle as a key concern, yet we do not mean to say that "anything goes" in terms of archival research and historiographic writing. Although no single historiography can be the "correct" one, although new archives and archival materials are recovered by every generation of scholars, all responsible archival research and the resulting historiography must be based on facts, research, and primary materials. After all, "[g]enuine historical scholarship demands that the central questions underlying the investigation should be potentially answerable with factual evidence" (Hume 411).[11]

Thus, even as rhetoric and composition scholars work on that axis we refer to as "history," an axis pitted by the skeptical probings of postmodern and post-stutctural critiques, our discipline continues to place real value in historical knowledge, in understanding research methods, in reading widely to the point of reading promiscuously, in contextualizing our research; in short, in doing our homework. Linda Ferreira-Buckley admonishes us to do just that. "Years ago," she writes, "our histories were undertheorized; today I fear they are underresearched" (28).

As we hope our discussion of the archival drama indicates, Burke's pentad offers a rich conceptual heuristic through which rhetoric and composition scholars can continue to scrutinize our research practices and articulate our histories. After all, historiographers want to make truth claims. We do care whether a given account is genuinely credible, probable, even true, because what is ultimately at stake is not only constructing a "usable past" that speaks to present concerns, but also treating that past ethically while getting it right (as far as doing so is possible). In the process, rhetoric and composition scholars might uncover some treasures among the written, visual, or material artifacts that our subjects have left behind, or we might decide once and for all how things "really" were in bygone times. Even more significant, if we consciously and carefully activate the materials in the archives, we might discover ways to address the present scholarly moment meaningfully and announce the near future insightfully.

Notes

1 We wish to thank *CCC* editor Deborah Holdstein, the anonymous *CCC* reviewers, and Jack Selzer, whose advice helped us revise this essay.
2 J. Clarke Rountree's practical Burkean criticism helped Cheryl and Jess respond to one of Burke's most basic questions: "What is involved, when we say what people are doing and why they are doing it?" (*Grammar* xv).
3 Kitzhaber's 1953 groundbreaking dissertation was transformed into *Rhetoric in American Colleges, 1850–1900* by John T. Gage in 1990. Kitzhaber mapped out the history of nineteenth-century American composition theories and practices, using archived textbooks and journal articles as his primary sources. His dissertation would transform twentieth-century appreciation of school rhetoric, proving that composition had a tradition worth examining and revaluing. Berlin and Brereton both extend Kitzhaber's work. Berlin dived into the archives to examine textbooks, exams, surveys, and course and professional materials, bringing to our consciousness the forward-looking, process-oriented, but nearly forgotten work in composition studies conducted by Fred Newton Scott, Joseph Villiers Denney, and Gertrude Buck. Brereton's *The Origins of Composition Studies in the American College, 1875–1925* brought to light the "public record," retrieving from the archives "what composition specialists said to each other, to their students, and to concerned citizens" (xv). These long-archived common materials (magazine articles, scholarly reports, textbooks, teachers' testimony, student papers, writing curricula, and course instructions) comprised "the common knowledge of composition teachers and administrators" (xv).
4 In "History in the Spaces Left," Royster and Williams critique the ways historiographies of composition "cast a shadow" on the work of African Americans. Royster and Williams, then, shine a light on the contributions Hallie Quinn Brown, Hugh M. Gloster, and Alain Locke made to composition practice and pedagogy (581). Gere turns our disciplinary gaze to alternative sites of writing and rhetorical instruction. Johnson gives us a dazzling array of nineteenth-century parlor rhetorics. Russell uncovers the pedagogies for writing in academic disciplines. Other historians include Lucille M. Schultz, who explains the writing pedagogies for and practices of young nineteenth-century writers. Together with Jean Ferguson Carr and Stephen Carr, Schulz analyzes the nineteenth-century literacy textbooks used at home and at school. Finally, Patricia Donahue and Gretchen Flesher Moon provide the composition histories of small colleges and universities.
5 So far, the positive results of studies like these are at least three: (1) they rewrite rhetoric and composition history; (2) they stimulate our thinking in terms of which historical moments, people, and places merit our scholarly attention—and a place in our field's history; and (3) they reflect the ways historiographic practice shifts in relation to the questions and imperatives of the present moment. As Thomas P. Miller and Joseph Jones remind us, "Our histories are not what they were but neither are we" (436).

6 The drama is played out in the interaction of archival materials, the researcher's current perceptions, and the researcher's prejudices (Connors), which results in an "attitude" or "archivists with different attitudes" (Severino).
7 Even the most basic research practices (choosing an archive, locating materials, re/reading documents) constitute trained incapacities that "blind" us to alternative ways of locating, interpreting, and recovering sources. We are limited by our interpretive abilities as well as by the resource materials we locate, cannot locate, or do not know about.
8 In our archival research, we've also been troubled by history. Whether we have worked at the Newberry library (Chicago, IL), the Houghton Library (Cambridge, MA), the National Library of Scotland and the University of Edinburgh Library (Edinburgh, Scotland), the Center for Southwest Studies (Albuquerque, NM), the Cumberland County History Society (Carlisle, PA), the American Antiquarian Society (Amherst, MA), the Webb County Heritage Foundation (Laredo, TX), or the Kenneth Burke Papers at the Paterno Library (University Park, PA), we have missed connections, followed false leads, and been confused by the texts themselves. Nearly every trouble became eventually clear.
9 The Boston Public Library, the New York Public Library, the Library of Congress, as well as the archives and libraries at Boston University and the Universities of Minnesota, Michigan, Wisconsin, Massachusetts at Boston and at Amherst, and, of course, the Pusey and Widener Libraries at Harvard.
10 As Susan Sánchez-Casal and Amie A. Macdonald teach us, "by surfacing how our social location both enhances and obstructs [our claims to know . . . we] consider the productive instability of the link between experience and epistemology" (9).
11 Later he warns his readers to "note that this is a very carefully hedged statement," which he goes on to explain.

Works Cited

Altick, Richard D. *The Scholar Adventurers*. 1950. New York: Free Press, 1966.

Berlin, James A. *Rhetoric and Reality: Writing Instruction in American Colleges 1990–1985*. Carbondale: Southern Illinois UP, 1987.

———. *Writing Instruction in Nineteenth-Century American Colleges*. Carbondale: Southern Illinois UP, 1984.

Bizzell, Patrica, and Bruce Herzberg, eds. *The Rhetorical Tradition*. 2nd ed. New York: Bedford, 2001.

Brereton, John C., ed. *The Origins of Composition Studies in the American College, 1875–1925*. Pittsburgh: U of Pittsburgh P, 1995.

———. "Rethinking Our Archive: A Beginning" *College English* 61.5 (1991): 574–76.

Burke, Kenneth, "Dramatism." *International Encyclopedia of the Social Sciences* (1968): 445–51.

———. *A Grammar of Motives*. Berkeley: U of California P, 1969.

———. *Language as Symbolic Action*. Berkeley: U of California P, 1966.

———. *Permanence and Change*. 3rd ed. Berkeley: U of California P, 1984.

Carr, Jean Ferguson. "Afterword," Donahue and Moon 237–40.

Carr, Jean Ferguson, Stephen L. Carr, and Lucille M. Schultz. *Archives of Instruction: Nineteenth-Century Rhetorics, Readers, and Composition Books in the United States*. Carbondale: Southern Illinois UP, 2005.

Connors, Robert J. "Dreams and Play: Historical Method and Methodology." *Selected Essays of Robert J. Connor*. Ed. Lisa Ede and Andrea Lunsford. Boston: Bedford, 2003, 221–35.

Donahue, Patricia, and Gretchen Flesher Moon, eds. *Local Histories: Reading the Archives of Composition*, Pittsburgh: Pittsburgh UP, 2007.

Donawerth, Jane, and Lisa Zimmerelli. "Dialoguing with *Rhetorica*." *Peitho* 8.1 (2003): 4–6.
Enoch, Jessica. "On the Borders of Tradition: Female Teachers and Rhetorical Education. 1865–1911." Unpublished manuscript.
———. *Refiguring Rhetorical Education: Women Teaching African American, Native American, and Chicano/a Students, 1865–1911*. Carbondale: Southern Illinois UP, 2008.
Ferreira-Buckley, Linda. "Serving Time in the Archives." *Rhetoric Review* 16.1 (1997): 26–28.
Gage, John T. Introduction. Kitzhaber vii–xxii.
Galen of Pergamum. *On the Usefulness of the Parts of the Body*. Trans. Margaret Tallmadge May. 2 vols. Ithaca: Cornell UP, 1968.
Gannett, Cinthia, Elizabeth Slomba, Kate Tirabassi, Amy Zenger, and John C. Brereton. "'It Might Come in Handy.' Composing a Writing Archive at the University of New Hampshire: A Collaboration between the Dimond Library and the Writing-across-the-Curriculum/Connors Writing Center, 2001–2003." *Centers for Learning: Writing Centers and Libraries*. Ed. James Elmborg and Sheril Hook. Chicago: Association of College and Research Libraries. 2005. 115–37.
Gere, Anne Ruggles. "Kitchen Tables and Rented Rooms: The Extracurriculum of Composition." *College Composition and Communication* 45.1 (1994): 75–107.
Glenn, Cheryl. *Rhetoric Retold: Regendering the Tradition from Antiquity through the Renaissance*. Carbondale: Southern Illinois UP, 1996.
———. *Unspoken: A Rhetoric of Silence*. Carbondale: Southern Illinois UP, 2004.
Henze, Brent, Jack Selzer, and Wendy Sharer. *1977: A Cultural Moment in Composition*. West Lafayette: Parlor, 2008.
Hogg, Charlotte. *From the Garden Club: Rural Women Writing Community*. Lincoln: U of Nebraska P, 2006.
Hollis, Karyn. *Liberating Voices: Writing at the Bryn Mawr Summer School for Women Workers*. Carbondale: Southern Illinois UP, 2004.
Howard, Jean. "Towards a Postmodern, Politically Committed, Historical Practice." *Uses of History: Marxism, Postmodernism, and the Renaissance*. Ed. Francis Backer, Peter Hulme, and Margaret Iverson. Manchester, Eng.: Manchester UP, 1991. 108–09.
Hume, Robert D. "The Aims and Limits of Historical Scholarship." *The Review of English Studies*. New Series 53.21 (2002): 399–422.
Jacobs-Huey, Lanita. "The Natives Are Gazing and Talking Back: Reviewing the Problematics of Positionality, Voice, and Accountability among 'Native' Anthropologists." *American Anthropologist* 103.4 (2002): 791–804.
James, Elizabeth. "history." *1:50 000: sixteen short poems*. London: Vennel, 1992. n.p.
Johnson, Nan. *Gender and Rhetorical Space, 1866–1910*. Carbondale: Southern Illinois UP, 2002.
Kitzhaber, Albert R. *Rhetoric in American Colleges, 1859–1900*. Dallas: Southern Methodist U, 1990.
Limón, José. "El Primer Congreso Mexicanista de 1911: A Precursor to Contemporary Chicanismo." *Aztlán* 5.1&2 (1974): 85–117.
Mattingly, Carol. "Telling Evidence: Rethinking What Counts in Rhetoric." *Rhetoric Society Quarterly* 32.1 (2002): 94–108.
Miller, Thomas P., and Joseph G. Jones. "Review: Working Out Our History." *College English* 67.4 (2005): 421–39.
Nietzsche, Friedrich. "On the Uses und Disadvantages of History for Life." *Untimely Meditations*. Trans. R. J. Hollingdale. Cambridge: Cambridge UP, 1983. 57–123.
Phelps, Christopher. "My Dream Archive." *The Chronicle of Higher Education* 53.18 (2007): 1.

Rountree, J. Clarke. "Coming to Terms with Kenneth Burke's Pentad." *The American Communication Journal* 1.3 (1998). 5 Aug. 2009 <http://acjournal.org/holdings/vol1/iss3/burke/rountree.html>.

Royster, Jacqueline Jones. *Traces of a Stream: Literacy and Social Change among African American Women*. Pittsburgh: U of Pittsburgh P, 2000.

———. "When the First Voice You Hear Is Not Your Own." *College Composition and Communication* 47.1 (1996): 26–40.

Royster, Jacqueline Jones, and Jean C. Williams. "History and the Spaces Left: African American Presence and Narratives of Composition Studies." *College Composition and Communication* 50.4 (1999): 563–84.

Russell, David. *Writing in the Academic Disciplines: A Curricular History*. 2nd ed. Carbondale: Southern Illinois UP, 2002.

Sánchez-Casal, Susan, and Amie A. Macdonald. "Introduction: Feminist Reflections on the Pedagogical Relevance of Identity." *Twenty First-Century Feminist Classrooms: Pedagogies of Identity and Difference*. Ed. Amie Macdonald and Susan Sánchez-Casal. New York: Palgrave MacMillan, 2002. 1–30.

San Miguel, Guadalupe, Jr. *"Let Them All Take Heed": Mexican Americans and the Campaign for Educational Equality in Texas, 1910–1981*. Austin: U of Texas P, 1987.

Schultz, Lucille M. *The Young Composers: Composition's Beginnings in Nineteenth-Century Schools*. Carbondale: Southern Illinois UP, 1999.

Severino, Carol. "Review: Archivists with Different Attitudes." *College English* 62.5 (2000): 645–53.

Sharer, Wendy. "Disintegrating Bodies of Knowledge: Historical Material and Revisionary Histories of Rhetoric." *Rhetorical Bodies*. Ed. Jack Selzer and Sharon Crowley. U of Wisconsin P, 1999. 120–42.

———. *Vote and Voice: Women's Organizations and Political Literacy. 1915–1930*. Carbondale: Southern Illinois UP, 2004.

Varnum, Robin. *Fencing with Words: A History of Writing Instruction at Amherst College During the Era of Theodore Baird. 1938–1966*. Urbana: National Council of Teachers of English. 1996.

14.
INVISIBLE HANDS: RECOGNIZING ARCHIVISTS' WORK TO MAKE RECORDS ACCESSIBLE
Sammie L. Morris and Shirley K. Rose

Seasoned researchers know that it's a good idea to contact an archive before visiting to do research. This ensures that needed collections will be available onsite during the actual visit to the archives and allows the researcher to begin a conversation with the archivist about any additional relevant resources available. Starting such a conversation (the "reference interview") with the archivist in advance helps make a visit to the archives more efficient and fruitful. This reference role of archivists is generally understood, if not fully exploited, by most archival researchers.

For many researchers, however, the archivist's processing of collections, which includes all work done by the archivist to make a collection available to researchers, remains a mystery. The researcher may understand, for example, that certain preservation steps are taken with collections after they are received by the archives, but other steps are not always evident. We believe that if archival researchers know how to recognize the outcomes of archivists' processing and understand the principles behind processing decisions, they will have a better understanding of the archival materials they study.

Understanding archival theory and principles and knowing the best practices derived from them will help researchers anticipate potential problems and assess the potential usefulness of the archival materials they consult. It is especially important for researchers to know how to work with a repository's archivist if the materials they wish to examine are not yet processed. As an archivist (Sammie) and a researcher (Shirley) who worked together on a recent project, we've come to believe that if archival researchers can be better equipped to recognize the outcomes of archival practice, they can better interpret the materials they study and become better researchers. Our purpose here is to help researchers recognize and understand the work of the archivist's "invisible hands." Using the processing of the James Berlin Papers,[1] a collection of documents created by rhetorician James Berlin during his academic career as a case study, we explain how the two primary principles governing archival work—provenance and original order—inform archival-processing practices from selection through description.

Morris, Sammie L. and Shirley K. Rose. "Invisible Hands: Recognizing Archivists' Work to Make Records Accessible." *Working in the Archives: Practical Research Methods for Rhetoric and Composition.* Eds. Ramsey et al. Illinois: Southern Illinois Press, 2010: 51–78. Print.

We begin by describing the context for processing the James Berlin Papers, along with the goals of the processing project and its outcomes. Decisions made during the collection processing are explained as they relate to making it physically and intellectually accessible to researchers. We also hope to illustrate the importance to researchers of learning more about the reasoning behind archivists' decision making and about how to recognize the ways a collection changes after passing through the archivist's invisible hands. Researchers who understand what has guided archival decisions will be better prepared to ask the right questions about a collection and how it has been altered from the time it was acquired by the archives. With answers to these questions, researchers can feel more confident in drawing conclusions from a collection that may be used as evidence in their scholarly endeavors. We hope to spark a dialogue between our readers and the archivists with whom they work that will ultimately lead to better access to and research use of archival collections.

Background of the Project

The Office of the Provost at Purdue University supports a fellowship program, the Faculty Program of Study in a Second Discipline, that offers faculty an opportunity to extend their scholarship through study in a separate field by providing released time for engaging in study on the West Lafayette, Indiana, campus. As an English department faculty member, Shirley won a fellowship for spring 2006 for one semester's study of archival practice under Sammie's direction as the Purdue University archivist in order to develop practical experience to complement an understanding of archival theory. As an archival researcher in the humanities, Shirley had published essays based on the examination of archival materials related to rhetoric and composition and essays on theoretical issues related to records management and administration of writing programs. She had also taught two graduate seminars on documentation strategies for writing programs. Although she developed some knowledge of archival theory through informal study, she had not had an opportunity to study the theory in a systematic way or to develop hands-on experience in archival processing, applying theoretical principles in specific, concrete contexts.

Shirley had three primary objectives for her program of study: to develop sound practices in archival processing, such as accessioning, preservation, arrangement, and description; to enhance her theoretical understanding of principles and issues in archival practice; and to develop interdisciplinary connections between archival theory and rhetorical theory by working to articulate a theory of the archives as rhetorical practice. Although the Society of American Archivists has recognized the relevance of theory in areas such as sociology, philosophy, political science, law, accounting, anthropology, and economics, as well as science and the arts, the relevance of rhetorical theory to archival practices has not been explicitly recognized by the professional archivist community. Yet, because rhetorical theory addresses the creation, interpretation, and use of documents in specific contexts, it promises to be especially useful to archival practitioners.

As the Purdue University archivist, Sammie's role in the fellowship project was to provide advice and guidance to Shirley in processing a specific collection, the James

Berlin Papers. This included explanation of archives accessioning practices, including the legal transfer of the collection to the archival repository, along with guidelines for arranging, preserving, and describing the papers according to archival theory and principles. Sammie and Shirley met twice a week over the course of the semester to answer questions relating to the project. Sammie provided guidance on ordering the correct types of preservation supplies and on creating the finding aid[2] (archival inventory) describing the contents of the papers. Although the primary goal of the project was to allow Shirley to gain hands-on experience processing archival materials, Sammie also benefited from the project by gaining a better understanding of the viewpoint of the researcher. Our essay is an outcome of those discussions.

The James Berlin Papers

Shirley chose to process the James Berlin Papers for her fellowship project, which had been placed in her custody by Berlin's widow several years earlier. We will use Shirley's work on the project, under Sammie's supervision, as an example of the need for researchers to have an understanding of archivists' practices.

As most of our readers will know, James Berlin was an important scholar of the history of rhetoric and composition and a leading theorist of cultural studies composition pedagogies. He was a member of the English Department at Purdue University when he died suddenly of a heart attack in February 1994. The Berlin Papers comprise seven cubic feet of materials from Berlin's academic career, including teaching materials, research materials, and collegial correspondence dated from 1978 through 1994, with the bulk of the materials dating from Berlin's work at Purdue from 1986 to 1994.

Understanding Provenance

To understand the materials in any archival collection, researchers must know as much as possible about their provenance, the chain of custody of the materials, including what happened to them (and when) from the time they were originally created up to the point of being accessioned or added to the archival repository. This will allow the researcher to evaluate the authenticity and integrity of the materials as evidence.

For example, knowing that the materials in the James Berlin Papers were placed in Shirley's custody in 1998 by Sandy Berlin, the widow of James Berlin, helps an archival researcher to establish their authenticity as reliable documents created by Berlin. Knowing they are the contents of the file cabinets in Berlin's faculty office on campus at the time of his unexpected death will help a researcher understand why most of the materials date from 1986 or later. More specifically, knowing that some of the teaching materials were removed from Berlin's office files and later returned by faculty colleagues who took over his classes within a few days of his death will help a researcher understand why a few folders are organized differently from the others.

General information about the provenance of a collection is usually included in the public finding aid for a collection; but often the archivist or other staff will have access to additional, more specific information and will be able to give a more detailed account of the collection's history. Many archival repositories maintain a "collection file" for each collection, in which, along with other relevant information, they include a more detailed account of the collection's provenance—specifically, who among the staff has worked on the collection. There is even a good chance that the archives staff member with whom a researcher consults will have been involved in acquiring the materials or will have contributed to some or all of the processing for the collection and will be able to give a firsthand account of some of its history. As Frank G. Burke notes, in some cases, "the curator becomes the ultimate finding aid" (55).

In some cases, a researcher can also contribute to identifying the provenance of a collection by clarifying the relationships of previous owners of the collection. For example, sometimes a repository has records of a collection being donated by a particular person but does not know that person's relationship to the original creator[3] of the collection. In these instances, a researcher who is familiar with the background and family relationships of the creator of the collection can help clarify who the donor was and his or her relationship to the creator.

Researchers rely on the ability to draw conclusions about a person's life by examining the papers of that person. Items found in the person's papers are assumed to have been owned by the person and kept for some reason. These items can be used as evidence in learning about what types of subjects were important to the person and can sometimes reveal information about a person's interests that may not appear in secondary sources such as biographies or encyclopedia entries. For these reasons, it is crucial that the papers of one individual or organization never be intermingled with those created by another person or organization, even if the subjects within the papers are similar. This principle of provenance is one of the two most significant theories guiding archives work and has its roots in the beginnings of the archives profession.

During the French Revolution (1789–99), there was a large increase in the creation and use of records. The French, recognizing that records such as land deeds were critical to protecting the rights of the public, sought to preserve the evidence contained in their records. They felt that the public had the right to examine the records produced and kept by their government. As a result, formal archival practice was established. The principle of provenance, or *"respect des fonds"* in French, was an outgrowth of the French Revolution and literally means "respect for the group." This principle is fundamental to contemporary archives work and exists to protect the integrity and authenticity of archival records as evidence by retaining the nature of the relationship that exists among records by the same creator. Although the principle of provenance was a result of the French Revolution, archivists generally did not begin applying the principle to their work until the second half of the nineteenth century (Posner). The impact of the French Revolution on the archives profession cannot be overstated, because out of it came the principle that the public had the right to access the records of its government. This increased governmental accountability to the people.

Understanding Original Order

The second foundational principle informing an archivist's work is the principle of respect for "original order," which refers to the original creator's arrangement of the materials. Like provenance, it is a principle that guides all professional archives work, and it exists for a similar reason: to document the relationships among the records themselves. Original order is also important because the arrangement of a collection can sometimes reveal things about the person or organization that created and used the records.

Archivists take care to determine and maintain the original order to the extent possible given their responsibilities both to preserve the materials from deterioration and to make them accessible to researchers. Archivists do not impose their own organizational principles upon materials that are already organized but rather devote their efforts to identifying and clarifying the organizational principles followed by the creator, recognizing that the arrangement itself may be of interest and significance to researchers. For archival researchers interested in rhetorical issues, original order may be of even greater interest than for other researchers because it can reflect the original context or rhetorical situation of the materials. It is critically important, then, for researchers to know whether original order has been maintained in the materials they examine.

For example, as was evident from the materials themselves and confirmed by colleagues who worked closely with him, Berlin's professional papers—those related to his teaching, research, and faculty service—were organized into file folders that were titled by subject and filed in alphabetical order. When Shirley developed the plan for arranging the papers, Berlin's existing file order was maintained to the extent possible. Understanding how what was "possible" was determined can serve as a useful example for researchers unfamiliar with archival arrangement. Detailed information regarding how a collection's arrangement may have changed after being processed is typically not included in a publicly accessible finding aid, and researchers may wish to consult the archivist for these types of specifics.

It's perhaps self-evident that researchers from different disciplines come to archives with different kinds of questions and therefore need different kinds of information about the collections there. Rhetoric and composition researchers are no different. Because of their interest in discursive genres, rhetoric and composition researchers are likely to want more information about archival document types and forms. Because of their interest in rhetorical contexts, they are likely to have extensive and specific questions about the provenance of records and be especially interested in the form in which records were originally created and the purpose for which they were created. They will also want as much information as possible about the history of how a collection has evolved from the time of the original creation of its contents up through processing decisions made by the archivists in whose custody the collection resides.

As any student of rhetoric is well aware, a knowledge of the rhetorical situation, or the context and events that gave rise to discourse, is critical to understanding that discourse. Researchers examining materials in a collection will draw inferences about the intellectual relationships among the materials from their physical relationships to each other. Materials in files organized alphabetically by subject will have a different relationship to one another than materials in files placed in chronological order. For example, Berlin arranged his folders containing copies of typescripts by academic colleagues alphabetically by the author's last name. He could have chosen other organizational methods—he might have ordered them by date of his receipt of them, or he might have organized them according to the subject of the manuscripts. One can imagine reasons either of these alternative orders might have been useful to Berlin as the original creator of the files, but the fact that he ordered them alphabetically by author's names tells us something about how he anticipated possibly consulting them at a future date, which in itself reflects Berlin's conceptual organization of intellectual content of the files: Relationships among authors are more salient than relationships among subjects.

Because respect for the original order of archival materials is a fundamental principle of archival practice, determining whether and to what extent original order has been altered is one of the archivist's highest priorities in working with a collection. Determining the original order is a kind of educated guesswork based on the archivist's knowledge of the creator's life and activities and the circumstances of creation of the materials. This determination enables the archivist to make good decisions about appropriate arrangement and description and to make good judgments about refiling materials that appear to be misfiled or removing materials that have no relevance to the life of the creator of the records. *Original order* is sometimes more a concept represented in an intellectual model of the collection (through the collection's finding aid) than it is a description based on actual physical proximity. Thus, it is more important to "know" the original order of materials than to actually physically keep materials in their original order.

For the researcher, understanding this about the archivist's work will be critically important to knowing what conjectures can safely be drawn about the relationships among materials. Furthermore, the researcher should consult the archivist to learn what he or she can about the rationale for the arrangement of collection materials. In addition to the public finding aid, the archivist may also have access to the original container list created when the collection was accessioned and other accessioning and processing notes that will reveal the order the collection was in when it was received by the archives.

Determining who may have used the files and altered their original order after they left the creator's custody is not always an easy task, particularly when papers are kept by a family over an extended period of time or custodianship has changed between the time the creator organized the files and the time they were acquired by the archival repository. In some cases, even the archivist will not be aware of how original order has been compromised prior to the materials arriving at the archives. A separate, but equally interesting, problem is the collection that arrives with no original order at all. The collection may have been organized in the past, but perhaps when the materials were packed, they were jumbled together and switched around in order to make them fit better into boxes. Or worse, perhaps the creator had no discernable arrangement scheme—perhaps the creator knew how to locate his or her own files, but the system was indecipherable for anyone else. In the interest of making the collection accessible, archivists will sometimes have to make choices about arranging these types of collections. When this happens, archivists rely on their training to guide them into arranging the collection in a way that is most likely to reflect the creator's own view of the relationships among materials. For this task, the archivist must "reconstruct" original order through researching the life and activities of the creator prior to establishing an arrangement scheme. Most archivists will already have researched the creator anyway in order to better understand the materials in the collection during processing or description.

Because significance can often be attributed to the order of materials, it is critically important that when researchers use archival collections, they maintain the order in which they find materials even if they cannot identify an ordering principle or the original order appears to have been disrupted. Otherwise, the next person who consults the materials—who may well be the researcher himself or herself, back for a second look—will be misled. If a researcher believes materials have been disarranged, he should call it to the attention of the archivist, who will be able to make an informed judgment about the order.

Archival Preservation Principles

While archival preservation materials and techniques vary, some practices are standard; a researcher might, in fact, be able to recognize whether or not a collection has been processed by noting the preservation measures that have been taken. Although techniques and materials change with improvements in technology and accelerated aging tests, archivists' decisions about appropriate preservation steps are informed by two general principles: chemical and physical damage to materials should be prevented, stopped, or slowed where possible without undermining the integrity of the records' content and form; and, to the extent possible, preservation steps should serve to make materials more accessible to researchers rather than less accessible. Archivists follow the motto of conservators and medical practitioners when considering treatment: "First do no harm." No action an archivist or conservator takes to preserve, repair, or stabilize archival material should be responsible for harm to the material over the long term, and ideally any preservation steps taken should be reversible. For this reason, only specific types of adhesives and other conservation supplies are used when treating archival materials. The idea is not just to repair a torn page but also to ensure that the materials used in that repair do not cause future damage such as staining or embrittlement of the page over time.

Some of the preservation steps taken with the James Berlin Papers will illustrate the application of these principles. The removal of metal paper clips and staples was a high-priority task because, after ten years, they had already begun to leave rust deposits on the papers. Removing staples and paper clips introduces some risk of separating materials that were originally together, but that can be ameliorated by replacing metal fasteners with plastic paper clips or folding acid-free, lignin-free paper around packets of papers that must remain together. Berlin's teaching materials included a number of newspaper clippings of articles related to the economy and education; because the high acidic content of newsprint causes it to deteriorate quickly—and to damage other paper it touches—photocopies of these clippings were made, and the originals were discarded. Though photocopying and then discarding the original clippings might seem to undermine the integrity of the original materials, it was justified for three reasons: the newsprint would damage the other materials, newspapers are mass produced and thus clippings have informational value but not artifactual value, and the clippings themselves were not created by Berlin. The *collection* of the clippings—that is, their selection and organization—was created by Berlin, and the integrity of that collection could be maintained with photocopies of the clippings.

Following standard practices and using standard materials, Shirley also replaced original folders and cardboard file boxes with acid-free, lignin-free folders and boxes, which slow the natural aging process of paper. These steps also make the materials much more accessible to researchers, because the standard folder sizes and uniform folder-tab length minimize the likelihood of overlooking a file, and the archival manuscript boxes are a convenient size for transporting and reviewing.

The steps described above were all consistent with standard practices and fairly common. Frequent users of archival materials will recognize them in the materials they consult. Two other preservation steps taken with the collection are less common and, because they are both more obvious and irreversible, seem more aggressive or proactive and therefore likely to raise more questions from users of the materials. The Berlin Papers included two wire spiral-bound notebooks containing notes from Berlin's participation in the 1978 National Endowment for the Humanities Seminar led by Richard Young at Carnegie Mellon University and a dozen or so legal-size yellow pads of notes. In consultation with Sammie, Shirley decided to cut and remove the rusting wire spiral from one of the notebooks that had already damaged several of the notebook pages. Removing the wire spiral risked undermining the order of the notebook pages and the papers inserted between the pages, so Shirley lightly penciled sequential page numbers on each notebook page and insertion. Also in consultation with Sammie, Shirley removed the cardboard backings from the yellow notepads to minimize the damage the highly acidic cardboard would do to the notepad pages. This step left the notepad binding still intact so that original page order could be maintained. Though these steps were appropriate and justified, they may seem more aggressive than other preservation steps because they alter the form of the materials and cannot be reversed. Furthermore, these are actions obviously not taken by the creator himself. For these steps, the archivist's hands became visible. However, a distinction must be made between altering the backing of a standard yellow legal pad and altering the form of, for example, a page on which Berlin wrote. The yellow pad itself was not created by Berlin, nor did removing its backing alter the appearance of the actual pages on which Berlin wrote.

Researchers need to be able to distinguish preservation steps taken by archivists from those taken by the records creator in order to avoid jumping to erroneous conclusions about the format or condition of materials. For example, in most cases, creators do not use or have access to professional archival preservation supplies such as acid-free, lignin-free folders, so their presence in a collection suggests a certain level of processing work by an archivist. As with many of the other steps of processing, some account of the preservation measures is likely to be provided in the collection file maintained by the archivist. Even if this is not the case, an archivist who does not know firsthand what preservation steps were taken during processing will very likely still be able to distinguish professional preservation work from steps taken by the records creator and will be able to advise a researcher who inquires about the preservation steps that have been taken. Researchers who become aware of preservation risks within an archival collection, such as torn pages, staples or metal paper clips, rubber bands, highly acidic newspaper or other damaging materials, should bring these to the attention of the archivist.

Archival Arrangement

As we explained earlier, the arrangement of archival materials is determined to a great extent by their creator and his or her context. This section describes how original order governed specific arrangement decisions for the Berlin Papers. Because James Berlin was a college professor, his professional work throughout his career had been assigned to the three general categories of research, teaching, and service. Regardless of how Berlin himself intellectually integrated his work across these categories or found them problematic, these categories organized his professional life insofar as he was assigned to specific classes each semester, served on specific committees, and worked on specific research projects. Each of these activities generated its own discrete materials; thus, the traditional triad for college faculty work also informed Shirley's decisions and choices for the archival arrangement of these materials.

A second example of how the creator's original order determined arrangement is in Shirley's decision to arrange the teaching materials by course number after dividing them into groups based on the institution where Berlin taught the courses. This division by institution could have easily been placed in chronological order. But because Berlin often reused teaching materials when he taught a course numerous times, grouping materials by course was more in keeping with how Berlin would have arranged the files and thus determined Shirley's final decision about arrangement. Yet, because chronology is also relevant, Shirley drew from various sources in the collection materials to create a chronological list of courses taught by Berlin from 1981 through 1993. That list became part of the collection file and can be consulted by any user of the collection in the future, if he or she knows to ask for it. That list is not filed with the collection itself because it was not created by Berlin, and a researcher is unlikely to learn of its existence if he or she doesn't ask about the contents of the repository's own files on the collection—another reason a researcher should not skip the reference interview with the archives staff or forgo an onsite visit to the archives if possible.

Archival Description

Description is the general term archivists use to describe the activities involved in creating a narrative account of the contents of a collection. Archivists prefer the term *description* to the library term, *cataloguing*, because describing archival materials involves more than creating catalog records, a complexity that rhetoric and composition researchers can appreciate. Archival description can include creating finding aids, collection guides, machine-readable cataloging records (MARC), encoded archival description (EAD), and other files and/or documents describing the collections themselves. Description is not simply a matter of listing the contents of boxes and folders; its purpose is to record the information necessary to composing a narrative account of the collection. In other words, description documents—which provide information about the creator of the documents and the context of their creation—provide information from which a story about the collection and its contents could be constructed.

Usually, this work of description begins at the point of accessioning materials into the archival repository's holdings, with a brief and general statement noting the number and size of the containers and their contents and continues through the creation of a finding aid prepared with the audience of potential users or researchers in mind. Several factors govern an archivist's decisions about the extent of description, and an awareness of these factors can help a researcher to accurately interpret the finding aids and other descriptive documents. Some factors relate to available resources such as staff expertise and time for doing description, which often translates into financial resources. Here again, the more communication between researcher and archivist, the better the choices made. Other factors relate to the archivist's assessment of potential users' interests in the collection materials. Effectively, the archivist must make cost-benefit analyses in order to determine where to direct limited resources.

The purpose of description is to let researchers know the general content of the collection, not the content of individual documents within the collection, although it is sometimes difficult to distinguish between the two. For example, Shirley had to decide whether or not to mention the existence of copies of William Blundell's *Wall Street Journal* article "The Days of the Cowboy Are Marked by Danger, Drudgery, and Low Pay" in various files in the Berlin papers, because she knew that a researcher familiar with Berlin's work would be likely to immediately recognize this title as a text used in the writing courses in which Berlin was developing a cultural-studies pedagogy for composition studies.[4]

The location of multiple copies of the "Days of the Cowboy" essay in the Berlin papers also serves to illustrate that while some materials in a collection have intrinsic value, other materials are important only because of their relationship to the collection's creator. Although the essay copies are self-evidently not one-of-a-kind materials, their presence among the teaching materials for one of Berlin's courses has evidentiary value because they could be interpreted as evidence that the course was one in which Berlin used a cultural-studies pedagogy.

The "Days of the Cowboy" essay also illustrates how the archivist's familiarity with the creator's work can influence decisions about processing a collection from appraisal through arrangement to description. As a specialist in contemporary rhetoric and composition studies, Shirley was familiar with Berlin's published scholarship, and as a Purdue faculty member, she was familiar with the curriculum of the graduate rhetoric and composition program, the mentoring program for first-year composition instructors in which Berlin taught, and the daily practices of life in the English Department. This meant that her context for identifying, interpreting, and evaluating collection contents was especially rich. Often, the archivist who processes a collection does not have the advantage of working from so rich a context, and when that is the case, researchers using a collection may discover that they can provide valuable information that can be used to revise or supplement finding aids.

Decisions about describing items found in archival collections must be made throughout the processing phase, so archivists must be trained to recognize items in collections that are either confidential by law or may infringe on the privacy rights of individuals. For example, while processing materials, archivists often must make decisions about how extensively to describe materials that are confidential. This is particularly important for materials that can legally be made accessible after the passage of sufficient time. The public finding aid should not include any information that would effectively undermine the confidentiality of the materials, yet enough information must be included to help ensure that potential users know of the materials' existence if appropriate. For example, the James Berlin Papers included confidential materials of several different kinds, each requiring a different means of arrangement and description. Information about students' course enrollment and grades is protected by law, so Shirley removed course rosters from folders of teaching materials in order to make the remainder of the folder contents accessible to researchers. Separation sheets noting the removal of the rosters were placed in each folder, and the rosters were then collected in a separate folder and filed with other confidential materials from the Berlin papers.[5] Other confidential materials found in the Berlin Papers included tenure and promotion reviews Berlin wrote for colleagues around the country. Such letters are typically considered confidential by their writers and readers. Though individual institutions' actual practices in this regard vary, and, typically, a review writer would be informed about whether his or her letter would be treated confidentially, the Berlin papers included no information about which of these reviews Berlin had written with the expectation that they would be kept confidential. Therefore, Shirley decided that all of them should be filed with the confidential materials and remain inaccessible for seventy years, a standard length of time used by archivists for restricting information that may infringe on privacy rights, as well as a sufficient amount of time to ensure the letters had no potential to affect the professional careers of their subjects. For these materials, however, no separation sheet was filled out and left with remaining materials because to do so would be a clear sign that a letter had been written, undermining an important element of the confidentiality of the process of tenure and promotion review. Instead, Shirley prepared a list of the folders of tenure and promotion reviews and related materials that were placed with confidential materials and included this list in the collection file. This provides an example of an instance in which consultation with the archivist, who will have access to the contents of the collection folder, could be particularly helpful to a researcher.

The collection folder often contains additional details about the collection that will be of interest to researchers and especially likely to be significant to scholars of rhetoric and composition. Information about the history of the collection, such as the details of its acquisition, and rationales for processing decisions, such as arrangement choices, are often included in the collection file and can provide explanations for aspects of a collection that might otherwise be puzzling or mysterious. For example, the collection file for the James Berlin Papers includes an account of Shirley's work with the collection over several years, explaining that when she first received Berlin's papers from Sandy Berlin in 1998, she worked with several graduate students in a "Documentation Strategies in Writing Programs" seminar to develop an initial general inventory of the materials, place them in sturdy standard-sized cardboard file-storage boxes, and remove rusting paper clips. That account clarifies that, although the seminar members' work focused primarily on developing recommendations for processing and included minimal hands-on work with the materials, Shirley did have a general idea of the overall contents of the collection.

When Shirley's fellowship project began in 2006, her first step in developing a description of the collection was to create a complete list of the file folders (using folder names already assigned by James Berlin or others) in each box. The second step was to develop more detailed notes on the folder contents that would be used later in the scope and content notes for the collection. It is important to note that listing each item in the collection was not part of the project; instead, notes were taken on types of materials found in the collection, inclusive dates, overall subjects included, and so forth. Once that was done, Shirley had the basis for identifying suitable series titles for describing the arrangement and content of the papers. Though some of the materials had clearly been displaced, most of Berlin's original organization seemed to be still evident and suggested the following six series titles as the major components of the collection:

> *Series 1. NEH Seminar Materials, 1978–1979.* Documents Berlin's participation in the seminar. Included are meeting handouts, notes, and readings.
> *Series 2. Teaching Materials, 1981–1994.* Documents Berlin's teaching career, with most materials related to his tenure at Purdue University (1987–93). Included are materials related to his development of a cultural-studies composition pedagogy for graduate teaching assistants.
> *Series 3. Research Materials, 1984–1994.* Includes handwritten research notes from composition-related journals, annotated copies of articles, unpublished drafts, and notes for conference papers.
> *Series 4. Collegial correspondence, 1979–1994.* Includes letters and notes from colleagues and copies of works in progress sent to Berlin for review.
> *Series 5. Faculty Governance and Community Activism, 1987–1994.* Includes faculty meeting minutes, proposals, and materials related to governance and activism.
> *Series 6. Confidential Student Records, Correspondence, and Committee Work, 1981–1994.* Contains student records (course rosters and grade sheets, dissertation prospectuses, exams), letters of recommendation, tenure and promotion reviews, and confidential notes from faculty searches. (Rose 5–6)

Shirley ordered the series according to best archival practice by ranking the series according to importance to the creator: she placed materials that represented the creator's overall achievement and contributions first. In addition, materials created by Berlin such as his teaching materials ranked higher in the hierarchy of the finding aid than materials not created by him such as the faculty-governance materials. Due to the importance of Berlin's attendance at the NEH seminar to rhetoric and composition, this series was placed first.

Familiarity with standard archival description practices benefits researchers by helping them more efficiently locate information in typical archival finding aids. A researcher needs to know the various documents of description and their purpose to determine what kinds of information can be gleaned from them. First of all, it's important to understand that even a descriptive document so apparently straightforward as a list of folder titles is a report on the archivist's examination of the materials and has been shaped by the sense the archivist is making of the apparent order and organization of the folders. A finding aid is a text that is not transparent but must be interpreted by a researcher. At the same time, standard practices of description have evolved, and a set of conventions is developing—in part as a result of technology's effects on the profession's descriptive practices—and the capabilities for developing searchable electronic databases radically alter researchers' virtual access to finding aids and, in some cases, digital versions of documents themselves.

A finding aid may be viewed as a map of a collection, designed to help the user find his or her way. The main purpose of the finding aid is to let researchers know that a collection exists, where it can be found, and how to access it; ideally, the finding aid will also provide a general idea of the collection's contents so users can judge the material's relevance to their research projects. However, it must be kept in mind that archivists are trained to describe collections at different levels: *fonds* (collection or record-group level), *series* (major categories within the collection), *box* (general summary of each container's contents), and *folder* (general summary of each folder's contents). Although researchers are usually interested in specific items in a collection, archivists are strongly discouraged from describing collections at the item level.[6] Researchers may wonder why archivists do not describe in detail each letter, photograph, artifact, diary, or other item in a collection. After all, it is undoubtedly easier for the researcher to know if the exact item he or she seeks is contained in the collection. Archivists do not describe to this level because of lack of resources. There are too few staff members to document every piece of paper in a typical archival collection, usually thousands of individual documents, photos, and related materials. This can be likened to the cataloging of books: When books are described in library catalogs, they are described in an overall summary—each page of the book is not described because it would be time and cost prohibitive. The same is true for archival collections—they are most often described as an overarching unit, with some detail added but usually not to the individual page level. Ultimately, the researcher must be willing to invest time into finding details that may not be included in a summary catalog record.

Most archival repositories are understaffed and face an enormous backlog of unprocessed collections that are practically inaccessible to researchers due to their lack of description. The archivist must choose between devoting limited staff resources to creating a small number of detailed, item-level finding aids for select collections and leaving the bulk of the collections undescribed and therefore inaccessible or using staff time to create quicker, more summarized descriptions or finding aids of the bulk of the collections but relying on researchers to delve into the collections themselves to discover particular documents. Neither choice is ideal, but archivists usually decide to spread out their staff resources over many collections rather than spending all of their staff time describing in great detail a select grouping of collections in their repository. Researchers should be aware of the benefits of this—after all, if the archives devoted the bulk of its staff resources to describing only a select few collections, what collections might remain invisible to researchers because they are not described or cataloged yet? Additionally, archivists must prioritize which collections to process first and to what level. In prioritizing processing, the archivist considers the mission, goals, and objectives of his or her institution; the collection development policy that provides guidance and outlines collection strengths; and the current and potential future use of the collections themselves. In addition, some collections are more problematic for processing due to their size, the nature of their content, their lack of arrangement, or the condition of the collection. For example, if a collection was in complete disarray and would require considerable time and effort to put in useable order, it might be lower priority due to time and staff constraints. Often, the collections with the highest potential for research use are processed earlier out of a commitment to accessibility. The level of processing will also differ among collections. For example, collections that contain unusually valuable documents, such as autographs by celebrities or historic figures, may be described at a more detailed level for security purposes so that if an item is missing, the archivist will have a record that it at one time was part of the collection. And collections that are digitized, as more and more are each year, are often described in more detail.

Researchers also need to understand that more than thirty years ago, typical finding aids appeared to be created as much for the archivists themselves as they were for researchers. For example, many older finding aids included numerous abbreviations that only archivists could decipher. This is because in the past serious researchers tended to visit the archival repository and speak directly to the archivist about the collections. The archivist would often keep notes and supporting documents about a collection that would help him or her assist the researcher in using the collection. Over time, archivists began to compare differences in finding aids created by different repositories, and they started focusing on making the finding aids easier for researchers to use. Attempts were made to use less archival jargon, improve the format and layout of finding aids, and to include more-helpful information for researchers so they could work more independently of the archivist. Now that finding aids are often posted on the Internet, their level of descriptive content, visual design, and layout are more important than ever, because many researchers are likely to refer to them without first consulting the archivist. It is especially interesting for rhetoric and composition scholars to see the changes that have taken place in finding aids since the creation of the Internet and to acknowledge the dramatic increase in researcher queries for particular collections that may have not been used heavily in the past before the finding aids for those collections were made available online. Even with these changes, however, a researcher should not forego direct consultations with the archivists in whose custody the research materials are held.

Researchers should be aware that various finding aids/descriptive documents created at the time of original accessioning of materials for current audiences or research situations may not address all subjects of interest to researchers of today and tomorrow. Archivists must base their decisions about what aspects of a collection need to be mentioned on their assumptions about who is likely to be using the collection and for what purpose. As research topics grow and change over time, finding aids created decades ago may or may not address current research topics such as women's studies, ethnic studies, and so forth.

Making Effective Use of Archival Finding Aids

By becoming familiar with the typical components and layout of finding aids, researchers can more effectively utilize finding aids to locate the information they are seeking. Although finding aids differ greatly across archival repositories in form, style, layout, and language, good finding aids all contain certain basic elements: introductory and administrative information; biographical or historical sketch of the author or creator of the collection; scope and content note providing a brief overall summary of the collection; and a container list or inventory of the contents of the collection. (See the appendix to this chapter for an annotated version of part of the finding aid for the James Berlin Papers.)

The introductory and administrative section includes information on how the collection is to be used: for example, if there are any restrictions on access to the collection. Often, archival collections are stored outside the main repository in offsite storage, due to space restrictions. A good finding aid will let researchers know if they need to contact the archives in advance of their visit to allow time to retrieve offsite materials. The administrative section of a finding aid may also include information on how the collection was acquired—in other words, its provenance.

The biographical or historical sketch is usually a brief biography or history of the person or organization that created or brought the materials together as a collection. Researchers already familiar with this information often skip over this general introduction to the creator, but it can contain important information. Sometimes, archivists will include a timeline relating to the person or organization, and this may be helpful to researchers.

The purpose of the scope and content note is to provide a quick summary to the overall collection. It includes information on how the collection is arranged, a description of the series or major parts within the collection, any major subject areas or important people or events covered, a range of inclusive dates for the collection, and types of materials included, such as documents, photographs, artifacts, and so forth.

The heart of the finding aid is the container list or inventory. Here, contents of the boxes, series, and/or folders are listed out in greater detail. Although it is rare to include listings of actual items in the collection, some repositories do provide this information. The container list or inventory is often the first place a researcher looks for the information, and it is helpful to know that in most archival finding aids, this information is located toward the end of the finding aid. A researcher seeking something very specific in the collection—such as a letter with a particular date from a particular correspondent—will find it most helpful to scan the series descriptions first, to see if "correspondence" is a series in the collection and if so, where it will be located in the more detailed container list.

Finally, although rare, some finding aids include indices that list personal and corporate names and topical subjects. These are often found at the end of the finding aid after the container list. Often, different archives describe or catalog their holdings differently.

The project of processing the James Berlin Papers presented a unique opportunity for a researcher and an archivist to work together to understand each other's perspectives when approaching archival collections. Reflecting on the experience, the most important insight Shirley gained was recognizing how her decisions about processing had to be informed by knowledge and understanding of the materials themselves. Because archival materials are one-of-a-kind, there is no one right way to arrange or describe them, and the archivist will always have to make his or her own decisions about how to proceed, informed by an understanding of the materials, their creator, and the context of their creation. Though professional archivists have, over time, developed a set of agreed-upon best practices that continue to evolve as technologies evolve and be refined as historical understanding is refined, those best practices are more like guidelines and principles than like a rulebook.

Shirley also learned how time- and labor-intensive the work of archival processing is. Not including the time spent rereading some of Berlin's publications or reading about archival theory and practice in the professional literature, Shirley devoted about a hundred hours to work on physically arranging and describing the James Berlin Papers. She acknowledges that as a novice, she worked less efficiently than a seasoned professional archivist would because she hadn't determined the most streamlined procedures for handling materials. To be fair, she felt that she lost some time because she would occasionally revert out of her novice archivist's role and back into her more familiar role as researcher. She would often find that she was reviewing materials more for the researcher's purpose of answering specific questions or analyzing documents for evidence to support arguments than for the archivist's purpose of identification and description.

Shirley also found that it took time to learn how to do the appropriate level or degree of description. She learned that appropriate description of folder contents was not a matter of listing every item in the folder but of characterizing the folder contents in a way that would help a researcher locate the materials if they were of interest. To do this, of course, she had to construct this figure of the "researcher" from her own experience of research, from her knowledge of the significance of Berlin's work in contemporary composition and rhetoric, and from her knowledge of the contents of the James Berlin Papers themselves.

Shirley is now much better able to understand that the professional archivist's intellectual work comprises a series of judgment calls from accessioning materials to providing access to those materials. Of course, archivists must make judgments about their priorities for expending their always limited funds, time, and staff. Yet, even in an ideal world of limitless resources, archivists would still have to make choices about how to arrange and describe those materials to best reflect their original state. And, ideally, the outcome of those choices would be finding aids that were so extensive (yet easy to read) and so precisely attuned to multiple users' interests as to seem transparently composed, so that readers would need no further help finding materials. Thus, ironically, under ideal circumstances, the archivist's best work might well be invisible to most researchers.

For her part on the project, Sammie learned how rhetoric and composition researchers differ from most researchers in the amount of context and detail they require about steps taken during processing archival collections. While the average researcher may not care how a collection was acquired by the archival repository, or why the collection is organized a particular way, or what preservation steps have been taken by the archivist, it has become clear to Sammie that rhetoricians need such information for drawing conclusions from their research. In addition, as she discussed archives work in more detail with Shirley, Sammie began to think about how exposing the details of the archivist's often "invisible" work might benefit the archives profession itself. For example, by explaining what decisions have been made when processing a collection and what theories and principles guided those decisions, the archivist is not only better able to justify her actions but also to illustrate to researchers the amount of time, resources, and expertise needed to make collections accessible. In addition, when archivists include more information in finding aids about the steps that have been taken in processing collections, it increases the accountability of the archivist's work by presenting it for critique and discussion. It also helps prevent researchers from drawing false conclusions and assuming that steps taken by the archivist were taken by the creator or author of the papers.

Many researchers may not understand that, unlike file clerks, archivists base their actions on not only their practical training for processing collections and describing them but also the theoretical foundation of the archives profession. Archivists must themselves be good researchers to be effective archivists; after all, how can an archivist adequately write a biographical sketch of the record's creator without researching the creator's life? How can the archivist reconstruct the original order of the creator's papers without understanding the different facets of the creator's activities? Archivists often feel undervalued, but perhaps by documenting more of the work they do in publicly accessible finding aids, they will achieve more recognition for their efforts.

In addition, the profession as a whole should open itself up for study by being more forthright about steps taken in processing collections. Just as the archives profession was an outgrowth of the need to make the government accountable to its people, offering evidence of its activities through access to its official records can make the archives community more accountable for its actions. This can only happen when archivists are more forthcoming about the steps they take processing collections. This is not to say that archivists as a rule purposefully seek to hide their actions from those outside the profession; instead, it has been a result of archivists' assumptions that researchers do not have the time or inclination to be interested in that level of detail.

We hope this brief explanation of professional archivists' work will help our readers to see the extent and significance of the often invisible work archivists do every day to preserve and make collections accessible for research and to better understand why so many archival collections remain "hidden" to researchers. If nothing else, we hope that our essay will prompt a dialogue between researchers and archivists that will ultimately result in increased accessibility and use of archival collections—bringing the work of archivists' invisible hands within reach of many more researchers' hands.

Notes

1 A pdf of the finding aid for the James Berlin Papers is available at <http://www.lib.purdue.edu/spcol/fa/pdf/berlin.pdf>.
2 A *finding aid* is "a tool that facilitates discovery of information within a collection of records." The *finding aid* is "a description of records that gives the repository physical and intellectual control over the materials and assists users to gain access to and understand the materials" (Pearce-Moses 168).
3 *Creator* is the term archivists use for "author" or "artist."
4 Berlin discusses his use of this article in his *Rhetoric Review* essay "Poststructuralism, Cultural Studies, and the Composition Classroom."
5 *Separation sheets* are forms that let the researcher know that an item or items were originally part of the folder's contents but were removed during processing. Ideally, separation sheets should identify the reason for the removal and the new location for the items that were separated.
6 Museum professionals differ from archivists in this manner, instead relying on their training for describing each item in their collections.

Works Cited

Berlin, James. "Poststructuralism, Cultural Studies, and the Composition Classroom." *Rhetoric Review* 11.1 (1992): 16–33.
Blundell, William E. "The Days of the Cowboy Are Marked by Danger, Drudgery, and Low Pay." *Wall Street Journal* 10 June 1981, sec. A: 1+.
Burke, Frank G. *Research and the Manuscript Tradition.* Lanham, MD: Scarecrow, 1997.
Pearce-Moses, Richard. *A Glossary of Archival and Records Terminology.* Chicago: Society of American Archivists, 2005.
Posner, Ernst. *Archives in the Ancient World.* Chicago: Society of American Archivists, 2003.
Rose, Shirley K. "Inventory to the James Berlin Papers, 1978–1994." James Berlin Papers, Archives and Special Collections. Purdue University Libraries. 2006. <http://www.lib.purdue.edu/spcol/fa/pdf/berlin.pdf>.

15.
EMERGENT TAXONOMIES: USING TENSION AND FORUM TO ORGANIZE PRIMARY TEXTS
Tarez Samra Graban

In early 2004, through a cooperative effort between the county archives and the university where I was a doctoral student, I was given access to eleven boxes of miscellaneous papers and artifacts surrounding the political, philanthropic, and legal activities of a nineteenth-century American suffragist, Helen Gougar (1843–1907). The cooperation began as a twenty-five-student seminar with a service-learning component and resulted in hundreds of cumulatively logged hours spent processing over twenty different collections on behalf of the archives. Initially, the seminar focused on the theoretical workings of "the archive" and soon became a praxis-driven exploration of the intellectual challenges that archives pose for researchers in different disciplines, made richer by the fact that many of the collections we worked on contained intertextual links from one to another.

I knew nothing of Gougar before discovering her there—nothing other than that she was a local legend who employed fairly biting rhetoric from time to time, including clubbing the newspaper editor with her umbrella and shrieking her displeasure in the courtroom during an unsubstantiated slander suit—and thus considered myself well positioned to be impartial and efficient in my work. However, because of my dual involvement as archivist and researcher (i.e., I approached the collection with the primary task of processing it and with the secondary task of making it a research subject), organizing the Gougar Collection at times felt more like disrupting it than giving it order.

Throughout this process, I had an obligation to remain true to its arrangement and sensitive to its silences, yet I was also aware of its possibilities for future research, particularly as I began to pinpoint textual evidences showing that Gougar played a more significant role in rhetorical history than we may think. I wanted not to personify Gougar but to uncover her vital participation with other public personae, yet I could not infer participation or discursive relationships that were not already evident in the order of existing materials. In short, I could not insinuate that a letter or speech or

---

Graban, Tarez Samra. "Emergent Taxonomies: Using Tension and Forum to Organize Primary Texts." *Working in the Archives: Practical Research Methods for Rhetoric and Composition*. Eds. Ramsey et al. Illinois: Southern Illinois Press, 2010: 206–219. Print.

activity was significant *to the collection* just because it began to take on a historical significance in my own mind.

The Need: Resolving Conflicts of De/Reconstruction

Carolyn Steedman's broad discussion of archival "memory" bears witness to how dilemmas like mine can sometimes drive an archival researcher's work. While we consider them to be fairly value-neutral, the acts of *biography, research,* and *remembering* can be understood as a rigorous exhuming of the dead's stories—reconstructed, taken, and then left (57). These acts tend to reconstruct the archival researcher's own desires for a particular collection; furthermore, they allow memory to subsume truth, for example, assigning significance to a particular document that may not have had it before or remembering a particular artifact within a photo that never showed it. My principal question should have been, "What is the most intrinsic way to *arrange* this information?" But I was most driven by the question, "What is the best way for rhetorical researchers to *access* the information that is here?" As my knowledge of Gougar's activities increased, I found it harder to prevent that question from driving my work.

It is precisely this question that causes the archivists and researcher's missions to sometimes conflict. Archivists process collections by maintaining obvious relationships, typically resulting in record groups and series numbers because this helps them to arrange documents into consistent patterns. Rhetorical researchers and discourse analysts working with archived texts may fail to understand how these organizational patterns make sense to the collection's creator and why that structure needs to be maintained—particularly when vital or dynamic relationships could be discovered in a reorganization of the texts. The conflict becomes a question of purpose and function: How should researchers proceed if they need more than the text to help them locate the discourse? Can the collection serve as an artifact of discourse or as a grouping of discursive contexts? Should the collection serve as more than a record of intrinsic relationships?

Aside from arrangement, another conflict between archivists and researchers is the importance of provenance—or originary source—to a collection's purpose and functionality, specifically for governing its arrangement and description and essentially for keeping the "chain of custody" of a series of documents intact (Brunton and Robinson 223). This chain of custody represents what was meaningful to the collection's creator and has more to do with the order in which items are found rather than an order in which the documents might serve a research topic or question. I have found that this order is not so easy for rhetoric and composition researchers to discern, let alone accept. For those researchers especially interested in discourse analysis, not disrupting the chain of custody often means suppressing the urge to mix or combine the archives of one agency or person with those of another. And for rhetorical theorists who strive to understand how texts function and are purposed together, it means having to study them apart. In short, researchers and theorists need methods that are more clearly developed for expanding the boundaries of a collection without blocking the archivist's mission to preserve and protect.

Thus, this essay offers one method for organizing texts according to their enduring rhetorical value without disrupting their provenance. It does so by utilizing the taxonomical system that emerges from the collection itself. It is my hope that this method as I describe it will help researchers and theorists to recognize their archival work through the same lens as Carolyn Heald's *diplomatics*—that is, as a research methodology that privileges certain facts in the interpretation of a collection by organizing texts within contexts that are broader than the collection, yet without imposing limits on the collection being studied. *Diplomatics* is the practice of reading texts whose principal function is documentary, and Heald argues for it as postmodern activity in surmising that—contrary to how we may understand their role—archivists have already been involved more in cultural and social deconstruction than in mere arrangement and preservation of texts (95). Recognizing archival organization as a deconstructive act underscores the need for taxonomical systems that emerge from the productive tension between document sets and the social strata out of which they were created.

The Taxonomy: Theoretical Foundations in a Contextualist Paradigm

This method relies on three assumptions. First, the best way to understand how certain texts in a collection inform other texts is by letting a new framework for analysis emerge from the texts themselves. Second, rhetorical analysis is situational as well as functional (Fahnestock and Secor 178), which implies that even a singly authored text is best understood via the audience and moment out of which it was constructed and further when we can discern these from features inherent in the text itself. Third, discourse analysis is the study of how language is organized in texts and contexts (Barton, "Linguistic" 57), which in turn implies that our goals with archived texts are similar to Ellen Barton's goals with any text—we examine them in light of their authorial contexts, and we are interested in how linguistic and rhetorical "rich features"—features "from all levels and registers of language"—allow us to identify, name, and evaluate a writer's strategies on all levels of language ("Inductive" 24).

To better describe how this taxonomy emerged in the Gougar collection, I will outline several steps, beginning with my application of Cindy Johanek's contextualist research paradigm for rhetoric and composition studies. Johanek developed this paradigm from the productive tensions often experienced by compositionists who see themselves as teachers and researchers simultaneously (1). These tensions occur when dichotomous methods or beliefs threaten to take over the research or when the situation provokes the question, "What makes good research in the discipline?" By adopting more fluid understandings of discipline and context, Johanek proposes that compositionists can become less burdened by making research fit a purely quantitative or qualitative framework and more focused on innovating the kinds of questions that are needed to sustain the field (9). For example, they can question lore without discounting its significance on their inquiry, they can employ stories and narratives as legitimate forms of data gathering, and they can let questions of audience and presentation help guide these forms of data gathering. Thus, rather than applying a static method to a question, Johanek proposes a method that arises from the question—and from the processes and definitions that continue to drive it (186).

Although Johanek developed her paradigm largely to allow compositionists to situate their research in changing social and political contexts, the archival researcher also often situates his or her research in fluctuating contexts and historical moments. That is, the archival researcher's project is also often defined by inquiry rather than by method, and that inquiry sometimes strains against available methods. I propose that the archival researcher can paradigmatically realize the strengths and limitations of the historical moments depicted in what he or she is sorting, instead reframing the subject in less stable social and political contexts, where context means more than just place and is, as Johanek might say, "defined by its own power and its own variability" (3). The archival researcher can benefit from enacting Johanek's art of questioning of rhetorical contexts rather than by relying on prescribed dichotomies or anticipated findings (113) and without rearranging what the collection's creator has done.

Reframing my research as contextualist helped me to formulate questions about Gougar's texts by letting their various audiences, motivations, and outcomes determine what questions I should ask. One particular challenge I faced was situating Gougar's performances in the suffrage history we already know, fragmented and complex as that history is. The evidence provided in those eleven boxes did not present a very consistent figure. Gougar seemed to exemplify rhetorical practices that were shaped by combinations of different discourses and styles. Acknowledging the ongoing complexity of Gougar's participation in suffrage rhetoric was the first step towards getting at the questions that would become critical in organizing her texts. Thus, the emergent taxonomy must first define *context* broadly, to include "interlocutors and their social roles, their purpose, the genres of their oral or written texts, their institutional relations and frameworks, the prior text or talk, the setting, and other relevant factors" (Barton, "Inductive" 24).

Because the context from which questions about a population arise also determines how the population should be analyzed, Johanek places "Rhetorical Issues" such as audience, researcher, and evidence at the top of a matrix, and situates "Research Issues" of publication, methods, purpose, and question to one side of the matrix (112). Any intersection of rhetorical/research issues on the matrix results in a metaepistemology of sorts, where the analytical framework goes beyond the scope of what an archivist *thinks* he or she should ask. Metaepistemology is concerned with questioning the basic concepts employed in epistemology, concepts of *knowledge, truth, belief, justification,* and *rationality.* For the archivist, these tend to be determined by the given order of a set of texts. For the rhetorician, discourse analyst, or researcher, these are determined more by a(n ideo)logical order. That difference is key.

In order to more systematically approach the Gougar Collection with broader discursive goals that didn't disrupt the internal management of the collection, I used Johanek's matrix to formulate a question based on the most practical intersection of issues between researcher/method:

- How can I best search and organize my findings on over a thousand pages of text in fewer than three months? (To avoid an unwieldy and indiscriminate process of note taking, I needed a method that would also serve my future data management.)

The quickest way for me to proceed was to create a hierarchy of materials from largest to smallest (i.e., container to unit to folder to document or item) noting the *original* physical order of materials before deciding how detailed a description I should apply to the collection as a whole. This hierarchical arrangement began with an initial "first-pass description," and it was in several of these first-pass descriptions that I began to see a problematic organization emerge—problematic not only from my perspective as a discourse analyst who wanted to organize the collection according to how the texts related but also because previous efforts to process the collection had obfuscated any clear chain of events. From accession records showing early and late donations, it became apparent that at least one other archivist and author had started the work twenty-five years earlier.

My first-pass description of each folder, file, and text tended towards the rhetorical—as if questions of authorship and relationship and not questions of physical order constituted the collection. More often than not, these questions strained against the physical and chronological arrangement of the materials at hand. For example, I was intrigued by the location of certain *cartes-de-visite,* by the loopy handwriting on the backs of photographs telling narratives about who was pictured, by brief identification statements in the margins of letters or on the flaps of envelopes, by faded notes on older accession records indicating who had been in searching the collection before (who was speaking to whom in these notes?). But from the questions in these first-pass descriptions, more concrete discursive tensions and social strata began to emerge:

- Why is there no reference to Gougar's lecture activity after [Elizabeth Cady] Stanton's and [Susan B.] Anthony's volume 4 of *History of Woman's Suffrage*?
- Kriebel notes a "rhetoric to Henry Ward Beecher" (p. 50) and a "rift with Susan B. Anthony" (p. 66)—in what documents did these occur?
- Exactly what role did Gougar play in the 1892 and 1900 presidential elections?
- Are the irony patterns in her letters to [Benjamin] Harrison, Reverend [B. Wilson] Smith, and other male politicians the same?
- Who were her other principal correspondents?

My task soon became finding out how Gougar's rhetoric did (or did not) impact the larger movements with which she was involved. The social, personal, and factual questions that ensued show Johanek-like intersections among my sensitivity to the collection as an object, my concern with utilizing an analytical method that is transparent, and my desire to uncover textual evidences that were substantial yet "new" (i.e., to more adequately substantiate what Gougar's place was in rhetorical history):

Researcher/Purpose

- What is the best place for me to begin given my trajectory for analysis?

Audience/Question

- What forms of textual evidence (via internal and external references) does my audience need to see to understand Gougar's role in the suffrage movement?
- How do I make Gougar's extratextual connections with major suffrage figures more visible?

Evidence/Method

Questioning the authorship of and activity within this burgeoning collection—including trying to discern three different sets of handwriting on the backs of some documents—confirmed an important reality of archival work, and that is that a collection's donor need not be the same as its creator and almost always is not the same as its subject. Applying Johanek's rubric to these questions in turn showed a valuable evidence/method interaction in the following:

- What information about the collection can I get from within the collection itself?
- What information should I locate from outside the collection (e.g., secondary sources, other linked collections)?
- Who has used these materials before and for what purpose?
- How am I being guided by what Gougar has published—what am I prioritizing as a first source of knowledge? What other sources might I be leaving out?
- What am I inferring about the holes in this collection—such as lack of personal letters and family correspondence?

I call this interaction valuable because it led me to devise an internally consistent method for organizing Gougar's work. In other words, it led me to draw conclusions about her rhetorical participation based on the relationships that were evident in this collection at this time. My organizational tool, then, would have to be contextual and flexible and could change as further archival evidences emerged.

The Tool: Tension and Forum in Taxonomical Grids

While the rhetorical and research interactions on Johanek's matrix helped me to initially sort and catalog Gougar's texts without changing the physical arrangement of the collection, I still required a taxonomical framework that would uncover traceable features of her discourse in order to determine broader classifications for those items beyond the categories an archivist sets. For little known or unknown suffrage texts, such a taxonomy would need to privilege how the social, personal, and factual dimensions of the researcher's inquiry contend with certain characteristics that may or may not align with what we know as the suffrage "standard." For example, I considered this subset of questions:

1. Where did she stand on marginalizing issues, such as abolition, labor, and immigration?

2. How did her writings simultaneously reflect and resist popular nineteenth-century reform rhetoric?
3. What moves, characteristics, or strategies could have positioned her as a major rhetorical figure? As a dissenter?

I tried to provide alternative ways of naming and evaluating Gougar's strategies. Two guiding ideas helped me to discern Gougar's audiences, and in demonstrating how they work on my own research project, I posit them as the next step in devising an emergent (rhetorical) taxonomy.

The first is Karlyn Kohrs Campbell's notion of *double bind*,[1] a term implying that the opportunities and occasions for women to speak were at odds with discourse defending their participation in the public sphere. In "Gender and Genre: Loci of Invention and Contradiction in the Earliest Speeches by U.S. Women," Campbell offers a reading of two women's speeches, Priscilla Mason's salutatory oration (circa 1794) and Deborah Sampson Gannett's public lecture (circa 1802), to argue two claims: first, the double bind that women faced as speakers actually spurred their inventional creativity by providing an opportunity for transcendence, and, secondly, the ensuing conflict they experienced between justifying their violation of taboos and speaking appropriately limited their ability to be seen as rhetorical artists (480). According to Campbell and Jamieson ("Rhetorical Hybrids"), whose concept of generic hybrid Campbell employs for her analysis of Mason and Gannett, in order to address the issue they embodied (whether women should have the right to speak in public), their discourse had to be consistent with audience expectations while justifying a violation of their gendered roles. Mason and Gannett had to "violate norms" for particular ways of acting and speaking and to speak in "unfeminine" masculine voices (491), yet they did so by appearing to speak in ways appropriate to their occasion and sex. I needed an archival classification system that was sensitive to these tensions.

The second guiding idea is James Porter's notion of forum. Unlike the classical rhetorical notion of audience as a one-way recipient of any text, Porter's forum allows me to consider Gougar's audiences as actors in or targets of certain ironic exchanges. It further allows me to consider Gougar's methods as uniquely feminist because she appears to be writing and speaking what is acceptable while using the irony to violate expected discourse conventions. Finally, it allows me to consider a classification based on the many situations in which she wrote.

Acknowledging the double bind or dual purpose of most of Gougar's performances and applying Porter's notion of forum analysis to Gougar's texts. I identified six "tensions," or strategic responses to audience and situation according to factors such as background (organizational affiliation, philosophy or expression of belief, reputation, membership, readership); speaker/writer status and credentials; addressee/assumed audience status and credentials; topic; form; and style ("Intertextuality" 46–47). These strategic responses (SRs) include the following:

1. Provoking women of means out of ambivalence into action and reprimanding dominant movements for their faltering efforts towards suffrage (1876–88)[2]

Emergent Taxonomies 225

2. Appealing to women pragmatists by demonstrating the domestic and economic benefits of women's legal participation (1879–1900)
3. Undermining arguments against suffrage by condescending to gendered stereotypes of regional women in order to overturn them (1879–1907)
4. Appealing to male intellectuals by de-moralizing suffrage and repositioning Midwestern suffrage efforts as politically progressive (1881–1907)
5. Appealing to political power holders through electoral lobbying and by mentoring male politicians in social reform (1882–1900)
6. Criticizing U.S. policy makers by showing disparaging effects of immigration laws on state suffrage and by highlighting the progress of woman suffrage abroad (1888–1907)

While it would still be valuable to study Gougar's performances according to the terms, styles, and tropes already identified in the performances of her contemporaries (e.g., Frances Willard, Elizabeth Cady Stanton, and Lucy Stone), it is significant that within her own collection a classification for rhetorical practice emerged on its own.

The six-part classification allowed me to privilege the following categories which in turn influenced the organization of a flexible grid (shown in the table) that would track future documents I discover and denote significant relationships between them in what genres Gougar wrote or spoke most prominently: the nature and characteristics of her audience(s); the number and nature of references she made to people, places, or the movement at large; dominant arguments (hers and/or the movement's) in her texts; and her use of register (in this case, irony and sarcasm) to convey those arguments. Each category on the grid offered a way to track evidence that would guide a multilayered analysis into specific features of Helen Gougar's discourse. Internal and external references also helped me to position Gougar's speeches and writings within and alongside the suffrage movement as a whole.

Organizational Grid

Classification	SR 2: Appealing to women pragmatists by demonstrating the domestic and economic benefits of women's legal participation (1879–1900)
Text	"Industrial Training for Women" Address given for the Tippecanoe County Homemakers' Association at Trinity M.E. chapel on 29 January 1900 (Kriebel 188).
Source	*Lafayette Evening Call*, 3 February 1900
Record	117:2004.01 Helen Gougar Collection Newspaper 75.17.26: Folder of assorted clippings of Helen Gougar's writings and speeches from 1890–1900. C.f. Gougar's introduction to sister Edna Jackson Houk's Book 75.17.3 C.f. the B. Wilson Smith Papers (14:82.05)
Genre(s)	Public Address Newspaper Reprint

Audience/ Characteristics	Gougar delivered this lecture between a series of trips to Joplin, Missouri, where she held business and speaking engagements for the WCTU. It became one of her most requested lectures. Gougar would later write columns under the title "Weekly Chat with the Call Readers" for the *Lafayette Evening Call* from 11/30/1903 to 12/15/1903. The paper became the *Weekly Call* in December 1903 and suspended the "chats" until 2/14/1904, before finally discontinuing them (Kriebel 198).
References to Suffrage Figures and Events	Passage B, line 3 (reference to *Uncle Tom's Cabin*) Passage B, line 4 (critics of Harriet Beecher Stowe misunderstand her role as little more than an overpaid domestic)
Argument	*Commonplace:* Logical expansion of the "women's sphere" into public life for the public good, and the positive effects to be gained from women's participation in political and economic life (Lomicky 103). Domestic and individual health contribute to the health of a strong nation. "In short she would represent the typical 20th century woman and stand for the highest civilization attained, for the status of woman always marks the status of her nation." *Gougar:* Promotes women's participation in education but preaches a particular kind of woman: someone who has liberty (but not license), temperance in all things, working over street-loafing. Differs from the WCTU by saying women can/should be able to participate on the basis of natural endowments and intellect, not on the basis of moral superiority. She outlines the curriculum she thinks all free schools (state institutions) should put into place for female students. Although this curriculum involves domestic training towards practical and common sense, individual health, and bodily comfort, not every woman is naturally endowed to be a housekeeper. "Inasmuch as there is no sex indicated in the divine decree that by sweat of the brow we must eat, and as I find that necessity knows no sex, I ask that there shall be no sex in the social or written laws pertaining to the industrial training of the young or old."
Notable Ironic Strategies	Uses exaggeration and metaphor to challenge stereotypes of Midwestern women (redirects her audience's attention to common but absurd beliefs about women's place) Embeds a high-context coarseness and bluntness in an otherwise plain style (uses understatement alongside exaggeration) Employs derisive adjectival construction to describe critical subjects (rather than using self-deprecation) Draws connection between women's rights and abolitionist possibilities "Strik[ing] the shackles from the lives of 4,000,000 slaves" and "washing dishes and ordering the domestic affairs of a home" are used within the same sentence, creating incongruity between women's social potential and men's domestic aims

While these categories are contextually appropriate given my specific research inquiry, I suggest them more generally even for texts not authored by women or little-known figures because they offer the researcher different levels of explanatory power. Practically speaking, these were the kinds of information I could glean fairly quickly, and they would allow me to do extensive cross-referencing of Gougar's texts. Most significant, they don't assume fixed or concrete categories. As more texts emerge and become subsumed into the collection demonstrating Gougar's rhetorical venues, these categories—and the six-part classification they came from—can and should change. (As a case in point, between 2004 and 2006 the list of SRs grew from five to six when I discovered references to three critical essays Gougar had penned on immigration policy, written after 1900 and from abroad, and in 2007, I happened across a collection of nineteenth-century newspapers featuring fifty-three short articles dating as early as 1882 that Gougar had written on foreign policy).

The organizational grid is not the same as a detailed collection inventory or even a finding aid. Both of those essential processing documents can and do make transparent how a collection works, and a detailed inventory can be gridlike to emulate a database that makes cross-referencing the content of items possible, but Johanek's and Porter's theorizing equips archival researchers to create other genres, allowing us to interpret documents in more than just their original order and beyond the creator's or archivist's leanings.

What distinguishes the taxonomical grid from other processing documents is its equal attention to the research trajectory and the inherent rhetorical nature of the collection. It allows the researcher to bring to archival work the important question of who is/was the audience for this collection. I note the following other benefits of creating organizational grids based on the taxonomical tensions inherent in a collection:

- holding the researcher accountable to the parameters of a collection without being limited by them
- allowing the researcher to augment limited public records by cross-referencing relationships to other figures, collections, documents, or performances
- compelling the researcher to look within the collection for information on how and how much to classify rhetorical performances, rather than imposing an external set of criteria
- focusing the researcher's analysis on the subject's performances by contextualizing them in other found texts
- causing the researcher to note pursuant areas of questioning
- preventing the researcher from trying to write only one coherent narrative of the subject's life or of approaching the subject's performances with the desire to personify through the limited evidence available

The Outcome: Recursive and Flexible Analysis

To summarize, my whole method consists of four steps:

1. I apply Johanek's matrix of rhetorical and research issues to do a first-pass description of the collection's contents and to organize the questions that

ensue—that is, questions pertaining to method, authorship, and activity. In so doing, I differentiate between the collection's provenance and arrangement and the kinds of evidences I will need to glean in order to satisfy my overarching query.

2. I initially examine these evidences as cotextually and contextually derived, where the cotext is provided by references to—but outside of—the collection, and context is provided by materials existing within the collection. In my case, acknowledging Campbell's double bind and Porter's forum as co/contextual factors in Gougar's work helped me to focus methodologically on the tensions she was negotiating with her writings. But in any case, the point is to acknowledge identifiable, flexible relationships that occur between the subject and the subject's context (e.g., tension, forum, situation) as the topmost classification in the taxonomy.

3. From these relationships (i.e., Gougar's strategic responses), I select organizational categories that bear on the question of audience, that can be marked discursively and linguistically, and that can be noted fairly quickly. These categories are also flexible and unstable inasmuch as they can change when and if more texts are added to the collection. For example, knowing that I am dealing with an archival subject who worked alongside but not always with the women we remember as "pioneering" figures in the suffrage movement, I chose to examine how Gougar's arguments did or did not conform with what was considered commonplace and to note how she used irony when her contemporaries did not. However, had Gougar already been one of the "pioneering" figures and had I been interested in how she positioned herself as a member of the movement, I would instead focus on the number of references she made to other suffrage figures, her method of attributing or citing ideas, and the type of forum in which she performed most frequently.

4. I apply the grid to a representative sample of texts in the collection, in order to select a minicorpus that best demonstrates the organizational categories and, eventually, to rethink and revise those categories in light of new textual evidence.

Beginning researchers who are new to a collection often do not know where to start, and even veteran researchers are often unaware of places to seek out alternative texts or are not practiced in how to mine unprocessed collections for inventive, productive taxonomical systems. Thus, they are at risk of glossing the essential characteristics of a collection by attempting to apply a prescribed organization to it or by evaluating its contents according to extant constructs. So one outcome of an emergent taxonomical method is that it helps researchers to recover authentic rhetorical features of understudied texts. Accounting for the relationship among "style, register, and situation" provides for fuller descriptions of how our archival subjects did and could communicate, not merely how they *should* communicate (Clarke 18).

However, this method can and obviously should be applied beyond just those texts. If what results from this volume is the realization that rhetoric and composition scholars are gradually gaining more access to archival collections—either because their projects are revisionist, or their institutional duties require that they create an archive from scratch, or their discursive or linguistic interests lead them to obscure but unprocessed work, or even because they view archival work as a kind of classroom-to-community engagement—then we should be aware of the difficulties of doing both processing and research in tandem with each other.

But we should also be aware that proceeding taxonomically can help us to more richly map intertextual activity in a collection by understanding documents within their social networks, yet without disrupting the nature of that collection if it is processed, and without erasing important provenance clues if it is not. In short, it helps us to devise a systematic method for organizing texts (and, hence, for classifying rhetorical practices) according to the communicative constructs inherent in that collection. It is in relating the documents within a taxonomical grid and not in disrupting the documents from a particular order where significant discursive relationships can be established and explored.

Notes

1 Because the collection I use was principally authored by an understudied figure in the American Suffrage Movement, I employ Campbell's "double bind" as a product of (feminist) revisionist historiography. However, broader and more general applications of this methodology can still utilize the notion of rhetorical tension in order to determine how the archival subject upholds or violates discursive norms.
2 These dates reflect Gougar's range of involvement in each strategic response based only on the archival records available to me. They are approximate rather than binding parameters and subject to revision whenever new documents surface.

Works Cited

Barton, Ellen. "Inductive Discourse Analysis: Discovering Rich Features." *Discourse Studies in Composition*. Ed. Ellen Barton and Gail Stygall. Cresskill, NJ: Hampton, 2002. 19–41.

———. "Linguistic Discourse Analysis." *What Writing Does and How It Does It: An Introduction to Analyzing Texts and Textual Practices*. Ed. Charles Bazerman and Paul Prior. Mahwah, NJ: Erlbaum, 2004. 57–82.

Brunton, Paul, and Tim Robinson. "Arrangement and Description." *Keeping Archives*. Ed. Judith Ellis and D. W. Thorpe. 2nd ed. Port Melbourne, Australia: Thorpe/Australian Society of Archivists, 1993. 222–47.

Campbell, Karlyn Kohrs. "Gender and Genre: Loci of Invention and Contradiction in the Earliest Speeches by U.S. Women." *Quarterly Journal of Speech* 81 (1995): 479–95.

Campbell, Karlyn Kohrs, and Kathleen Hall Jamieson. "Rhetorical Hybrids: Fusions of Generic Elements." *Quarterly Journal of Speech* 68 (1982): 146–57.

Clarke, Danielle. *The Politics of Early Modern Women's Writing*. Harlow, England: Pearson, 2001.

Fahnestock, Jeanne, and Marie Secor. "Rhetorical Analysis." *Discourse Studies in Composition*. Ed. Ellen Barton and Gail Stygall. Cresskill, NJ: Hampton, 2002. 177–200.

Heald, Carolyn. "Is There Room for Archives in the Postmodern World?" *American Archivist* 59 (1996): 101.

Johanek Cindy. *Composing Research: A Contextualist Paradigm for Rhetoric and Composition*. Logan: Utah State UP, 2000.

Kriebel, Robert C. *Where the Saints Have Trod: The Life of Helen Gougar.* West Lafayette, IN: Purdue UP, 1985.

Lomicky, Carol S. "Frontier Feminism and the *Woman's Tribune:* The Journalism of Clara Bewick Colby." *Journalism History* 28.3 (2002): 102–11.

Porter, James E. "Intertextuality and the Discourse Community." *Rhetoric Review* 5.1 (Autumn 1986): 34–47.

Steedman, Carolyn. *Dust: The Archive and Cultural History.* New Brunswick, NJ: Rutgers UP, 2002.

SECTION 4

RETHINKING THE ARCHIVES

16.
OCTALOG III: THE POLITICS OF HISTORIOGRAPHY IN 2010
Panel Organized by Lois Agnew, Laurie Gries, and Zosha Stuckey

Introduction

The field of rhetoric has historically been defined by competing visions of language and education—and by the conviction that these debates have significance for public life. James J. Murphy highlighted this point at the beginning of Octalog I (1988) when he noted the field's consistent engagement with the idea that "what is at stake ... ought to be discovered for the good of the community" (5). The Octalogs have provided a space for exploring varied notions concerning rhetoric's role in serving a common good and assessing the contentious nature of that undertaking. These conversations have included a wide range of perspectives concerning rhetoric's role in public and private life, methods of researching and writing rhetorical history, and the values that surround our work. They have suggested that our field's notion of "truth" is multiplicitous and incomplete.

Octalog I sparked new scholarship by asking us to uncover and recover histories that have been neglected or hidden. The panelists highlighted assumptions about power, knowledge, and struggle that are embedded in every construction of history. They discussed the importance of creative research methodologies, what constitutes evidence, who and what should be included in our histories, and how researchers' positions and goals affect their interpretations. Octalog II (1997) extended these discussions by pointing us toward the importance of local, contested, and marginalized histories and rhetorical practices and encouraging us to listen for the silences that have been left out of well-known historical accounts. The discussions urged a continued awareness about how moving the margins to center revises our sense of rhetorical history.

Octalog III builds on these earlier conversations. As Arthur E. Walzer notes in his reflection on the event, "all participants welcomed the expansion of rhetoric beyond what Graff and Leff have characterized as a white, male, European demographic." Yet Octalog III shows that we are still negotiating multiple and contested understandings of what constitutes the history of rhetoric, how to study it, and rhetoric's role in forming and promoting the common good. Octalog III urges us to move beyond our initial

---

Agnew, Lois, Laurie Gries, and Zosha Stuckey. "Octalog III: The Politics of Historiography in 2010." *Rhetoric Review* 30.2 (2011): 109–134. Print.

attempts to recover multiple and contested histories by exploring how the dynamics of power and issues of identity formation influence the historiography of rhetoric. The eight panelists and respondent specifically ask us to interrogate how our own dispositions and epistemologies shape our perceptions of the past and press us toward new methodologies and sites of inquiry. Especially as we continue to cross and move between borders in our research, participants press us to ask: why these histories? As we answer that question for ourselves and our students, participants urge us to consider the ethics that interrogate our choices, our assumptions, and our methods of researching and teaching history.

The Octalog participants also remind us that we research and teach in political and economic times that necessitate rethinking our ways of doing, writing, and teaching rhetorical history. They prompt us to ask how we can challenge dominant paradigms both within and beyond our discipline and maintain our commitment to inclusivity against a backdrop of inevitable acculturation. They challenge us to keep pressing on the traditional ways of doing rhetorical history, both as we look back to sites that have been traditionally taken up and toward new sites that ought to be studied. In addition, they urge us to consider the value of dialogue, difference, and interdependence that emerges from such work. Finally, this panel reflects the productive work of doing rhetorical history that has emerged since Octalog II, particularly in relation to bodies, space, and rhetorics of the other. Yet, as we continue our pursuit of an expansive and reflective approach to rhetorical scholarship and history, there is still much messy work to be done. As Victor Vitanza suggests, Octalog III ultimately pushes us to take risks in our scholarship that may lead us in directions that we cannot yet imagine.

We have printed below the revised statements presented by each of the Octalog panelists, along with Victor Vitanza's response. Some of these revised statements include reflections on the event; other panelists' reflections are included in a final section at the conclusion of this article.

Lois Agnew
Laurie Gries
Zosha Stuckey
Syracuse University

ETHOS IN THE ARCHIVES

Vicki Tolar Burton

Oregon State University

Like *Smith Magazine*'s six-word memoir, my historiography of rhetoric is brief: Cross borders. Lift rhetors. Study systems. These imperatives are not new—they were eloquently set forth by scholars in Octalogs I and II, and shape many histories of rhetoric. Octalog III embodies and enacts some directions border-crossings have taken. My work has crossed borders into the archives of eighteenth-century British Methodism in search of preaching women and working-class rhetors. In the Manchester archives, within the method of Methodism, I found a democratizing system of spiritual literacy that arguably laid the foundation for the British trade union movement. This system both sponsored and controlled rhetors, supporting and later silencing the preaching women, and containing other women rhetors by the accretion of male texts over female voices (Tolar Burton).

Since Octalog II, when Linda Ferreira-Buckley called for more attention to archival methods, historians have responded with significant work on methodology. I'm thinking, for instance, of Buchanan, Glenn and Enoch, Ranney, and collections by Kirsch and Rohan, and by Ramsey, Sharer, L'Eplattenier, and Mastrangelo.

Today, I want to interrogate archival work by bringing the pressure of *ethos* to bear on practices of border crossing. As we cross into the archives of others, what is the *ethos* of the historian of rhetoric? In the earliest days of Greek civilization, the days of Homer and Hesiod, *ethea,* the root of *ethos,* meant "a dwelling place." The notion of *dwelling* shapes Aristotle's story of the strangers who went into the wilderness in search of the wise philosopher Heraclitus, only to find him living in poverty. Sensing that his visitors were disappointed with what they saw and intended to leave, Heraclitus reached out, inviting the travelers to *dwell* with him, saying, "Here too the gods are present" (Hyde xix).

As historians of rhetoric, who are we in this story? We imagine ourselves as Heraclitus, reaching out to strangers and recognizing the sacred in the ordinary. But sometimes when we cross borders into the archives of others, we may be more like Aristotle's strangers. We embark on our research travels with high expectations. Then we arrive in the archives, and things are a bit of a mess—disorganized, uncataloged, overwhelming. Like the traveling strangers, we are in danger of not seeing what is before us, of missing our chance to dwell. Here, too, the gods are present.

In our field "crossing borders" has become an assumed good. But borders are also crossed by inept tourists, invaders, imperialists, and Starbuck's franchisers. We had best think carefully about our *ethos* as border crossers, especially as rhetorical studies go global.

Michael Hyde suggests, "The ethical practice of rhetoric entails the construction of a speaker's *ethos* as well as the construction of 'dwelling place' or a ground of being 'for collaborative and moral deliberation'" (xviii). The ethical practice of archival research makes the same demands. Led by scholars like Brice Heath, Geertz, Street, Vitanza, Bizzell, and Royster, we practice research with principles such as respect for the local, non-exploitation of people and cultures, respect for the challenges of language difference, and the ambiguity of working in translation. We admit the partialness and situated nature of our knowledge.

As our research goes global, through what lenses do we examine the texts and practices that we encounter? Do questions that apply to Aristotle or American composition studies work equally well for Asian and Arabic rhetorics? Our *ethos* is formed in part by the questions we ask.

We enact good will by observing the etiquette of the host archive. We enact a deeper *ethos* of knowledge and character by a willingness to dwell with the documents, to practice slow reading as we lift the rhetors from their musty folders, seeking clues to their rhetorical situations and literacy practices. But travel is expensive, so researchers are tempted to hurry, to get to everything fast, to possess the archive. This is the way of hubris and folly. Slow down. Breathe. Dwell. Before my first trip to the Manchester archives, I asked Anne Gere for advice. She said, "Always assume you will need to go back."

Jim Berlin advised us to study systems, place discourse within its community, identify sources of power to speak and to silence. Deborah Brandt reminds us that sponsors of literacy may want a return on their investment. Dwelling with the material archive—city, buildings, artifacts—we scrutinize the systems and motives of the archive's collectors and sponsors. Likewise, let us examine our own place in systems of grants, tenure and promotion, access and publication, acknowledging that we may sometimes conceal the partialness of our knowledge under the cloak of academic authority. Do we respeak archival subjects, ourselves practicing the rhetoric of accretion?

Now many researchers are crossing digital borders, lifting e-rhetors, and studying elusive systems of electronic sponsorship. Whether in bricks and mortar or digital archives, we enact our most generous *ethos* by mentoring others, inviting them to dwell and discuss. Here, too, the gods are present.

THE CIRCULATION OF DISCOURSE THROUGH THE BODY

Jay Dolmage

West Virginia University

I see rhetoric as the strategic study of the circulation of power through communication. In the very first Octalog, James Berlin offered a very similar definition of rhetoric, defining it as: "the uses of language in the play of power" (6). I am pretty sure that when I read the first Octalog in my very first year of graduate school, I stole Berlin's definition, and I have been subtly rotating it and leveraging it for my own purposes ever since.

So I want to keep this theft in mind and at hand.

Berlin also suggested, in that first symposium, that rhetoric "reveals the conflicts of a historical moment"; later he praises another panelist for "acknowledging the narrativity of ... historical writing" (12, 35). And Susan Jarratt agreed, suggesting that "there are stories that are guiding these things [these things being histories]" (26).

So I sit here today with my own ideas about historiography and my own definitions of rhetoric. Yet I do so as I weave together several earlier perspectives, writing myself into a guiding story. I am conscious of some theft and likely oblivious to other small crimes, yet willing to plead a preemptive guilt.

I want to suggest that this collage says something about the politics of historiography: My own perspectives are the creative and sometimes conscious layering of other people's stories and ideas. When I can do this with some cunning and ingenuity, I am doing my job as a *rhetorical* historian.

I see rhetorical history as the study not of *just* a selected archive of static documents or artifacts, but a study *also, always* of the negotiations, valences, shifting claims and refutations, canons and revisions that orbit any history.

As a rhetorical historian, I seek to discover as many layers of meaning as possible in order to interrogate the interestedness of each version of a given story, not in order to choose one version. I think we learn a lot not from asking which history is most real, and not *just* from asking which histories to look for, but we learn from gathering and parsing the histories that are most fraught and varied, tense, duplicitous and difficult, and celebrating their contestation.

So my further suggestion is that when we look through rhetorical history for what is most tense and contested, we most often come to stories about the body. Wherever we find the body rhetorically contested, and wherever we find rhetorical contestation about the body's role in meaning-making, we see intensely fraught negotiations. These constellations of value and their variable gravities are exactly what we should be looking for—and we should be asking questions not to resolve this argument and set the universe in order but to better understand ourselves by locating those things we disagree, worry, and wrestle about most vehemently.

For instance, in my effort to locale the role of disability in rhetorical history, I've come to see that disability has a rhetorical push and pull, not just wherever we might recover disabled bodies but also when we find any supposedly "abnormal" body— foreign, raced, feminized, sexualized or desexed, contagious. Disability is often used rhetorically as a flexible form of stigma to be freely applied to any unknown, threatening, or devalued group. In these ways the "abnormal" or extraordinary body is highly rhetorical. So we need to look for it actively and engage the rhetorical body in our historiography—indeed in all of our research and in all of our classrooms. If we follow this impulse, we would create rhetorical history that reclaims stories from the margins and from apocrypha, as I have tried to do in reclaiming disability in rhetorical history. But a differently embodied historiography does not just find new stories; it is a new way to circulate these stories in order to generate a new ontology, a new epistemology, a new rhetoric.

Here I'll offer a litany and an invocation.

The litany: Tension around the body exists, first, because efforts to define rhetoric have so often denied and denigrated the body; second, because this denial has always been laughably impossible; third, because modern body values and anxieties have always been mapped back across rhetorical history; and finally because studying any culture's attitudes and arguments about the body always connects us intimately with attitudes and arguments about rhetorical possibility. That is, to care about the body is to care about how we make meaning.

The invocation: Rhetoric is always embodied. When I say this, I mean, first, that all meaning issues forth from the body and that second, communication reaches into the body to shape its possibilities. The body has traditionally been both a rhetorical instrument and a rhetorical experiment, even as bodies have always been insistently material. The corpus of history has most often been shaped to look like an ideal body: proportional, autonomous, never needing the assistance of others, strong—and of course white and masculine and upright and forward-facing. But if you find the *rhetorical* body, you find a field of tension, a site of trial and trouble; find the body in history and you need rhetoric not just to uncover layers of evidence but also the negotiation, argument, and translation between them. Then, writing from bodies we would do history differently, not just in recognizing other bodies throughout our stories in new complexity and eminence but also because our histories might more closely represent our bodies themselves—bodies that are flawed, incomplete, vulnerable, and unique, always in need of others, interdependent, rhetorically constructive and constructed.

I see rhetoric as the strategic study of the circulation of power through communication; this was the statement that I pilfered to begin my comments. Let me filter this theft a bit further as I end: I believe that we should see rhetoric as the circulation of discourse through the body. When we do so, we may find the conflict and variation that impels any rhetorical endeavor.

FINDING NEW SPACES FOR FEMINIST RESEARCH

Jessica Enoch

University of Pittsburgh

In her contribution to Octalog II, Cheryl Glenn called for the "regendering" of rhetorical history as a means to create an expanded, inclusive rhetorical tradition. The ensuing years have seen feminist scholars take up this work in earnest, with their explorations largely falling into two dynamic categories. First, scholars have recovered the rhetorical significance of female rhetors from an increasingly varied spectrum of raced, classed, and cultured backgrounds. As scholars engage in these acts of recovery, they do not simply add women to the history of rhetoric. Rather, they use their recoveries to revise our thinking about rhetorical theory and practice. The second way scholars have regendered rhetorical history is by rereading rhetoric's traditions through the lens of gender. Here, scholars explore, for example, how masculine ways of performing rhetoric gained precedence and how rhetorical pedagogies have often been feminized and, consequently, dismissed.

These two modes of historiography have made tremendous challenges to traditional understandings of rhetorical theory, practice, and history. And there is still much work left to do. As we continue to pursue these research trajectories, however, it's also vital to build from this work and imagine new ways of writing feminist history. For, as Glenn explains, every historiography and historiographic method is performative in that it "subtly shape[s] our perception of rhetoric englobed" (*Rhetoric* 7).

Here I imagine a new feminist historiographic practice, one that examines the rhetorical process of gendering. This mode of historiography interrogates the rhetorical work that goes into creating and disturbing the gendered distinctions, social categories, and asymmetrical power relationships that women and men encounter in their daily lives. Attending to such concerns expands the purview of feminist research. Instead of working to recalibrate the rhetorical tradition, this project focuses on the everyday rhetorical processes that create difference and grant privilege. While there is certainly a range of historiographic possibilities to explore, I consider what it would mean to historicize the rhetorical processes that engender space.

A feminist rhetorical history of space starts from the premise that spaces are not neutral backdrops for human dramas but are, borrowing from Michel de Certeau, "practiced places"—practiced in ways that play out assumptions regarding gendered behavior and social expectations (117). Working from such a premise, this project examines what I call spatial rhetorics: the discursive and material means used to engender spaces with value. Spatial rhetorics suggest the purpose of a space; the actions, behaviors, and practices that should happen inside that space; and the people who should occupy it. Methodologically, the work is to study the language that designates a space, the materials that construct and adorn it, and the activities enacted inside it. The ultimate goal is to investigate how the composition of space creates, maintains, or renovates gendered differences and understandings.

This historiographic project might seem familiar. Spatial concerns have been foremost in the work of scholars who analyze the constraints women have faced when attempting to claim masculine and male-dominated rhetorical spaces such as the pulpit, platform, and podium (Buchanan; Mountford; Shaver). For this new historiography, however, the gendering of rhetorical spaces is just the beginning. Its inquiry extends to other sites critical to the personal, professional, and political welfare of women and men, such as the schoolhouse, university, voting booth, childcare center, women's shelter, and home. Additionally, examining these sites means that scholars consider not only what spatial rhetorics say about masculine and feminine behavior but also how these rhetorics comment on the full range of social categorizations, including those of race, class, culture, sexuality, and physical ability. To give two examples: We might study the physical construction of Harvard's campus to understand how it reinforced the idea that the school was a preserve of white, aristocratic masculinity; or we might examine how black female rhetors such as bell hooks have revised white feminist visions of the home as a site of domestic entrapment to see it instead as a space of resistance that can "heal the wounds inflicted by racist domination" (384).

The stakes of this project are high indeed. As theorists such as Mary Ryan have argued, "[T]he appropriation of the social spaces of everyday life is an essential precondition for the political empowerment of subordinated groups" (92). Historicizing the rhetorical processes that engender spaces, then, offers critical insight to varied ways this appropriation and empowerment has occurred. Furthermore, in relation to the overarching aims of feminist historiography, this project gains a different kind of significance. It serves as an example of how we might continue to imagine new ways to write histories that explore the complex imbrication of gender and rhetoric.

WHEN WILL WE ALL MATTER: A FRANK DISCUSSION OF PROGRESSIVE PEDAGOGY

Ronald L. Jackson II

University of Illinois–Urbana Champaign

I write this statement with a spirit of caring and hope. I care that power as a form of dominance has raided our epistemologies and left us naked with only one garment of epistemological singularity that some of us recognize as "mainstream rhetoric." Others know it by its abbreviated name "rhetoric." I care that how we practice effective pedagogy pertaining to the study of rhetoric most of the time routinely ignores theoretic contributions from non-White scholars and therefore provides students with partial stories, partial truths, and nonprogressive training. I care that the legacy we are preparing to leave our children is rife with political, cultural, and social unfreedom. I care that as I speak to many rhetorical scholars about culturally progressive pedagogy, their eyes glaze over and they issue a battery of excuses and rationales why they cannot give serious consideration to a multicultural pedagogy when teaching classical and contemporary rhetoric.

Obviously, because there are multiple cultures in our world, there must be multiple classics because what is classical in one culture is not necessarily classical in another. Lest we think this is a tactical play on words, we need to recognize that rhetoric did not emanate in Greece or Rome. How could it unless of course the origins of humankind can be found in Greece or Rome, or unless we are willing to concede that no human being held the capacity to think, to organize ideas, or to compose arguments prior to Greeks and Romans? That has been the historical narrative. However, we all know that the writer who with every stroke of the pen moves our imagination controls the principal messages in a narrative.

Today, I come to you with hope, hope that we will once again rise to a challenge put to academics many centuries ago. The challenge was to consider assembling academic institutions that would train students to bind themselves to a creed of global civic participation, to prepare our students to engage with a world before them that is constantly changing, to equip students with the kind of moral integrity and independent thinking that will interrogate wrongdoing, reconcile poor judgment, and embrace all forms of social difference.

Rhetoric is a vast and varied field of inquiry. One of its many multitentacled dimensions is that of culture. Even narrower than that is the area of culture we have come to know as African-American rhetoric, which is where my work emanates. At this Octalog III, I am most concerned with discussing the nature, function, and usefulness of rhetorical studies. It seems to me we still teach rhetoric the way we always have. We still train students to ignore nonmainstream (that is, non-White) rhetorical traditions. As professors and scholars, we also tend to sidestep our responsibility to be epistemologically responsible and just within this vast terrain of rhetorical studies. So the principal questions we must insist on asking every year is what counts as rhetorical scholarship? Whose rhetorical legacies and traditions get to be centered in the curriculum such that students cannot leave without learning them? Does it matter or is it culturally relevant how we teach what rhetoric is and how it functions in our society? These are questions with which we must grapple if we ever hope to be relevant and responsible. The challenge is to engage in a paradigm shift. Our challenge as intellectuals is to consider new perspectives. Oftentimes that means inviting and embracing new epistemologies.

Where We Must Go from Here

Many whiteness researchers have discovered that whites see no separation between what it means to be white and what it means to be American. Their reflex is to consider the two as synonyms (Jackson; McIntosh; Nakayama and Krizek). On the other hand, Blacks, Latinos, Asians, and even Native Americans do not think of their cultures as synonymous with what it means to be American. How could they?

What is perceived to be at stake is cultural solidity, often articulated as "our way of life." At present, my fear is that the average students whom we consider the best of our most progressive students graduate with a set of social conditions they must learn to resist, a set of promises they must learn to tune out, and a set of ideals they must learn to cling to for dear life, hoping that some of it will save them.

We must become the Citadel of intellectual integrity, moral aptitude, and civic preparation. It is true that our legacy is inscribed on our children's souls, and yet we must avoid this slippery slope of divested morality or else we will find ourselves repeating the same. Solutions must include remembering: We must remember the past perils of pedagogical violence so they can later be avoided; we must remember that when we unravel privilege, we have a colonialist subject standing there; we must remember epistemic violence is attached to a power/knowledge matrix, which includes its own body politic; we must remember that forgetting is ignoring symptoms of a disease that is deteriorating our social bodies. We must also remember that identity and difference are predicated on subjectivity, and it is our responsibility to critically interrogate how we consume messages that affect our consumption of difference.

THE RHETORIC OF RESPONSIBILITY: PRACTICING THE ART OF RECONTEXTUALIZATION

LuMing Mao

Miami University

Thanks in part to the contributions made from the first and second Octalog at the CCCC, our field has been turning to non-Western, indigenous rhetorical traditions to help reexamine the history of rhetoric and reconceptualize rhetoric's forms, purposes, and functions. In spite of the progress made so far, several key questions remain to be fully addressed. For example, what practices in these other traditions should we exactly focus on? Not every communicative practice that is non-Western or indigenous can either deserve our critical attention or promise to help advance our cause of writing the other ways of knowing and being into the history of rhetoric in the twenty-first century. How, then, does our object of study reveal our own experience, our own affiliation, and our own authority and legitimacy? How do they in turn privilege and prevail upon what we study?

Equally important, how should we go about engaging these practices? Is it methodologically possible for us to study such practices free of ethnocentrism and etic biases as long as we claim to be self-reflective or even openly critical of the rhetoricity of our own enterprise? Almost by the same token, how can we represent or celebrate these other practices, many of which have hitherto been ruled anything but rhetoric, without putting them on a pedestal or without denying them their own heterogeneous, if not conflicting or even problematic, traditions? Is there some standard or heuristic out there that can stand outside, or stand up to, this perennial self-other binary?

And related, in what ways do our ongoing dialogues and entanglements across national, political, and linguistic boundaries inflect and influence our engagement with these other practices? Do the conditions of the global necessarily impinge upon the effort to write a different kind of history that is closely tied to the local ways of doing and being? How can the production of such a history help usher in a new set of relationships and a new paradigm of cross-cultural dialogue?

I suggest that we practice the art of recontextualization to respond to these questions. By this I mean a critical reevaluation of both the self and the other, interrogating who we are and where we have been and unpacking how local political, economic, and sociocultural exigencies help determine particular contexts and individual performances. By this I further mean tenaciously engaging the contingencies of the present and recognizing how they can potentially shape our new historiography of rhetoric while still preserving or perpetuating the existing asymmetrical structures of power. I want to suggest that practicing the art of recontextualization constitutes a processual model that productively troubles our own modes of thinking and that seeks to privilege experiences over facts and relations of interdependence over structures of sameness or difference. An inevitable corollary of this model, then, is a strong ethical imperative.

Finally, practicing the art of recontextualization in the global contact zones does not mean yoking the other with the global in the name of "seizing the kairotic moment," at the risk of uprooting the other from its own native environment. Nor does it mean that we remain uncritically tethered to the local milieu for the sake of "going (and staying) native" to the point of failing to consider the influence of the global. Rather, practicing the art of recontextualization means negotiating, both dialectically and perpetually, between developing a localized narrative and searching for its new and broader significance within and outside its own tradition; between looking for rhetoric where it has been categorically ruled non-existent and rejecting a concomitant temptation to reduce experiences into facts and equate heterogeneous resonance with either sameness or difference; and between using the other for transformative agendas and resisting methods and logic that continue to silence or make invisible the same other. This is, I submit to you, the ultimate form of the rhetoric of responsibility.

THIS IS A STORY ABOUT A BELIEF . . .

Malea Powell

Michigan State University

This is a story.

Because I must be brief, I'm going to skip some of what I consider to be essential elements of story—easing in, slowly drawing an audience to me—and skip right to a fairly contentious and imprecise claim followed by a set of barely elaborated explanations that are themselves pretty contentious and imprecise.

The claim. In our discipline, scholars who study, theorize, and write histories about race are almost always assumed to be *not* talking about rhetoric—at least, we are told, not the kind of rhetoric that is generally useful to everyone or thought to generate theoretical frames and methodological practices that will be used by folks who "really" or "just" study rhetoric. As short-sighted and blatantly racist as such assumptions might be, most of us *other* scholars just go politely about our business, grumbling to one another but carefully avoiding any direct acknowledgement of such attitudes. I'm breaking that polite avoidance here because I've observed first-hand the slow creep of these assumptions as they move from scholarship about race to include scholarship about ethnicity, sexual orientation, able-ness, language practices, digital technologies, material culture—anything that seems to threaten the primacy of the text over the materiality of the body or the kind of meaning produced by/through bodies. This worries me. The reason this worries me is because of what I've learned from my own work in American Indian rhetorics—cultures that don't change, die. Our discipline's inclination to fetishize the text above the body, combined with a narrowness of vision that insists on connecting every rhetorical practice on the planet to Big Daddy A and the one true Greco-Roman way does not exactly build a sustainable platform for the continued vibrance of our disciplinary community.[1]

So right about now, some of you probably violently disagree with me. You might see yourselves as advocates of diversity with a pretty expansionist view of rhetoric studies. You might say: "But we don't do this; we've diversified! We have women's rhetorics and African-American rhetorics and we even have a couple books about 'other' rhetorics from antiquity! Just look at the folks gathered here at the Octalog to discuss 'the future of rhetorical studies'!" You might even point to my presence here as proof of the existence of "otherness" in rhetoric studies, in fact. Some of you might have different objections. You see yourselves as maintaining a boundary between studying rhetoric and studying everything (anything) else, or you might be the rare bird who actually studies classical Greco-Roman traditions in their full cultural situatedness and original languages. Some of you might want to ask me what I *mean* when I use the word *rhetoric* if I don't hearken back to Aristotle's supposed consolidation of the term.[2] And because I hardly have the time to offer a nuanced and complicated response to any of those objections, I want to offer this instead.

Working from theorists like Homi Bhabha[3] and Roy Harvey Pearce filtered through the meaning-making practices of indigenous North Americans,[4] helps me see these kinds of objections to my contentious and imprecise claim as grounded in a belief I do not share. A belief that there is *a* rhetorical tradition around which all other rhetorical traditions constellate. A belief that *all* rhetorical scholarship must somehow, some way, show a genealogical or thematic relationship to that mythical Greco-Roman origin story in order to be counted as "really" (or "just") about rhetoric. This belief itself is an outgrowth of a much larger, more insidious belief—a belief about civilization, about the duties and character of civilized wo/men, a belief that made it possible for the colonization of the Americas to take place, a belief that writes particular destinies as "manifest," and others as impediments. The imperial narrative that produces this belief is founded in the same intellectual fires that "revived" rhetoric during the Greco-Roman re-turns and re-writings that characterized the Scholasticism and then the European Renaissance. This belief is literally *written* in the same colonial spaces where the revised version of classical rhetoric found a way to travel to North America—in the writings of Scottish colonials whose work, if we believe Win Horner and a slew of other scholars, became the basis for a kind of writing instruction that tried to organize the savage chaos of the "new" world through the "elements" of rhetoric (see Horner; Whately).

Here it's important to remember that what our discipline has produced is what Pearce would call "a certitude" about our destiny—a study of our own civilizing discourse that gives those who come after us "an enlarged certitude of another, even happier destiny—that manifest in the progress of American civilization over all obstacles" (xvii). How easy, then, it is to make the claim that our discipline has allowed "other" rhetorics space on the stage in order to study them in quite the same way—in order to produce a certitude about the strength of *a* single rhetorical tradition, dressed up and feathered by its gradual incorporation of difference into that narrative of certitude—a narrative that continues to sustain us in the face of the chaos that confronts us every day here in the twenty-first century. This certitude is a problem. It's a methodologically unacceptable way to theorize rhetorical scholarship because it keeps us trapped in genealogies of colonialism.

It's important to understand that I'm not arguing for us to make space for other rhetorics. Even at its most radical, that multicultural story about "the history/histories of rhetoric/s" is merely a complicated rhizome spreading out under the fertile ground of *the* rhetorical tradition that ultimately treads that same path, what I think of as "the narrow arrow," from Greece to the Americas. What I'm arguing here is that we have to learn to rely on rhetorical understandings different from that singular, inevitable origin story. We have to try harder to overcome the behaviors that sustain colonial discourse in our contemporary practices, which means we need to theorize, and that theory can't always be directly tied to classroom practices that are, again, an outgrowth of a paracolonial ideological state apparatus.[5] We need to theorize, and that theory can't engage in textual fetishism—neither by relying on alphabetic print texts nor by textualizing non-alphabetic objects. We need, in fact, to move our conversations and our practices toward "things," to a wider understanding of how all made things are rhetorical, and of how cultures make, and are made by, the rhetoricity of things.⁶

Newee; thank you.

Notes

1. So, this phrase has gotten a lot of attention. First during and immediately after the Octalog panel in the Tweetstream, then in f2f and continuing social-media interactions after. Most younger scholars express excitement to hear someone say what they've been thinking all along; many "established" scholars express dismay at my lack of respect. Disciplinarity does do its job, does it not?
2. I will, however, offer my definition of rhetoric. Just for the record, when I use the word *rhetoric*, I am evoking a *shorthand* that encompasses thousands of years of intellectual production all over the globe—a set of productions that we have only just begun to understand—and that generally refers to systems of discourse through which meaning was, is, and continues to be made in a given culture.
3. In *Signs Taken for Wonders*, Homi Bhabha reminds us that "[t]here is a scene in the cultural writings of English colonialism which repeats so insistently" that it *"inaugurates* a literature of empire." That scene, he tells us, is always "played out in the wild and *word*less wastes" of "the colonies" and consists entirely of the "fortuitous discovery of the English book" by colonized peoples; this scene marks the book as an "emblem," one of the colonizers' "signs taken for wonders" (29).
4. See especially Lisa Brooks; Joy Harjo; Thomas King; Nancy Shoemaker (ed.); Linda Tuhiwai Smith; Robert Warrior; and Shawn Wilson.
5. For an examination of "paracolonial," see Vizenor.
6. A totally unsatisfying and provocative opening into my current work that argues for situating specific rhetorical events in the continuum of rhetorical practices (alphabetic and non-alphabetic) that hold particular cultures together over time.

RHETORIC AS A HISTORY OF EDUCATION AND ACCULTURATION

Arthur E. Walzer

University of Minnesota

The first Octalog featured "the politics of historiography." The session was dominated by criticism of our pioneering histories by Kennedy, Corbett, and Vickers, which were faulted as methodologically uncritical and limited for their focus on theoretical texts by white European males. In the decade between the first Octalog and Octalog II, historians expressed a greater self-consciousness about methods. Many of the authors of these new histories (for example, Atwill, Schiappa, and Glenn) were participants in Octalog II. While these revisionist histories criticized the traditional rhetorical tradition and included contributions of women, they retained the chronology, geography, and genres of the traditional tradition. The new heroes—the Sophists, Isocrates, Aspasia—lived just down the street from the old. Based on the work of the panelists invited to participate in Octalog III, the limitations of the first wave of revisionist histories are now being addressed. This expansion is welcome. But is it possible at the same time that we are welcoming this expansion to revitalize the traditional tradition?

The traditional rhetorical tradition was modeled after philosophy and literature: from philosophy, a narrative of great men, great ideas; from literature, critical reading of "great speeches that transcend their age." I am a child of this tradition and am not inclined to matricide. Nevertheless, perhaps this approach has run its course. It may never have been the best approach for a discipline interested in the history of literacy. But the history of literacy is also the history of rhetoric at least until the eighteenth century. The history of Western rhetoric should not be neglected.

I propose that we conceptualize the tradition in a different way. The history I propose would focus on how instruction in rhetoric has created historically appropriate subjectivities. In the short time left, I will give three examples.[1]

Example 1. Under the great man/great ideas approach to Roman rhetoric, we study Cicero's speeches to identify the sources of their transcendent style and how Cicero's eloquence relates to his philosophy of education. But as W. Martin Bloomer has argued, the most enduring legacy the Romans have bequeathed to us is "not a lapidary prose style" but a competitive system of rhetorical performance—declamation—that did not create many transcendent orators but did socialize the Roman boy to his role within Roman Imperial culture. Crucial to this process of acculturation were rhetorical exercises of *ethopoeia*—exercises in which students performed and rehearsed the roles of slave owner, father, advocate—becoming comfortable in their role as paterfamilias. Education in rhetoric shaped a politically appropriate subjectivity.

Example 2. Declamation was part of the rhetoric exercises known as the *progymnasmata* that formed the basis of rhetorical education through the Renaissance. We have sometimes studied the *progymnasmata* to see if their integrated sequence might be a model for a writing curriculum today. But we could study these exercises in terms of their political use in the Renaissance. A most interesting example is Erasmus's encomium on marriage, which he included in his textbook on letter-writing (*De conscribendis epistolis*) as an example of a letter of persuasion. In the context of Luther's challenge to clerical celibacy, Erasmus's letter was considered heretical, but Erasmus disingenuously claimed that the letter was merely an exercise in declamation intended to teach students how to structure an argument and argue *utramque partem* (van der Poel). Education in rhetoric played a covert political/social role.

Example 3. Historically, rhetoric is a complete art for shaping students—influencing how they think through the canon of invention, how they express themselves through the canon of style, and how they move and sound through the canon of delivery. In the eighteenth century, the fifth canon became especially prominent, enlisted in the effort to fashion the polite subject, as Dana Harrington has shown in a recent issue of *Rhetorica*. Politeness was a matter of feeling and taste—shaping the subject toward appropriate emotional response and civil behavior to others. Thomas Sheridan preached that polite response and its appropriate expression could be taught, especially somatically. Sheridan and other elocutionists would train students' faculties by having students enact the tones and gestures that embodied politeness in giving a speech or in reading aloud. One is tempted to invoke Foucault: Rhetoric was complicit in rendering the body as a political field. But the elocutionists' instruction could also be seen as liberatory—as a force in the transformation of the public sphere in the eighteenth century.

Historicizing rhetoric in the way I propose is not new; one might say that this approach is inherent in the idea of *paideia*. But the project as I envision it would be undertaken without the evangelism and elitism that once characterized the study of *paideia* in the context of ancient Greece. We would proceed, not in the spirit of Jaeger but under the sign of Bourdieu.

Note

1 I take inspiration from Richard Graff and Michael Leff; Thomas Habinek; Jean Ferguson Carr, Stephen L. Carr, and Lucille Schultz; and Susan Miller.

NEOLIBERALISM, HIGHER EDUCATION, AND THE RHETORICAL/ MATERIAL RELATION

Ralph Cintron

University of Illinois at Chicago

Professor Tom Miller raised an important question from the audience. He noted that the speakers, with the exception of me, seemed hopeful. He concluded that much of the convention did not seem to question how it rested on neoliberal paradigms. I answered by elaborating what I think to be the political and economic contexts that are eroding the innovations in public education from the last half century. The argument, which needs more careful analysis than what I can provide, is that publicly funded universities and colleges—along with vast sections of the public sector—have been dismantled by the combination of a populist antitax movement and a segment of the wealthier class that wants to maximize profits. The first group consists of working and middle-class folks who interpret government action as tyrannical, resenting even filling out census forms. The second group wants to maximize profit by rolling back the taxation of wealth (hedge fund managers pay only fifteen percent on their profits), privatizing public services (the rise of charter schools; garbage pickup used to be public sector employment), and advocating deregulation.[1] Neoliberalism, a capacious term, wants to starve the beast of government and make the economy more efficient and flexible by privatizing social security, culling pension funds, ensuring on-time deliveries of goods and services rather than warehousing, and chasing cheap labor through outsourcing.

Where I teach, state funding has plummeted over the decades until today it is about sixteen percent. The university is developing plans for consolidating departments and units. Similar talk is occurring in many other public universities. There are two major consequences that seem to be unfolding from these national discussions:

(1) Legislators and the public in general are targeting graduate teaching in the humanities as less essential than undergraduate teaching. English departments are particularly vulnerable because they cannot automatically justify

the study of literature, literary theory, or even cultural studies to cost-saving administrators. The positioning of composition and rhetoric may be different, for we study and teach specific skills. Indeed, many of our first composition and rhetoric PhD programs began in the late 1970s and 1980s as one response to an influx of "nontraditional" students, a movement that first appeared with the GI Bill. Nevertheless, our field may undergo structural changes due to public pressure to emphasize undergraduate teaching and not graduate teaching or research. Indeed, our campus recently fought off a proposal that threatened to eliminate tuition and fee waivers for graduate students, a proposal that, in effect, would have killed our graduate program.

(2) Since the 1950s the production of BAs, MAs, and PhDs among the not privileged has arguably changed the "face" of the American professional class and radically altered what counts as knowledge, particularly in the social sciences. But students are taking on ever-larger proportions of their own education. In sum we may be seeing the privatization of public education and, consequently, a hardening of the divide between those who can afford and those who cannot. Remember, at one point the University of California at Berkeley was free. Needless to say, these changes in public university funding and their consequences will be site specific.

Professor Miller's critique of the entire convention, including our panel, hit at one of the vulnerable cores of composition studies and rhetorical studies. Both mobilize a certain social uplift in the name of progressive politics. The politics of social uplift, otherwise known as "empowerment," is at the core of neoliberalism, for neoliberalism can justify a disinvestment from the public sector once everyone becomes her own entrepreneur. Consider the overlap between George W. Bush's "ownership society" and our field's "own your own text, culture, or identity." So identity movements, uplift, and empowerment—the focus of many of our panel presentations and the conference itself—have been positively used to fight historical injustices but are also seamless with neoliberal agendas.

Democracy is, among other things, a vast argument machine and desire machine, and its most important products are the democratic rhetorics, such things as equality, rights, transparency, freedom, and so on. "Freedom is ... constantly produced. [Liberalism] proposes to manufacture it constantly, to arouse it and produce it, [along with the] constraints and the problems of cost raised by this production" (Foucault 65). The progressive left, including the panelists and me as well, have simply followed the logic of incitement rooted in the democratic rhetorics, which have historically enabled the disadvantaged to advance their material conditions in the face of otherwise hierarchical and sedimented power relations. But I am impatient with this work when its focus is limited to rhetorical dimensions or identity formation and does not include material analyses of political economy. Our field provides little training in such matters. We are too much about words. We might also turn to urban theory, economics, social theory, political theory, and empirical methods. All of my teaching and research these days is a search for ways to meld rhetorical and material analyses whether in matters of taxation, banking regulations, citizenship status, housing initiatives, or in understanding the nation state as a set of territorial, political, and economic stabilities in contexts of transnationalism. So, a call here for rhetoric to move out of any disciplinary location—and I have seen some success in this: the deinstitutionalization of rhetoric from English and communications and its reconstitution elsewhere. But a wilder call: Kenneth Burke explored a poetics in which the whole of daily life—its thoughts, actions, and objects—became enactments of the rhetorical. I repeat: His was a poetics, not an ontological claim. Well, of late my students and I have been examining how price performs the rhetorical action of reification in order to settle the elusive concept of worth; or how rights are metaphors, storehouses of social energy, that deny their origins in desire; or how both libertarianism and Marxism are the *inventio* of liberalism; and how all three fetishize freedom. If one starts to unearth the conceptual grounds and material conditions upon which our beliefs and actions lie, one may, shockingly, discover that identities are only a tertiary production of these mechanisms.

Note

1 See http://wealthforcommongood.org/wp-content/uploads/2010/04/ShiftingResponsibilily.pdf for more information.

RESPONSE[1]

Victor Vitanza

Clemson University

This occasion of a Third Octalog is a moment that calls for *epideictic* discourse. Primarily praise. Let's rebegin, however, with a **flashback** to Octalog, a flashback that comes to us from various future anteriors. Octalog was not considered the first of three+. It was Octalog! Bear with me: A flashback: I will have said something like this: *I've come not to bury* **THE** *politics of historiography, but to praise what otherwise wants to be said. Yet, I dig a grave issue, when it is perhaps an unbearable lightness of a certain uncertain attitude that I want to perform. The revenant will have returned* (cf Derrida, *Specters of Marx* 4). Etc. . . . And so we did our thing back then. But surely you must know, you must feel, there are specters whose improper-proper names haunt this third octalog. But there's not near world enough in what goes for time in the program.

We each have five minutes. Can you imagine in another world with another ethnologic sense: The life-span of a "little fly, called an ephemera" (Franklin). A few moments, not in terms of a full day! How grave can it be! I could **try to respond to** eight presenters in five minutes. Instead, I've responded at length privately in writing to each of them and placed my affirmative comments for each in an envelope, which I have just now distributed to them ... Vicki, Ralph, Jay, Jessica, Ron, LuMing, Malea, Arthur.

I would dis-rupt *the time that remains*. To Messianic Time. I have little faith in Chronological time. Contrary to the flashback that I opened with, I do not deliver in chronological time, but invest in *the future anterior* of times to come.

Item one: Octa-loggers **reclaim** your *éthea*, that is, your wildness, that which you were before becoming domesticated into y.our professional, academik *ethos*.[2] Octa-loggers, *address the other that is indefinite*. Not only *within you* and all around you, but especially *in Logoi*. Rethink the notion of *responsibility* by beginning perpetually to develop y.our abilities *to respond to the other that is indefinite in Logoi, not just in ethos and pathos, but in Logoi*![3]

Item two: Octa-loggers, **follow** what wants, desires, to be said. No matter how wild *your truths without principles* might be expressed through your variously perverse historiographies! Be wild. Be wilder at first and thereafter. Bewilder not only those around you, but even, if not more so, your so-called "self." I have in mind what Althusser has called "a wild/savage practice." Think finitude! Writing is, after all is said and undone, the very site of finitude's excesses.

Item three: Ergo, post-Ego, **beware** of chrono-logic. Embrace anachronisms. Embrace messy-antics. Beware, specifically, of those in philology who pretend that chronology, chrono-logic, has exclusive validity and value when it comes to historiographical readings of times past, remembrances of times lost. Traditional philologists, old or new, cannot themselves remain faithful to their god Chronos. Who eats his futures! Traditional philologists are the great pretenders of time-travel to the past, when, more so, and every moment so, they, with others, live in a future anterior, a *what will have been*—namely, in a past that is forever re-situated in a future. With a past coming to us from a future.

So, **Let be thought** this morning a para-philology not unlike, yet quite different from, those of Paul de Man and Edward Said. Both of whom called for a return to philology. But their particular calls are not *logoi*'s call. Rather surreal.ally, *logoi*'s peculiar call is for a revisionist—yet, ever sub/versive—para-philology that is de-based, ungrounded, in finitudes, by ways of *being alongside, besides itself*, wherein so-called agents as well as agencies become "adjacencies," ex-statically next to, impertinently so, what has been called philology. **Let there be less thought** about achieving a *point of stasis*—which historiographers have yet to achieve anyway—thanks to the gods who are perpetually at odds with each other. Such a point of *stasis* would only be a *static* trap for establishing an "us" as inside, perpetually as *enstasis*. Rather, **Let there be exultations.** For the *revenant* is coming. **Let there be** ek-stasis ... more so, every moment so. *Ek-stases* and Ecstasies!

Notes

1 For Jim and Bob ... Susan, Sharon, Richard, Jan, Nan, and Jerry (chair), Octalog, 1988, St. Louis.
2 *Éthea*, where animals belong, in their wildness. I'm using Charles Scott's *The Question of Ethics* for reading, as CS cites such in the *Iliad* (6.506–11). The horse wants to return to its *Nomós*. field, as opposed to *Nómos*, law (Scott 143). I've consulted Charles Chamberlain's "From Haunts to Character."
3 I would claim, therefore, that it is our responsibility to search out our other-abilities, our impotentialities, to address the other that is indefinite. I'm not referring to potentialities, that is,

Techné or *Dynamis*. Rather, I am referring to what Aristotle notes only in passing as *Adynamis*, or Impotentiality (see *Metaphysics* 1046e, 25–32). This, then, would be the para-methodology of misology! As well as the wildness that I refer to! In reference, as Giorgio Agamben says, *Adynamis*, or Impotentiality, would address all that has NOT YET been intuited, thought, acted on in ethico-political lived experiences (see *Potentialities*). Or forgotten! At least, in our wide, impotentially wild field.

Reflections Following Octalog III at CCCC

Vicki Tolar Burton: One astute questioner in our abundant audience asked several panelists what was meant by the "we" in our papers. If there is a gift from this Octalog, it is an understanding that the "we" of rhetoric has become more capacious—yet clearly not capacious enough. I want to connect this present lack to future pedagogy. Introducing Octalog III, Chair Lois Agnew said that students begin her graduate course in rhetorical history by reading Octalogs I and II. Now is added Octalog III, with new questions for historical rhetoric, new pedagogies, research methods, and territories for rhetorical exploration. I imagine spirited discussions as students place our papers in dialogue with each other, with earlier Octalog speakers, and with their own visions of what rhetoric can be and do. Respondent Victor Vitanza encouraged us to "go wild" with our research, meaning, I think, to take risks, to re-imagine our work—to rap it, to rhyme it, to turn it on its head. My hope is that Octalog III's audiences will go into the wilderness of new archival and rhetorical frontiers with Vitanza's spirit of wildness, with a traveler's curiosity and appetite for knowledge, with Heraclitus' commitment to dwell ethically with texts, speakers, and audiences, and with courage to address the messiness of our times.

Jay Dolmage: During this third Octalog, I was struck by several important ways in which ideas enfolded, echoed, anticipated, and responded to one another. So, just as I grounded my own comments upon a theft from a previous Octalog, I hope to center future work around theft from *this* Octalog—with some selection and deflection, of course. In particular, I am energized by the challenges posed by my peers: from Ronald Jackson, the call to recognize the harm racism does to both bodies and the "body politic"; from Jessica Enoch and Vicki Tolar Burton, the need to see the ways that bodies shape and are shaped by social spaces; from Art Walzer, the suggestion that we might find liberatory potential even in classical pedagogies and practices that have been seen as repressive of bodily expression; from LuMing Mao, the argument that the us/them duality that impels so much bodily denigration must be transformed into a "proactive heuristic"—a way of seeing all bodies as "coterminous and interdependent"; from Malea Powell, the provocative challenge to move beyond flat and linear historiography, and instead shape a method as malleable and unpredictable as the body itself; from Ralph Cintron, the call to "name a citizenship of movement and presence"; and finally, from Victor Vitanza, the affirmation of wildness, partiality, and messiness. Perhaps opportunistically, I see these all as invitations to engage the body rhetorically, and in particular to challenge the normative body of rhetorical scholarship.

Jessica Enoch: The conversations of Octalog III elucidated for me two major historiographic concerns. First, not only is historiographic writing rhetorical, but it should also be overtly persuasive. While scholars have made this point in previous contexts, it takes on a different nuance in this contemporary moment (Berlin; Bizzell; Jarratt). The Octalog III panelists made clear that our field is (or should be) rich with histories: histories of rhetorical education, of "Other-ed" or non-Western communities, of women, and even of gendered spaces. As the discipline's past grows in these divergent ways, now more than ever it is important for the historian to persuade her readers why her particular history is worthy of the field's attention: Why *this* history? What does it say to readers today? How does it contribute to or (re)direct scholarly conversations? Second, as the historian crafts arguments regarding the relevance of her historiography, she must also consider the methodological questions that arise when pursuing new research areas. Such questions include not only what counts as evidence, and what is (or could be) the primary text, but also what ethical concerns emerge in investigating this group, working in this archive, or pursuing this kind of interdisciplinary scholarship. Addressing these questions seems paramount to the scholar's work, especially at this moment when the potential for historiographic expansion is both so necessary and so possible.

Ronald L. Jackson: Rich with profoundly important intellectual statements about the future of rhetoric, the Octalogs have attempted to paradigmatically shift how we do rhetoric. This Octalog was greeted with a spectacular standing-room only audience. Although not that diverse culturally, the audience remained interested and responsive. We had at least three panelists discuss the significance of a radically progressive multicultural pedagogy. I urge everyone who reads these words and attends these events to do some critical self-interrogation and rigorously revise your pedagogy to be more aggressively culturally inclusive. It is only then that we truly educate our students to be effective citizens.

LuMing Mao (*From "Going Native" to Cultivating a Transrhetorical Dialogue*): In espousing the art of recontextualization for writing a new historiography of rhetoric, I have drawn inspiration from the work of the comparative philosopher David Hall and the sinologist Roger Ames. They have proposed for the study of Chinese culture an *ars contextualis* ("art of contextualization") that rejects any overarching context determining the shape of other contexts and that "permits the mutual interdependence of all things [in Chinese culture] to be assessed in terms of particular contexts defined by social roles and functions" (248). No less important to me is the work by scholars who have challenged us to critically examine how and why non-Western, indigenous rhetorical practices are being constructed and how and why such constructions become, importantly rather than merely additively, constructive for this new historiography. The art of recontextualization calls for perpetually moving between rhetorical borders with no overarching context or standard from one tradition influencing or determining the shape of many from other traditions. However, such a practice is not foolproof. We can become so entrenched in our own tradition that we either unknowingly fail to make the crossing or end up, after crossing, seeing the other with one's very own "I" (eye). We can also feel so enlightened by the other that we begin to hyper-correct the other in hopes of correcting the ills that have troubled our own tradition. Overzealousness could be another form of perpetuating the structures of dominance that such a rhetorical border-crossing aimed to transform in the first place. Admittedly, "going native" has become the gold standard for the study of the other in ethnography. The art of recontextualization for writing the new historiography of rhetoric is not so much about "going native" as about going places to cultivate a transrhetorical dialogue. There we stop coveting a rhetorical communion—an epistemological impossibility—and we begin to practice and advance interdependence-in-difference where both the self and the other turns, overlaps or interruptions notwithstanding, to develop a new language and to learn to recognize and draw from each other's social, political, and linguistic affiliations and affordances.

Art Walzer: It seems to me that Octalog III was marked by a confirmation of the expansion of the scope and function of rhetoric as a discipline that is currently well underway. All participants welcomed the expansion of rhetoric beyond what Graff and Leff have characterized as a white, male, European demographic. But the challenge of attempting to understand cultures different from one's own is clearly the source of some anxiety as scholars fear, in Emmanuel Levinas's phrase, turning the Other into the Same. A second theme in our session, building on the work of revisionist historians of Octalog II, was the movement away from a focus on the reading of great works to a focus on the relationship of rhetoric to power, not only in the overtly political arena but in education, where rhetoric has historically played a dominant role. Here the challenge (it seems to me) is to acknowledge that acculturation is inevitable and to understand how it liberates as well as limits.

Works Cited

Berlin, James. "Octalog I: The Politics of Historiography." *Rhetoric Review* 7.1 (1988): 11–12.
Bhabha, Homi. "Signs Taken for Wonders: Questions of Ambivalence and Authority Under a Tree Outside Delhi, May 1817." *Europe and its Others: Proceedings of the Essex Conference on the Sociology of Literature,* July 1984. Vol. 1. Ed. Francis Barker, Peter Hulme, Margaret Iversen, and Diana Loxley. Colchester: U of Essex, 1985. 89–106.
Brooks, Lisa. *The Common Pot: The Recovery of Native Space in the Northeast.* Minneapolis: U of Minnesota P, 2008.
Buchanan, Lindal. *Regendering Delivery: The Fifth Canon and Antebellum Women Rhetors.* Carbondale: Southern Illinois UP, 2005.
Carr, Jean Ferguson, Stephen L. Carr, and Lucille Schultz. *Archives of Instruction: Nineteenth-Century Rhetorics, Readers, and Composition Books in the United States.* Carbondale: Southern Illinois UP, 2005.
Certeau, Michel de. *The Practice of Everyday Life.* Trans. Steven Rendall. Berkeley: U of California P, 1984.
Chamberlain, Charles. "From *Haunts* to *Character*." *Helios* 11.2 (1984): 97–108.

de Man, Paul. "The Return to Philology." *The Resistance to Theory*. Minneapolis: U of Minnesota P, 1986. 21–26.

Derrida, Jacques. *Specters of Marx*. Trans. Peggy Kamuf. New York: Routledge, 1994.

Foucault, Michel. *The Birth of Biopolitics: Lectures at the College de France*. Ed. Michael Senellart. Trans. Graham Burchell. New York Palgrave, 2008.

Franklin, Benjamin. "The Ephemera: An Emblem of Human Life" *The Oxford Book of American Essays*. Ed. Brander Matthews, New York: Oxford UP, 1914. http://www.bartleby.com/109/l.html.Web.

Glenn, Cheryl. *Rhetoric Retold: Regendering the Rhetorical Tradition from Antiquity to the Renaissance*. Carbondale: Southern Illinois UP, 1997.

Graff, Richard, and Michael Leff. "Revisionist Historiography and Rhetorical Tradition(s)." *The Viability of the Rhetorical Tradition*. Ed. Richard Graff, Arthur E. Walzer, and Janet M. Atwill. Albany: SUNY UP, 2005. 11–30.

Habinek, Thomas. *Ancient Rhetoric and Orator*. Oxford: Blackwell, 2005.

Hall, David L., and Roger T. Ames. *Thinking through Confucius*. Albany: SUNY P, 1987.

Harjo, Joy. *A Map to the Next World*. New York: Norton, 2000.

Harrington, Dana. "Remembering the Body: Eighteenth-Century Elocution and the Oral Tradition." *Rhetorica* 28 (2010): 67–96.

hooks, bell. "Homeplace (a site of resistance)." *Available Means: An Anthology of Women's Rhetoric(s)*. Ed. Kate Ronald and Joy Ritchie. Pittsburgh U of Pittsburgh P, 2001. 383–90.

Horner, Winifred. *Nineteenth-Century Scottish Rhetoric: The American Connection*. Carbondale: Southern Illinois UP, 1993.

Hyde, Michael J. "Introduction: Rhetorically We Dwell." *The Ethos of Rhetoric*. Columbia: U of South Carolina P, 2004. xiii–xxviii.

Jackson, Ronald L. "White Space, White Privilege: Mapping Discursive Inquiry into the Self." *Quarterly Journal of Speech* 55.1 (1999): 1–17.

Jarratt, Susan. "Rhetoric and Feminism: Together Again." *College English* 62.3 (2000): 390–93.

King, Thomas. *The Truth About Stories*. Minneapolis: U of Minnesota P, 2003.

McIntosh, P. "White Privilege and Male Privilege: A Personal Account of Coming to See Correspondence through Work in Women's Studies." *Race, Class, and Gender: An Anthology*. Ed. M. Anderson and P. H. Collins. Belmont, CA: Wadsworth, 1994. 94–106.

Miller, Susan. *Trust in Texts: A Different History of Rhetoric*. Carbondale: Southern Illinois UP, 2008.

Mountford, Roxanne. *The Gendered Pulpit: Preaching in American Protestant Spaces*. Carbondale. Southern Illinois UP, 2003.

Nakayama, T. & R. Krizek. "Whiteness: A Strategic Rhetoric." *Quarterly Journal of Speech* 81.3 (1995): 291–319.

"Octalog: The Politics of Historiography." *Rhetoric Review* 7 (Fall 1988): 5–49.

"Octalog II: The (Continuing) Politics of Historiography." *Rhetoric Review* 16 (Fall 1997): 22–44.

Pearce, Roy Harvey. *Savagism and Civilization: A Study of the Indian and the American Mind*. Berkeley: U of California P, 1988. Rev. ed. of *The Savages of America*. 1953.

Ryan, Mary. *Women in Public: Between Banners and Ballots. 1825–1880*. Baltimore: Johns Hopkins UP, 1990.

Said, Edward. "The Return to Philology." *Humanism and Democratic Criticism*. New York: Columbia UP, 2003. 57–84.

Scott, Charles. *The Question of Ethics*. Bloomington: Indiana UP, 1990.

Shaver, Lisa. "Women's Death-Bed Pulpits: From Quiet Congregants to Iconic Ministers." *Rhetoric Review* 27.1 (2007): 1–34.

Shoemaker, Nancy, ed. *Clearing a Path: Theoretical Approaches to the Past in Native American Studies*. New York: Routledge, 2001.
Smith, Linda Tuhiwai. *Decolonizing Methodologies: Research and Indigenous Peoples*. London and New York: Zed, 1999.
Smith Magazine. http://smithmagazine.com. 1 February, 2010. Web.
Tolar Burton, Vicki. *Spiritual Literacy in John Wesley's Methodism: Reading, Writing, and Speaking to Believe*. Waco, TX: Baylor UP, 2008.
van der Poel, M. "For Freedom of Opinion: Erasmus' Defense of the *Encomium matrimonii*." *Erasmus of Rotterdam Society, Yearbook Twenty-Five (2005)*. Oxon Hill, MD, 2005. 1–17.
Vizenor, Gerald. Manifest *Manners: Postindian Warriors of Survivance*. Middletown, CT: Wesleyan UP, 1994.
Warrior, Robert. *The People and the Word: Reading Native Nonfiction*. Minneapolis: U of Minnesota P, 2005.
Whately, Richard. *Elements of Rhetoric*. London: B Fellowes, 1841.
Wilson, Shawn. *Research Is Ceremony: Indigenous Research Methods*. Fernwood P, 2008.

17.
TRAINING IN THE ARCHIVES: ARCHIVAL RESEARCH AS PROFESSIONAL DEVELOPMENT

Jonathan Buehl, Tamar Chute, and Anne Fields

Prologue

On 23 July 1959, a third-page headline in the *Ohio State Morning Lantern* announced a story about a summer student: "Coed Introduces Indians to Paleface's ABC's." Wedged between an article about a new campus laboratory, a story on Russian entertainers visiting Chicago, and an advertisement for Florida real estate, the short profile explained that Miss Trula Detweiler—a third-grade teacher working on a master's degree in elementary education—lived and taught on the Navajo Reservation in Ganado, Arizona, during the school year.

As its headline might suggest, the article is a product of its time. Its first sentence is a riff on the racist children's rhyme "Ten Little Indians," Detweiler is characterized as an inquisitive but "soft spoken redhead," and the Navajo are portrayed as foolishly superstitious, quiet, and reserved. Through a playful but chauvinistic style, the article attempts to tell a positive story. After describing the reservation's "modern" school facilities and the role of federal funding on the reservation, it explains how education is changing in Ganado:

> There is a new interest in education on the reservation and the parents encourage the children to go to school each day. A few of these Indians go on to the college and come back to their reservation as nurses, secretaries, and teachers.
>
> (Wonfor 3)

Education and literacy are agents of change in this brief story of development and racial uplift.

Fifty-one years later, eight graduate students discussed this story during a session of their class on research methods in rhetoric, composition, and literacy studies. Having serendipitously found the Detweiler story while researching another topic, their instructor brought the artifact to class to spur a discussion about historical research. *What kinds of questions does this artifact invite?* The students' initial questions were

---

Buehl, Jonathan, Tamar Chute, and Anne Fields. "Training in the Archives: Archival Research as Professional Development." *CCC* 64.2 (2012): 274–305. Print.

biographical and historical: Who was Trula Detweiler? How did she get to Ganado? How did she end up in a graduate program in Ohio? Where was "the college" mentioned in the story? What was taught in its writing classrooms? What might this story tell us about literacy and education in this era? Eventually, the discussion turned to methodological concerns: What threads can we trace from this story? Where might we find more information? What kinds of material would be relevant?

These students were adept in using electronic resources to locate digitally visible information—those records revealed through online searches. Within minutes they found an obituary archived in MennObits, a digitized list of obituaries maintained by the Archives of the Mennonite Church USA. Trula Zimmerly née Detweiler passed away in 1997. Born in 1929, Detweiler turned thirty the day before the *Lantern* article appeared. At the time of her death, she belonged to a Mennonite congregation near Akron, and her survivors included her husband, four children, and two grandchildren. *Could they flesh out the details of Detweiler's story? Would their accounts be reliable? Who else might be interviewed?*

Other searches revealed more about the history of education in Ganado. According to the National Park Service, a Presbyterian mission school opened there in 1906. The Sage Memorial Hospital School of Nursing—the first nursing school for Native American women—opened in Ganado in 1930. This new information took the conversation in new directions. For example, although the nursing school had closed long before Detweiler arrived in Arizona, some students thought the school might be an interesting site for studying professional literacies or the rhetoric of health and medicine. Others wondered about relationships between religion, government, and education between 1906 and 1959. Were Detweiler's "modern" buildings parts of the mission school? Or did competing literacy sponsors operate in Ganado?

Following each digital thread raised new and provocative questions about literacy, culture, and education, but each thread also led to physical archives. Having read historical scholarship in rhetoric and composition for other courses, the students had good ideas about the kinds of documents that might yield relevant details about Detweiler or the Ganado schools. Some assumed the Ohio State University (OSU) Archives would have student records and administrative documents about graduate programs. Their digital searches led them to the Archives of the Ganado Historic Mission in Arizona, the Archives of the Mennonite Church in Goshen, Indiana, and the Presbyterian Historical Society in Philadelphia. However, like many archives, each of these facilities has limited or non-existent digitized resources. To pursue the leads emerging from the discussion would require in-person contact. The rubber of historical imagination would have to meet the archival road—a road unfamiliar to most students and many established scholars.

The discussion of Detweiler's story offered these students practice in thinking like historiographers; however, most of the relevant archives were too far away to explore in a course context. To practice working like historiographers, these students would research their own interests locally through a loosely structured exercise involving real archives. In the reading room of the OSU Archives, they would interact with archivists, struggle with finding aids, and comb through boxes and folders holding traces of our past. Writing studies scholars of every ilk can benefit from such practice, the intellectual and technical preparation it requires, and the moments of reflection it can induce.

Historiography and Archival Work: From Politics to Pragmatics to Pedagogy

Discussions of the politics of historiography have widened the scope of whose stories count and what counts as evidence when articulating histories of rhetoric and composition. A generation of scholars has been trained in the wake of the debates that crystallized as "Octalog I" and "Octalog II," and—if "Octalog III" is any index—writing the histories of our discipline(s) will continue to be a central and contested activity. Although political stances and ideological orientations vary widely, all historiographers share a common problem. Traditionalists, revisionists, postmodernists, recovery workers, localizers, and those who resist labels altogether—they all need evidence to write their histories. And they often seek that evidence in archives.

The need to use archives—and sometimes to create or contest or complicate them—has generated a wave of recent scholarship emphasizing the pragmatics of historiography. For example, the contributions to *Working in the Archives: Practical Research Methods for Rhetoric and Composition* (Ramsey et al.) describe approaches to the specific challenges of finding and arguing from historical material related to rhetoric and writing instruction. Similarly, the personal essays in *Beyond the Archives: Research as a Lived Process* (Kirsch and Rohan) show how researchers navigate archives methodically but with the help of passion, personal investments, and serendipity. Collectively, the chapters of *Local Histories: Reading the Archives of Composition* (Donahue and Moon) widen the scope of composition's disciplinary origins in America by engaging the archives of "non-elite" institutions, such as normal schools, liberal arts colleges, and historically black colleges; moreover, these essays are explicitly marked as examples of archival research and include lists of their archival sources (Moon 7). More recently, Patricia Sullivan has argued for recovering students' in situ reactions to writing instruction by finding and interpreting diverse archival sources, including notebooks, ephemera, and marginalia; such reconstructions require methodologies that resist oversimplifying the material traces of complex, historically situated, and highly personal artifacts (382–83). Although the growing body of scholarship on archival methods offers a plethora of practical resources, inspirational anecdotes, productive exemplars, and reflections on methods, no essay or chapter offers a sustainable model for training new scholars to work with archives, though Linda Ferreira-Buckley (582), Thomas P. Miller and Melody Bowdon (585), and Barbara L'Eplattenier (71) have called for one. There are anecdotal accounts of ad hoc archival education of graduate students and established researchers in rhetoric and composition scholarship. For example, Katherine E. Tirabassi (170–72), Sammie Morris and Shirley Rose (51–78), and Lisa Mastrangelo and Barbara L'Eplattenier (161–67) have described learning about archival research through special projects, collaboration grants, and interpersonal networks, respectively. These accounts reveal aspects of archival work and demonstrate the creative development of resources and relationships; however, their stories also reveal that our field has yet to articulate good and replicable models for teaching archival methods. Now that the field has a substantial body of scholarship on ways of *doing* in the archives, scholars of rhetoric and composition should further discuss ways of *teaching* and *learning* in the archives.

For us, such discussions should consider a role for archives in introductory courses on research methodology; however, these discussions should also consider how writing studies scholars can develop archival research skills at other points in their careers. Whether self-guided or instructor-led, archival training is important for all scholars of rhetoric and composition—not just for those interested in pursuing historical research.

To be clear, we do not define *training* narrowly—the one-time orientation to procedures or terms. Rather, archival training should be conceived in broad terms, and archives should be viewed as training sites where research skills and habits of mind can be taught and strengthened. Such training has practical and intellectual outcomes that include but extend beyond learning to work in an archives facility. Archival training helps researchers think methodically about texts and contexts—an important faculty for developing any research project. Moreover, archival training is an ideal tool for teaching students of any level to think about the material, temporal, and rhetorical constraints of research. Equally important, archival research encourages scholars to develop relationships with information specialists. These benefits of archival training can transfer to other types of research; thus, it can be a productive addition to a general course on research methodology or to any self-guided professional development plan.

In support of this argument, we offer a case study of a teaching module—collaboratively developed by a librarian, an archivist, and a rhetorician—that provides loosely structured practice with real archives.[1] Such practice introduced our students to practical aspects of historical research, but it also encouraged them to consider the rhetoric of historiography and the position of historiography within subfields of our discipline. We show how coordinating local resources—both material and human—can help scholars train to conduct creative and provocative historical research. We also show how archival research training helps researchers think critically about methods, methodology, and scholarly argumentation. Finally, we use group interview data to show what early career researchers want from historical research training and how such training changes their beliefs about research, teaching, and disciplinary practices. Although the lessons of this case apply most directly to course contexts, they also apply to self-guided training in archival research methods.

One Pedagogy of Historiography: A Course, a Collaboration, and a Module

The Course

The Ohio State University's English 795 is an introduction to research methods in rhetoric, composition, and literacy studies. The 2010 iteration of the course was divided into three modules: historical research, empirical research, and textual analysis. The collaboration described in this article pertained primarily to the first three-week module; however, the information-literacy skills practiced in this module were applicable to the entire course.

As a lower-division graduate course offered biennially at a doctorate-granting institution, the class typically enrolls graduate students at all stages of coursework. Areas of student interest can run the gamut of the field: digital media studies, history of rhetoric, literacy studies, composition studies, professional communication, and others. The specific research interests of students enrolled in this iteration of the class included veterans in the writing classroom, the history of composition programs, rhetoric in indigenous communities, the rhetoric of science, rhetoric and disability studies, literacy and social class, and multimodal composing. To support these diverse interests, the introductory methods course had to expose students to a diverse range of methods; thus, teaching archival research was only one component of the ten-week class, Nevertheless, the conversations initiated during the first module spilled over into later discussions of empirical research and textual analysis.

The Collaboration

The instructor for this iteration of the research methods course was Jonathan Buehl, an assistant professor in the Department of English. Jonathan wanted to develop a hands-on historical research project for the course; however, he was relatively new to OSU and did not know much about the archival resources and special collections available at the institution. After reading an announcement for the OSU Libraries' Course Enhancement Grant (CEG) program, Jonathan met with Anne Fields, associate professor of libraries and English subject specialist, to discuss ways this program might enhance his historical research module. She suggested enlisting the aid of Tamar Chute, associate professor and associate university archivist. After a few meetings, we knew that the OSU Archives would be an ideal site for collaboratively teaching the pragmatics of historiography and that such a collaboration would meet the CEG program's two most important goals: incorporating the OSU Libraries' resources into the classroom and fostering collaboration between librarians, faculty, and students. The committee reviewing Jonathan's CEG application also liked his idea of using the OSU Archives as a "lab" in which students could "get their hands dirty"—metaphorically, of course.

With the backing of the CEG program, Jonathan could collaborate with information specialists at a level situated between the typical extremes of light involvement—such as when a librarian visits a class for a single session on research databases or when an archivist leads an orientation to an archives—and formally arranged team teaching—such as when a librarian or an archivist participates in every class session. This mid-level involvement enabled a richer experience than a single librarian-led tutorial or a short tour of the archives could provide. Preliminary meetings allowed Jonathan to describe the intellectual commitments of rhetoric and composition for Tamar and Anne, which helped them to prepare for their roles in the module. Their preterm work with the students' research interests statements (described in the next section) allowed the module to "spin up" quickly. Most importantly, repeated contact with Tamar and Anne encouraged the students to see them as approachable human resources with whom they can and should develop professional relationships.

Although archival research methods could be taught with more involvement from library faculty, alternatives introduce different sets of issues. A full-term team-taught course focused exclusively on archival research could provide additional pedagogical opportunities; for example, students could practice accessioning and processing new material for the archives. However, teaching such a course at OSU would require much more advanced planning to coordinate multiple teaching schedules, and it might require interdepartmental agreements over resources and credit.

At any level of involvement, collaboration between faculty members—particularly those from different areas of an institution—can be complicated. In our case, the largest challenge was coordinating three different schedules to prepare for the module and to fit in visits by Tamar and Anne at appropriate times. We did not face other common issues of team teaching, such as determining which collaborator's department would receive credit for the course; however, instructors at other institutions might face such administrative hurdles or other local challenges.

The possible challenges of a team-teaching collaboration between composition scholars and information specialists are far outweighed by potential benefits. Without access to the expertise, resources, and knowledge of Tamar and Anne, Jonathan would have had a difficult time developing an authentic research experience involving both real archives and all of the students' diverse research interests. Moreover, the sustained involvement of Tamar and Anne was essential because a major goal of the module was teaching the students how to interact with information specialists.

The Module

The primary goals of the historical research module were 1) to expose students to the practical aspects of working in an archives facility and 2) to provide them with opportunities to practice arguing with and about archived material. More specifically, they were to learn what kinds of materials archives contain; how archives are created; how to find, access, and use archived collections; how to work with an archivist; and how to develop effective arguments from historical sources. In short, the module was designed to advance students' understanding of the communicative, conceptual, pragmatic, and rhetorical aspects of archival research.

Although archival research involves working with material artifacts, it also requires communication with human resources. Researchers must learn how to contact and converse with archivists and librarians; therefore, our module included multiple occasions to practice communicating with information specialists. Before the course began, the students provided Jonathan with brief descriptions of their research interests, which he forwarded to Anne and Tamar. Some descriptions were incredibly broad ("I want to study literacy practices"), while others were more specific ("19th-century American rhetorics, especially as practiced by 'outsiders'—women, Native Americans, African Americans"). Anne used the interest statements to develop sessions on information literacy. Tamar used the descriptions to locate relevant collections, and she then created electronic packets of archival records for each student. These packets were posted to the class wiki with a general list of inventories for university publications and broadly relevant archives, such as presidential papers. In some cases the material was entirely processed with a finding aid—a detailed inventory of a processed, or organized, collection. Other material was unprocessed with only an accession record (a brief, collection-level or box-level description).

Although student interests ranged from composition history to digital media studies, Tamar did her best to find relevant (and often fantastically relevant) material for each student. Even so, the university archives' collections meshed better with some students' interests than with others. In some cases, the archives simply did not have directly relevant material; in other cases, Tamar's unfamiliarity with rhetoric and composition jargon limited her ability to connect the students' research statements with material from the archives. (Thus, even in this structured experience, it became clear how important direct communication is to the success of an archival research project.) Nevertheless, the purpose of the assignment was not to further the students' specific research agendas. Instead, it was to introduce them to archives and archival research methods. Those students unexcited by the material initially suggested for them found relevant material in other posted finding aids. The archives used by the students included faculty meeting minutes and other administrative documents, collections of conduct books, book club meeting minutes, and the archives of research centers studying media education and people with disabilities. By speaking with Tamar and her staff, the students were able to navigate these rich and extensive archives.

Archival research requires both intellectual and technical preparation. To prepare for their archival work, students discussed selections from *Working in the Archives* (Ramsay et al.) as well as other articles and chapters. (Appendix 1 includes the complete reading schedule for the class.) Some discussions helped to define key terms (such as *finding aid* and *provenance*) and to prepare the students for their archival experience. Other discussions focused on strong examples of historiographical research. Still other discussions—such as our conversation about Trula Detweiler and the schools in Ganado—oriented the students to the process of working from historical artifacts to develop and pursue interesting research questions. With help from Anne, the class discussed how to work from thematic interests and research questions to locate productive research material.

Anne visited the class to help the students understand that archival research requires accessing information resources from multiple disciplines. She explained strategies for navigating the OSU Libraries' plethora of information resources, and she reviewed search methodologies using examples related to the students' interest statements. For instance, Anne explained how a research question on veterans returning to university classrooms after various wars could involve databases and print indexes in, at minimum, history, political science, and education. She hoped working through such examples would prepare the students for thinking in a more interdisciplinary way about potential research strategies and information resources. Having received similar library presentations in other contexts, the students were already familiar with basic search strategies, and they seemed confident in their information literacy. As we would later learn, however, that confidence would be tested when seeking information to support arguments based on archival material.

The students' technical and intellectual preparation also included managing the logistics of an archival visit. After discussing readings on archival methods and conducting preliminary research, the students requested boxes to be pulled in advance of a class visit to the archives. They generated preliminary research questions and documented why material in the selected boxes might help them approach these questions. Two days before the archives session, Tamar visited the class to review the pragmatic aspects of working in the archives. She discussed archival protocols, the anatomy of finding aids, and the processes that help and hinder archival researchers. Tamar explained that not all research takes the same path, and she stressed the importance of working with the archivist. This point is emphasized throughout the studies on archival methodology read by the students, and Tamar reiterated that active collaboration with an archivist can increase a researcher's efficiency and success. Tamar also explained that even experienced researchers do not always understand the idea of searching up the "food chain." For example, a researcher interested in some aspect of the English Department might not find relevant material in the department's collections. Instead, the archivist may have to pull material from college-level archives, from the provost's office, or even from the office of the president. Working up the "food chain" gives researchers additional opportunities to find the information they seek. Similarly, scholars often miss important nontraditional collections, such as those from student organizations. "Hidden" material can also be found in the correspondence of university presidents, administrators, and notable faculty. Tamar hoped that exposing the students to these strategies would help them when they visited the OSU Archives.

The class visit to the archives began with a tour, which included a trip to the stack area. With its 30-foot-high shelves, the 195-by-60-foot room is reminiscent of the final scene of *Raiders of the Lost Ark*.[2] Stacked rows of identical boxes seem to extend forever and archives staff require a hydraulic lift to reach most boxes. Seeing the storage facility reinforced for the students why contacting archives before a visit can improve the efficiency of research. After the tour, students had approximately ninety minutes to examine the contents of the boxes they requested and to ask questions of Tamar and her staff. After the session in the archives, the students could return to the OSU Archives on their own, but a return visit was not required for the module assignment.

Successful archival researchers need strong rhetorical skills both to fund and to publish their research; thus, our students also practiced writing about archives. At the end of the module, the students submitted a research log for the project and a short proposal related to their work. For the proposal, each student wrote a brief memo for an administrative audience—the English Department chair. This document was to describe the exigency for the project, to describe the preliminary findings of their work at the OSU Archives, and to request funds to support additional research at OSU or another archives. The assignment was designed so students could practice both arguing about archived material and describing research for administrative purposes, an important skill for academics. (Appendix 2 reproduces the assignment sheet.) The module's four-week schedule, the assignment's size and scope, and the nature of the materials did constrain students when writing about their research. For example, they did not have the time or space to practice developing complete arguments about history or historiography, which they might do in longer papers completed at the end of a full-term course. However, the summary and proposal assignment offered an authentic task for writing through their preliminary findings. All the students seemed to identify valuable threads during the archives session, and they could articulate how and why they would follow up on those threads. About half of the students chose to develop their historical research topics in the final project of the class—a detailed research plan and annotated bibliography.

Based on the students' seeming delight with the module and the success of their initial proposals, we believed they had successfully practiced the communicative, technical, and rhetorical skills required of archival research. However, we wanted to confirm our assessment by analyzing the students' views. We also wanted to know how this practice had developed their understanding of research methods and their beliefs about archives. The remainder of this article describes what we learned through group interviews with our students and considers the broader implications of using archives as training sites.

Methods

To generate a more complete picture of the module's strengths, weaknesses, and implications, we interviewed our students approximately six months after the class ended. We chose this approach because it provided the most efficient way to collect rich data about the experience. We hoped the reflections of these novice researchers might illuminate the practical and intellectual benefits of training in the archives.

Tamar and Anne conducted and recorded group interviews with seven students. By interviewing the students in groups, we could follow up on spontaneous threads suggested by one student that might prime the memories of others. Moreover, this approach gave students a chance to think about their experiences in relation to other students who might identify with a different subfield or research tradition.

Although Anne and Tamar worked from a script of questions, they allowed each conversation to follow its own course in order to gain as much insight as possible into the students' experiences. The interview script included the following questions:

- What did you know about archival research before the class?
- What new knowledge did you gain about archival research through the class?
- In what ways did the archival research unit change your attitudes toward historical research?
- Does having an understanding of historical research methods change the way you plan to work on your dissertation or thesis?
- In what ways do you imagine archives (of any kind) fitting into your research plans?
- In what ways did the archival research unit help you learn a new method of research?
- What do you see as the long-term benefits of the archival research unit?
- How might you incorporate archival research into your own undergraduate and graduate teaching?

Spontaneous follow-up questions included the following questions:

- In what ways was it beneficial for Anne and Tamar to visit the class in the weeks before the visit to the archives?
- What role should the subject specialist play in a class like this?
- Did doing historical research cause you to think differently about primary sources?

The interview comments were analyzed with a grounded-theory methodology (see Charmaz). We first coded the interview data individually. We then compared notes and reconciled open codes into axial codes, which we ultimately used to define a set of emergent themes. These themes are described in greater detail in the next section.

Participation was voluntary and confidential. Students were told not to use any first names, the audio files were digitally modulated, and some information was redacted so that Jonathan could never identify specific speakers. This protocol was approved by the Institutional Review Board of OSU. After we completed a draft of this article, the students had opportunities to comment anonymously on the article to clarify any misrepresentations.

Results and Discussion

The interview data revealed that the archival module was an extremely positive learning experience; moreover, six noteworthy themes emerged: (1) appreciating learning about the practical aspects of historical research, (2) diversifying information search strategies, (3) gaining a better understanding of the rhetoric of historiography, (4) understanding our discipline(s) by practicing historical research, (5) articulating what graduate students need from research methods training, and (6) imagining teaching with archives.

Theme 1: Appreciating Learning about the Practical Aspects of Historical Research

All students appreciated learning about the practical aspects of archival research, which included learning how to use finding aids, learning how to work with archivists and librarians, and understanding the material constraints of archival work.

We wanted the students to learn the uses and limits of finding aids, and their comments indicate that they did. Several students noted that working with real finding aids was vital to understanding these documents. Although some finding aids appeared in their course readings (e.g., the annotated finding aid in Morris and Rose's "Invisible Hands"), students quickly learned through practice that finding aids can range from detailed and precise to downright puzzling. Several students noted that Tamar's tutorial on finding aids was crucial and that she could spend even more time teaching students how to develop research strategies from these documents—especially for older and less detailed aids.

Understanding how to access the specialized knowledge of archivists and librarian specialists was another major lesson of the course. As one student observed, archivists and librarians are "human repositories of knowledge," and the archival unit showed students how valuable these human resources can be. For example, when asked about the new knowledge they gained from the project, one student responded, "What I really learned in this project was the intangibles of working with archivists." Another replied, "The human dimension of archival work—that it's this really positive relationship that you have with librarians."

The interview comments suggested that Anne—our subject specialist—could have been better integrated into the project and the course; nevertheless, the students ended up seeing her in a new light. For example, one student noted that a practical lesson of the class was "the idea of using the subject specialist as a resource." We found such comments interesting because these students had already met Anne at different points in their graduate careers: during orientation sessions, in introductory courses, and at TA trainings. The nature of these meetings might limit how students imagine interacting with her, and some of our students had never considered using Anne as a resource for their research. As one student noted, "There's a lot of emphasis on incorporating the library staff into the classes that you teach . . . but there is not as much emphasis on using those resources for your own research, where the stakes are higher." Such comments reinforce the importance of including subject specialists in research methods classes.

Based on the students' comments, we will schedule future librarian presentations after students have gathered their primary sources from the archives. At that point the students would have a context for learning to do further interdisciplinary research and for recognizing how the librarian can help them. In short, delaying the subject specialist's visit would shift its role from "just-in-case" instruction to an opportunity for "just-in-time" interaction. This more realistic demonstration of how librarians can help researchers might encourage the students to work with librarians in this way in the future.

Finally, students found it helpful to learn about the constraints that influence and direct archives-based scholarship. One student noted how both touring and working in the OSU Archives helped him or her understand the "physical restrictions that apply to archival research." Working in the archives demonstrated "why it is that you can't have 10 things at the same time and why if you want something you can't have it right now." Another student came to appreciate that "it takes a while to make good Xeroxes of fragile archival material." The same student lamented that he or she could not develop the class project into an article now because—to do the project right—he or she would need to visit many other archives, including potentially inaccessible corporate archives. On a graduate-student budget and schedule, traveling to distant public archives can be equally impossible. Although many of these constraints were described in their assigned readings (e.g., Gaillet's "Archival Survival"), the module activity forced students to experience how material circumstances can constrain research practices.

Theme 2: Diversifying Information Search Strategies by Rediscovering Browsing

Our students, like most of their peers, were accustomed to working independently—using research methods developed on their own or perhaps with the help of faculty and other students. Typically, they had located their research materials using online library catalogs and databases, and they had been narrowly focusing their searches, looking for what they "already knew was there" through author, title, or keyword searches. In the archives, however, one student noted, "The first pass through revealed nothing, but more was revealed with time." Another student was enthusiastic about how the unit allowed him or her to "go beyond the catalog." Each of these students had (re)discovered browsing, an information literacy strategy necessary for archival research.

In library studies, browsing is typically considered as one behavior in a set of information-seeking strategies. Various models of information-seeking list different behaviors and strategies, but most stem from David Ellis's model first articulated in 1989, which identifies six behaviors: starting, chaining, browsing, differentiating, monitoring, and extracting (176–77). Other researchers have extended and revised Ellis's model, and recently Xuemei Ge has proposed the addition of two additional behaviors: (1) preparing and planning and (2) information management (450–51). Other models, for example Allen Foster's nonlinear model of information-seeking, describe other patterns of information-seeking behavior, but some variation of browsing is always included.

Browsing behaviors vary depending on disciplinary and material factors. Browsing a library's open stacks in person is a traditional method of library research—a method well loved by many scholars in the humanities. Another traditional form of browsing is to scan works cited lists, bibliographies, footnotes, and even acknowledgments sections. Finally, online technology has provided additional opportunities for browsing. For instance, even without physically browsing a library's open stacks, a researcher can loosely browse the collection by clicking links to related call numbers, as well as by exploring links between subjects and other catalog headings.

Browsing in archives differs significantly from browsing in libraries. For instance, the archives' closed stacks prevent researchers from browsing the stacks in person. At first this lack of access may seem like a disadvantage, but it actually can encourage interaction with the archivist to determine what material should be pulled for research. Drawing on these interactions, the archivist can select a range of materials that will serve as a starting point for browsing. Finding aids and inventories to unprocessed collections invite the researcher to browse the archives' material in other ways. Even inside a box, the researcher often skims every page in a folder to see if his or her needs can be met by a document filed close to the others. Because documents may be located in many different folders (e.g., correspondence by Smith may be filed with other S correspondence, in its own folder, or in a correspondence folder arranged by date), researchers are forced to look in multiple places. Browsing within a collection increases the possibility of serendipitous discoveries and the resulting enrichment of research. Browsing can also result in productive examples for teaching, like Jonathan's serendipitous discovery of Trula Detweiler's story.

Through our archives unit, the students came to appreciate the value and pleasure of browsing as a complement to targeted searching. In this case, their excitement at discovering or rediscovering the pleasures of browsing—the ability to "go beyond the catalog"—may have reflected the fact that the OSU's main library had recently undergone a three-year renovation, which made browsing the collection inconvenient.

However, construction is not the only factor constraining a library patron's ability to browse. Many libraries face the twin challenges of dwindling space and tight budgets by housing books in off-site storage, choosing electronic over print formats, and collecting cooperatively. These necessary measures result in smaller physically browsable collections. Librarians and instructors must be aware of how such local pressures may impact student research habits. Indeed, it is wise for all researchers to consider how our physical and digital environments enable and constrain how we seek and find artifacts and information.

Theme 3: Gaining a Better Understanding of the Rhetoric of Historiography

The size and scope of the module assignment meant that the students' initial writing about their archival material was more descriptive than argumentative; nevertheless, the interview data suggest that students gained a better understanding of the processes of historiography and how to make historical claims. One student explained how the archival unit reinforced his or her belief that historical accounts are rhetorical endeavors:

> We tend to think of history as being a fixed thing, but it's really just claims based on evidence—and a very selective amount of evidence. And there are so many opportunities to rethink those claims or revise them or add to them in different ways.

This same student saw how training in the archives provided an opportunity to work through the rhetorical challenges of constructing historical accounts:

> [The archives unit] made me much more aware of how you have to use evidence to construct an argument—of what you can and can't say based on evidence you have from the archive. So you can make certain kinds of claims from looking at course catalogs, for example, but you can't make other kinds of claims about what was happening. I think that was made more evident by just seeing what was left over from the historical period.

In addition to gaining a better understanding of historical evidence, students gained a better understanding of the kinds of historical accounts the archives could help them construct.

Several students commented that working in the archives showed them that archival research does not necessarily mean arguing about the distant past. One student noted, "I knew the archive had things that are old; [this project] made me really aware that contemporary historical documents are also there, especially if you are looking at everyday materials." Another student shared a similar account of how his or her beliefs about historical research changed: "I worked with materials that were more recent history. I had an impression of historical work that was romantic and distant but that it wasn't a thing I could ever do myself; it was made much more accessible to me through the archival unit."

Students also came to realize that archival evidence is multimodal. One student commented on the value of a photograph in a file that primarily contained text documents: "That picture told me something that I suspected but that wasn't totally obvious from the text in the archive." Other archives included documents—such as annotated documentary scripts and comments about broadcast programming—that reveal multimodal composition strategies from specific periods. Finally, students recognized the pedagogical potential of the OSU Photo Archives, a point addressed under Theme 6.

Theme 4: Understanding Our Discipline(s) by Practicing Historical Research

The process of conducting archival research led some students to realize how their subfields approach historiography. Some of these realizations were predicted. For example, the students who self-identified as historical researchers felt they had become better acquainted with the "work in the trenches" required of historiographers of rhetoric and composition. Students aligned with other areas had reactions that we did not expect.

Students with other research interests were excited by their class projects, but they recognized that historical work was less valued by their areas. For example, one student was excited by the material in the archives but learned that a detailed treatment would have to wait. The student's adviser had explained that graduate students in his or her field were expected to do specific kinds of work—presumably qualitative research— early in their careers; the student would have to build authority in the field before he or she could make broader historical claims. Of course, the validity of the adviser's point is arguable; nevertheless, the comment demonstrates how archival research encouraged this student to reflect on the value of specific approaches for specific subfields.

Students also remarked about how specific subfields approach history and how they might contest the biases of those approaches. For example, one student noted that the process of archival research caused him or her to reflect on how much the history of the field centers on the study of specific important figures and organizations. Another noted, "I don't work in a field where archival research is common at all, so to be shown the possibilities [for my field] was really useful." Finally, a student planning a qualitative dissertation saw how archival material—such as recently archived records—could support his or her project. Such comments suggest that archival sources and archival training can be relevant for researchers in every field of writing studies.

Theme 5: Articulating What Graduate Students Need from Methods Training

The focus group interviews allowed the graduate students to offer candid comments about research methods training and graduate curricula. Although they were not prompted to do so, students in both focus groups compared their experiences during the archival unit with experiences from other classes.

Students in each group also explained how the structured practice of our module increased their confidence in using archival methods. Students compared the archival unit to three kinds of experiences: introductory courses on graduate study in English, other class projects based on special collections or archives, and independent trips to archives for other class projects. Some of these experiences occurred at OSU; others occurred at other institutions.

Several students commented that they wished their introductory courses had focused less on critical theory and more on the practical aspects of research, such as working in archives. One student suggested that introductory courses should replace their typical theoretical orientations with a "methodological orientation toward English studies [that is] as broad as possible." He or she argued that "only focusing on the text itself, regardless of material conditions and only on published texts—not records and all these crazy things that are in archives—really narrows down what you think—what interests you cultivate as graduate students." Another student contrasted the project from our module with typical projects:

> [This project] was very much "ground up." In a lot of grad school classes you doodle around with theory first and then you say "I'm going to go apply it to this text I found." Whereas this was more of an inductive process. The documents I was looking at—I didn't really know what I was going to think about them at the end. Whereas I feel like I often work with texts and already know what I'm going to say about them at the start.

Other students made similar comments about practicing inductive research. For example, one student noted that "'ground up' is a good way to frame it because [my archive] was one of those things that at first didn't yield anything, but the more I pressed it, the more it produced." Of course, deductive, theory-first approaches to textual artifacts offer immense pedagogical value. However, these comments suggest that students also benefit from class experiences requiring extended practice with inductive approaches.

When describing other courses that incorporated archives or special collections, students explained that the structure of those assignments sometimes limited their value as methods training. For example, several students described an assignment that involved only one artifact from a large special collection; the narrow focus of the project did not offer the opportunity for the students to interact with archivists. With our project, students could follow interesting threads by engaging both the material in the boxes and the expertise of the staff at the OSU Archives.

Finally, some students compared their experiences in our class with unguided experiences. For example, one student described visiting an archive without any practical preparation:

> I had been to an archive before [the class], but I went blindly; I didn't know anything about finding aids. I only knew that I needed to request stuff ahead of time. I had no concept of how much time it would take to work through archival material. So this class helped me a lot with understanding the practical aspects of archival research.

This student was not alone in appreciating guided practice with archives, as the description of Theme 1 suggests. Although such guided practice might not be a training option for researchers after graduate school, there are numerous opportunities for self-guided practice. Researchers new to archives should consider practicing in an archives facility and conversing with archivists in a low-stakes setting before taking more extensive and expensive research trips.

Theme 6: Imagining Teaching with Archives

All of these students were graduate teaching assistants preparing for careers as teacher-scholars, so it made sense to ask them about the pedagogical possibilities of archives. Their responses suggest that archives could be valuable tools for many undergraduate and graduate contexts.

For undergraduate classes, they suggested incorporating archival research into both composition classes and undergraduate courses on research methods. For example, photographs from different periods of university history could be engaging primary sources for first-year writing classes. However, just as quickly as they generated ideas for teaching with archives, they recognized obstacles to be overcome. For instance, the Archives' limited hours and its location on the far edge of campus makes field trips with undergraduate classes impractical. Moreover, the reading room is too small to accommodate a typical undergraduate class. Instructors wishing to teach with archives must consider such constraints.

After recognizing the specific challenges of teaching from the OSU Archives, the students considered the pros and cons of working around them. Some proposed using digitized materials; however, this solution would deprive their students of the experience of "getting their hands dirty" in the archives, which could be especially important in a research methods class. Another proposed solution would be to bring a selection of materials into the classroom. Several terms later, one student implemented this solution in a second-level composition class. Tamar visited the class with examples of archival material, and the undergraduate students analyzed digitized copies of other documents from the university archives as part of their individual class projects. This student demonstrated that there are ways to work around some of the material constraints of archives-based teaching, but such approaches require developing a collaborative relationship with an archivist. Indeed, collaborating with an archivist on a teaching project would be a productive way for postgraduate researchers to practice working in the archives.

Having had such a positive experience with archival research, these students could easily imagine teaching archival research methods at the graduate level later in their professional careers. In fact, they assumed that they should be teaching a hands-on archival research project in such classes, and they commented that our module increased their confidence to do it well. Moreover, they were so enthusiastic about the integration of archival research into this course that they asked if Tamar could offer a workshop on incorporating archival materials into their classes.

As our six themes suggest, when scholars practice archival research they engage archives from multiple perspectives: archives as material and spatial entities, archives as structured and unstructured information, archives as sources of evidence, archives as disciplinary formulations, and archives as tools for teaching and learning. These varied perspectives suggest that an archival research experience can enrich a scholar's general understanding of research methods and methodology.

Of course, archival research is but one set of skills scholars apply in charting the past and future of our disciplines. For example, if a student pursued the implications of Trula Detweiler's story, he or she would face research challenges beyond working in distant archives staffed with unfamiliar archivists. This student would also need to conduct research interviews if his or her account would incorporate stories from Detweiler's family or from the teachers and alumni of Ganado's schools. He or she might need qualitative and quantitative tools for processing interview data and analyzing artifacts discovered in the archives. Further, an understanding of the politics and the stakes of historiography would help this student navigate the risks and responsibilities entailed in writing history. Thus, we do not imagine archival research methods as superseding all other methods. Nevertheless, training in the archives offers practical and intellectual preparation for thinking critically about how our fields make knowledge. To conclude this essay, we consider the implications of framing archives as training spaces.

Training in the Archives: Sustaining the Archival Turn

In her editor's introduction to the February 2012 issue of *College Composition and Communication*, Kathleen Blake Yancey contemplated the recent rise of archival scholarship in composition studies:

> What interests me in part is the variety of contexts in which we are using or sharing or introducing archives: for research and in theory and for programs and with our students in classrooms. What interests me as well is how we are using the metaphor of *archive* as well as the physical or material archive itself. I'm not sure it's a trend, but I am wondering if the field is, perhaps, serious about taking an archival turn.
>
> (364, her emphasis)

Like Yancey, we are intrigued by both the diverse uses and associations of archives. If the fields of writing studies are to sustain an "archival turn" across varied contexts of research, teaching, and administration, then scholars need to consider *why* and *how* they might engage the archives on their own and with their students. Regularizing such engagement might reconfigure *what* archives mean as sites of scholarly and pedagogical praxis.

Our students' comments about their archival experiences suggest compelling answers to the "Why archives?" question. Even a brief engagement with the archives has lasting pragmatic and intellectual benefits. By working in the archives, scholars learn to think methodically about texts and contexts while facing physical and temporal constraints. They practice increasingly neglected information literacy skills (such as browsing) while developing relationships with invaluable human resources. They develop a more nuanced understanding of historiographical argumentation, and they learn to find and work with materials that can bolster their claims and complicate the histories of our discipline(s). They might come to think critically about how historical methods relate to their fields and to think creatively about undergraduate and graduate pedagogy. In short, archival research training provides far more than focused practice with finding aids and time constraints. Although training in archival methods is necessary for historiographers, it is relevant for all scholars in our discipline, regardless of their subfields or research plans.

The "how" of archival training must depend on local resources, personal interests, and curricular needs; however, archives are flexible and scalable resources for teaching and learning. As our students imagined (and even realized in their own classes), archives are productive sites for undergraduate classes in composition, writing studies, or research methodology. If visiting the archives is not feasible or desirable for these classes, material can be digitized to facilitate research assignments or to create rich cases for class projects and discussions. Archives are equally flexible resources for graduate pedagogy. Our module was one of three components in an introductory research methods class, and we will continue to follow that model. However, the archival research unit could be integrated into courses with historical content themes or expanded into a full-term graduate course on historical research methodology. Finally, archives are good sites for autodidacts wishing to develop their archival research skills, to learn more about the history of their institutions, or to develop relationships with intramural colleagues in other disciplines.

The outcomes and opportunities of archival training suggest a reconsideration of what archives can and do mean for writing studies. As Yancey suggests, *archives* resonate with both literal meanings and figurative associations (364). Archives are physical spaces, but they are also institutions, sources of invention, and personal constructions. Archives are repositories of records, but they are also the repositories "of record" and thus sites of memory and power. As Derrida reminds us, the first archives were the homes of the Greek *archons*—magistrates who protected, interpreted, and policed the records and law of a literate culture (2). We must be mindful that archives, like universities are often "insides" defined by what (and who) is "outside."

Despite the necessary division and selection of archiving, archives can also represent pleasure and possibility, personal investment and public participation. Archives are sites of dreaming, playing, and rambling (Connors 23). They are gift-bearing spaces that offer "resistance to our first thought, freedom from resentment, and the possibility of reconfiguring our relation to history" (Wells 58). Archives fuel the historical imagination and provide the evidence for complicating the narratives of our past. Moreover, the concept of "archives" is not confined to describing institutional storage facilities. Archives can also be constructed by collecting materials or contextualizing family artifacts. Further, digital technologies have expanded how archives can be accessed, created, and populated.

In short, archives resonate with multiple and sometimes contradictory associations. Each permutation presents intellectual, methodological, and rhetorical resources and challenges. Such multiplicity makes the archives ideal training spaces for the discipline of writing studies.

Appendix 1: Archival Module Reading Schedule

This appendix lists the reading assignments completed by the students before and during the archival module. The archival module was the first of three, and it commenced after two days of general discussion about research methods (Days 1 and 2 on the following schedule). As we noted in our discussion section, we will schedule Anne's class visit to occur after the students visit the archives rather than on Day 2 in future iterations of the class. This change will require adjusting the days when specific texts are read; however, we do not imagine significant changes to the reading list.

Day 1—Introduction to Research Methodology

Burke, Kenneth. "Terminsitic Screens." [From *Language as Symbolic Action.*] *The Rhetorical Tradition.* Ed. Patricia Bizzell and Bruce Herzberg. Boston: Bedford/St. Martin's. 2001. 1340–48. Print. (Supplemental)

Cross, Geoffrey, Carol S. David, Margaret Baker Graham, and Charlotte Thralls. "Thinking and Rethinking Research Methodology." *Business Communication Quarterly* 59.3 (Sept. 1996): 105–16. Print.

Kirsch, Gesa. "Methodological Pluralism: Epistemological Issues." *Methods and Methodology in Composition Research.* Ed. Gesa Kirsch and Patricia A. Sullivan. Carbondale: Southern Illinois University Press. 1992. 247–69. Print. (Supplemental)

Rickly, Rebecca. "Messy Contexts: The Required Research Methods Course as a Scene of Rhetorical Practice." 3rd International Santa Barbara Conference on Writing Research. Writing Research Across Borders. 22–24 Feb. 2008. UC-Santa Barbara. Web. 5 Feb. 2010. <http://www.writing.ucsb.edu/wrconf08/Pdf_Articles/Rickly_Article.pdf>.

Sullivan, Patricia, and James E. Porter. "Introducing Critical Research Practices." *Opening Spaces: Writing Technologies and Critical Research Practices.* Greenwich: Ablex, 1997: 1–14. Print.

Toulmin, Stephen. "From The Uses of Argument." *The Rhetorical Tradition.* Ed. Patricia Bizzell and Bruce Herzberg. Boston: Bedford/St. Martin's, 2001. 1410–13. Print. (Supplemental)

Day 2—Research Questions

Blakeslee, Ann, and Cathy Fleischer. "What's Your Question?" *Becoming a Writing Researcher.* Mahwah: Lawrence Erlbaum, 2007. 13–36. Print.

Bizup, Joseph. "BEAM: A Rhetorical Vocabulary for Teaching Research-Based Writing." *Rhetoric Review* 27.1 (2008): 72–86. Print.

Rude, Carolyn. "Mapping the Research Questions in Technical Communication." *Journal of Business and Technical Communication* 23.2. (April 2009): 174–215. Print.

Day 3

Bordelon, Suzanne. "Composing Women's Civic Identities during the Progressive Era: College Commencement Addresses as Overlooked Rhetorical Sites." *College Composition and Communication* 61.3 (Feb. 2010): 510–33. Print.

Connors, Robert. "Dreams and Play: Historical Method and Methodology." *Methods and Methodology in Composition Research*. Ed. Gesa Kirsch and Patricia A. Sullivan. Carbondale: Southern Illinois University Press, 1992. 15–36. Print.

Connors, Robert. "The Rise of Technical Writing Instruction in America." *Journal of Technical Writing and Communication* 12.4 (1982): 329–52. Print. (Supplemental)

Gaillet, Lynée Lewis. "Archival Survival: Navigating Historical Research." *Working in the Archives: Practical Research Methods for Rhetoric and Composition*. Ed. Alexis Ramsey, Wendy Sharer, Barbara L'Eplattenier, and Lisa Mastrangelo. Carbondale: Southern Illinois University Press, 2009. 28–39. Print.

Glenn, Cheryl, and Jessica Enoch. "Invigorating Historiographic Practices in Rhetoric and Composition Studies." *Working in the Archives: Practical Research Methods for Rhetoric and Composition*. Ed. Alexis Ramsey, Wendy Sharer, Barbara L'Eplattenier, and Lisa Mastrangelo. Carbondale: Southern Illinois University Press, 2009. 11–27. Print.

Day 4

Morris, Sammie, and Shirley Rose. "Invisible Hands: Recognizing the Archivists' Work to Make Records Accessible." *Working in the Archives: Practical Research Methods for Rhetoric and Composition*. Ed. Alexis Ramsey, Wendy Sharer, Barbara L'Eplattenier, and Lisa Mastrangelo. Carbondale: Southern Illinois University Press, 2009. 51–78. Print.

Ramsey, Alexis. "Viewing the Archives: The Hidden and the Digital." *Working in the Archives: Practical Research Methods for Rhetoric and Composition*. Ed. Alexis Ramsey, Wendy Sharer, Barbara L'Eplattenier, and Lisa Masterangelo. Carbondale: Southern Illinois University Press, 2009. 79–90. Print.

Tirabassi, Katherine. "Revisiting the 'Current-Traditional Era': Innovations in Writing Instruction at the University of New Hampshire." Diss. University of New Hampshire, 2007. Ann Arbor: UMI, 2007. Print.

Zinkham, Helena. "Finding and Researching Photographs." *Working in the Archives: Practical Research Methods for Rhetoric and Composition*. Ed. Alexis Ramsey, Wendy Sharer, Barbara L'Eplattenier, and Lisa Mastrangelo. Carbondale: Southern Illinois University Press. 2009. 119–34. Print.

Day 5

Masters, Thomas. "Reading the Archive of Freshman English." *Working in the Archives: Practical Research Methods for Rhetoric and Composition*. Ed. Alexis Ramsey, Wendy Sharer, Barbara L'Eplattenier, and Lisa Mastrangelo. Carbondale: Southern Illinois University Press, 2009. 157–68. Print.

Ritter, Kelly. "(En)Gendering the Archives for Basic Writing Research." *Working in the Archives: Practical Research Methods for Rhetoric and Composition*. Ed. Alexis Ramsey, Wendy Sharer, Barbara L'Eplattenier, and Lisa Mastrangelo. Carbondale: Southern Illinois University Press, 2009. 181–94. Print.

Tirabassi, Katherine. "Journeying into the Archives: Exploring the Pragmatics of Archival Research." *Working in the Archives: Practical Research Methods for Rhetoric and Composition*. Ed. Alexis Ramsey, Wendy Sharer, Barbara L'Eplattenier, and Lisa Mastrangelo. Carbondale: Southern Illinois University Press, 2009. 169–80. Print.

Day 6 – Field Trip—Meet in the OSU Archives

Day 7 – Reflecting on the Archival Experience

Johnson, Nan. "Autobiography of an Archivist." *Working in the Archives: Practical Research Methods for Rhetoric and Composition.* Ed. Alexis Ramsey, Wendy Sharer, Barbara L'Eplattenier, and Lisa Mastrangelo. Carbondale: Southern Illinois University Press, 2009. 290–300. Print.

Appendix 2: Assignment Sheet for the Archival Research Module

Module 1: Historical Research Project

As you will soon learn firsthand, the OSU Archives is a rich resource for scholars studying rhetoric, composition, and literacy. In this first project, you will plan an archival visit, explore a very small portion of the Archives' holdings, document your research activities, and argue for the significance of a larger project based on your pilot work.

University Archivist Tamar Chute has used the research statements you sent me to identify materials that might relate to your scholarly interests. You will use some of this material in developing your project.

Project Objectives

In completing this assignment you will . . .

- learn about historiography and historical research methods in RCL.
- learn how to find, access, and use archival collections
- learn how to work with an archivist
- practice developing effective arguments from historical sources

Project Deliverables

The Research Log: Create a wiki page to document your progress on this project. Back up your work in a Word file. **NB: The research log will be a "messy" document. Do not agonize over its format or the precision of its prose.**

Your log should include the following items before you compose your email request to Tamar:

1. At least one paragraph describing the collections that seem most promising for your research interests.
2. A short list of research questions. Include questions that this material might help you answer and/or questions that the material seems to inspire.
3. A short (300–400 words) summary of any information you can find about this topic, person, or event from online resources.

4. A short paragraph explaining why you will ask for a specific box/folder from a specific collection.

By the end of the module, your log should include the following items:

5. A description of what you found. (A short summary of your notes is sufficient.)
6. A summary of any new questions raised by the materials.
7. A short list of sources that might help explain the context or significance of the materials.

The Archives Request Email: Send an email to Tamar by 4/8, and copy me on the message. In the email, ask Tamar to pull specific material for you by referring to the finding aid.

The Project Plan Summary: Imagine that you are requesting funding from your department for a follow-up visit to the OSU Archives or another archive. (The location will depend on where your archived material leads you.) As part of this request, you must write a brief statement (250–500 words) that explains the topic and rationale of the project. Explain the significance (or failure) of your first trip, and argue for the significance of the specific resources you want to see in your next trip. (For example, it is a unique resource, a source for comparative analysis, a source for quantitative data, etc.)

Timetable

March 31—Create a wiki page linked to your personal page called "[Last Name] Archival Research Log." Review the finding aids. Begin thinking about questions that might be addressed by some of your archival material. Anne will visit our class.
April 5—Post preliminary research questions to the log.
April 8—Phase 1 of the research log should be completed. Send request emails to Tamar.
April 12—Tamar will visit our class to discuss working in the Archives.
April 14—Archives session. (We need to coordinate carpooling to the OSU Archives facility.)
April 19—Archives debriefing, discussion, and workshop.
April 23—Due: Final draft of the project plan summary; wiki research log.

Notes

1 We recognize that we are not the first people to ever suggest using archives as a site for teaching. As early as 1987, Bruce W. Dearstyne encouraged his fellow archivists to cooperate with historians and other professionals to create courses, workshops, and seminars to show students how to use archival sources (84). Since then, archivists have offered case studies of undergraduate courses (e.g., Zhou) and discussions of assessment strategies for archives-based classes (e.g., Krause). Scholars in women's studies (e.g., Kleinman), Victorian studies (e.g., Senf), and history (e.g., McCoy) have also

described incorporating archival research into their classes. Like contributions in the archival literature, these articles concentrate on undergraduate students and specific assignments. Although teaching undergraduates to use archival material is important, particularly if they continue their education into graduate work, connecting graduate students to the archives can be instrumental in the completion of theses and dissertations. It also may help them in the future with their own teaching and postgraduate research.

2 Archivists generally cringe when their stack areas are compared to the warehouse at the end of *Raiders of the Lost Ark*. The idea that material would be placed in a box and never used is completely antithetical to the purpose of archives and the archival vocation.

Works Cited

Charmaz, Kathy. "Grounded Theory as an Emergent Method." *Handbook of Emergent Methods*. Ed. Sharlene Nagy Hesse-Biber and Patricia Levy. New York: Guilford P, 2008. 155–170. Print.

Connors, Robert. "Dreams and Play: Historical Method and Methodology." *Methods and Methodology in Composition Research*. Ed. Gesa Kirsch and Patricia A. Sullivan. Carbondale: Southern Illinois UP, 1992. 15–36. Print.

Dearstyne, Bruce W. "What Is the Use of Archives? A Challenge for the Profession." *American Archivist* 50.1 (1987): 76–87. Print.

Derrida, Jacques. *Archive Fever: A Freudian Impression*. Trans. Eric Prenowitz. Chicago: U of Chicago P, 1998. Print.

Donahue, Patricia, and Gretchen Flesher Moon, eds. *Local Histories: Reading the Archives of Composition*. Pittsburgh: U of Pittsburgh P, 2007. Print.

Ellis, David. "Modeling the Information-Seeking Patterns of Academic Researchers: A Grounded Theory Approach." *The Library Quarterly* 63.4, Symposium on Qualitative Research: Theory, Methods, and Applications (1943): 469–86. Print.

Ferreira-Buckley, Linda. "Rescuing the Archives from Foucault." *College English* 61.5 (1999): 577–83. Print.

Foster, Allen. "A Nonlinear Model of Information-Seeking Behavior." *Journal of the American Society for Information Society and Technology* 55.3 (2004): 228–37. Web. 13 July 2011.

Gaillet, Lynée Lewis. "Archival Survival: Navigating Historical Research." *Working in the Archives: Practical Research Methods for Rhetoric and Composition*. Ed. Alexis Ramsey, Wendy Sharer, Barbara L'Eplattenier, and Lisa Mastrangelo. Carbondale: Southern Illinois UP, 2009. 28–39. Print.

Ge, Xuemei. "Information-Seeking Behavior in the Digital Age: A Multidisciplinary Study of Academic Researchers." *College & Research Libraries* 71.5 (2010). 435–55. Print.

Kirsch, Gesa, and Liz Rohan, eds. *Beyond the Archives: Research as a Lived Process*. Carbondale: Southern Illinois UP, 2008. Print.

Kleinman, Lynne. "Writing Our Own History: A Class in Archival Sources." *Feminist Collections*: 16.3 (1995): 16. Print.

Krause, Magia G. "Undergraduates in the Archives: Using an Assessment Rubric to Measure Learning." *American Archivist* 73.2 (2010): 507–34. Print.

L'Eplattenier, Barbara. "An Argument for Archival Research Methods: Thinking beyond Methodology." *College English* 72.2 (2009): 67–79. Web. 19 July 2011.

Mastrangelo, Lisa, and Barbara L'Eplattenier. "Stumbling in the Archives." *Beyond the Archives: Research as a Lived Process*. Eds. Gesa Kirsch and Liz Rohan. Carbondale: Southern Illinois UP, 2008. 161–70. Print.

McCoy, Michelle. "The Manuscript as Question: Teaching Primary Sources in the Archives—The China Missions Project." *College & Research Libraries* 71.1 (2010): 49–62. Web. 19 July 2011.

Miller, Thomas P., and Melody Bowdon. "A Rhetorical Stance on the Archives of Civic Action." *College English* 61.5 (1999): 591–98. Web. 19 July 2011.

Moon, Gretchen Flesher. "Locating Composition History." *Local Histories: Reading the Archives of Composition*. Ed. Patricia Donahue and Gretchen Moon. Pittsburgh: U of Pittsburgh P, 2007. 1–13. Print.

Morris, Sammie, and Shirley Rose. "Invisible Hands: Recognizing the Archivists' Work to Make Records Accessible." *Working in the Archives: Practical Research Methods for Rhetoric and Composition*. Ed. Alexis Ramsey, Wendy Sharer, Barhara L'Eplattenier, and Lisa Mastrangelo. Carbondale: Southern Illinois UP, 2009. 51–78. Print.

"Octalog: The Politics of Historiography." *Rhetoric Review* 7.1 (1988): 5–49. Web. 19 July 2011.

"Octalog II: The (Continuing) Politics of Historiography." *Rhetoric Review* 16.1 (1997): 22–44. Web. 19 July 2011.

"Octalog III: The Politics of Historiography in 2010." *Rhetoric Review* 30.2 (2011): 109–34. Print.

Ramsey, Alexis, Wendy Sharer, Barbara L'Eplattenier, and Lisa Mastrangelo, eds. *Working in the Archives: Practical Research Methods for Rhetoric and Composition*. Carbondale: Southern Illinois UP, 2009. Print.

Senf, Carol. "Using the University Archives to Demonstrate Real Research." *Changing English* 12.2 (2005): 297–307. Web. 19 July 2011.

Sullivan, Patricia. "Inspecting Shadows of Past Classroom Practices: A Search for Students' Voices." *College Composition and Communication* 63.3 (2012): 305–86. Print.

Tirabassi, Katherine E. "Revisiting the 'Current-Traditional Era': Innovations in Writing Instruction at the University of New Hampshire, 1940–1949." Diss. U of New Hampshire, 2007. Ann Arbor: UMI, 2007. Print.

"Trula Irene Detweiler Zimmerly." *MennObits.com*. "Gospel Herald Obituaries." Archives of the Mennonite Church USA. Web. 19 July 2011.

United States. Department of the Interior. National Parks Service. "National Historic Landmark Nomination: Sage Memorial Hospital School of Nursing, Ganado Mission." Web. 7 May 2011.

Wonfor, Marilyn. "Coed Introduces Indians to Paleface's ABC's." *Ohio State Morning Lantern* 23 July 1959: 3. Web. 19 July 2011.

Wells, Susan. "Claiming the Archive for Rhetoric and Composition." Rhetoric *and Composition as Intellectual Work*. Ed. Gary Olson. Carbondale: Southern Illinois UP, 2002.55–64. Print.

Yancey, Kathleen Blake. "From the Editor: A Blueprint for the Future: Lessons from the Past." *College Composition and Communication* 63.3 (2012): 361–64. Print.

Zhou, Xiaomu. "Student Archival Research Activity: An Exploratory Study." *American Archivist* 71.2 (2008): 476–98. Print.

18.
ARCHIVAL RESEARCH IN COMPOSITION STUDIES: RE-IMAGINING THE HISTORIAN'S ROLE
Kelly Ritter

The archival history of composition studies, at backward glance, often makes little narrative sense—even as readers of this history expect that it "must follow a chrono-logic ... [and] must be made to hang together by an infinitely complex web of cause/effect relationships" (North 69).[1] Composition historiographies therefore attempt to narrativize past events in order that they might be revealed, per Hayden White, as "possessing a structure, an order of meaning, that they do not possess as pure sequence" ("The Value of Narrativity" 5). But these narratives are fraught with questions of subjectivity, representation, and *truth*—in that all archival historians attempt to sew together events according to cause and causality, when in fact composition and rhetoric perpetually resists a master narrative that would allow for this neater ordering of effect.

Though all fields arguably face historiographic difficulties of truth-telling and narrative ordering, composition studies is especially vulnerable to such impasse due to its relative youth, low on the academic hierarchy even as it is responsible for far more, institutionally, than just the (infamous) first-year course. It houses a problematic tripartite structure not yet completely shaken out by even the best narrative attempts: Composing is at once a physical, cultural practice (writing outside academe): an academic subject: and an area of research within a larger scholarly field (transforming midcentury, according to Stephen North, from composition to Composition). Due to these three branches of inquiry, composition studies struggles to maintain one central dialogue about its origins and milestones that satisfies the representative needs of all possible interested parties: students, faculty, administrators, community members, scholars, and critics. Further framing the very "story" of composition relies upon the coherence of relationships resisted by the multiple definitions of *composing* itself, especially evident in widespread perceptions of its first-year course as remedial or subcollegiate, and in the difficulty with which those outside the field conceive of the demands and intellectual goals of upper-level undergraduate and graduate work in writing, rhetoric, and language study.

Historiography is thus an attractive and energizing means of narrating composition studies' noisy, multivocal story of making meaning out of fragments of literacy

---

Ritter, Kelly. "Archival Research in Composition Studies: Re-Imagining the Historian's Role." *Rhetoric Review* 31.4 (2012): 461–478. Print.

practices. Indeed, Linda Ferreira-Buckley argued in 1999 that we not only should pay more attention to our archival histories but that we also must carefully train graduate students in archival methodologies to ensure a continuance of such scholarship (577). Her call is echoed in Shirley Rose's 2002 call for WPAs to become archivists themselves ("Preserving Our Histories"). Yet even the most careful training in historiographic methods has its logical limits. In addition to deciding what *types* of historical evidence best tell composition's story (Textbooks? Writing program materials? Other administrative artifacts? Student texts?), scholars are faced with methods of *presentation*. Historians enter the archives in order to re-present the history of a field that resists consensus on its origin stories, and thrives on countering master narratives.

As such, one would expect the field's resulting historical work to be dynamic, provocative, and, importantly, dialogic. But as Barbara L'Eplattenier has noted, unlike more historic events or movements in our culture, our ability to counternarrate is limited by situational ethos, as "the fields of rhetoric and composition often do not have multiple histories on a topic. Instead, we have one excellent text that now serves as *the* text; the ethos of the researcher is paramount in our acceptance of that text and our use of it as a foundational text" (74). In response to this, and to the problem facing composition and rhetoric historians in general—who do not have a "critical mass within departments"—L'Eplattenier calls for scholars of the archives to make their methods more available and transparent to fellow researchers, to illustrate their methodologies "in a systematic and incremental way that both highlights the uniqueness of archival study and creates the depth and breadth of knowledge required to begin generalizing about the tools our discipline needs and uses" (68).

Voicing similar concerns over representation and the situated *ethoi* of archival historians, Lisa Mastrangelo and Lyneé Lewis Gaillet argue that the notion of "presentism"—that all archival studies must have an immediate (and significant) impact on the present, either pedagogically or theoretically speaking—is another call to revise our methodologies. Mastrangelo and Gaillet ask, "[M]ust historical scholarship make implicit connections to the present? Can historical research simply be fun/interesting/strange/informative for its own sake?" (21). They further query, "Have we been so concerned about our place within the academy that we feel the need to create a 'usable past'?" (22).

These challenges to our standard archival practices require effort toward a response, and one can imagine the paths to responding as myriad. One avenue of exploration might be the role of personal position in archival research. Another might be the documentation and archival practices that emerge from specific cultural predilections. Still another might pursue the practice of oral history collection as a means for understanding how and why certain narratives are documented and others not. But my concern here is with L'Eplattenier's broader implication, namely that archivists frequently avoid acknowledging the limits of representation and response within their research, and thus remain within archival pockets, at neat historiographic distances, going forward as if their archival subjects could be "known" in impossible ways. Mastrangelo and Gaillet acknowledge just how much historians feel pressed to make their research über-meaningful, as it were, faced with colleagues (including tenure and promotion committees) who desire a tangible connection between archival materials and present-day programs and pedagogies. The rationale and methods behind archival work are thus often subsumed by a greater impetus to cohesively narrate archival stories, which in turn sometimes are presented as untroubled by situational ethos, following a trajectory that seamlessly ends in the present.

Janice Lauer voiced her own objections to this stance in "Octalog II," commenting that in stories regarding the development of rhetoric and composition, she "encounter[s] those that try to stuff dynamic developments into static categories; that claim definitive status; that distort to promote a thesis . . . and that ignore many voices as they whisper to a few within a limited strand of scholarship" (30). Later in her remarks, Lauer posits, "To what extent, we might ask, is our effort to foreground our own ideology complicitous with writing a "definitive" story imbued with this ideology?" (31). While Lauer lays bare the ideological agendas that necessarily affect our telling of archival histories—questioning, perhaps, the insistence that "bias is value" made by Jan Swearingen in "Octalog I" (29) or James Berlin's argument that "all histories are partial accounts, are both biased and incomplete" (12)—less often do field historians today counterbalance their findings with larger questions of bias as relevant to *personal position,* such as: What is my relationship, as an historian, to the story I tell? What role do I play as the self-assigned narrator of the story of an institution, a community, or a people? Further, what processes and values were in place when these archives were created—what other stories, if any, were attempting to be told?

These are questions we avoid asking because we do not typically question the inherent value of storytelling itself. In both "Octalog I" and "Octalog II" (and as present in arguments for greater ethnic/cultural identity representation in archival research in "Octalog III"), the question of historians as narrators is never debated; instead, the questions become how to narrate *well.* We see our job as historians, by definition, as one of narrative recovery and occasionally narrative-driven activism. But what if the purpose and desired outcome of archival work was *not* to achieve a narrative whole—whether to create a story that rebels against "master" narratives, or to tacitly agree upon a master narrative that seems to say what we think/hope composition studies is/says/does? What if instead of pushing on historical texts, artifacts, and objects to get us to a satisfying "plot," as Susan Miller would argue is our general aim, composition historians instead viewed archival spaces as sites of communal representation with historical scholars at the helm, poised to report from the location and embed themselves in the multivocality of the past?

To begin to reconcile some of these opposing (and seemingly insolvable) queries, I look toward an approach that might resituate the positionality of the historian herself. I propose that composition historians should consider redefining their work in conversation with the principles and theories of archival scholarship writ large, and more specifically through the relatively new concept of *archival ethnography,* a term recently activated by the field of library and information science.[2] Reseeing historiography through these methodological lenses—approaching the archives as "real institutions" and privileging the position of the archivist as part of his/her own community, available for study—allows composition historians to face inevitable narrative contradictions head on, with responsibilities residing in theoretical conversation with the collectors of data themselves (Schwarz and Cook 2). Re-imagining the historian's role in this light makes the role far less ethically burdensome: to present data, evidence, and past practices, as well as their resulting paradoxes, disappointments, and contradictions, so as to paint a full and unadulterated picture of a particular community in a particular chronological time. The historian then presents, not *re*-presents, a community created by the external force of the archivist herself, rather than as a naturally appearing phenomenon.

Far from ignoring community in their work presently, I would argue that archival historians typically overprivilege the human dimensions of their research, highlighting aspects of stories such that they fit into categories that are not always comfortable, or accurate. Like Joe Harris, I believe that the "idea" of community can give scholars a language for exclusion, as it is a term with no "positive opposing" definition (Williams qtd. in Harris 99) and therefore soon becomes an "empty and sentimental word" as he asserts in *A Teaching Subject* (99). Further, as Harris argues, troubling of the boundaries and parameters of community's discourse and membership can be productive rather than destructive, as "not threats to [a community's] coherence but as normal activity" (106). Using this framework, one might view the historiographer in his or her typical undertakings as a double-voiced rhetor, whereas I advocate for something closer to a ventriloquist. Positioning material research practices in the archives as denarrativized could free our field's historians from the heavy burden of narratology, and better allow a full (if internally competing) history of composition studies to emerge for valuable inquiry.

Ethnography without People: Representation through Documentation

Questioning the value of narrative in composition studies history, I argue, opens us to new paradigms in archival work. Hayden White deems the *doxa* of historiography to be thus: the annals, the chronicle, and the "history proper," with neither annals nor chronicles serving as true or palatable representations of past actions (4). White notes that

> [w]hile annals represent historical reality as if real events did not display the form of story, the chronicler represents it as if real events appeared to human consciousness in the form of unfinished stories. And the official wisdom has it that.... [the historian's] account remains something less than a proper history if he has failed to give to reality the form of a story.
>
> (5)

In composition studies, we search in vain for that "proper history," but ultimately it refuses to be told. Student writing contradicts textbooks; textbooks contradict program documents; program documents undercut and argue against administrative artifacts; and public writing—the most vexing, if exciting, component of all—often speaks in conversation with none of the above. As Ferreira-Buckley notes in "Rhetorical Historiography and the Octalogs," "History is far from settled because it is shaped by their perspectives, positions, theories, and so on. That is to say, their account, like all accounts, are subject to challenge and hence to revision, small and large" (247).

To participate in what library science calls *archival ethnography* means taking an ethnographic approach to viewing the archives and their creators and curators. To do so, we must first come to terms with the ways in which archival work is, in fact, deeply ethnographic in its practices, albeit usually without living human (subject) voices to speak and be heard. The work of history in composition studies is complicated by the sometimes-competing processes of discovery and interpretation. Scholars uncover material from the archives that must be narrated, somehow "told" to others, but that narration is limited by time and space. An archival scholar can never be "there" in the moment of an artifact's creation. She is always excavating and offering products of another culture of which she cannot be a part, much like the ethnographer. If we accept this foundational complication of our core methodology, we must further ask, what are the responsibilities of the archivist-as-ethnographer to call attention to the gaps and even misdeeds that question a history of the "normal" or the proper ordering of events and people? What if her story, in other words, is not something others want to *hear*?

Thinking of our historiographic work in composition studies as fundamentally ethnographic adds a necessary human—and fallible—dimension to the interpretative work that we must do in order to represent in particular the experiences of those people and institutions for whom few have previously endeavored to speak. A summary of the basic tenets of ethnography evinces some overt similarities in the methods of archival scholars and the methods of field work. As John Van Maanen explains, there are three "distinct activity phases," or movements, associated with ethnography:

> The collection of information or data on a specified (or proposed) culture [fieldwork] . . . the construction of an ethnographic report or account and, in particular, to the specific compositional practices used by the ethnographer to fashion a cultural portrait . . . [and] the reading and reception of an ethnographic text across various audience segments. Each phase raises distinctive and problematic concerns for the subjects, the producers, and the consumers of ethnography.
>
> (Van Maanen 5)

When we apply these definitive phases to archival historiography, we see overlap. Information and/or data are collected through the troves of an archive or archives; a "cultural portrait" is fashioned from these data; and the resulting document is released to various "audience segments"—including, in some cases, descendants of persons represented by the archives and/or communities who have a stake in the materials of a particular archive (for example, veterans who might benefit from a recovery and rhetorical analysis of journals of fellow veterans, housed at a particular institution or repository).

But unlike traditional ethnographers, composition historians are rarely face-to-face with their subjects, particularly those scholars working in early- or pre-twentieth century archives.[3] Historians may draw upon oral histories or interviews to augment a particular archival collection, for example, but the bulk of archival historians' work will be, by definition, out-of-time, without the benefit of physical immersion in a community or communities under study, and without dialogic exchange with persons inhabiting those communities. The best that most archival historians can do in terms of dialogue is a reading of the written products left behind, products both public and private, never meant to be viewed by noncommunity members. Whereas ethnographers are interlopers who must be accepted by a community, at least to some degree, archival historians are spies, recording and reporting without the community's express permission, exposing not only artifacts but also the real human experiences hidden behind those artifacts.

This interloper position has not gone without comment in composition historiography, most recently in two essays in the collection *Working in the Archives*. Neal Lerner contends that the "social process" of archival work means that "archival research is not merely about the artifacts to be found but is ultimately about the people who have played a role in creating and using those artifacts ... [including] a host of other players in the social world represented" (195–96). Describing his effort to find the "story" of Robert Moore, an early director of the Writing Clinic at the University of Illinois, Lerner notes the complexity of "finding" Moore—as an historical character, and as a real person. He uses Moore's case to argue that "[f]or composition studies, partial histories are both an indication of gaps in be filled in and a caution to mistrust the certainty of those who claim to know. After all, our field is built on knowing and forgetting ..." (203). Lerner goes further to make an explicit connection between archival research and ethnographic work, claiming that Stephen J. Ball's definition of the "social stance" in ethnography, that which involves "risk, uncertainty, and discomfort," also describes the stance of the archival researcher. Lerner ultimately wants to know, in the close of his essay, whether "the persons being studied, those who contribute to the archives, or those in the present have some stake in the stories being told?" (204).[4]

Lerner makes clear that the *people* behind the archives are the most important consideration in our historical research. In doing so, Lerner aligns himself less with historians and more with journalists, sociologists, and of course ethnographers. This concern for accurate, adequate representation of subjects is also vocalized in Linda Bergmann's essay "The Guilty Pleasures of Working with Archives," found in this same collection. Bergmann recounts her experiences working with the private papers of Marcia Tillotson, a literature scholar, and Elizabeth Agassiz, the author of an expedition narrative as well as the biographer of her scientist husband (220). She recalls feeling particularly sheepish about gaining access to and reading Tillotson's personal letters, in that "[r]eading the letters as 'story' invoked in me another sense of guilty pleasure, the kind ... [found in] rummaging through the drawers of the parents of children for whom I babysat in high school." Bergmann notes that "these letters were not written for public consumption, and yet here I was, a stranger who was 'consuming' them" despite the author's explicit directive to her own mother that making her letters public would constitute "an act of betrayal and exposure" (222).

The two terms that Bergmann puts in quotes here—"story" and "consuming"—reveal a discomfort with the positionality of the archival historian herself. Bergmann is compelled to make the letters *into* a "story" and later is burdened with the guilt of "consuming" the personal words of her subject, words never meant to be public. Archival researchers can empathize with the feelings behind both of these acts, but too infrequently make such difficulties explicit in their writing. Yet as we survey boxes of documents explicitly meant for a particular person's (or group's) eyes only—or for no eyes other than those of the author—we know this paradox of representation. Based on my own experience with archived private correspondence that made its way into my scholarship, I agree with Bergmann's view of using Tillotson's letters—quoting broad terms used by the former *New York Times Magazine* "Ethicist" columnist Randy Cohen: "When and how can we be sure that the 'interests of the living' are 'profoundly important' enough to ignore the intention of the dead writer?" (223). Cristina Kirklighter even more pointedly argues that this same conflict of interest affects ethnographers in composition studies, questioning "How can ethnographers 'tell the truth' when doing so reflects negatively on the communities or when they cannot get respondents' written permission to be published?" (xiii).

Bergmann concedes that the "material reality of the archive" affects how researchers and subjects interact, even across time and space. She argues that

> [o]ne touches the actual paper and reads the actual words directly as they were written, and it is hard not to feel part of the particular, personal audience for whom they were written. This all-too-strong human sympathy can color the reading of unpublished work and impact responses to it.
>
> (230)

Like Lerner, who "emerge[s] from these long [archival] sessions with only a partial knowledge of these previous worlds and disoriented to my present one" (195), Bergmann articulates the wrenching position in which archival researchers often find themselves: They are not a completely reliable "storyteller" of the person/group/community in which they have been immersed, and they are no longer a completely reliable, or "objective," reporter of factual information appearing in those archives and critical to audiences in the present day. The historiographer exits the archives as a liminal being, one stuck in a defective, seductive time machine.

Consider how the liminality of the archival researcher in composition studies compares to the position of scholars in the second stage of traditional ethnographic work: fieldworking. Van Maanen describes this stage, or the act of "writing it up," as one that

> has undergone changes over time from a relatively unreflective, closed, and general ("holistic") description of native sayings and doings to a more tentative, open, and partial interpretation of member sayings and doings. . . . The genre itself is marked by a number of compositional conventions including, for example, the swallowing up and disappearance of an author in the text, the suppression of the individual cultural member's perspective in favor of a typified or common denominator "native's point of view," *the placement of a culture within a rather timeless ethnographic present*, and a claim (often implicit) for *descriptive or interpretive validity based almost exclusively on the author's own "being there" experience.*
>
> (7, emphasis added)

Kristi Yager, theorizing teacher research in composition studies writ large, argues that these impulses toward "being there" already are always-already present and that they complicate notions of representation and validity. Yager quotes Pratt and comments that

> anthropologists and composition's teacher researchers face the same problems, problems best explained and exemplified through two tropes that have been employed to establish authority and to represent others ... the literary tropes of the hero which in ethnographic writing typically take one of two forms: the "royal arrival" or the "old-fashioned castaway."
>
> (38)

Yager further argues that researchers' adherence to this trope (which one finds most frequently in research of marginalized student populations) "is not an inherent problem" in terms of self-identification. It is a problem, however,

> for a kind of research that professes to represent the "real" learning experience or situation of others, of students. When the hero trope becomes the primary means of structuring research, the plot, angle of vision, and the lessons learned tend to focus on the teacher's perspectives, feelings, confusions, and revelations. The subjectivity of the teacher-researcher dominates the writing of the research, and therefore can. . . . obscure the thoughts, feelings and revelations (or lack thereof) of the students.
>
> (43)

Certainly in presenting the literacy history of communities of students, teachers and other institutional or extra-institutional groups, this notion of subjectivity is paramount—from the perspective not only of the composition historian herself but also from the archivist who assembled said documents and who made choices about which documents and artifacts were, in fact, revelatory and which were not.

I offer the values and methods of archival ethnography as a possible bridge between the problematic narrator position that works as a default for composition historians—who are without the benefit of interaction with their research subjects but who are privy to many details of these subjects' lives that are worthy of presentation and respectful dissemination, as free from bias and researcher positionality as is possible—and a mere clinical reporting of archival histories, á la White's "annals" mode. If composition historians were to consider the profitability of this approach to the study of communities-in-relation, they might uncover a more capacious path in representation, or at least a new angle into the why and how of representing historical, nonpresent beings and events in a more objective manner.

Linda Gracy, one of the scholars associated with the scholarly attention to archival ethnography in library science, describes such a practice as

> a form of naturalistic inquiry which positions the researcher within an archival environment to gain the cultural perspective of those responsible for the creation, collection, care, and use of records. A corollary. . . . is the concept that creators of documents, users of documents, and archivists form a community of practice—the archival environment—for which social interaction creates meaning and defines values. Archival ethnography may be practiced in a

variety of environments—any social space where the creation, maintenance, or use of archival records forms a locus of interest and activity.

("Documenting Communities of Practice" 337)

Key to Gracy's description, for composition historians, is the idea of gaining a "cultural perspective" of those who created, collected, and cared for the records under study. Aside from the recent *Working in the Archives* collection noted previously. Kirsch and Rohan's *Beyond the Archives: Research as a Lived Process* and Shirley Rose's work on WPAs as researchers and archivists, little mention is made in composition studies historiography regarding the role of the *archivist* and the social and material function or the archives that we employ. Considering more deeply the relationship between what is selected for inclusion in archives—and what is left *out*—is certainly germane to our field, given that the types of materials often helpful in studying past composition practices (student work, teachers' notes) are the very items sometimes deemed less "important" to archival depositories. Better understanding the differences between caring for and cataloguing archives and studying them as researchers also opens up our notion of "narration." What do archivists value that we should consider emulating? Conversely, what can we *teach* archivists about the things we value, as a discipline, and would like to have preserved for future study?

Secondary to Gracy's notion of cultural perspective on care and collection of records is her allied idea of a "community of practice," specifically that such a community can "creat[e] meaning and defin[e] values." Gracy's concept seems ripe for application in composition studies, since we are certainly a community in which archival research "forms a locus of interest and activity." If we were to look at the archives as *creating* meaning rather than *narrating* the values we believe to have been historically in place in our field, we might see this work as more archeological in nature—more discovery and presentation, rather than validation or proof. Archival studies of composition's history are on the rise, as we are just now "old" enough as a field to gain some perspective on not just nineteenth-century (fabled) origins of the first-year course, but also twentieth-century academic movements and other allied scenes of literacy. Composition studies scholars occupy a unique position in terms of researching their field's history, having undergone as many "waves" of theory and practice in the last sixty years as many other fields have in much longer spans. If we act upon the methodologies inherent in archival ethnography, those that use archives for *creating* meaning and community, we can recover but not necessarily reclaim those pasts for future use. In addition, we can better weave in those nontextual documents— for example, surviving oral histories and other human-based artifacts—to augment the traditional scope of archival research and data collection relied upon by scholars of other academic fields.

Employing a similar community-centered agenda for archival research, Sue McKemmish, Anne Gilliland-Swetland and Eric Ketelar augment Gracy's seminal overview of library science practices by describing archival ethnography in terms of the critical concepts of memory and forgetting, namely that

> [s]ocieties institutionalize their collective archives according to their own evidence and memory paradigms. These paradigms influence what is remembered and what is forgotten, what is preserved and what is destroyed, how archival knowledge is defined, what forms archives take, [and] how archives are described and indexed.
>
> (146)

McKemmish et al. conclude that archival ethnography "could be used to study cultures of documentation, the forms of records and archives, the recordkeeping and archiving processes that shape them, the worldviews made manifest in their systems of classification, the power configurations they reflect, and associated memory und evidence paradigms" (158).

McKemmish et al.'s argument that archives illustrate a community's "memory paradigms" is critical to the enterprise of archival research in composition studies—wherein "memory" is a contested term in relation to pedagogical practices and trends, and particularly student ability; the lore of the ever-deficient student, for example, illustrates the need for our community to continually remind itself that the past *is* present, and that our disciplinary practices are often at odds with public, lore-fueled perceptions of the same. Further, McKemmish et al. remind us that archives represent what is remembered and what is *destroyed*—the holes that all archival researchers encounter—is relevant to the work of composition historians. Selecting the most relevant, important, or timely theories and practices for immediate as well as future consideration includes recovering "gaps"; as extant within the institutional narrative as a whole, these gaps are part of the challenge of constructing and maintaining a field's history that is characterized by incoherence and, importantly, selective inattention to institutional and departmental/disciplinary memory, particularly as a field primarily associated with the transient population of first-year writers. This concern goes back to Gracy's advice to understand archival *practices* alongside archival research.

Indeed, Gracy argues that "it is possible to study archival processes and practices in situ—within communities of practice—rather than as idealized conceptions of archival theory" (335–36). This method privileges the human elements of archiving itself in the context of what records ultimately result. Further, Gracy recognizes that

> research questions have tended to promote the archival endeavor as ideally objective work, where individual or collective subjectivity must be either ignored or rooted out. Perhaps many of us are still unduly influenced by the belief in the sanctity of the processes of record creation and recordkeeping, fondly desiring to make them purely logical procedures which can thus be theorized, normalized, and generalized (not to mention dehumanized). It may be difficult and messy to admit that record creators make and manage records in an illogical fashion, and that archivists sometimes do not treat records in the most objective manner possible.
>
> (362)

Composition historians can apply this sensibility more generally to current archivists working in large collections, or more specifically to *past* archivists who had a greater stake in what kind of materials were saved, or were lost. We know that it has been difficult to convince broader academia of the value of historicizing our field via student writing and other pedagogical materials. But historians have also had the experience of seeing the most prominent, famous, or well-regarded figures being archived ahead of others. Department heads might have entire boxes of files unto themselves in a particular institutional archive, for example, while writing program administrators may have a slim folder at best. Acknowledging more freely that the archivist him or herself—and the presence of *multiple* archivists for a series of multidecade files from, say, an English department—remind us that whatever "truth" in history we might be trying to represent through analysis of an archive, it is limited by the subjectivity and general care of those who came to these spaces before us.

Also key to Gracy's use of the term *archival ethonography* is her observation that the practices of these two research methods (archival study and ethnographic study) are, in fact, innately connected. Gracy notes that "[m]ore recently, anthropologists, sociologists, and others have applied ethnographic methods to a wider range of "cultures," including those found within urban environments, organizations, and modern work cultures. This expansion of the ethnographic agenda reflects a new understanding of culture and community" (336–37). Van Maanen would take this claim even further, in determining what constitutes an ethnography (archival or otherwise), as he asserts that "[a] text is *axiomatically an ethnography* if it is put forth by its author as a nonfiction work intended to represent, interpret, or (perhaps best) translate a culture or selected aspects of a culture for readers who are often but not always unfamiliar with that culture" (14, emphasis added). Using this rather capacious definition, the various books, chapters, articles, and digital presentations of archival histories in composition studies that we create are, in fact, ethnographies, in that they "translate" as well as represent a slice of the field's past for uninitiated readers.

What constitutes a "community" as conscribed by the archives in composition studies, and as articulated in Gracy's defense of archival ethnography and Van Maanen's base definition of ethnographic products, above? The question an archival researcher should ask regarding this issue of community is, why are some voices privileged and not others, and more importantly, what does the archivist who articulates these voices want to tell us? What stories were told, but not saved in records? Alternatively, what stories were saved, but not transmitted by another researcher with access to and control over records? And finally, as an historian of composition studies, what documents should I be now *contributing* to the continued repository of our field—a challenge most prominently put forth by Shirley Rose but also by those involved in the National Archives of Rhetoric and Composition at the University of Rhode Island.

Here is where the concept of ethnography comes most into play in archival work, particularly in a field as historically fraught as composition studies. How a community is built by the archival ethnographer has much to do with how the community is viewed by its own inheritors, those who put the archives together and those who come to them for later use. Like an anthropologist, an archival ethnographer works with what is available, and in doing so not only re-presents the history of the people and places (and events) narrated within these archives, but also shapes a past community in order to revoice its legacy, and materialize its beliefs and values. Consequently, the archival ethnographer also assumes the values and position of the original archivist, knowing only what remains, never what was lost. As such, composition historians would be wise to better understand the positionality of archivists themselves, and broaden their fields of inquiry to include, if not privilege, archival methods and theories amongst or beyond the resulting narrative(s) so often sought in our historiography.

Conclusion: Changing the Terms of the Discussion

In arguing for composition historians to accent, or at least seriously consider, the methodologies of archival ethnography as both a procedural and communicative alternative to storytelling practices, I am asking that we fundamentally change the way we talk and even think about historical research. I am also asking that we de-emphasize our reliance upon narratology when we approach our field's archives, and thereby release some of the pressure we put upon ourselves to offer "true" subject representation in our archival studies. One such existing model for this kind of approach may be found in John Brereton's *The Origins of Composition Studies in the American College, 1875–1925: A Documentary History*.

While Brereton begins his book with an historical overview of the social and material conditions of this period and its key players, he limits himself to very little editorializing within the chapters—which themselves are, as the book's subtitle implies, presented in a "documentary" fashion for readers. We get long chunks of reproduced sections of textbooks, student writing, committee reports, and early treatises on composition and/versus rhetoric in college instruction. We get occasional editorial interjections—Brereton's voice is heard minimally—yet there is no explicit, overarching imperative to tell a "truth" of the discipline. If anything, the materials that Brereton selects often seem contradictory in various ways (the strong interest in a possible graduate concentration in rhetoric expressed by survey respondents in the 1901 MLA report, for example, versus the more-common narratives of the "drudgery" of teaching first-year writing in the colleges). Brereton's book is not, ultimately, a perfectly "objective" presentation of composition history; he had to select the materials *he* wanted to tell *this* history. But his ability to resist a heavy-handed narration of the materials—and his general decision to let the materials *speak for themselves*, rather than be largely spoken about—is an interesting step toward what archival ethnography might look like, were these materials in *Origins* focused on a smaller, more easily defined group of individuals who worked, lived, or studied together in one moment in our field history. Additionally, where earlier hands have been at work—for example, editors of student writing within textbooks, arguably kinds of archivists in their own right—Brereton recognizes that interference, and comments upon it (minimally) in the entry's preface.

It is interesting to ponder why more studies of Brereton's kind have not been published since this book appeared in 1996, wherein an author or editor "reassembles" archival documents for review and education, rather than coherent narration. What is holding archival historians back from laying bare more of our key documents? To reframe this question, what causes us to produce articles, books, and edited collections of intricately *narrated* histories of particular local groups, institutions, communities rather than simply immerse ourselves, insofar as it is possible, in the past experiences of these groups, institutions, and communities, and represent what happened, offering as few "truthful" conclusions as possible?'

Shifting this discourse of narration—built upon longstanding values of historians not just in composition studies but in any other field wherein disciplinary histories are critical to understanding the institutional present—to a discourse of methods will not be easy. We will need to open up our conversations to fields outside of our own, as well as consider archival work as but one spot on a continuum of representation of our field's work. We will also have to think about what we value in our published work. Are we willing to make available more nontraditional forms of archival representation for scholarly dissemination and value in highstakes arenas, such as promotion and tenure (including, incidentally, that which may be represented through digital archives)? Based on a survey of the current market of books and collections employing archival materials, we seem, as a field, to be emerging past the notion that our origin story is univocal or monolithic. More publishers are embracing local case studies in archival work and are open to singular studies of historical moments operating outside the Harvard genesis narrative, for example. But still our work in these books and collections is almost completely characterized by storytelling. I thus call for my fellow historians to look at archival study in a new way—a more interdisciplinary, multirepresentational way—in order that we keep dynamic and dialogic the continuing trove of artifacts that serve as remembrances of our field.

Notes

1 I am grateful to the *RR* peer reviewers of this article, Dr. Hugh Burns and Dr. Brad Lucas, for their valuable feedback and guidance.
2 In her essay "Preserving Our Histories of Institutional Change," Shirley Rose argues that composition and rhetoric archivists develop closer relationships with library science professionals in order that they might better understand the very construction of the archives, and the choices made in assembling individual archival repositories; she also argues that WPAs need to be archivists themselves and should transmit materials to subsequent and fellow WPAs. Her argument, however, does not use the term *archival ethnography,* nor does it advocate for a relabeling or reification of the ways in which archival work gets *done* in the field of composition and rhetoric, as I am articulating in this essay.
3 A fascinating (if inadvertent) enactment of this is in James J. Murphy's opening vignette in "Rhetorical Historiography and the Octalogs," when he notes that two attendees at the 1998 Octalog whispered to one another, describing the Octalog participants about to speak, 'I don't care anything about this subject—I just want to know what THEY look like.' I realized suddenly that I was not a person, but a footnote. I was a stance, a position, a reference point" (239). Murphy's existence as an historical "footnote" is an example of another way historiography can go wrong: in the simple recovery of figures *as* figures, persons in a narrative that itself does not give *actual* voice to its original narrator.
4 A striking example of archival work that enacts this very question is Henze, Selzer, and Sharer's *1977: A Cultural Moment in Composition,* which examines the first-year composition program at Penn State University during the 1970s in the context of concurrent developments and conflicts in the field. Using program archives as well as interviews with former faculty and staff, Henze el al. challenge the limits of archival representation by attempting to assemble a local past that speaks *to* that history as well as *with* its present. In their introduction the authors remark that "linear Grand

Narratives [of composition studies]. . . . are somewhat less serviceable for preserving the astonishing range of practices, personalities, and messy particulars that strove for a hearing, however temporarily, within the mixed aggregate that has been known as composition," noting, as I have here, the conflicts of history that sometimes are elided in narratives of the field (44). *1977* in part also answers my desire for multiply-represented archival voices through its notable "Sidebars" feature that provides brief insights from leading composition and rhetoric scholars regarding the "moment" that was 1977, both inside and outside Penn State, and their activities and perspectives whilst in that moment. But the book also, and importantly, represents the difficult enterprise of researching and writing about one's graduate (or home) institution and accurately representing the views of those voices still living, yet also represented in the archives. Thus it privileges in its methodologies—perhaps more than any other recent historiography—Lerner's concerns for the people behind archival work.

Works Cited

Agnew, Lois, James J. Murphy, Cheryl Glenn, Nan Johnson, Jan Swearingen, Richard Leo Enos, Jasper Neel, Linda Ferreira-Buckley, Janice Lauer Rice, Janet M. Atwill, Kathleen Ethel Welch, Roxanne Mountford, Thomas Miller, and Victor J. Vitanza. "Rhetorical Historiography and the Octalogs," *Rhetoric Review* 30.3 (2011): 237–57.

Agnew, Lois, Laurie Gries, Zosha Stuckey, Vicki Tolar Burton, Jay Dolmage, Jessica Enoch, Ronald L. Jackson II, LuMing Mao, Malea Powell, Arthur E. Walzer, Ralph Cintron, and Victor Vitanza. "Octalog III: The Politics of Historiography in 2010." *Rhetoric Review* 30.2 (2011): 109–34.

Bergmann, Linda S. "The Guilty Pleasure of Working with Archives." *Working in the Archives: Practical Research Methods for Rhetoric and Composition.* Ed. Alexis E. Ramsey, Wendy B. Sharer, Barbara L'Eplattenier, and Lisa S. Mastrangelo. Carbondale: Southern Illinois UP, 2010. 220–31.

Brereton, John. *The Origins of Composition Studies in the American College, 1875–1925: A Documentary History.* Pittsburgh: U of Pittsburgh P, 1996.

Enos, Richard Leo, Janet M. Atwill, Linda Ferreira-Buckley, Cheryl Glenn, Janice Lauer, Roxanne Mountford, Jasper Neel, Edward Schiappa, Kathleen Ethel Welch, and Thomas P. Miller. "Octalog II: The (Continuing) Politics of Historiography." *Rhetoric Review* 16.1 (1997): 22–44.

Ferreira-Buckley, Linda. "Rescuing the Archives from Foucault." *College English* 61.5 (1999): 577–83.

Gracy, Karen E. "Documenting Communities of Practice: Making the Case for Archival Ethnography." *Archival Science* 4 (2004): 335–65.

Harris, Joseph. *A Teaching Subject: Composition Since 1966.* Upper Saddle River, NJ: Prentice Hall. 1997.

Henze, Brent, Jack Selzer, and Wendy Sharer. *1977: A Cultural Moment in Composition.* Lafayette, IN: Parlor P, 2007.

Kirklighter, Cristina, et al. "Introduction." *Voices and Visions: Refiguring Ethnography in Composition.* Ed. Cristina Kirklighter. Cloe Vincent, and Joseph M. Moxley. Portsmouth, NH: Boynton-Cook, 1997, i–xiii.

Kirsch, Gesa, and Liz Rohan, eds. *Beyond the Archives: Research as a Lived Process.* Carbondale: Southern Illinois. UP, 2008.

L'Eplattenier, Barbara. "An Argument for Archival Research Methods: Thinking Beyond Methodology." *College English* 72.1 (2010): 67–79.

Lerner, Neal. "Archival Research as a *Social* Process." *Working in the Archives: Practical Research Methods for Rhetoric and Composition.* Ed. Alexis E. Ramsey, Wendy B. Sharer, Barbara L'Eplattenier, and Lisa S. Mastrangelo. Carbondale: Southern Illinois UP, 2010. 195–205.

Mastrangelo, Lisa, and Lyneé Lewis Gaillet. "Historical Methodology: Past and 'Presentism'?" *Peitho* 12.1/2 (Spring–Fall 2010): 21–23.

McKemmish, Sue, Anne Gilliland-Swetland, and Eric Ketelaar. "Communities of Memory: Pluralising Archival Research and Education Agendas." *Archives and Manuscripts* 33 (2005): 146–74.

Miller, Susan. *Textual Carnivals: The Politics of Composition.* Carbondale: Southern Illinois UP, 1991.

Murphy, James J., James Berlin, Robert J. Connors, Sharon Crowley, Richard Leo Enos, Victor J. Vitanza, Susan C. Jarratt, Nan Johnson, and Jan Swearingen. "Octalog I: The Politics of Historiography." *Rhetoric Review* 7.1 (1998): 5–49.

North, Stephen. *The Making of Knowledge in Composition. Portrait of an Emerging Field.* Portsmouth. NH: Boynton/Cook, 1987.

Rose, Shirley K. "Preserving our Histories of Institutional Change: Enabling Research in the Writing Program Archives." *The Writing Program Administrator as Researcher: Inquiry in Action and Reflection.* Ed. Shirley K. Rose and Irwin Weiser. Portsmouth, NH: Boynton/Cook, 1999. 107–18.

Schwartz, Joan M., and Terry Cook. "Archives, Records, and Power: The Making of Modern Memory." *Archival Science* 2.1 (2002): 1–19.

Van Maanen, John. "An End to Innocence: The Ethnography of Ethnography." *Representation in Ethnography.* Thousand Oaks, CA: Sage, 1995. 1–35.

White, Hayden. "The Value of Narrativity in the Representation of Reality." *The Content of the Form.* Baltimore: Johns Hopkins P, 1987. 1–25.

Yager, Kristi. "Composition's Appropriation of Ethnographic Authority." *Voices and Visions: Refiguring Ethnography in Composition.* Ed. Cristina Kirklighter, Cloe Vincent, and Joseph M. Moxley. Portsmouth, NH Boynton-Cook, 1997. 37–44.

19.
(PER)FORMING ARCHIVAL RESEARCH METHODOLOGIES
Lynée Lewis Gaillet

> *[T]here is an emerging subspecialty of the field of rhetoric and composition: archival studies. Composition has clearly taken an archival as well as a social turn.*
> John C. Brereton and Cinthia Gannett, "Review: Learning from the Archives"

Complicating existing narratives about archival research, moving from the fortuitous nature of Robert Connors's 1992 "directed ramble ... August mushroom hunt" metaphor for searching in the archives (23) toward clearer conceptions of the calculated work primary investigators do, is the goal of twenty-first-century archival research. Cutting-edge scholarship identifies issues associated with archival methodologies while integrating practical advice for working in the archives. While this special issue of *CCC* is specifically devoted to research methodologies, in archival investigation examining methodologies and methods in tandem is critical given the nature of primary research, as this essay demonstrates. In "An Argument for Archival Research Methods: Thinking beyond Methodology," Barbara L'Eplattenier explains the importance of integrating discussions of methods and methodology: "Just as methodology allows us to theorize the goals of our research, methods allow us to contextualize the research process or the researched subject and materials. Methods make the invisible work of historical research visible" (69). Illustrating the "social turn" in archival research, Cheryl Glenn and Jessica Enoch explain in "Drama in the Archives: Rereading Methods, Rewriting History" that "histories do change—in response to the dominant values of institutions, cultures, and historiographers (history writers) themselves" (321). A dual archival/social remapping of rhetorical terrain depends upon shifts in researchers' integrated goals and practices. Increasingly, scholars interested in primary investigation are (1) revisiting primary and canonical materials with a new set of research questions in mind, (2) mining a broader range of archives than heretofore considered, (3) viewing (and adding to existing) archives in ways that *make* knowledge rather than simply finding what's already known, and (4) taking advantage of new technologies to expand the scope and possibilities inherent in archival investigation. Furthermore, it is imperative that readers trust the ethos of the archival researcher, given that triangulating

---

Gaillet, Lynée Lewis. "(Per)Forming Archival Research Methodologies." *CCC* 64.1 (September 2012): 35–58. Print.

archival data is often difficult to do, and understand what the researcher "counts" as evidence. Because archival researchers are only now consciously examining the interplay of method and methodologies, along with trying to make their goals and practices transparent, this essay doesn't presume to offer a prescriptive portrayal of archival research. Instead it raises both methodological and method questions and issues for consideration, looks to the insights of experienced archival researchers on these matters, and suggests areas for future research.

Some Background

The oft-cited 1999 *College English* (*CE*) issue devoted to archival work—which includes articles by John Brereton, Linda Ferreira-Buckley, Steven Mailloux, Thomas Miller and Melody Bowdon, and Vicki Tolar Burton—brought investigations of archival researchers' work to a broad constituency of English studies scholars. These researchers raised questions and issues that only now are being addressed:

> [W]e still aren't sure what should be in our archive, or how access can be broadened, or which tools we should bring to our task of exploring the past. In fact, we aren't sure exactly what we already have in our archive, or how in fact we even define the term.... [W]e need to begin asking what is missing from the archive and how it can get there. And we can also ask some questions while there is still time to act: Are there things we should be working to preserve right now? What can we do now to make sure current practices and materials will be accessible in the archives of the future?
>
> (Brereton 574)

Twenty-first-century scholarship devoted to in-depth and interdisciplinary explorations of the ways and means of archival research and the roles researchers play within the process are beginning to interrogate rhetoric and composition archival research in ways Brereton suggested; see Patricia Donahue and Gretchen Flesher Moon's *Local Histories: Reading the Archives of Composition* (2007), Gesa E. Kirsch and Liz Rohan's *Beyond the Archives: Research as a Lived Process* (2008), and Alexis Ramsey, Wendy Sharer, Barbara L'Eplattenier, and Lisa Mastrangelo's *Working in the Archives: Practical Research Methods in Rhetoric and Composition* (2010) for wide-ranging, frank, and personal discussions from archival researchers about the work they do. These collections change the trajectory of archival research in rhetoric and composition by defining this methodology in practical terms, adding a human face to the scholarship, and raising questions about definitions and uses of "archives" and ethical considerations associated with investigating primary materials. Furthermore, contributors' stories are critical to current examinations of the gatekeeping function of archives and the urgent need to maintain and make available primary materials.

Working in the Archives addresses lacuna in archival research. Not until the 2010 publication of this collection has the field witnessed such wide-ranging, useful information about why and how to research archives. Included are essays about finding and gaining access to materials; important discussions about digital and hidden collections on the Web; chapters addressing working with photographs, letters, and student writing; taxonomies for organizing findings; personal accounts about archival research projects; and, perhaps the most enlightening for me, a coauthored essay by archivist Sammie Morris and researcher Shirley Rose entitled "Invisible Hands: Recognizing Archivists' Work to Make Records Accessible." These coauthors introduce researchers in both the humanities and social sciences to archivists' terms and practices, suggesting ways that investigators might recast themselves as archivist-researchers. Interestingly, Luke J. Gilliland-Swetland, archival librarian and museum curator, outlines in "The Provenance of a Profession: The Permanence of the Public Archives and Historical Manuscripts Tradition in American Archival History," two competing opinions of the role of the archivists within the archival professional community: "one that views archivists as members of a larger community of historian-scholars with a responsibility to interpret the documents in their care, and one that defines archivists as information-management professionals with a responsibility to act as 'gatekeepers' for the materials under their control" (121). Roles of researchers and archivists are shifting and expanding as they come under scrutiny. Taking a much broader view, James Purdy in "Three Gifts of Digital Archives" claims that "[i]f we view the Web itself as 'the most important archive ever created' (Miller and Bowdon 594) or 'the largest document ever written; stored in a digital archive' (Gitelman 128), we and our students daily serve as archivists and archival researchers" (Purdy 23).

Interdisciplinary scholarship addressing archival research raises as many questions as it answers, including the following topics:

- ways to locate and interpret archival materials
- ways to accurately describe and portray the condition of primary materials
- ways to refine research questions given the messiness of archival research
- ways to triangulate findings
- connections among researchers, collectors, and archivists
- ways to organize and store findings
- what counts as evidence in archival research
- who gets represented (by whom); who gets silenced and why
- what sorts of methodologies are acceptable in archival research
- ways to revise methods of archival research given new technologies
- ways scholars cast their relationships with materials under scrutiny
- the potential harm in crossing cultural borders
- ways to add to existing archives
- ways to address the gatekeeping function of archives

This rather unwieldy list suggests multiple directions for future research and inquiry. By complicating the theories and practices of archival research, we tell fuller, more inclusive and transparent stories of both the work we do and our findings. This essay attempts to collate and address some of the recurring issues associated with rhetoric and composition archival research.

Current Issues in Archival Research

How Do We Define "Archive"?

Contemporary archival researchers push the boundaries of defining what counts as an archive. No longer are "sanctioned" collections (housed in special collections and recognized research libraries) or traditional venues for rhetorical performance and agency the sole purview of the archival researcher. Katherine E. Tirabassi explains:

> [M]y first direct encounter with the UNH Archives, as part of a collaborative team designing a local writing program archive, reshaped my definitional views of archival research in significant ways.... The generative work of creating this archive reshaped my view of an archive as an inert repository of artifacts to a layered, historical record of dynamic stories. I saw firsthand how artifacts already housed within a university archive could be reimagined with a fresh perspective by a researcher asking a different set of questions than those implied by the archive's established categories. I also saw that artifacts could be added to the archive to extend the historical picture of a given collection or collections.
>
> (170–71)

Archives are now viewed as primary sources for creating knowledge rather than mere storehouses for finding what is already known. History professor James O'Toole explains, "Any archivist who has supervised a collection knows that an ingenious researcher can find uses for records that no creator, collector, or curator ever imagined" (52). Rhetoric and composition scholars, who often investigate materials not originally assembled with writing instruction or instructors in mind, are familiar with creating new knowledge out of collected materials. Consider Kelly Ritter's gendered readings of the Yale, all male, Awkward Squad (basic writing) archives. Her experiences working in archives where her presence "was never intended nor particularly foreseen" left her with a new set of methodological questions (192): 1) what does a homogenous archive have to say to a deliberately excluded investigator who has a research agenda very different from the original purposes of the collection; 2) how can researchers answer "Brereton's call to 'begin asking what is missing from the archive and how it can get there' (574)"; and 3) how can "restricted history . . . open doors for us, as scholars, to reinterpret the histories of our field and ask, 'What can we gain by confronting the discomfort we feel when these historical assumptions are overturned, if unexpectedly, by archival research?'" (193).

Interestingly, in *Rhetoric and Composition as Intellectual Work,* contributors Susan Miller and Susan Wells tout archival scholarship as proof that the work compositionists do is rigorous and scholarly: "[I]f we claim expertise about relations between specific writers, their processes and their texts, we easily grow and successfully divert out-worn attempts to marginalize our teaching and research" (52). Rhetoric and composition scholarship often and necessarily works outside the box, using archival materials in ways that perhaps weren't intended by the collector and often producing what Linda Ferreira-Buckley labels "a revolutionary shift in who counts" (578). Certainly historical literacy studies in which scholars investigate figures and populations falling outside the traditional rhetorical canon expand notions of who and what matters. Wells shows how works by Cheryl Glenn, Jackie Jones Royster, Thomas Miller, and Sharon Crowley expand what is known by recovering historical people, places, and practices by reading "*around* a historical text, in contemporaneous history and analogous collections, often to discover positive value in what is *not* evident. Writing studies leads archivists to look for evidence of writing practices, of pedagogy, and of individual modes of composing, for the sake of identifying the plausible cultural work a text may have accomplished" (45). This redefinition of the role archives play in cultural scholarship is interdisciplinary. Consider Beverly Moss's *A Community Text Arises*, in which Moss adopts an ethnographical methodology to study the literacy practices of three African American churches. Using sermons as community textual evidence and observation as a primary research tool, Moss locates the church within the larger African American community, analyzes literacy practices revealed in sermons, and provides significant cultural, theological, and social commentary.

Judith M. Panitch, research and special projects librarian at the University of North Carolina at Chapel Hill, reminds us that "archives, as 'sites of memory,' are very much products of their time, invested with a meaning that may be changed—as during the French Revolution—by changing beliefs and values" (102). The work of Ann Laura Stoler, professor of anthropology and historical studies at the New School for Social Research, exemplifies this claim. Stoler, who investigates colonial cultures through archival productions, focuses on "archiving as a process rather than archives as things," explaining that "new approaches to colonial studies within the broader 'historical turn' of the last two decades" look "towards a politics of knowledge that reckons with archival genres, cultures of documentation, fictions of access, and archival conventions" (267). Wells shows us how contemporary archival work demands rethinking and explains how the archive "resists knowledge in a number of ways. It refuses closure; often it simply refuses any answer at all. . . . It prompts us, as contending scholars, to resist early resolution of questions that should not be too quickly answered" (58). Comparing this "resistance" of archival methods to similar resistance in ethnographic studies, Wells demonstrates how archives allow for a "loosening of resentment," combating feelings of being underappreciated or undervalued that occur across disciplines. Recovery work in particular leads to legitimacy, "speaks more loudly than the arrogance that neglects" people, texts, practices, and places in the first place. Finally, Wells asserts that archival research allows us to refigure the discipline of rhetoric and composition by more broadly investigating what constitutes the field (59–60).

How Does Our "Positionality" Color the Kinds of Projects We Take On? In crossing cultural, racial, political, and gendered borders, in what ways do we need to tread carefully in terms of representation?

Kirsch and Rohan's collection of eighteen essays, *Beyond the Archives*, takes up issues of "positionality," or the researcher's stance in regard to subject matter, in nearly every chapter. In expanding the range of archival methodologies and tools available to researchers and redefining what constitutes an archive, the contributors foreground their individual relationships to research questions and materials—relationships that often lead to expanding existing notions of what counts as archives and adding voices and venues to scholarly conversations. Two talks at the 2010 meeting of the Coalition of Women Scholars in the History of Rhetoric and Composition (and printed in *Peitho*) illustrate this point. Michelle T. Johnson in "Beginning with the End in Mind: Why I Chose a Career at an HBCU" and Rhea Estelle Lathan in "For Colored Girls who Considered the Academy when Suicide Wasn't Enough: Unceasing Variations in an Early Afrafeminist Academic Career" explain how their research choices are "situated within the nexus" of identity (Lathan 6). By pointedly discussing the reasons they select particular research projects, their personal relationships to the materials at hand, and their prejudices and assumptions, archival researchers write truer narratives—bringing a rich perspective to subjects under investigation while in many cases discovering topics new to rhetorical studies, unexamined collections, and novel venues for rhetorical agency.

Noted historian Wendy Sharer eloquently encourages archival researchers to blend personal experience and professional work, particularly when writing about family archives; she suggests "that we seek out and celebrate the roles that our emotions play in our selection of research projects" rather than soft-pedaling or apologizing for our connections with familial projects (54). Sharer's dissertation, "Rhetoric, Reform, and Political Activism in U.S. Women's Organizations, 1920–1930," based on archival materials found under her grandmother's bed, won the CCCC 2002 James Berlin Memorial Outstanding Dissertation Award. Undeniably, scholars bring a set of preconceived notions, experiences, and perspectives to their topic choices. Even when attempting to have an agenda-free research plan, our humanity often gets in the way. Recent scholarship also addresses issues of positionality when researchers tackle community archives other than their own. Sue Hum and Arabella Lyon succinctly sum up the problems of speaking for others. They explain that when scholars begin working outside their areas of specialization, which often happens in archival research, the chances of misrepresentation increase. Embracing the work of Linda Alcoff, Hum and Lyon suggest that researchers investigating other communities must (1) listen rather than speak and teach, (2) critically examine their standpoints and locations, (3) be receptive to criticism and willing to demonstrate accountability, and (4), most importantly, understand the weight of their claims (160). Adopting a revisionist or recovery methodological stance demands full investigation of the culture or community under scrutiny, along with a healthy dose of respect for cultures different from one's own. Engaging in description of archival materials rather than judgment is particularly important when the researcher is speaking from a position of privilege (Hum and Lyon 160). David Gold's investigation of historically black and women's colleges illustrates the point.

Gold explains that for him "subject position and identity are important, but they do not define [the researcher] entirely" ("Accidental," 16). In "The Accidental Archivist: Embracing Chance and Confusion in Historical Scholarship," Gold shares his experiences being a self-identified "Italian Jew raised in Miami" researching historically black and women's colleges as the subject of his dissertation. Although discouraged and warned by senior scholars that he was committing "career suicide," Gold forged ahead. As he studied these institutions and communities, he discovered a kinship with his subjects, given his own familial and socioeconomic circumstances: "I became determined to write histories that would not merely expand the body of historical knowledge in my field but also do justice to the diverse experiences of students and educators at previously marginalized institutional settings" (17). Gold's revised dissertation, *Rhetoric at the Margins: Revising the History of Writing Instruction in American Colleges, 1873–1947*, won the CCCC 2010 Outstanding Book Award, proving that researchers can effectively study communities to which they do not belong, but they must be cautious and honest while engaging in careful self-examination of their methods and motivations.

In discussing Eastern rhetoric, Bo Wang encourages scholars to examine cultural rhetorics moored to time, place, and politics. In particular, she laments that so much existing research into Eastern artifacts and practices adopts a Western perspective, ignores Asian pedagogy, and dismisses dialogue between East and West (173). Interesting sources examining changes in cultural methodologies include Sucheng Chan's "The Changing Contours of Asian-American Historiography," which traces alterations in the landscape of Asian American historiography practices from the 1850s to the present—including a bibliography of recent work addressing trauma, Asian diasporas, and the social dynamics of Asian culture. In *Rescuing History from the Nation: Questioning Narratives of Modern China*, Prasenjit Duara offers an account of the relationship between nationalism and the concept of linear history. Focusing primarily on China, but also including discussions of India, Duara argues that historians of postcolonial nation-states who adopt linear, evolutionary (and invented) histories have written repressive, exclusionary, and incomplete accounts. Likewise, American Indian scholar Malea D. Powell tells us to listen to ghosts, to refrain from hypothesizing about the artifacts and evidence we find, and instead to examine how cultures of people "who were made less than" appropriated rhetorical actions for their own purposes—in the case of her research subjects, to survive (38). Model analyses of primary texts associated with American Indian rhetoric includes Siobhan Senier's *Voices of American Assimilation and Resistance*, in which the author examines the writings and oratory of three women—white novelist Helen Hunt Jackson, Paiute autobiographer and performer Sarah Winnemucca, and Clackamas Chinook storyteller Victoria Howard—who resisted the federal government's assimilation of Native Americans. Ernest Stromberg's groundbreaking collection *American Indian Rhetorics of Survivance: Word Medicine, Word Magic* presents thirteen multifaceted readings of Native American rhetoric through the lens of autobiographies, memoirs, prophecies, and storytelling traditions.

Finally, Krista Ratcliffe in the contemporary chapter of *The Present State of Scholarship in the History of Rhetoric* explains the importance of theorizing research methods and asking "Who is speaking? For whom? About what? And with what authority or vision?" (199). These questions are important ones for researchers investigating any communities outside their own. Archival researchers must immerse themselves in study of the place, time, and culture they are researching. Talking with members of the community when possible, broadly reading any contemporary materials, addressing pertinent issues of time and place, and triangulating data so that claims have merit are essential in representing cultures and communities.

Is There Harm in Borrowing Methodologies From Other Disciplines?

Experienced archival researchers generally agree that there is little harm in borrowing methods from other disciplines unless the borrowing is superficial—but they speak about the need to proceed cautiously when appropriating other disciplines' research methods. Cheryl Glenn explains, "We in the humanities should not limit ourselves ... to traditional library and archival research." She acknowledges that "we've always been drawing from other fields, picking up their disciplinary lenses to see better what we've recovered. We've long used psychoanalytic, feminist, critical-race, and language-acquisition theories, for example" (message to the author). The 2010 edition of *The Present State of Scholarship in the History of Rhetoric and Composition* serves as a useful reference for researching how this borrowing and assimilation of other disciplines' methodologies—throughout historical periods and across the disciplines—is represented in a myriad of individual scholarly projects grounded in diverse approaches to archival research. In particular, Ratcliffe's chapter on twentieth- and twenty-first-century rhetoric is divided into twenty subheadings, most of which embed borrowings to some degree. However, Thomas Miller cautions that we may have misappropriated methodologies from other fields. He explains, for example, how "[o]ften, too often, archivists claim to be ethnographers when all they provide is an exposition and a couple of interviews with some historical particulars on a place and a time"; ultimately, he embraces borrowing, explaining that "[a]s we have come to understand that there is no authentic source, no originary place or *arche,* our grasp of *the archeological* method has become as unbounded as our sense *of archive.* Through this process, we begin to move beyond disciplinary norms to corroborate our methods against the broader experiences of our times and engage with the collective experience in new ways" (message to the author).

But is there harm in this blending of methods? Does it threaten our identity as a field? Does this borrowing make us a brood parasite, a cuckoo laying our eggs in other disciplinary nests? Barbara L'Eplattenier stresses that in tailoring methods from history and ethnography for our own needs, we "should also recognize that Rhetoric and Composition has its own tradition of methods and methodology that may not conform to other disciplines' ideas of valid research" (message to the author). Likewise, Sharer rejects the idea of disciplinary ownership of methods, claiming as long as research tools "are used responsibly, thoughtfully, and critically," then they are available to all (message to the author). Misunderstanding a methodology or "superficial borrowings" can easily lead to schisms among researchers from varying disciplines. Jordynn Jack, associate professor at the University of North Carolina at Chapel Hill and author of *Science on the Home Front: American Women Scientists in World War II,* points to recent "discussion about this [issue] in rhetoric of science and science studies, especially the tendency to rely on popularized scientific books or findings taken at face value (rather than considered from a rhetorical perspective)" (message to the author). As early as 1995,

Elizabeth A. Flynn in "Feminism and Scientism" cautioned against methodological borrowings from other disciplines that aren't compatible with the goals of rhetoric and composition research. Most fields share what might be labeled an alienation problem, but as prolific archival researcher Katherine Adams reminds us, borrowing and "interdisciplinarity is essential when we look at writing instruction or public rhetoric." She advocates that we overtly discuss borrowings in our methodologies, which will indicate that "the researcher is stretching to learn" (message to the author). To illustrate, Robert R. Johnson in "Complicating Technology: Interdisciplinary Method, the Burden of Comprehension, and the Ethical Space of the Technical Communicator" discusses "the responsibility of understanding the ideologies, contexts, values, and histories of those disciplines from which we [technical communicators] borrow before we begin using their methods and research findings" (75).

Reading scholarship from other disciplines, particularly by archivists and librarians, is key to understanding issues that unify all archival researchers. However, actually working with researchers in other disciplines and placing a concentrated focus on collaboration among scholars with related interests offers a logical way to more thoroughly understand alternative research methods and create mutually satisfying ways to gather and interpret data across disciplinary divides. The success of *Working in the Archives*—written by compositionists, historians, librarians, administrators, communication scholars, high school educators, records managers, visual literacy experts, and government employees—illustrates this point and provides a framework for sharing our expertise across disciplines.

How Can the Archivist's Work Alter Existing Notions of "Text"? How might we appropriate everyday places and artifacts as sites for archival investigation—to add to existing archives?

Brereton and Gannet discuss the differences between "traditional institutional archival sites (the big A archives)" and "out-of-the-way places ... (the small *a* archives)" (675). For the archival researcher, the concept of texts is tied to representations of communities and cultures, collections, and artifacts. Those materials can include letters, pictures, newspapers, statues, government documents and records, committee reports, tools, pottery, interviews, musical recordings, textiles, clothing, quilts, maps, coins, cookbooks, medical reports, etc. ... and, yes, traditional materials typically housed in manuscript libraries. Primary research, examining a wide range of materials and texts, is at the heart of archival investigation and leads to a more inclusionary conception of revisionist and recovery research methods. Glenn argues "that the only way for us to write histories of rhetoric that are truly inclusive and representative of all the people who use (have used) rhetoric purposefully [is] to look beyond the writings of the powerful, political, and aristocratic" (message to the author). Similarly, Jack suggests that the best way to expand notions of text and begin thinking about alternative spaces for investigation is to start "with one's own community." She explains how she and her students began archival investigation with local archives and "used those to spur an investigation into southern women's rhetorical practices" (message to the author). Recent rhetoric and composition scholarship addressing issues of space and place illustrate both Glenn and Jack's challenge to examine archives outside the mainstream and in situ.

Two interesting collections published in 2003, Robert E. Brooke's *Rural Voices: Place-Conscious Education and the Teaching of Writing* and Bruce McComiskey and Cynthia Ryan's *City Comp: Identities, Spaces, Practices,* demonstrate how students and their teachers make meaning that is connected to local exigencies and responsive to societal issues—whether those students and teachers are working in rural or urban settings. Contributors examining writing instruction in at least thirteen cities across the US and, conversely, in a concentrated study of Nebraska teaching practices sponsored by the National Writing Project's Three-Year Rural, Country Schools Program prove Susan Miller's claim that "in writing studies a student theme is not interesting as a historical instance of ability, of assigned topics, or of teachers' comments, unless we account for its archival locale" (46). In 2002, Miller claimed that researchers who study archives of writing instruction must adopt "a new set of descriptive questions" (46):

> What genres, purposes, information or exchanges were written in a specifically demarcated time, place, and political/economic context? Who wrote them? (That is, how is this writer, identifiable or not, situated in relation to prior reading experience, writing lessons, and contemporaneous expectations for class, gender, and racial discourses?) What evidence is there that a writer took form, content, and, even, specific language from already empowered models that create textual authority?
>
> (46)

These questions, posed by Miller a decade ago and motivated by an interest in situated practice, now guide archival methodology.

Social movement rhetoric, another trend within recent scholarship, investigates local archival materials and populations often falling outside what Glenn labels the "powerful, political, and aristocratic"—and in line with Miller's insistence upon investigating local and material circumstances. Contributors to two recent collections—Michelle Smith and Barbara Warnick's *The Responsibilities of Rhetoric* and Sharon McKenzie Stevens and Patricia M. Malesh's *Active Voices: Composing a Rhetoric for Social Movements*—illustrate this line of research. Consider these chapters in the Stevens and Malesh collection: Malesh's own "Sharing Our Recipes: Vegan Conversion Narratives as Social Praxis" in which she examines the power of constructing and telling conversion stories for those who are "insiders" and "outsiders" of social movements; Mary Ann Cain's "'Creating Space' for Community," which integrates identity narratives (of the Three Rivers Jenbé Ensemble) within a discussion of classroom/nonacademic spaces for learning about "difference"; and Moiro K. Amado-Miller's analysis of the language and actions of historical "disorderly women" as a lens for a "strong reading of the rhetorical figure *antistrephon*"—the act of using one's opponent's words against him or her. Likewise, in the Smith and Warnick collection, Gregory Clark's "Rustic Experience and the Rhetorical Work of National Park Architecture," offers an interesting examination of environmental rhetoric in which sermonic spaces are rhetorically manipulated to invoke reverence among park visitors. Also examining liminal spaces and public rhetorical artifacts, Brian McNely in "La Frontera y El Chamizal: Liminality, Territoriality, and Visual Discourse" takes up issues of "rhetorical stratigraphies" associated with the contested physical spaces represented by the Chamizal National Memorial (near El Paso, Texas) and graffiti on physical border markers between El Paso and Juárez. Not only do archival researchers such as these now stipulatively define texts for their own research purposes (regularly adding their own photos of artifacts and venues under investigation), but they also expand traditional notions of rhetorical delivery by studying alternate venues and liminal places for enacting rhetorical agency.

What are Limitations of Storing and Examining Artifacts Online?

Purdy explains: "Literacy in a networked, digital world ... will increasingly involve the ability to ethically, critically, and effectively create, navigate, evaluate, and use digital archives" (25). To turn a fine-tuned ear to required next-generation technologies for conducting archival research, we need to read scholarship produced by library archivists and attend conferences specifically addressing archivists' "ways of knowing"—conferences that traditionally fall outside our disciplinary field. As mentioned, professional archivists have much to tell us about how to go about finding and interpreting primary materials, particularly as our investigations increasingly rely on digital hunts.

Elizabeth Yakel, professor at the University of Michigan School of Information in the areas of Archives and Records Management and Preservation of Information, succinctly discusses ways (and limitations) of accessing primary documents on the Web in "Searching and Seeking in the Deep Web: Primary Sources on the Internet." She includes information for planning a search strategy (rather than relying on traditional search engines); useful sources, including directories, online bibliographic directories, and finding aids (along with warnings about their limitations); and digitized primary sources. Yakel introduces terms that may not be familiar to even seasoned historians and archival researchers, including "synonym generation, chaining, name collection, pearl growing, and successive segmentation" and explains that by understanding archivists' terms, researchers can gain fuller access to online repositories and learn how to link disparate collections (113).

Limitations of digital research include the inability to adequately gauge the size, shape, and smell of archives; the possibility that, given budget limitations, libraries and other repositories won't have the personnel or financial resources to update materials to accommodate new technological formats; limited access to marginalia (which is often faint and doesn't reproduce well); and lack of finding aids or access to librarians' expertise. Another, perhaps more esoteric, limitation concerns place. Kirsch and Rowan admit that the impetus of many archival research projects is influenced by serendipity and chance, along with location and creativity (5). This "serendipitous" nature of archival research is the focus of Lori Ostergard's interviews with experienced archivists, "Open to the Possibilities: Seven Tales of Serendipity in the Archives," which illustrate "the unpredictable interplay between serendipity and process" (40)—encounters that most often occur in physical spaces. Conducting only digital searches limits opportunities for chance findings in much the same way looking up a book online is very different than perusing library book shelves. While it is difficult to capture the romantic physical elements of archival research online (smell of old books, tactile sensations, quiet and reverent atmosphere), and maintaining long-term access to online documents is a real concern given changing technology, digitizing archives does allow access to collections and artifacts for a far greater number of researchers, lessens the expense and travel difficulties associated with visiting faraway collections, greatly benefits interdisciplinary research, and potentially allows researchers to augment existing archives.

Co-directors Brad Lucas and Margaret Strain of the Rhetoric and Composition Sound Archives (RCSA), a "national organization dedicated to the collection, production, and preservation of audio, visual, and print interviews that document the history of rhetoric and composition studies," offer an excellent discussion of the practical, theoretical, and ethical aspects of considering and evaluating alternative texts—in this case oral interviews—in "Keeping the Conversation Going: The Archive Thrives on Interviews and Oral History." They discount charges that oral interviews are flawed examples of primary evidence because of issues of reliability, subjectivity, and validity—offering convincing arguments that oral evidence should be given the same consideration and attention as print texts and providing researchers with the methods and tools to conduct, edit, and store oral interviews that are ethically sound, reliable primary sources (260). In particular, researchers considering alternative texts and those studying artifacts as text must consider issues of archive preparation, setting and location, disclosure, IRB approval, technology, transcription, and representations. Lucas and Strain thoroughly address these matters and discuss ways for archivists and researchers to work in tandem to promote scholarly research.

Unfortunately, the promise held out by this excellent project (like so many digital collections) is limited by its brief content, difficulties in accessing it online, and funding. Our field needs funded, organized, and accessible resources like RCSA to ensure longevity of and accessibility to diverse archival sources. Initiatives such as the Immigrant Archive Project—sponsored by the Latino Broadcasting Project and dedicated to preserving immigrants' stories in their own words (and videos)—serves as an excellent example of creating, maintaining, and accessing a broader archival canon. Ultimately, the advantages of online research far outweigh the limitations and encourage us to seek solutions to locating, codifying, preserving, and interpreting digital archives.

How Can We Codify Methods of Corroboration and Issues of Reliability in Archival Research? What role does storytelling play in archival research?

Brereton and Gannett warn that "archivists need to acknowledge their own definitions and agendas in the ongoing creation or use of any archive"; they urge archival researchers to document their methodologies and methods, including "the narratives of archival construction itself" (677). Likewise, Julie Garbus admits that for many archival researchers "methodologies remain our secret" (88). She explains how issues of time and money, along with the conflict between wanting to tell a convincing story and detailing the messiness of archival research, complicate the documentation of research methodologies. Brereton and Gannett's interchangeable use of the labels "archivists" and "archival researchers" is interesting and certainly builds on new scholarship implying that primary researchers in some cases also need to become archivists. This new breed of "archivist-researcher" studies existing materials and artifacts while also creating or compiling materials into new collections, reflecting specific scholarly interests.

Furthermore, the compilation of primary and secondary research sources and codification of materials and methodologies is central to the role of the archivist-researcher. Lisa Mastrangelo explains "that archival documents need to be triangulated with general documents on your topic in order to avoid making major history blunders. . . . Selective use of materials leads to 'erroneous conclusions.'" Interestingly, she notes the lack of oversight by publishers when it comes to fact-checking archival sources (message to the author). Corroboration of data is critical to avoid skewed histories; however, production and copy editors rarely ask for the kinds of validation of archival sources that constitute common author queries when working with published materials. In discussing "what counts as evidence in archival research," noted historian Nan Johnson looks "for the definitive generalization." She explains, "If I am discussing women's education at schools of elocution, the study of one institution is not sufficient to make an argument for typicality but the study of ten institutions is" (message to the author). *Triangulation* is the watchword among archival researchers in codifying data; interestingly, archival researchers frequently discuss triangulation in connection with storytelling—based on rich, thick investigation and corroboration of data. Adams explains how storytelling captures the essence of archival methodology:

> Archival research is all about storytelling because through all the documents that you study, you are figuring out the nature of a life, whether it be public or private, for a summer or for fifty years. Documents must grow into storytelling or they are not really worth writing about. But the path of document to story, of course, is a treacherous one, with inferences made by the writer, often based on her own prejudices, and thus her own story.
>
> (message to the author)

Researchers' back stories about the processes of discovering materials, the rationale and reasons for their selected narrative structure, and tales of rigorous research paired with the sometimes serendipitous nature of archival investigation are critical to producing ethical and transparent scholarship.

Thomas Miller claims that "as with archiving, storying is about framing—about contexting"; he explains that archivists and "ethnographers spend time coming to know a people and their place in the world, weaving all the texts they can find into a 'thick description' that they triangulate against the teller and the told to garner a felt sense of how a people understands their collective experience" (message to the author). Unified storytelling is critical to interpreting and disseminating data. Suzanne Bordelon, author of *A Feminist Legacy: The Rhetoric and Pedagogy of Gertrude Buck,* warns that "[g]iven the storytelling and argument-laden nature of historiography, we need to be careful to balance an appealing style, a strong story with historical depth." To successfully do this, she suggests that we may need to excerpt heavily from primary sources "so that readers can examine the evidence themselves and arrive at their own conclusions" (message to the author). To illustrate, Jane Donawerth in *Conversational Rhetoric: The Rise and Fall of Women's Tradition, 1600–1900* argues that before women began writing composition texts for mixed-gendered audiences, they engaged in a rhetorical theory based on "conversation, letter writing, testimony and preaching, elocution, and eventually public speaking" (1). Donawerth includes excerpts from a wide range of "small *a* archives" and cites the work of scores of women rhetors spanning three hundred years. Studies like the 2012 *Conversational Rhetoric* emphasize a multilayered story replete with examples of archival data that depends upon interpretation from both researcher and reader.

How Do Scholars Researching Archives Organize and Store Data, Add to Existing Archives? How can we make sense of what we find and easily revisit materials?

Very little has been written about organizing archival evidence within rhetoric and composition; however, anyone examining manuscript collections and the wealth of secondary and tangential information in order to immerse oneself in a period or place—or triangulate data—quickly realizes the difficulty in storing or making sense of findings. Other ever-present circumstances facing primary researchers further complicate organizational strategies: (1) we often don't know what we'll find in the archives (despite finding aids) or what information will be important later and (2) the practical reality that researchers often don't have access or finances to revisit a physical place or collection. Thomas Miller explains, "To 'make sense of what we find,' and how to find it, we need to think about archiving texts as a mode of contexting—of situating utterances in fields of discourse that are grounded in social transactions and institutional hierarchies. Virtual texts challenge our materialist methodologies to configure spaces and places that are engaged with lived experience" (message to the author). Given the sheer volume of materials present on the Web, Purdy claims that "[i]n digital archives researchers do not have to work as hard to find relevant materials; instead they have to work hard to determine which available materials are useful.... Research becomes less about finding particular texts and more about sorting, assessing, and vetting them" (29).

Tarez Samra Graban in "Emergent Taxonomies: Using Tension and Forum to Organize Primary Texts" offers comprehensive theoretical underpinnings and practical grids for cataloging what we find. In addition, she ethically organizes materials based on original arrangement, silences in the collection, and "chain of custody" (206–7). Nan Johnson, in "Autobiography of an Archivist," offers a much more physical and visual representation for organizing data and framing research questions—but one that proves useful as well; she describes her method of physically arranging and labeling collected data in a wheel or rim in order to determine order and patterns. Morris and Rose discuss ways to inventory uncataloged materials, providing as illustration a most useful inventory of James Berlin's papers (71–78). Building archives of collected materials is important work and represents one of the most-needed areas of scholarly attention within discussions of archival method. Again, consulting professional archivists and librarians is a logical place to start; journals such as *Archivaria* and the *American Archivist* regularly address issues of documentation and storage—along with theoretical issues associated with the role of the archivists. Randall C. Jimerson's *American Archival Studies: Readings in Theory and Practice* (2000), which includes twenty-eight essays written by scholar-archivists from many disciplines on a wide range of archival issues, and James M. O' Toole and Richard J. Cox's collection *Understanding Archives and Manuscripts* (2006) offer divergent opinions and advice covering a myriad of topics from documenting, storing, and preserving strategies to theories for appraising archives to considerations of researchers' needs.

Only rarely do archival researchers see themselves overtly as archivists (and vice versa), when in fact professionals from both fields regularly engage in dual acts. The emerging trend in archival scholarship to tell research stories and share experiences about means for codifying, interpreting, and appropriating materials under investigation becomes critical as emerging digital technologies invite Web users to make meaning by adding information to existing archives and providing easy access to do so.

Conclusion

In this essay, I have discussed issues that repeatedly surface in the scholarship on archival research. Other troublesome concerns meriting further attention, according to Brereton and Gannett, include "federal restrictions on the uses of student texts" and "the current state of the archives in composition studies" (678). Additionally, the messiness of many archives prohibits discovery and access, while limited library funds allocated for organizing and maintaining archival collections stand in the way of cataloging or preserving acquired materials in a timely manner. The training of archival researchers is an increasing concern in recent scholarship as well; survey courses in composition and rhetoric methodologies routinely gloss over archival research or align it only with historical investigations. As Sharer explains, "Many of us ... who are currently doing archival research in composition and rhetoric have developed/learned our research methods on our own—by reading about research methods in other fields, by studying archiving practices, by stumbling around in a trial-and-error process, etc." (message to the author). Legal and ethical issues, material conditions, and educational concerns represent three areas ripe for future investigation in archival research.

Ultimately, archives shape identity. Expanding definitions of archives, digital means for easily adding to existing archives, the increasing numbers of researchers who see themselves as archivist-researchers, and codified information for working in the archives pave the way for composition and rhetoric scholars to make new knowledge through archival research. By abandoning gatekeeping notions traditionally associated with archival research, we can move toward Glenn and Enoch's hope that "if we consciously and carefully activate the materials in the archives, we might discover ways to address the present scholarly moment meaningfully and announce the near future insightfully" (337). Brereton tells us that "[o]ur term 'archive' is hardly static"; the same can be said of archival methodologies. Researchers are now dynamically redefining the role archival investigations play in the scholarship of rhetoric and composition.

Works Cited

Adams, Katherine. Message to the author, 10 Aug. 2011. Email.

Amado-Miller, Moiro K. "Disorderly Women: Appropriating the Power Tools in Civic Discourses." Stevens and Malesh 69–91.

Bordelon, Suzanne. *A Feminist Legacy: The Rhetoric and Pedagogy of Gertrude Buck.* Carbondale: Southern Illinois UP, 2007. Print.

———. Message to the author. 4 Aug. 2011. Email.

Brereton, John C. "Rethinking Our Archive: A Beginning." *College English* 61.5 (May 1999): 574–76. Print.

Brereton, John C., and Cinthia Gannett. "Review: Learning from the Archives." *College English* 73.6 (2011): 672–81. Print.

Brooke, Robert E., ed. *Rural Voices: Place-Conscious Education and the Teaching of Writing.* New York: Teachers College P, 2003. Print.

Cain, Mary Ann. "'Creating Space' for Community: Radical Identities and Collective Praxis." Stevens and Malesh 181–96.

Chan, Sucheng. "The Changing Contours of Asian-American Historiography." *Rethinking History* 11 (2007): 125–47. Print.

Clark, Gregory. "Rustic Experience and the Rhetorical Work of National Park Architecture." Smith and Warnick 201–13.

Connors, Robert. "Dreams and Play: Historical Method and Methodology." *Methods and Methodology in Composition Research.* Ed. Gesa Kirsch and Patricia Sullivan. Carbondale: Southern Illinois UP, 1992. 15–36. Print.

Donahue, Patricia, and Gretchen Flesher Moon, eds. *Local Histories: Reading the Archives of Composition.* Pittsburgh: U of Pittsburgh P, 2007. Print

Donawerth, Jane. *Conversational Rhetoric: The Rise and Fall of a Women's Tradition, 1600–1900.* Carbondale: Southern Illinois UP, 2012. Print.

Duara, Prasenjit. *Rescuing History from the Nation: Questioning Narratives of Modern China.* Chicago: U of Chicago P, 1995. Print.

Ferreira-Buckley, Linda. "Rescuing the Archives from Foucault." *College English* 61.5 (May 1999): 577–83. Print.

Flynn, Elizabeth A. "Feminism and Scientism." *College Composition and Communication* 46.3 (1995): 353–68. Print.

Gaillet, Lynée Lewis, ed., with Winifred Bryan Horner. *The Present State of Scholarship in the History of Rhetoric: A Twenty-First Century Guide.* 2nd ed. Columbia: University of Missouri P, 2010. Print

Garbus, Julie. "Vida Scudder in the Archives and in the Classroom." Ed. Patricia Donahue and Gretchen Flesher Moon. *Local Histories: Reading the Archives of Composition.* Pittsburgh: U of Pittsburgh P, 2007: 77–93. Print.

Gilliland-Swetland, Luke J. "The Provenance of a Profession: The Permanence of the Public Archives and Historical Manuscripts Tradition in American Archival History." Jimerson 123–41.

Gitelman, Lisa. *Always Already New: Media, History, and the Data of Culture.* Cambridge, MA: MIT UP, 2006. Print.

Glenn, Cheryl. Message to the author. 2 Aug. 2011. Email.

Glenn, Cheryl, and Jessica Enoch. "Drama in the Archives: Rereading Methods, Rewriting History." *College Composition and Communication* 61.2 (2009): 321–42. Print.

Gold, David. "The Accidental Archivist: Embracing Chance and Confusion in Historical Scholarship." Kirsch and Rohan 13–19.

———. *Rhetoric at the Margins: Revising the History of Writing Instruction in American Colleges, 1873–1947*. Carbondale: Southern Illinois UP, 2008. Print.

Graban, Tarez Samra, "Emergent Taxonomies: Using Tension and Forum to Organize Primary Texts." Ramsey et al. 206–19.

Hum, Sue, and Arabella Lyon. "Recent Advances in Comparative Rhetoric." *The Sage Handbook of Rhetorical Studies*. Thousand Oaks: Sage. 2009. 153–65. Print.

Immigrant Archive Project. Latino Broadcasting Company. 2011. Web. 24 Jan. 2012.

Jack, Jordynn. Message to the author. 8 Aug. 2011. Email.

———. *Science on the Home Front: American Women Scientists in World War II*. Urbana: U of Illinois P, 2009. Print.

Jimerson, Randall C., ed. *American Archival Studies: Readings in Theory and Practice*. Chicago: Society of American Archival, 2000. Print.

Johnson, Michelle T. "Beginning with the End in Mind: Why I Chose a Career at an HBCU." *Peitho* 13, no. 1 (Spring 2011): 8–9. Web. 4 July 2012.

Johnson, Nan. "Autobiography of an Archivist." Ramsey et al. 290–300.

———. Message to the author. 29 July 2011. Email.

Johnson, Robert R. "Complicating Technology: Interdisciplinary Method, the Burden of Comprehension, and the Ethical Space of the Technical Communicator." *Technical Communication Quarterly* 7.1 (1998): 75–98. Print.

Kirsch, Gesa E., and Liz Rohan, eds. *Beyond the Archives: Research as a Lived Process*. Carbondale: Southern Illinois UP, 2008. Print.

Lathan, Rhea Estelle. "For Colored Girls Who Considered the Academy When Suicide Wasn't Enough: Unceasing Variations in an Early Afrafeminist Academic Career." *Peitho* 13, no. 1 (Spring 2011): 6–7. Web. 4 July 2012.

L'Eplattenier, Barbara. "An Argument for Archival Research Methods: Thinking Beyond Methodology." *College English* 72.1 (2009). 67–79. Print.

———. Message to the author. 10 Aug. 2011. Email.

Lucas, Brad E., and Margaret Strain. "Keeping the Conversation Going: The Archive Thrives on Interviews and Oral History." Ramsey et al. 259–77.

———. dirs. *Rhetoric and Composition Sound Archives*. Texas Christian U. 2007. Web. 12 July 2011.

Mailloux, Steven. "Reading Archives, Reading Typos." *College English* 61.5 (1999): 584–90. Print.

Malesh, Patricia M. "Sharing Our Recipes: Vegan Conversion Narratives as Social Praxis." Stevens and Malesh 131–45.

Mastrangelo, Lisa. Message to the author. 19 July 2011. Email.

McComiskey, Bruce, and Cynthia Ryan, eds. *City Comp: Identities, Spaces, Practices*. Albany: State U of New York P, 2003. Print.

McNely, Brian. "La Frontera y El Chamizal: Liminality, Territoriality, and Visual Discourse. Smith and Warnick 96–114.

Miller, Susan. "Writing Studies as a Mode of Inquiry." *Rhetoric and Composition as Intellectual Work*. Ed. Gary Olson. Carbondale: Southern Illinois UP, 2002. 41–54. Print.

Miller, Thomas. Message to the author. 3 Aug. 2011. Email.

Miller, Thomas P., and Melody Bowdon. "A Rhetorical Stance on the Archives of Civic Action." *College English* 61.5 (1999): 574–76. Print.

Morris, Sammie L., and Shirley K. Rose. "Invisible Hands: Recognizing Archivists' Work to Make Records Accessible." Ramsey et al. 51–78.

Moss, Beverly. *A Community Text Arises: A Literate Text and a Literacy Tradition in African-American Churches.* New York: Hampton. 2003. Print

Ostergaard, Lori. "Open to the Possibilities: Seven Tales of Serendipity in the Archives." Ramsey et al. 40+. Print.

O'Toole, James. "The Symbolic Significance of Archives." Jimerson 47–72.

O'Toole, James M., and Richard J. Cox. *Understanding Archives and Manuscripts.* Chicago: Society of American Archivists, 2006.

Panitch, Judith M. "Liberty, Equality, Posterity? Some Archival Lessons from the Case of the French Revolution." Jimerson 101–22. Print.

Powell, Malea D. "Down by the River, or How Susan Lafleshe Picotte Can Teach Us about Alliance as a Practice of Survivance." *College English* 67 (2004): 38–60. Print.

Purdy, James. "Three Gifts of Digital Archives." *Journal of Literacy and Technology* 12.3 (2011): 24–29. Web. 11 Feb. 2012.

Ramsey, Alexis, Wendy Sharer, Barbara L'Eplattenier, und Lisa Mastrangelo, eds. *Working in the Archives: Practical Research Methods in Rhetoric and Composition.* Carbondale: Southern Illinois UP, 2010. Print.

Ratcliffe, Krista. "The Twentieth- and Twenty-First Centuries." *The Present State of Scholarship in the History of Rhetoric: A Twenty-First Century Guide.* Ed. Lynée Lewis Gaillet, with Winifred Bryan Horner. Columbia: U of Missouri P, 2010. 185–236. Print.

Ritter, Kelly. "(En)gendering the Archives for Basic Writing Research." Ramsey et al. 181–94.

Senier, Siobhan. *Voices of American Indian Assimilation and Resistance: Helen Hunt Jackson. Sarah Winnemucca, and Victoria Howard.* Norman: U of Oklahoma P, 2003. Print.

Sharer, Wendy. Message to the author. 4 Aug. 2011. Email.

———. "Rhetoric, Reform, and Political Activism in U.S. Women's Organizations, 1920–1930." Diss. Pennsylvania State U, 2001. Print.

Smith, Michelle, and Barbara Warnick, eds. *The Responsibilities of Rhetoric.* Long Grove: Waveland P, 2010. Print.

Stevens, Sharon McKenzie, and Patricia M. Malesh, eds. *Active Voices: Composing a Rhetoric for Social Movements.* Albany: State University of New York P, 2009. Print.

Stoler, Ann Laura. "Colonial Archives and the Arts of Governance: On the Content in the Form." *Archives, Documentation, and Institutions of Social Memory: Essays from the Sawyer Seminar.* Ed. Frances X. Blouin Jr. and William G. Rosenberg. Ann Arbor: U of Michigan P, 2006: 267–79. Print.

Stromberg, Ernest, *American Indian Rhetorics of Survivance: Word Medicine, Word Magic.* Pittsburgh: U of Pittsburgh P, 2006. Print.

Tirabassi, Katherine E. "Journeying into the Archives: Exploring the Pragmatics of Archival Research." Ramsey et al. 169–80. Print.

Tolar Burton, Vicki. "The Speaker Respoken: Material Rhetoric as Feminist Methodology." *College English* 61.5 (1999): 545–73. Print.

Wang, Bo. "A Survey of Research in Eastern Rhetoric." *Rhetoric Review* 23 (2004): 171–81. Print.

Wells, Susan. "Claiming the Archive for Rhetoric and Composition." *Rhetoric and Composition as Intellectual Work.* Ed. Gary Olson. Carbondale: Southern Illinois UP, 2002. 55–64. Print.

Yakel, Elizabeth. "Searching and Seeking in the Deep Web: Primary Sources on the Internet." Ramsey et al. 102–18.

INDEX

academic skeptics 24
accession *see* archival accession
accession record *see* archival accession record
activism: civic 138; narrative-driven 282; socio-political 138
Adams, Katherine 303, 307
Addison, Joseph 22
Adisa, Opal Palmer 84, 86
Adorno, Theodor W. 18
affirmative action 68
African American: churches 299; community 79, 172, 299; women 3, 82, 83, 85, 100, 131, 191
agency, historical 183
Agnew, Lois 7, 92, 128, 234, 251
Air Force Association 158
Alabama State University 32
Alcoff, Linda 135–6, 300
Althusser, Louis 250
Altick, Richard D. 190
Ambrose, Stephen 160
American Archivist 308
American Legion 158
Ames, Roger 252
annals 283, 287
Annual Conference on Rhetorical Criticism 127
Anzaldúa, Gloria 84
archaeology 21, 23, 99, 123–5
Archimedes 13
archival: accession 201–2, 205, 209, 214–15, 261; accession record 222, 262; chain of custody 202, 219, 308; description 208–9, 212; digitization 1; education 258, 291; ethnography 7, 282–4, 287–91; exploration, praxis-driven 218; gatekeepers 297; historian 280–1, 283–5, 291; integrity 202–3, 206–7; inventory 202, 211, 214, 227, 262, 308; materials, field-specific 185; method (*see* method, archival); methodology (*see* methodology, archival); preservation 6, 149, 154, 156, 190, 200–2, 206–8, 216, 220, 306; processing 200–1, 215; protocols 263; research method (*see* method, archival); research methodology (*see* methodology, archival); scholarship 3, 183, 272, 282, 298, 309; serendipity 2, 173, 185, 258, 305; silences 218, 233, 236, 308; theory 200–2, 215, 289; training 1, 8, 111, 173, 259, 269, 273
Archivaria 308
Archives on the History of Writing and Writing Instruction 190
archives: digital 8, 212, 236, 257, 265, 273, 290, 292, 296–7, 305–6, 308–9; informal 189
archivist historian 171
archivist-as-ethnographer 284
archivist-researcher 4, 6
archons 273
Arens, Katherine 111
Argumentation and Advocacy 104
Aristotelian rhetoric 13, 20, 29, 35, 43, 106–7
Aristotle 13, 18, 24, 26, 28, 45–6, 48, 62–3, 70, 73, 102, 106, 112, 121, 235, 244; Efficient Causes 13; Final Causes 13; Lyceum 17, 24; *polis* 13, 15; *Rhetoric* 16; *têchnê* 93
Arnold, John H. 175
Arnold, Thomas 111–12, 115
ars dictaminis 29
Art Institute of Chicago 165
Aspasia of Miletus 3, 64–5, 67, 70–3, 80, 132–4, 193, 245
Atlantic Monthly 53
Atwill, Janet 3, 63, 91, 92, 109, 245
authenticity 24, 202–3

Bacon, Francis 30, 45–6
Bain, Alexander 51
Ball, Stephen J. 285
Ballif, Michelle 8, 68
Barlowe, Jamie 68
Barnard's 52
Barrett, Harold 67, 127–8
Barton, Ellen 220–1
Baskerville, Barnett 122–3
Benedict, Ruth 137
Benjamin, Walter 45
Bennett Jr., W. Burr 161
Bennett, William 48
Bergmann, Linda 285–6
Berlin, James 2–3, 6, 18, 25–6, 29, 33, 36–7, 41, 52, 61, 63, 66, 92, 95, 107, 177, 183, 187, 200–2, 204–12, 214–17, 236, 252, 282, 300, 308
Bhaba, Homi K. 84
Bibb, T. Clifford 32
Biesecker, Barbara A. 5, 68–71, 97, 156
Birmingham, Elizabeth 5, 165
Bizzell, Patricia 20–1, 63–4, 67–9, 71, 74, 131, 133–5, 156, 173, 235, 252
Black, Edwin 104
Blair, Carole 69–70, 97
Blair, Hugh 22, 114
Bloomer, W. Martin 246
body politic 22, 34, 241, 251
Bordelon, Suzanne 307
Bordo, Susan 70, 72, 97
Bourdieu, Pierre 93–4, 247
Bowdon, Melody 136, 173, 258, 296–7
box (level of description) 212, 214, 262
Brandt, Deborah 236
Brereton, John 7, 115, 173, 183, 187, 189–90, 291, 295–6, 298, 303, 306, 309
Brice Heath, Shirley 235
British Academy 114
Britt, Beth 100
Brockriede, Wayne 104
Brooke, Robert E. 304
Brooks, Kevin 92
Brown, Stuart 73, 108
Browne, Sir Thomas 22
browsing 266–7, 272
Bryant, Donald C. 122
Bryn Mawr College 187
Buchanan, Lindal 235, 239

Buehl, Jonathan 7, 256, 260
Burke, Edmund 128
Burke, Frank G. 203
Burke, Kenneth 6, 48, 63, 102, 183–96; dramatism 6, 183–4, 186, 190; pentad 6, 183–4, 195–6; poetics 249; ratios 6; terministic screens 14, 53–4, 78, 184, 192, 274; trained incapacities 6
Burkean comedy 43
Burton, Vicki Tolar 7, 234–5, 251, 296
Butler, Judith 159

Cain, Mary Ann 304
California State University, Hayward 127
Cambridge University 95, 114
Cambridge University Press 114
Campbell, George 22
Campbell, Karlyn Kohrs 6, 68–9, 130, 136–7, 224, 228
capitalism, monopolistic 25
Caplan, Harry 127–8, 139
Carnegie Mellon University 15, 207
Carpenter, Ronald 103
Carr, Jean Ferguson 186, 189
cataloguing 6, 209, 288
Cavendish, Margaret 132–3
Center for Southwest Research 194
Cereta, Laura 68
Chan, Sucheng 301
Chicago Historical Society 166
Christian, Barbara 83
Chronicle of Higher Education 165
chronicles 283
Chute, Tamar 7, 256, 260, 276
Cicero 63, 102, 108, 112, 246
Cintron, Ralph 7, 247, 251
civic engagement 8, 81, 136, 187, 229
Cixous, Hélène 16, 22, 43, 68
Clark, Gregory 173, 304
Clark, Suzanne 68
Clarke, Danielle 228
Clarke, Kenneth 119
classical studies 24, 38, 117, 123, 126, 240, 243, 251
classicists 45, 61, 93, 109, 118
Clemson University 249
close reading 4, 123
Coalition of Women Scholars in the History of Rhetoric and Composition 300

coeducation 57–8
Cohen, Randy 286
Coleridge, Samuel Taylor 16
College English 4, 53, 55, 130, 173, 177, 296
Collingwood, Robin G. 115
Collins, Vicki 68
colonialism 244
common good 7, 13, 233
community: Aristotelian (*see* Aristotle, *polis*); community, cultural 79–82, 125, 131 2, 137, 185, 260, 299–300, 302–3; discourse/rhetorical 19, 57, 64–5, 74, 78, 131, 190, 236, 283; marginalized 3, 80, 109; of practice 287–9; professional 92, 96, 147, 201, 297; scholarly 15, 21, 26, 41, 96, 100, 119, 124–6, 131, 134, 185, 216, 243, 282, 287, 297; of women 64–5, 68, 187, 252
composition, multimodal 260, 269
composition and rhetoric *see* rhetoric and composition
composition studies 19–20, 41, 50–1, 53, 62, 105, 147–9, 152, 183, 188, 209, 220, 235, 248, 260, 272, 280, 282–90, 292, 306, 309; ethnographic study of 284, 286
Conference on College Composition and Communication (CCCC) 1–3, 8, 18, 53, 74, 86 87, 91, 106–11, 115, 119, 127, 189, 241, 251, 272, 295, 300–1
confidential materials (handling within an archive) 210
Connors, Robert J. 2–3, 14–15, 19–20, 25, 28–9, 31, 34, 36, 38, 41, 43, 50, 107, 185, 187, 191, 273, 295
Construction News and Western Architect 166
contextualist research paradigm 6, 220
Cooper, Anna Julia 86
Corax 21, 63, 125
Corbett, Edward P.J. 3, 63, 68, 92, 138–9, 245
Cornell School of Rhetoric 127
Cornell University 128
Council of Writing Program Administrators 147
Court, Franklin 95
Covino, William 63
Cox, Richard J. 309
critical thinking 8
criticism: external 2, 56–7; formalist, 60; internal 2, 56–8; literary 33–4, 58, 122–3; New Criticism 60, 123; rhetorical 69, 103–4, 117, 122–3, 127, 136

cross-cultural dialogue 242
Crowell, Laura 127–8, 139
Crowley, Sharon 2, 6, 15, 20, 26, 30, 38, 40, 63, 67, 107, 172, 177, 187, 299
Culler, Jonathan 34
cultural boundaries 80, 84
cultural literacy *see* literacy, cultural
current-traditional pedagogy 1, 106
Cushman, Ellen 100

D.C. Heath 51
daily theme 57
Darwin, Charles 30
Davis, Angela 85
Davis, Miles 85
de Certeau, Michel 65, 133, 239
de Man, Paul 250
de Oliveira, Rosiska Darcy 139–40
de Pizan, Christine 68
deep web 8, 305
Deleuze, Gilles 22, 45, 94
Democritus 24
depth of field 47–8
Derrida, Jacques 115, 134, 136, 158, 167, 249, 273
Descartes, René 112
Detweiler, Trula 256–7, 262, 267, 272
diachronic readings 4, 124
dialectic 3, 13–14, 17–18, 21, 26–7, 29, 38, 41–3, 46, 48, 78, 80, 109, 124, 136, 242; Marxian 43
digital borders 236
Diotima of Mantinea 68, 106, 133, 137
diplomatics 6, 220
discourse: analysis 6, 219–20; community 57; cross-boundary 3, 78–9, 85, 195
documentary records 8
documentation strategy 149–54
Dolmage, Jay 7, 236, 251
Donahue, Patricia 173, 258, 296
Donawerth, Jane 189, 308
Donne, John 48
double bind 6, 224, 228
dramatism *see* Burke, Kenneth, dramatism
Du Bois, W.E.B. 82
Duara, Prasenjit 301

Eble, Michelle 8
Ede, Lisa 127

education 71, 86, 102, 108, 117, 124, 147, 170, 185, 207, 226, 233, 245–8, 253, 257, 262, 309; American 52; archival (*see* archival, education); change 57, 185, 256; classical 96, 126; elementary 256; establishment 19; goals or standards 47; graduate 121; journals (*see* journals, education); lack of 119; literacy (*see* literacy education); media 262; Mexican 185; practices 47, 94, 185; rhetorical 185–6, 191–3, 246, 252; statistics 56; Victorian 94; women 307

Educational Review 52
Efficient Causes *see* Aristotle, Efficient Causes
EGI tradition (Empedocles-Gorgias-Isocrates) 106
Ehninger, Douglas 66, 71, 97
Elliot, Clark 149
Ellis, David 267
encoded description (EAD) 209
English Journal 53, 55
English Public Record Act 112
Enoch, Jessica 6–7, 183, 235, 238, 251–2, 295, 309
Enola Gay controversy 5, 158–9, 161
Enos, Richard Leo 4, 34, 37–9, 42, 63, 67, 73, 99–100, 117, 132, 138–9, 171, 177; classicist 45; panel organizer 3, 91–2; panelist 2, 15, 20, 26, 29, 31, 34, 42, 107; "Recovering the Lost Art" 132
Enos, Theresa 32, 73–4, 91–2; panel organizer 3, 91
ephemera 53, 56, 185, 249, 258
Erasmus 246
Erikson, Erik 70
ethea 235, 250
ethnography 100, 194, 253, 284–7, 290, 302, 307; archival (*see* archival, ethnography); of composition studies (*see* composition studies, ethnographic study of); dialogic 194; distinct activity phases 284; research (*see* research, ethnographic); resistance to 299; social stance 285
ethopoeia 246
ethos 26, 28, 125, 177–8, 234–6, 250, 281–2, 295
etiquette, 236
exemplars (disciplinary) 92–3, 127, 258

Fell, Martha 68
female tokenism 68

feminism 40, 64, 70, 72, 134, 172, 272, 303; methodology (*see* methodology, feminist); research (*see* research, feminist); as a resistance to post-modern critique 65; rhetoric 69, 104, 193; scholarship 68, 70, 97; theory 70, 97, 139, 193
Ferreira-Buckley, Linda 1, 3–4, 7, 91, 94, 109, 111, 132, 134–5, 140, 171, 173–4, 195, 258, 281, 283, 296, 298
Feyerabend, Paul 44
Fields, Anne 7, 256, 260
Final Causes *see* Aristotle, Final Causes
finding aid 8–9, 149, 171–5, 205, 209–10, 212–16, 257, 262–3, 265, 270, 273, 277, 305, 308; archivist acting as 203–4, 210; container list 212, 214–15; internet 212–13, 305; inventory 202, 227, 267; public 203–5, 210, 216
Fischer, Walter 34
Fisher, Stephen 174
Flax, Jane 70, 97
Flower, Linda 29, 35–6, 44
Flynn, Elizabeth A. 303
folder (level of description) 212, 214–15, 222, 225
fonds (level of description) 212
formalist criticism *see* criticism, formalist
forum 6, 218, 223–4, 228, 308
Foster, Allen 267
Foucault, Michel 3, 43, 111, 114, 134, 136, 246, 248
French Revolution 113, 203, 299
Freshwater, Helen 158
Frink, Henry 58

Gagarin, Michael 118
Gaillet, Lynée Lewis 1, 7–9, 266, 281, 295
Gale, Xin Liu 4, 130, 132, 134, 177
Galen of Pergamum 186
Gannett, Cinthia 190, 224, 295, 306, 309
Garbus, Julie 306
Ge, Xuemei 267
Geertz, Clifford 95, 235
gender: analysis 73; hierarchy 131, 137; identity 3, 71, 131, 133, 139, 141; politics 22, 69, 72, 96, 135, 137, 140–1; and power (*see* power, related to gender); roles, fixed 72, 139, 224; studies 3, 64–5, 69–72, 97; theory 70–1, 96–7
gendering, societal 72

Genung, John 58
Gere, Anne Ruggles 183, 196, 236
Gibbon, Edward 42
Gilliland-Swetland, Anne 288
Gilliland-Swetland, Luke J. 297
Glenn, Cheryl 3–4, 6, 63–4, 91, 96, 109, 127, 130–2, 137, 176–7, 183, 235, 238, 245, 295, 299, 302–4, 309
Gold, David 300–1
Goody, Jack 118
Gorgias 21, 41–2, 67, 106, 125, 133
Gougar, Helen 6, 218, 220–3, 225–8
Graban, Tarez Samra 6, 218–28
Gracy, Linda 287–90
Graff, Richard 233, 253
Gramsci, Antonio 114
grand narrative 73 (*see also* narrative, master)
Gries, Laurie 233
Griffin, Marion Mahony 5, 165–70
Griffin, Walter Burley 5, 166–7
Grimaldi, William M.A. 28
Grimké, Sarah 68
Guattari, Felix 94

Habermas, Jürgen 44, 114
Haley, Alex 86
Hall, David 252
Harding, Sandra 132–3, 136, 138
Harper, Frances 53, 85
Harper's 53
Harrington, Dana 246
Harris, Joseph A. 283
Harrison, Jane 137
Harry Ransom Humanities Research Center 114
Harvard Book List 25
Harvard Exams 25
Harvard genesis narrative 292
Harvard University 53, 57, 61, 187, 239
Harwit, Martin 158–60
Havelock, Eric 118, 125
Hayden, Wendy 8
Haywood, Eliza 22
Heald, Carolyn 6, 220
Hegel, Georg 16, 42–3
Henze, Brent 118
Heraclitus 235, 251
Heritage Turnpike 64
hermeneutics 38, 136, 147
Herodotus 112

Herzberg, Bruce 63, 68
Hesiod 94, 235
Heyman, I. Michael 158–60
Higgins, Andrew 160
Hill, Adams S. 54, 58
Hill, D.J. 30
Hirsch, E.D. 25–6
historically black colleges 258, 300
historiography 1–8, 13, 15, 17, 20, 21–6, 30, 32–3, 37, 40, 47, 65–8, 72, 91–2, 98–9, 101–2, 104–5, 109, 124, 195, 233, 237–8, 245, 252, 279, 284; as an active endeavor 123; Asian-American 301; dialectical 38; epistemology of 3; feminist 3–4, 68–9, 130, 136, 138, 173, 239; hermeneutical 38; linear 251; meta- 121; methodology (*see* methodology, historiographical); and pedagogy 259, 280, 285, 288, 291; politics of (*see* Octalog); pragmatics of 258, 260; praxis of 48; research of (*see* research, historiographical); rhetorical 3, 7, 42, 103, 130–2, 134, 136, 141, 234, 236–9, 242, 252, 259, 264–5, 268, 283, 307; speculative 124; tensions within 194; tradition of 2; training in 122; linear 301; revisionist 20, 47, 48, 96, 115, 173, 192, 229, 245, 253, 258 history, rhetorical 3–4, 28, 37, 64–7, 69, 73, 96–8, 106, 131–5, 137–8, 141, 156, 172, 218, 222, 233–4, 237–9, 251
Hogg, Charlotte 187–8
Hollis, Karyn 187
Homer 21, 99, 118, 120, 125, 235
homología 44
hooks, bell 84–5, 140, 239
Horner, Winifred Bryan 95, 138, 244
Houlette, Forrest 95
Housman, Alfred Edward 61
Howell, Wilber Samuel 117–19, 125
Hughes, Langston 83
Hum, Sue 300
HUTS (Households Using Televisions) 105
hybrid people 84
Hyde, Michael 235

identity 7, 134, 139, 141, 248, 300, 304, 309; disciplinary 120, 131, 302; ethnic/cultural 131, 282; expansion 101; gender (*see* gender, identity); loss of 97; negotiation of 78, 156, 234, 241; movements 248

Iliad 21, 99, 124
illiteracy 40, 51
illusoriness 28
Immigrant Archive Project 306
Institutional Review Board (IRB) 265, 306
interdisciplinarity 101, 120, 303
interdisciplinary collaboration 4
interestedness 190–2, 195, 237
International Society for the History of Rhetoric 119–20
intertextual readings (of primary materials) 4
intertextuality 4, 6, 98–9, 102, 124, 161, 218, 224, 229
invention 5, 20, 112, 119, 156, 224, 246, 273; collective 156
Iowa State University 92
Isocrates 67, 102–3, 106, 109, 126, 245
Ivie, Robert L. 122

Jack, Jordynn 302–4
Jackson II, Ronald L. 7, 240–1, 251–2
Jaeger, Werner 247
James, Mark 92, 128
James Berlin Papers 6, 200–2, 206, 210–11, 214–15
Jameson, Fredric 29, 66
Jamieson, Kathleen Hall 224
Jarratt, Susan C. 2, 4, 16, 22, 27–8, 30, 34, 37, 45, 63, 67, 69, 107, 115, 130–2, 136, 177, 236, 252
Jevons, Frank Byron 125–6, 140
Jimerson, Randall C. 309
Johanek, Cindy 6, 220–3, 227
Johnson, Michelle T. 300
Johnson, Nan 2, 17, 23, 26, 31, 38, 40, 47, 56, 63, 107, 183, 307–8
Johnson, Robert R. 33–4, 303
Jolliffe, David 61
Jordan, June 85
Journal of Education 52
journals, education 8, 52–3, 55
justice 18, 32, 44, 46, 93, 109, 113, 134, 136, 248, 301

Kahl, Mary 69
Kairos 5
Kangkang, Zhang 139
Karnow, Stanley 104
Kellner, Hans 65–6, 73
Kelly-Gadol, Joan 133–4

Kennedy, George A. 63, 245
Kerford, G.B. 67
Kerkham, Eleanor 189
Kesner, Richard M. 149
Ketelar, Eric 288
Kinneavy, James L. 28, 63, 109
Kirklighter, Cristina 286
Kirsch, Gesa 9, 173, 235, 258, 288, 296, 299, 305
Kitzhaber, Albert R. 52, 61, 183, 189
Knapp, James A. 157
Kristeva, Julia 16, 43, 68
Kuhn, Thomas 66, 92
Kundera, Milan 43

L'Eplattenier, Barbara E. 5–6, 8–9, 171, 235, 258, 281, 295–6, 302
Lacan, Jacques 16, 43
LaCapra, Dominick 157
Laclau, Ernesto 94
Lathan, Rhea Estelle 300
Latino Broadcasting Project 306
Lauer, Janice 3, 32, 35, 44, 49, 91, 98, 109, 138, 282
Laws, Hubert 85
Lecercle, Jean-Jacques 16
Leff, Michael 233, 253
Lerner, Neal 285–6
Levinas, Emmanuel 253
Lévi-Strauss, Claude 118
Lewis, Roger 114
liberal arts colleges 258
librarian 1, 9, 188, 259–61, 265–6, 268, 303, 305, 308; 297; research 95; special collections 7; special projects 299; subject 8
library, community 188
library science 284, 287–8
liminal spaces 305
liminality (of the researcher) 286, 305
Limón, José 185
linguistic form 133
linguistic phenomena 124
linguistics 34, 43, 101, 117, 220, 228–9, 242, 253
Lipscomb, Drema 68
literacy 15, 17, 24, 40, 71, 105–6, 108, 110, 118–19, 125–6, 173, 191, 246, 256–7, 260, 276, 287–8, 305; crisis 51, 53, 60; cultural 25; education 106, 257; information 259, 261, 267, 272; political 187; practices 105, 115, 187, 236, 261–2, 280–1, 299; spiritual 235;

sponsors 236, 257; studies 9, 78, 147, 256, 259–60, 298; teaching of 7, 24; technology 105; visual 303
literary criticism *see* criticism, literary
literary narrative *see* narrative, literary
literary theory 16, 33, 45, 92
lived experience 3, 82, 134–5, 140, 165, 251, 308
Logan, Shirley 130, 140
logos 16, 28, 102, 105–6
Loraux, Nicole 73
Lorde, Audre 83–5
Lucas, Brad 306
Lunsford, Andrea 68, 127, 130
Luther, Martin 246
Lyceum *see* Aristotle, Lyceum
Lyon, Arabella 300
Lyons, Scott 100
Lyotard, Jean-François 44, 156

Macaulay, Thomas 111, 115
machine-readable cataloging records (MARC) 209
Mailloux, Steven 173, 296
Malesh, Patricia M. 304
Mao, LuMing 7, 241, 251–2
mapping 3, 65–6, 73–4
Marcus, Jane 27
marginalia 258, 305
Marrou, H.I. 126
Martin, Emily 100
Marx, Karl 16, 44, 113, 249
Marxism 41, 43, 45, 47–8, 249; neo- 30, 33, 40–1, 48; post- 33
Mary & Leigh Block Museum of Art 165
Mason, Priscilla 224
Massachusetts Institute of Technology (MIT) 166
Mastrangelo, Lisa S. 8–9, 171, 174–5, 235, 258, 281, 296, 307
materiality 5, 141, 157, 173, 243
Mattingly, Carol 177, 193
McCann, Les 85
McComiskey, Bruce 10, 304
McHenry, Elizabeth 115
McKemmish, Sue 288–9
McNely, Brian 305
Melville, Herman 22
Merleau-Ponty, Maurice 157
meta-discipline 16, 34

metaepistemology 221
metatheory 4
method: anthropological 114; archeological 302; archival 1, 4, 7–10, 100, 171, 174, 188, 235, 259, 261–3, 269, 272–3, 282, 284, 287, 290–1, 295, 299, 306–8; chaining 267, 305; contextual 124; feminist 130; name collection 305; pearl growing 305; successive segmentation 305; synonym generation 305
Methodism 188, 235
methodological *ethos* 178
methodology: afrafeminist 193; archival 1, 8, 10, 263, 281, 288, 291, 295, 297, 299, 304, 306–9; feminist 4, 64, 68–9, 71, 131–4, 141, 303; grounded-theory 265; historiographical 64, 131, 172, 282–3
methods section 5–6, 175–8
Mexican Revolution 185
Mexican-American War 105
Miami University 16, 241
Michigan State University 243
microhistories 10
Miller, Susan 63, 282, 298
Miller, Thomas P. 3, 73–4, 92, 95, 106, 136, 172–3, 184, 192, 247, 258, 296–7, 299, 302, 304, 307–8
Milton, John 94, 102
Mohanty, Chandra Talpade 83–4
Moon, Gretchen Flesher 258
Morris, Sammie L. 6, 200, 258, 265, 297, 308
Morrison, Toni 85
Moss, Beverly 299
Moss, Roger 67
Mossell, Gertrude 85
Mott, Lucretia Coffin 68
Mouffe, Chantal 94
Mountford, Roxanne 3, 68, 91, 99, 109, 239
multimodality 8, 119, 260, 268–9
Murphy, James J. 2, 13, 17, 20, 24, 26, 31–2, 35–6, 42, 45, 91, 96, 107, 233
Murray, Lindley 39

Nancy, Jean-Luc 156
narrative 7, 15, 22, 34–5, 59–61, 63, 66–8, 73, 83, 95–7, 99, 105, 115, 152, 156, 177–8, 189, 208–9, 242, 244, 280–2, 295, 306; in composition studies 283, 285; dominant 73, 244, 289, 291; educational 193; gender 73; grand 44, 73, 99, 156–7; Harvard genesis

(*see* Harvard genesis narrative); historical 54, 60, 66, 73, 102, 115, 156–7, 159, 177–8, 222, 227, 240, 246, 273, 281, 300; identity 304; literary 17, 23; master 63, 70, 97–8, 280–2; paternal 64–6, 68, 73–4; recovery 282; research 192; structure 95–6, 174, 307; subversive 190
narratology 283, 291
National Air and Space Museum 158–9
National Archives of Rhetoric and Composition 112, 290
National Communication Association 117
National Council of Teachers of English (NCTE) 86–7
National Union Catalog 55
National Writing Project 304
nationalism 249, 301
Native American 7, 191, 194, 241, 257, 261; rhetoric (*see* rhetoric, Native American)
Neel, Jasper 3, 63, 67, 92, 101, 109, 115
networking (as a research method) 189
New Criticism *see* criticism, New Criticism
New Deal 50
New School for Social Research 299
New York Times Magazine 286
Newkirk, Thomas 57, 61
Newman, John Henry 46
Nichols, Marie Hochmuth 127
Nietzsche, Friedrich Wilhelm 111, 113, 136, 192
normal schools 258
North, Stephen 280
Northern Arizona University 15
Northwestern University 165

O'Brien, Mary 70
O'Toole, James M. 150, 298
Octalog I: The Politics of Historiography 1–3, 6, 13, 91–4, 96, 99, 107–9, 128, 173, 177, 233–4, 245, 249, 258, 282
Octalog II: The (Continuing) Politics of Historiography 1–3, 91, 233–5, 238, 241, 253, 258, 282
Octalog III: The Politics of Historiography in 2010 7, 233, 240, 243, 249, 251–3, 258, 282
Odyssey 21, 99, 124
Ohio State University 92, 257, 259
Olsen, Tillie 82
Ong, Walter 17, 24, 35, 67, 118

Oregon State University 234
organizational grid (as a method tool) 225, 227
original order 6, 149, 200, 204–6, 208, 216, 227
Ostergard, Lori 305
Other (Othering) 16, 37–8, 66–7, 74, 79, 102, 104, 131, 195, 234, 242–4, 250, 252–3

paideia 15, 21, 43, 125–6, 247
Panitch, Judith M. 299
Parker, Charlie 85
Parsons, Talcott 70
Partner, Nancy 66
paternal narrative *see* narrative, paternal
pathos 28, 250
Peaden, Catherine 68
Pearce, Roy Harvey 244
pedagogy 3, 8–9, 20, 32, 52–3, 73, 98–9, 134, 171, 190, 209, 211, 240, 251–2, 258–9, 273, 299, 301, 307; Asian 301
Pedagogy and Provenance 8
Peitho 300
Pennsylvania State University 91, 96
pentad (dramatism) *see* Burke, Kenneth, pentad
people of color 3, 94, 108–9, 115, 140, 192
Perelman, Chaim 63
Pericles 64, 71–2
peripetetics 24
personae 103–4, 218
personal position 281–2
philology 58, 123, 250
Philosophy and Rhetoric 120
Plato 17, 24, 26–7, 43, 48, 63, 72, 74, 102, 106, 115, 121, 125–6, 132–3
Plato's Academy 17, 24
PMLA 36, 45, 52, 95, 119
Poetics Today 157
polis see Aristotle, *polis*
Politics of Historiography *see* Octalog
Polk, James K. 105
Poole's Index 53
Popper, Karl 113
Porter, James 6, 100, 224, 227–8
positionality 3, 5, 7, 10, 23, 191–3, 282, 285, 287, 291, 299–300
postmodernism 4, 48, 64, 130–1, 134–6, 138, 172
Poulakos, John 67
Poulakos, Takis 63, 73
Powell, Malea 7, 100, 243, 251, 301

power 3, 7, 16, 38, 134, 136, 233, 240, 273, 289; and discourse 19, 22, 73; dynamics 10, 95, 234; in education 45; related to gender 63, 69–70, 72–3, 96–7; instilling of 40; in Marxism 48; methodological 4; and politics 37, 69–70, 72, 96–7; positions of 30, 33, 37, 63, 80, 96, 236, 242; relations 19, 41, 72, 248; rhetorical 14, 18, 33, 35, 37, 65, 70, 236, 238–9, 253
power/knowledge matrix 241
Pratt, Mary Louise 81, 287
PRE/TEXT 29, 37, 67
presentism 281
primary sources, digitized 8, 305
privileged groups 3, 45, 69, 71, 240, 248, 290
professional book 53
progymnasmata 246
Protagoras 61, 66, 93, 133
provenance 6, 48, 149, 175–7, 200, 202–4, 214, 219, 220, 228–9, 262, 297
psychology, cognitive 34–5
Purdue University 6, 14, 91, 98, 151, 201–2, 209, 211
Purdy, James 297, 305, 308

Quarterly Journal of Speech 122
quietism 40, 136
Quintilian 63, 102
Quon, Dennis 32

Ramsey, Alexis E. 8, 174, 235, 258, 275–6, 296
Ranney, Frances J. 235
Ratcliffe, Krista 68, 130–1, 136, 301–2
ratios (dramatism) *see* Burke, Kenneth, ratios
Reagan, Ronald 104
received wisdom 61
Redfern, Jenny 68
reference interview 200, 208
referential plentitude 156–7, 161
relativism 31, 39–40, 106, 113, 136
Renaissance 24, 27, 63, 68, 112, 127, 157, 186, 244, 246
Rensselaer Polytechnic Institute 100
research: deductive 29, 38–9; digital 8, 236, 257, 268, 305, 308; dominant practices 134; empirical 147, 248, 259–60; ethnographic 130; feminist 64, 68–9, 71–2, 131–4, 136, 139–40, 238–9; historiographical 4, 269; inductive 29, 30, 38–9, 270; inquiry based 7, 8; locally focused 8; on-site 8; program 145, 148, 152–4; qualitative 269
researcher-archivist *see* archivist-researcher
respect des fonds 203
Reynolds, Nedra 100
rhetoric and composition 1, 9, 49, 78, 95, 107, 131, 134, 141, 183, 256, 259, 276
Rhetoric and Composition Sound Archives (RCSA) 306
Rhetoric Review 42, 67, 91, 177
Rhetoric Society of America 108, 119
Rhetoric Society Quarterly 67, 69, 128, 173, 177
rhetoric: African-American 240, 243; Arabic 235; Asian 235; centralized 9, 71; Chinese 130, 137, 140; classical 15, 24, 37, 51, 58, 65, 71–2, 74, 92–3, 97, 108–9, 115, 127, 172, 224, 240, 244; democratic 248; Disability 237, 260; Eastern 106, 301; epistemic 36; Greek 93, 121, 125; marginalized 3, 70–1, 110, 130–1, 138, 140, 185; medieval 20, 36; Native American 100, 301; and power (*see* power, rhetorical); Renaissance 68, 112, 127, 186, 244, 246; Roman 121, 240, 243–4, 246; social movement 304; sophistic 25, 27, 29, 43, 67; spatial 239; Victorian 94; Western Paternal Narrative 68
Rhetorica 127, 246
rhetorical history *see* history, rhetorical
rhetorical tradition 3, 67–70, 73, 95–7, 107–9, 127, 132, 192, 238–41, 244–6
rhetors: female (*see* rhetors, women); women 6, 64–5, 68–71, 127, 130–4, 136–41, 187, 192–3, 224, 226, 235, 238, 243, 303, 308; working class 235
Richard S. Beal Collection 53
Richards, I.A. 63
Rippingham, John 220
Ritter, Harry 114
Ritter, Kelly 7, 280, 298
Robb, Kevin 125–6
Roen, Duane 138–9, 148
Rohan, Liz 173, 235, 258, 288, 296, 299
Roosevelt, Franklin D. 50
Rorty, Richard 66, 134, 136
Rose, Shirley K. 4–6, 145, 200, 211, 258, 265, 275, 281, 288, 290, 297, 308
Rosen, Stanley 27–8
Rousseau, Jean-Jacques 70

Royster, Jacqueline Jones 3, 9, 68, 78, 115, 130–1, 135–7, 140, 183, 191–4, 235, 299
Rushing, Janice Hocker 69
Russell, David 59, 183
Ryan, Cynthia 304
Ryan, Mary 239

Said, Edward 250
Samuels, Helen W. 149–50
Santayana, George 25, 42, 108
Schiappa, Edward 3, 63, 67, 92, 103, 109, 245
Schliemann, Heinrich 21, 99–100, 124–5
Schmitz, Robert Morell 114
Scholes, Robert 119
School Review 52
Scott, Fred N. 54, 58, 59, 61
Scott, Joan Wallach 70, 97, 133–4, 140
Scott, Robert L. 36, 66
Scottish rhetors/philosophers 172, 244
secondary sources 4, 52, 56–7, 61, 65, 67, 102, 120, 166–7, 173, 177, 185, 193, 203, 223, 307, 308
Selzer, Jack 188
Senier, Siobhan 301
serendipity 2, 173, 185, 258, 305
series (level of archival description) 211–12, 214–15, 219
service learning 8, 109, 218
Seven Sisters colleges 175–6
Shakespeare, William 49
Shanks, Michael 158
Sharer, Wendy B. 8–9, 173–4, 187–90, 235, 296, 300, 302, 309
Sher, Richard 114
Sheridan, Thomas 246
Shonagon, Sei 189
Shyamalan, M. Night 165
Simple stories 83
Sinfield, Alan 157
sixth sense, researcher's 1, 165, 169–70
Slomba, Elizabeth 190
Smith Magazine 234
Smith, Barbara Hermstein 92–4
Smith, Michelle 304
Smith-Rosenberg, Carroll 65
Smithsonian Institute 5, 151, 158
social change 4, 134, 136, 191
Society of American Archivists 201
Socrates 67, 69, 72, 101, 106, 132–3, 193

Sophism, Diotimic 106
sophists 26–7, 45, 67, 70, 106, 112, 115, 121, 245
sophists, Sicilian 67
Southern Communication Journal 69
SPA tradition (Socrates-Plato-Aristotle) 106
Speaker and Gavel 104
special collections 8, 260, 269–70, 298
Speech Communication Association 117
Spivak, Gayatri Chakravorty 84
Spon, Jacob 123
St. Augustine 63, 119
Stalin, Joseph 43
Stanton, Elizabeth Cady 68, 222, 225
Steedman, Carolyn 219
Steele, Richard 22
Stevens, Sharon McKenzie 304
Stewart, Donald 59–61
Stewart, Maria 85
Stoic Diodoros Kronos 24
stoicism 24
Stoler, Ann Laura 299
Stone, Lucy 225
Stough, Charlotte 112
Strain, Margaret 306
Street, Brian 235
Stromberg, Ernest 301
Stuckey, Zosha 233–4
students, undergraduate 8, 271, 273, 280
suffrage 68, 221–6, 228
suicide, academic 126, 168, 301
Sullivan, Patricia A. 173, 258
Swearingen, Jan 2, 17, 24, 27–8, 32, 36–7, 41, 58, 63, 67–8, 117, 130, 133, 137, 282
synthesis (of materials) 2, 56, 58–9
Syracuse University 234

Tacitus 42, 94
Tanesini, Alessandra 136
taxonomical methods (of research) 6, 58, 218, 220–1, 223–4, 227–9, 297, 308
têchnê *see* Aristotle, têchnê
telos 72
tension, 6, 66, 167–8, 185, 193–4, 218, 220, 222–4, 227–8, 308
terministic screen *see* Burke, Kenneth, terministic screens
Texas Christian University 91–2, 128
textbooks 8, 20, 30, 38, 46, 52–4, 56, 99, 185–8, 246, 281, 283, 293

Thompson, E. P. 114
Thoreau, Henry David 43, 87
Thucydides 16
Thurman, Howard 84
Tibbets, Paul 159
Tirabassi, Kate 190, 158, 298
Tisias 21, 63, 125
Toulmin, Stephen 102
trained incapacities *see* Burke, Kenneth, trained incapacities
triangulation 173, 307
Truth, Sojourner 68
Tuchman, Barbara 57

University of Arizona 91–2, 99, 106
University of British Columbia 17
University of California, Davis 14
University of Illinois at Chicago 247
University of Illinois Urbana Champaign 240
University of Iowa 187
University of Michigan 61, 125, 305
University of Minnesota 92, 103, 245
University of New Hampshire 14, 53, 56, 190
University of New Mexico 194
University of North Carolina at Chapel Hill 299, 302
University of Oklahoma 92, 105
University of Pittsburgh 238
University of Rhode Island 290
University of Tennessee 91–2
University of Texas Press 118–19
University of Texas, Arlington 16–17
University of Texas, Austin 91, 94
University of Washington 127
Utah State University Press 10

Van Maanen, John 284, 286, 290
Vanderbilt University 92, 101
Varnum, Robin 187
Veysey, Lawrence 58
Vickers, Brian 245
Victorian: educational practices 94; ideals 15; scholasticism 95, 126
Vitanza, Victor J. 2, 7, 16, 20–1, 25, 27, 31, 34–5, 37, 41, 61, 63, 73–4, 107, 234–5, 249, 251
voice (archival) 3, 21–2, 37, 46, 62, 67, 74, 78–80, 83–5, 98, 139, 235, 290

von Humboldt, Wilhelm 113
von Ranke, Leopold 113

Walker, Alice 85
Walker, John 52
Walzer, Arthur E. 7, 233, 245, 251, 253
Wander, Phil 104
Wang, Bo 301
Warnick, Barbara 127, 304
Watt, Ian 118
Watts, Isaac 20, 38
Weaver, Richard M. 63
Weiser, Irwin 4–5, 145
Welch, Kathleen 3, 63, 74, 92, 97, 105, 109
Wells, Ida 83, 115
Wells, Susan 273, 298–9
Wendell, Barrett 57–8, 61
Wertheimer, Molly Meijer 130
West, Cornel 84–5
West Virginia University 236
Whately, Richard 22, 244
White, Hayden 66, 113–14, 280, 283, 287
Whitman, Walt 22
Wigley, Mark 167
Willard, Frances 225
Williams, Jean C. 183
Williams, Patricia 85–6
Williams, Robert C. 174
Wills, Garry 114
Winterowd, Ross 63
Wollstonecraft, Mary 22–3, 68
women: African American 3, 82–3, 85, 100, 140, 191, 261; Chinese 130–1, 135–7, 139 40; communities of 64–5, 172, 187, 252, 300; education (*see* education, women); faculty 139; Native American 257, 261; nineteenth-century 115, 136, 193; philosophers 17, 27, 32; preachers 235, 239; professional 136; rhetors (*see* rhetors, women); Third-World 131, 140; writers 27, 37, 64, 67, 71, 115, 137, 167, 170, 187, 189, 227, 301, 308
women's colleges 176, 300
women's liberation 137
women's movements 137
women's studies 27, 114, 214
Woolf, Virginia 27
Woolley, Edwin 39
workbook 54, 59

working classes 1, 3, 109, 114–15, 140, 235
Wright, Frank Lloyd 166
writing program administration 4, 145–8, 152, 190
writing program administrator (WPA) 4–5, 145–54, 281, 288, 290
Wu, Hui 4, 130, 172

Xing'er, Lu 139

Yager, Kristi 286–7
Yakel, Elizabeth 8, 305
Yale University 187, 298
Yancey, Kathleen Blake 272–3

Zenger, Amy 190
Zimmerelli, Lisa 189
Žižek, Slavoj 158